ROUSSEAU'S POLITICAL WRITINGS

NEW TRANSLATIONS
INTERPRETIVE NOTES
BACKGROUNDS
COMMENTARIES

NORTON CRITICAL EDITIONS IN THE
HISTORY OF IDEAS

FOR A COMPLETE LIST OF NORTON CRITICAL EDITIONS, VISIT
www.wwnorton.com/college/english/nce.welcome.htm

A NORTON CRITICAL EDITION

ROUSSEAU'S POLITICAL WRITINGS

DISCOURSE ON INEQUALITY
DISCOURSE ON POLITICAL ECONOMY
ON SOCIAL CONTRACT

Translated by Julia Conaway Bondanella

NEW TRANSLATIONS
INTERPRETIVE NOTES
BACKGROUNDS
COMMENTARIES

Edited by ALAN RITTER

UNIVERSITY OF CONNECTICUT AND TRINITY COLLEGE

and

JULIA CONAWAY BONDANELLA

INDIANA UNIVERSITY

W · W · NORTON & COMPANY · *New York* · *London*

Printed in the United States of America.

The text of this book is composed in Electra, with
display type set in Bernhard Modern. Composition by Vail-Ballou
Manufacturing by The Maple-Vail Book Group
Book design by Antonina Krass

First Edition

Library of Congress Cataloging-in-Publication Data
Rousseau, Jean-Jacques, 1712–1778.
Rousseau's political writings.
(A Norton critical edition)
Bibliography: p.
Contents: Discourse on inequality—Discourse on
political economy—On social contract.
1. Rousseau, Jean-Jacques, 1712–1778—Collected works.
I. Ritter, Alan, 1937–   II. Bondanella, Julia
Conaway.   III. Title.
JC179.R7   1987   320'.01'1   87-20365

ISBN 0-393-95651-2

W. W. Norton & Company, Inc., 500 Fifth Avenue, New York, N.Y. 10110
www.wwnorton.com

W. W. Norton & Company Ltd., Castle House, 75/76 Wells Street,
London W1T 3QT

Contents

Preface

Rousseau's political writings, when first encountered, dazzle and perplex. They engagingly denounce established institutions, but caution against projects for change. They paint an enticing picture of a radically new arrangement, only to lament that it will self-destruct. Most notoriously, they mount an inspiring defense of freedom, while calling for the imposition of what sounds like oppressive force. Paradoxes like these seem to set Rousseau on both sides of key issues in political theory, and for centuries have kept him at the center of debate.

This Critical Edition provides first readers with the material they need to enter this debate as informed participants. It contains the three most important of Rousseau's political writings: *Discourse on Inequality* (1755), *Discourse on Political Economy* (1755) and *On Social Contract* (1762). The reader will also find here a sketch of Rousseau's life, selections from his autobiography, and a section, "Reactions to Rousseau," that includes impressions of his work and personality from illustrious contemporaries and early critics.

The notes and commentaries in this edition focus on Rousseau's attitudes toward democracy. In what sense does he espouse democracy? What sort does he prefer? How does he account for the weakness of democratic institutions in political experience up to his time? What, in his view, are the preconditions, prospects, and procedures for establishing a legitimate democratic state? How satisfactory is his project? These questions assume that Rousseau is a kind of democrat, an assumption not shared by most students of his political thought. For the burning question in Rousseau studies, from the start, has not been what kind of democrat he is but whether he is sufficiently committed to liberty and equality to qualify as a democrat at all.[1] Debate on this issue has most recently taken the form of a controversy over whether Rousseau is a totalitarian. But with the thaw in the Cold War and renewed international interest in democracy the time is ripe to focus attention on the democratic aspects of Rousseau's political thought.

While the interpretive focus of this Edition is on Rousseau the democrat, readers will find material for reaching their own conclusions, not only on this issue but on many others about the meaning of Rousseau that they themselves will raise.

A. R.

1. For a convenient collection of arguments from the outset on both sides of this controversy, see Guy H. Dodge, ed., *Jean-Jacques Rousseau:* *Authoritarian-Libertarian?* (Lexington, Mass.: D. C. Heath, 1971).

Translator's Note

The translations of *Discourse on Inequality, Discourse on Political Economy,* and *On Social Contract* that follow attempt to provide a close approximation of the French text in idiomatic, contemporary English. They should also provide the English reader with some sense of the brilliant clarity of Rousseau's style, the problematic aspects of his terminology, and the ambiguities of his thought.

Nowhere do these translations deviate in any significant way from the original to paraphrase in a personal poetic style what the translator thought Rousseau was trying to say, nor do they revert to archaic syntax or diction to achieve an "Enlightenment" flavor. I have tried throughout to keep in my ear the sound of Rousseau's sometimes breathless enumeration of examples. Unlike most other modern translators of Rousseau, I have avoided chopping up his sentences by inserting periods where he does not intend a full pause, and where such a pause would detract from or distort the power of his meaning. I have attempted always to balance faithfulness to the original with good stylistic practices in English.

In my work on these texts, I isolated a number of key terms and themes and attempted to translate them in a consistent fashion so that the reader can see how these key terms recur and develop within Rousseau's works. Among the key terms which I have attempted to translate in a reasonably consistent manner, those that follow recur throughout the texts in this edition: (1) *Un particulier* refers to the individual members of a community, and is translated as *private individual*, whereas the adjective *particulier* is often opposed to *général*, as in the general will and the particular will. Hence, I have normally rendered the adjective *particulier* as *particular* to contrast it with *privé (private)*, unless the context makes useful the contrast in English between *private* and *public*. (2) The distinction between *principe* as a rule of law and *maxime* as a rule of politics is maintained by translating the former as *principle* and the latter as *maxim*. (3) The term *convention* is rendered by the term *agreements* in order to avoid the connotation of *conventional* in English when Rousseau is referring to the legitimate agreements that serve as the cornerstone of the community. It should be noted, however, that Rousseau often opposes the terms *naturel* and *conventionel*, which are translated as *natural* and *conventional* or *civil*, since the distinction reflects the one Rousseau constantly makes between the life in the state of nature and that in civil society. (4) Although any wholly satisfactory equivalents are difficult to discover in English, the different connotations of the terms *amour-propre* and *amour de soi* are indicated by translating them respectively as *self-love* and *self-esteem*. (5) The term *moeurs* which refers to the manners and morals of a community has been rendered as *moral habits* to avoid the clumsiness of using the two nouns and to avoid confusion with the translation of *coûtumes* as *customs*. (6) The word *patrie*, which really has no equivalent in English but "native country," I have chosen to translate as *homeland*. (7) The noun *droite* is translated as either *law* or *right* depending upon the context; the adjective *droite* is usually rendered as *in the right*. (8) *Propriété* is rendered as *property* or *ownership* depending upon the context, since Rousseau's concern falls sometimes on legitimate title and sometimes on management or use.

These new translations of the *Discourse on Inequality*, *Discourse on Political Economy*, and *On Social Contract* are based upon the Pléiade edition of Rousseau's works, specifically upon the *Oeuvres complètes*, volume III (Paris: Éditions Gallimard, 1975). Rousseau's notes to the 1782 edition of *On Social Contract* have also been included, as well as notes IX, XI, XV, and XIX of those Rousseau appended to the *Discourse on Inequality*. These provide a first reader with crucial additional arguments.

I will be ever indebted to my co-editor for his endlessly patient readings of the translations in their various stages as well as his always dependable guidance in polishing the English prose. To Peter Bondanella go our thanks for his assistance in suggesting the project to us and for his support in the course of completing it. We appreciate Mark Musa's early advice on translating as well as Steve Forman's suggestions in the final stages of preparing this volume.

                                                        J. C. B.

ROUSSEAU'S POLITICAL WRITINGS

Discourse on the Origin and Foundations of Inequality Among Men

Rousseau published the *Discourse on the Origin and Foundations of Inequality Among Men* in 1755 as his entry in a contest sponsored by the Academy of Dijon for the best essay on the question: "What is the origin of inequality among men, and is it authorized by natural law?" Having won the first prize in a previous contest of the Academy, five years earlier, with his brilliant though discursive *Discourse on the Arts and Sciences,* he no longer needed to establish his reputation. Rousseau instead used the new contest as an occasion to begin a less immediately engaging but more systematic exposition of his social and political ideas. The resulting essay displeased the Academicians, who did not even read it to the end, but has since been recognized as both original and penetrating in its analysis of what causes social inequality and of how inequality poisons human life.

This *Discourse* is a work of critical diagnosis. It traces out and denounces the consequences of social, political, and economic inequality not only for our relations with others, but also for our psychological well-being. Yet the *Discourse* is no jeremiad. Though Rousseau certainly attacks social inequality, he is more concerned to explain its origin and chart its growth. His analysis of the many-staged process through which inequality develops is mainly a subtle and sometimes allusive ascription of cause. In his assessment of this process Rousseau is ambivalent. The condition of primitive equality may never have existed and cannot be regained; nor was it an unmixed good. As for the inequality and corruption of civilized life, these, truly, are abominations, though the developments that produced them also awakened the admirable human capacities to reason, create, and judge. No remedy for inequality is provided here, but the criticism and explanation which this *Discourse* presents amount to a diagnosis. The *Discourse* thus identifies the nature of the ailment for which *On Social Contract* seeks a cure.

Discourse on the Origin and Foundations of Inequality Among Men

"Non in depravatis, sed in his quae bene secundum naturam se habent, considerandum est quid sit naturale."

Aristole, *Politics,* I. 5. 1254a[1]

1. Aristotle, *Politics,* I. 5. 1254a. "We do not seek what is natural in depraved beings, but among those who comport themselves in conformity with nature."

Preface[2]

The most useful and least advanced of all the branches of human knowledge seems to me to be that of man, and I dare say that only the inscription[3] on the temple at Delphi contained a precept of greater importance and difficulty than all the great tomes of the moralists. Thus, I consider the subject of this discourse to be one of the most interesting that philosophy can propose, and, unhappily for us, one of the thorniest that philosophers can try to resolve, for how can the source of inequality among men be known, unless we begin by knowing men themselves? And how will man succeed in seeing himself as nature created him, through all the changes that the passing of time and events must have produced in his original constitution, and in separating what he owes to his own essence from what circumstances and his advances have added to or changed in his original state? Like the statue of Glaucus, which time, sea, and storms had so disfigured that it resembled less a god than a wild beast, the human soul, altered in the midst of society by a thousand constantly recurring causes, by the acquisition of a mass of knowledge and a multitude of errors, by the changes that came about in the constitution of the body, and by the continual impact of the passions, has, so to speak, changed in appearance to the point of being nearly unrecognizable; and instead of a being which always acts according to certain and invariable principles, instead of that celestial and majestic simplicity which its author imprinted on it, one no longer finds anything but the grotesque contrast between passion which thinks itself reasonable and understanding in a state of delirium.

What is even more cruel is that, since all the advances made by the human species constantly move it away from its primitive state, the more we accumulate new knowledge, the more we deprive ourselves of the means of acquiring the most important of all, and, in a sense, it is by virtue of studying man that we have become totally unfit to know him.

It is easy to see that it is in these successive changes of the human constitution that we must seek the earliest origins of the differences that distinguish men, who, by common consent, are naturally as equal among themselves as were the animals of each species before various physical causes had introduced in some of them the varieties that we now observe. In fact, it is inconceivable that these first changes, by whatever means they came about, should have, all at once and in the same manner, altered all the individuals of the species, but whereas some were improved or made worse, and acquired various qualities, good or bad, which were not inherent in their nature, others remained for a longer time in their

2. We have omitted the first prefatory section of the *Discourse on Inequality*, the *Dedication to the Republic of Geneva*, in which Rousseau depicts his native city as a homeland of freedom. As a description, the *Dedication* is very inaccurate, since eighteenth-century Geneva was an oligarchy, not the virtuous democracy Rousseau portrays. But, if read as a vision of what Geneva might become, should it follow his principles, the *Dedication* gives substance to Rousseau's conception of a legitimate state.

3. "Know thyself."

original state; such was the first source of inequality among men, and it is thus easier to give some general indications of its origins than to determine its true causes with any precision.

Let my readers not imagine, then, that I dare flatter myself with having seen what appears to me so difficult to see. I have hazarded a few guesses, less with the hope of resolving the question than with the intention of clarifying it and reducing it to its true proportions. Others will easily be able to go farther along this route, without it being easy for anyone to reach the end. For it is no small matter to distinguish what is original from what is artificial in the present nature of man, and to have a clear understanding of a state which no longer exists, which has, perhaps, never existed, and about which it is necessary to have accurate notions in order to judge our own present state properly. Anyone who undertakes to determine exactly which precautions to take in order to make solid observations on this subject would need even more philosophy than is generally thought, and a good solution to the following problem would not seem to me unworthy of the Aristotles and Plinys of our century: "What experiments would be necessary to gain some knowledge of natural man? And what are the means of carrying out these experiments in the midst of society?" Far from undertaking to resolve this problem, I believe that I have meditated sufficiently on the subject to dare respond in advance that the greatest philosophers will not be too good to direct these experiments, nor the most powerful sovereigns to carry them out; it is scarcely reasonable to expect such cooperation, especially with the perseverance or, rather, the confluence of understanding and good will necessary on every side for success.

This research, which is so difficult to carry out and which no one has really thought about until now, is, nonetheless, the only means left to us of overcoming a mass of difficulties that conceal from us the knowledge of the real foundations of human society. It is this ignorance about the nature of man which throws so much uncertainty and obscurity on the true definition of natural right, for the idea of right, says Mr. Burlamaqui, and still more that of natural right, are obviously ideas relating to the nature of man. Therefore, he continues, the principles of this science must be deduced from this very nature of man, his constitution and his condition.[4]

It is not without a sense of surprise or shock that we observe how little agreement prevails among the various authors who have treated this important subject. Among the most serious writers we scarcely find two who are of the same opinion on this point. Without speaking of the ancient philosophers who seem to have made it their business to contradict each other on the most fundamental principles, the Roman jurists indifferently subject man and all the other animals to the same natural law, because they take this term to mean the law that nature imposes on

4. Jean Jacques Burlamaqui, *Principes du droit naturel*, 1747, I. i. 2.

itself, rather than the law that nature prescribes; or rather, because of the particular sense in which those jurists understand the term "law," which they seem to have taken only as the expression of the general relations established by nature among all living beings for their common preservation. The moderns acknowledge as a law only a rule prescribed to a moral being, that is, a being intelligent, free, and prudent in his relations with others, and, consequently, they limit the jurisdiction of natural law to the only animal endowed with reason, that is, man. But with each one defining this law in his own fashion, they all establish it on such abstract principles that even among us there are very few people in a position to understand these principles, let alone able to discover them on their own, so that all the definitions of these learned men, who otherwise perpetually contradict each other, agree on this alone, that it is impossible to understand the law of nature and, consequently, to obey it, without being skilled in reasoning and a profound metaphysician, which only means that for the establishment of society, men must have made use of the kind of understanding that is developed only with great difficulty and by very few people within society itself.

With so little knowledge of nature and such dissension over the meaning of the word *law*, it would be very difficult to come to any agreement on a good definition of natural law. Thus all those definitions found in books, aside from a lack of uniformity, also have the fault of being drawn from several areas of knowledge that men do not naturally possess, and from advantages they cannot even imagine until after having left the state of nature. Writers begin by searching for rules which men would appropriately agree upon among themselves for the common welfare, and then they give the name of natural law to this collection of rules, without any other proof than the good which would presumably result from their universal application. Surely that is a very convenient way to compose definitions and to explain the nature of things by virtually arbitrary conventions.

But insofar as we are ignorant of natural man, it will be useless for us to try to determine the law that he received or the one which is best suited to his constitution. All that we can very clearly see with regard to this law is that for it to be a law, the will of anyone who is bound by it must be capable of submitting to it knowingly, and that, furthermore, for it to be natural, it must speak directly by the voice of nature.

Leaving aside, therefore, all the scientific books which teach us only to see men as they have made themselves, and pondering the first and simplest operations of the human soul, I believe I perceive in it two principles that are prior to reason, of which one makes us ardently interested in our well-being and our self-preservation, and the other inspires in us a natural repugnance to seeing any sentient being, and principally our fellow men, perish or suffer. It appears to me that the ability of our mind to coordinate and combine these two principles, without the need for introducing that of sociability here, gives rise to all the rules of natural right, rules that reason is then forced to reestablish on other foundations, when, by its successive developments, it has succeeded in smothering nature.

In this way, we are not obliged to make man a philosopher before making him a man; his duties towards others are not dictated to him solely by the belated lessons of wisdom, and as long as he does not resist the inner impulse of compassion, he will never do harm to another man, or even to any other sentient being, except in those legitimate cases where, since his own preservation is involved, he is obliged to give preference to himself. By this means, the old debate concerning the applicability to animals of natural law can be put to an end, for it is clear that, bereft of understanding and liberty, they cannot recognize this law, but since they share to some extent in our nature by virtue of the sensibility with which they are endowed, it will be thought that they must also participate in natural right, and that man is bound by some kind of duty towards them. It seems, in fact, that if I am obliged to do no harm to my fellow man, it is less because he is a rational being than because he is a sensitive being, since sensitivity is a quality which is common to man and beast and should at least give the beast the right not to be needlessly mistreated by the man.

This same study of original man, his true needs, and the fundamental principles of his duties, is also the only effective means of overcoming the host of difficulties that present themselves concerning the origin of moral inequality, the true foundations of the body politic, the reciprocal rights of its members, and a thousand other similar questions that are as important as they are obscure.

When human society is considered with a serene and dispassionate eye, it seems, at first, to display only the violence of powerful men and the oppression of the weak; the mind rebels against the harshness of the former; it is inclined to lament the blindness of the latter; and as nothing is less stable among men than those external relations, more often produced by chance than by wisdom, which are called either weakness or power, or wealth or poverty, human institutions appear at first glance to be founded on shifting sands; it is only by examining them closely, only after having cleared away the dust and sand surrounding the edifice, that we perceive the unshakable base on which it has been raised, and that we learn to respect its foundations. Now, without a serious study of man, his natural faculties, and their successive developments, we shall never succeed in making these distinctions, and in distinguishing, in the present constitution of things, what the divine will has done from what human art has claimed to do. The political and moral inquiries inspired by the important question I am examining are therefore useful in every way, and the hypothetical history of governments is, in every respect, an instructive lesson for man. In considering what would have become of us, left to ourselves, we should learn to bless Him whose benevolent hand, by correcting our institutions and giving them an unshakable foundation, has prevented the disorders that would otherwise result from them, and has brought forth our happiness from means that seemed apt to redouble our misery.

> Quem te Deus esse
> Jussit, et humana qua parte locatus es in re,
> Disce.[5]

Notice on the Notes

I have added a few notes to this work, according to my lazy habit of working in fits and starts. Sometimes these notes stray so far from the subject that it is not appropriate to read them with the text. I have therefore relegated them to the end of the *Discourse,* in which I have tried my best to follow the straightest path. Those who have the courage to begin again will be able to amuse themselves a second time by beating the bushes and attempting to run through the notes; there will be little harm done if others do not read them at all.[6]

Question

Proposed by the Academy of Dijon.

What is the origin of inequality among
men, and is it authorized
by natural law.

Discourse on the Origin and Foundations of Inequality among Men

It is man that I am to discuss, and the issue I am examining tells me that I am going to speak to men, for such questions are not proposed by those who are afraid of honoring the truth. I shall, therefore, defend the cause of humanity with confidence before the wise men who invite me to do so, and I shall not be displeased with myself if I prove worthy of my subject and my judges.

I conceive of two kinds of inequality among the human species; one I call natural or physical, because it is established by nature and consists of differences in age, health, physical strength, and qualities of mind or soul; the other may be called moral or political inequality, because it depends upon a kind of agreement and is established or at least author-

---

5. Persius, *Satires,* III. 73–71. "Learn what divinity has ordered you to be, and what your place is in human affairs."
6. Only Rousseau's most significant notes—IX, XI,

XV, and XIX—have been included. Also found among the footnotes are the additions to the *Discourse* made by Rousseau in the 1782 edition.

ized by the consent of men. The latter consists of the different privileges that some enjoy to the detriment of others, such as being more wealthy, more honored, more powerful than they, or even making themselves obeyed by them.

It is impossible to ask what the source of natural inequality is, because the answer is given in the simple definition of the word; it is even more impossible to find out if there is some essential connection between the two kinds of inequality, for that would amount to asking, in other words, if those who command are necessarily more worthy than those who obey, and if strength of body or mind, wisdom or virtue, are always found in the same individuals in proportion to power or wealth, a good question to be debated among slaves within hearing distance of their masters, perhaps, but unfitting for rational and free men seeking the truth.

What precisely is, then, the point of this discourse? To indicate in the progression of events the moment at which right replaced violence and nature was subjected to law; to explain the chain of miracles by which the strong could resolve to serve the weak and the people could purchase the semblance of peace at the price of true felicity.

Philosophers who have examined the foundations of society have all felt the need to go back to the state of nature, but none of them has reached it. Some have not hesitated to attribute the notion of the just and unjust to man in that state, without bothering to demonstrate that he had to have this notion or even that it was useful to him; others have spoken of the natural right of each to preserve what belongs to him, without explaining what they meant by the word *belong*; still others, who begin by granting the strongest authority over the weakest, have immediately gone on to discuss how governments arise, without considering the time which must have elapsed before the meaning of the words authority and government could have existed among men. All of them, in short, constantly speaking of need, greed, oppression, desires, and pride, have transferred to the state of nature ideas they have acquired in society; they speak of savage man and they depict civil man. It has not even entered the minds of most of our philosophers to doubt that the state of nature ever existed, whereas it is evident from reading the Holy Scriptures that the first man, having received his understanding and commandments directly from God, was not himself in that state, and that in giving Moses' writings the credence that every Christian philosopher owes them, it must be denied that men were ever in the pure state of nature, even before the deluge, unless they fell back into it through some extraordinary circumstance: a paradox which is highly embarrassing to defend and quite impossible to prove.

Let us begin, therefore, by setting all the facts aside, for they have no bearing on the question.[7] The research which can be conducted on this

---

7. What are the facts that Rousseau here vows to ignore? Some have thought they are the facts about man's early history as depicted in the Bible; others believe the facts referred to concern the effects of social living on personality. Rousseau may mean to ignore both sorts of facts, since neither sort sheds light on the character of people who live in social isolation. Notice later in this *Discourse* that he uses facts about extant primitive peoples to back up some of his conjectures.

subject need not be taken as historical truth, but only as hypothetical and conditional arguments, better suited to explain the nature of things than to reveal their true origin, just like those our physicists set forth every day upon the formation of the world. Religion commands us to believe that since God Himself took men out of the state of nature, they are unequal because He wanted them to be, but it does not forbid us to form conjectures drawn solely from man's nature and the beings which surround him about what might have become of the human race, if it had been left to itself. That then is what I am being asked, and what I propose to examine in this discourse. As my subject concerns man in general, I shall try to use a language that suits all nations, or rather, forgetting times and places in order to think only of the men to whom I am speaking, I shall imagine myself in the Lyceum of Athens, repeating the lessons of my masters, with such men as Plato and Xenocrates for judges, and the human race for an audience.

O Man, from whatever country you come, whatever your opinions may be, listen: here is your history as I thought I read it, not in the books of your fellow men, which are deceptive, but in nature, which never lies. All that comes from nature will be true; nothing will be false except what I have involuntarily put there on my own. The times of which I am going to speak are very remote. How much you have changed from what you once were! It is, so to speak, the life of your species that I am going to describe to you in accordance with the qualities which you received and which your education and habits could corrupt but not destroy. There is, I feel, an age at which the individual man would like to remain; you shall seek the age at which you would have desired your species to remain. Discontent with your present state, for reasons which promise still greater unhappiness for your unfortunate posterity, perhaps you would like to have the power to go back, and this sentiment will celebrate your early ancestors, criticize your contemporaries, and frighten those who will have the misfortune to follow you.

First Part

However important it may be, in order to judge the natural state of man accurately, to consider him from his origins and to examine him, as it were, in the embryo of the species, I shall not trace his structure through its successive developments; I shall not stop to seek within the animal system what he may have been at the beginning in order to have become what he is at last; I shall not examine whether, as Aristotle thinks, his elongated nails were at first hooked claws, whether he was hairy like a bear, and whether the range of his vision, which was directed toward the earth and restricted to a horizon of a few paces, revealed both the nature and limits of his ideas. I could make only vague and almost imaginary conjectures on this subject; comparative anatomy has still made too little progress and the observations of the naturalists are still too uncertain for the basis of a sound argument to be established on such foundations. Thus, without having recourse to the supernatural knowledge that we have on this point, and without considering the changes which must have occurred as much in the internal as in the external structure of man as he applied his limbs to new uses and fed himself upon new foods, I shall suppose him always to have been formed as I see him today, walking on two feet, using his hands as we do ours, casting his glance over all of nature, and measuring the vast expanse of heaven with his eyes.

By stripping this being, thus constituted, of all the supernatural gifts he could have received and of all the artificial faculties he could have acquired only by long progress, by considering him, in a word, as he must have come from the hands of nature, I see an animal less strong than some, less agile than others, but, on the whole, the most advantageously constituted of all; I see him eating his fill under an oak tree, quenching his thirst at the first stream, making his bed at the foot of the same tree which furnished his meal, with all his needs satisfied.

Left to its natural fertility and covered with immense forests that the axe has never mutilated, the earth offers at every step stores of food and shelter to animals of every species. The men dispersed among them observe and imitate their industry, and thus attain the instincts of the beasts, with the advantage that, unlike any other species which has only its own instinct, man, who has none which belongs to him alone, appropriates them all, lives equally well on most of the different foods that the other animals share among themselves, and, consequently, finds his subsistence more easily than any of them.

Accustomed from infancy to bad weather and the harshness of the seasons, inured to fatigue, and forced, naked and unarmed, to defend their lives and their prey from other wild beasts, or to escape from them by running, men acquire a robust and almost unalterable constitution; the children, bringing into the world with them the excellent constitution of their parents fortifying it by the same exercises that produced it, thus acquire all the vigor of which the human species is capable. Nature treats them precisely as the law of Sparta treated the children of citizens; it makes strong and robust those with good constitutions and lets all the others perish, differing in that respect from our societies, in which the state, by making children burdensome to parents, kills them indiscriminately before they are born.

As the savage man's body is the only instrument he knows, he puts it to various uses for which our bodies, through lack of exercise, are unfit, and it is our industry which deprives us of the strength and agility that necessity obliges him to acquire. Had he had an axe, would he have broken such strong branches with his hands? Had he had a sling, would he have thrown a stone so hard? Had he had a ladder, would he have climbed trees so nimbly? Had he had a horse, would he have been so swift a runner? Give civilized man the time to assemble all these tools around him, and he will undoubtedly overcome savage man with ease, but if you want to see an even more unequal contest, pit them against each other naked and unarmed, and you will soon see the advantage of having all one's strength constantly at one's disposal, of always being prepared for every event, and of always carrying one's whole self, so to speak, with one.

Hobbes claims that man is naturally intrepid and only interested in attacking and fighting. An illustrious philosopher[8] thinks, on the contrary, and Cumberland and Pufendorf also assure us, that nothing is as timid as man in the state of nature, and that he is always trembling and ready to flee at the least noise he hears or the least movement he perceives. That may be so for the things he does not know, and I do not doubt that he is frightened by all the new sights that greet him, whenever he is unable to discern the physical good or evil he may expect from them, or to compare his strength with the risks that he must run. Such circumstances are rare in the state of nature, where all things proceed in such a uniform manner, and where the face of the earth is not subject to those sudden and continual changes caused by the passions and inconstancy of united peoples. But living dispersed among the animals and soon finding himself in a position to pit himself against them, savage man soon makes the comparison, and, sensing that he surpasses them more in adroitness than they surpass him in strength, he learns to fear them no longer. Set a bear or a wolf against a savage, robust, agile, courageous as they all are, armed with stones and a good stick, and you will see that the danger will at the very least be reciprocal, and that after several such experiences, wild beasts, which do not like to attack each other will less willingly attack man, whom they will have found quite as ferocious as themselves. With regard to the animals that are actually stronger than man is skillful, he is, in relation to them, in the position of other weaker species, which are able to subsist, with the advantage for man, that being no less fit than they are for running and finding almost certain refuge in the trees, he may, in every situation, take or leave any encounter, and make the choice between flight or combat. Let us add that, apparently, no animal naturally makes war upon man except in the case of its own self-defense or extreme hunger, or evinces any of those violent antipathies toward him which seem to indicate that one species is destined by nature to serve as food for the other.[9]

Other more formidable enemies against which man lacks the same means of defending himself are the natural infirmities, infancy, old age, and illnesses of every kind, the sad signs of our weakness, of which the first two are common to all animals, whereas the last belongs principally to men living in society. On the subject of infancy, I will even observe that a mother, carrying her child with her everywhere, can feed it much

8. Montesquieu in *The Spirit of the Laws*, I. 2. In this work Montesquieu (1689–1755) develops a theory to explain the form a government takes which refers to the physical, economic, political, and moral conditions of a people.

9. This is no doubt the reason why negroes and savages do not become very uneasy about the wild animals they meet in the woods. In this respect, the Caribs of Venezuela, among others, live in the most absolute security and without the slightest disadvantage. Although they are almost naked, says François Corréal, they nevertheless expose themselves boldly in the woods, armed only with bow and arrow, but no one has ever heard of any of them being devoured by wild beasts [Rousseau's note, 1782].

more easily than the females of several other animals, which are constantly forced to come and go, greatly fatigued by seeking their own food in one place and suckling and feeding their young in another. It is true that if the woman happens to perish, the child is in great danger of dying with her, but this risk is common to a hundred other species, whose young are for a long time unable to go seek nourishment for themselves, and if infancy lasts longer among humans, life also lasts longer, and everything is still nearly equal in this respect, although there are other rules concerning the duration of infancy and the number of young, which are not part of my subject. Among old people, who are less active and perspire little, the need for food diminishes with the ability to provide it; and since savage life keeps them from gout and rheumatism, and as old age is, of all the ills, the one which human assistance can least alleviate, they finally pass away, without anyone being aware that they have ceased to exist, and almost without being aware of it themselves.

With respect to illnesses, I shall not repeat the vain and false declamations which most healthy people make against medicine, but I shall ask if there is any solid observation from which it may be concluded that in the countries where this art is most neglected the average lifetime of man is shorter than in those where it is cultivated with the greatest care. And how could that be, if we bring upon ourselves more ailments than medicine can furnish remedies! The extreme inequality in the manner of living, the excessive idleness of some, the excessive labor of others, the ease of exciting and satisfying our appetites and our sensual desires, the overly refined foods of the rich, which nourish them with constipating sauces and prostrate them with indigestion, the bad food of the poor, which they more often lack than not, so that they greedily overburden their stomachs whenever they can, late nights, excesses of every kind, immoderate outbursts of all the passions, hardships, spiritual exhaustion, innumerable pains and afflictions which are felt in every class, and which keep our souls in perpetual torment—this is the deadly proof that most of our ailments are of our own making, and that we could have avoided nearly all of them by preserving the simple, uniform, and solitary manner of living which was prescribed for us by nature. If nature destined us to be healthy, I venture to affirm that the state of reflection is contrary to nature and that the man who meditates is a depraved animal.[1] When we think of the good constitution of savages, at least of those whom we have not ruined with our strong liquors, when we realize that they rarely experience any illnesses other than wounds and old age, we are very inclined to believe that the history of human illnesses could easily be written by following that of civil societies. Such is, at least, the opinion of Plato, who judges, on the basis of certain

---

1. This provocative declaration has often been read as an unqualified attack upon reason. But the context shows that Rousseau is here attacking reason only insofar as it impairs health. Although it depraves us as animals, it need not deprave us altogether. In fact, Rousseau goes on to suggest, on p. 39, that the benefits of reasoning for people who live in society are considerable. Yet, compare below, on p. 29, where Rousseau says reason engenders self-love. Rousseau's evaluation of reason is a crucial but elusive aspect of his thought.

remedies used or approved by Podalirios and Machaon at the siege of Troy, that the various illnesses which these remedies must have inflamed were still not, at that time, known among men.[2]

With so few sources of disease, man in the state of nature has, then, little need of remedies and less still of physicians, and, in this regard, the human species is in no worse a condition than all the others; and it is easy to learn from hunters whether they find many infirm animals on their trips. They find some with large wounds which are well healed, or with broken bones and limbs which have recovered with no other surgeon than time and no other regimen than their everyday life, and they are no less perfectly cured for not having been tormented by incisions, poisoned with drugs, or exhausted by fasting. In short, however useful properly administered medicine may be among us, it is always certain that if the ailing savage left on his own has nothing to hope for but from nature, he has, in compensation, nothing to fear but from his disease, which often makes his situation preferable to ours.

Let us, therefore, guard against confusing savage man with the men we have before our eyes. Nature treats all the animals left to its care with a partiality that seems to show how jealous it is of this right. The horse, the cat, the bull, even the ass are generally taller, and all have a more robust constitution, more vigor, strength, and courage in the forests than in our homes; they lose half these advantages as they become domesticated, and it could be said that all our efforts to treat these animals well and to feed them serve only to debase them. It is thus with man himself. As he becomes sociable and a slave, he becomes weak, timid, and servile; his soft and effeminate manner of living completely exhausts both his strength and his courage. Let us add that between the savage and domestic conditions the differences from man to man must be even greater than that from beast to beast, for although the animals and man have been treated alike by nature, man gives himself more conveniences than the animals he tames, and these conveniences become so many special causes which make his degeneration more perceptible.

It is not, therefore, such a great misfortune for these first men, nor is it even such a great obstacle to their preservation, to be without clothes and shelter, deprived of all those useless things we believe so necessary. If they do not have hairy skin, they do not need it in the warm countries, and, in the cold countries, they soon learn how to appropriate the skins of beasts they have overcome; if they have but two feet for running, they have two arms to provide for their defense and their needs; perhaps their children walk late and with difficulty, but the mothers carry them with ease, an advantage lacking in other species, in which the mother, when pursued, is forced to abandon her young or to adjust her pace to theirs. Finally, unless we presuppose these singular and fortuitous conjunctions of events, which I shall subsequently discuss and which might very well never occur, it is clear, in any case, that the first person who made

___
2. And Paracelsus reports that diet, so necessary today, was first invented by Hippocrates [Rousseau's note, 1782].

himself clothes or lodging thereby gave himself things that were hardly necessary, since he had done without them until then, and since it is difficult to see why he could not have endured as a grown man the kind of life he had endured from his infancy.

Alone, idle, and always near danger, savage man must be fond of sleeping, and he must be a light sleeper, like animals which, thinking little, sleep, so to speak, whenever they are not thinking. Since his own preservation is almost his sole concern, his best-developed faculties must be those devoted principally to attack and defense, either to subjugating his prey or to protecting himself from being the prey of another animal; organs which are perfected only by softness and sensuality, on the contrary, must remain in a crude state, which makes him incapable of any kind of delicacy, and, as his senses are divided in this way, he will have extremely coarse senses of touch and taste along with the most acute senses of sight, hearing, and smell. Such is the condition of animals in general, and it is also, according to the reports of travelers, that of most savage peoples. Thus, we should not be astonished that the Hottentots of the Cape of Good Hope can sight vessels on the high sea with the naked eye at as great a distance as the Dutch with telescopes; or that the savages of America track Spaniards by smell as well as the best dogs; or that all these savage nations endure their nakedness with ease, sharpen their palate with red pepper, and drink European liquors like water.

Up to this point, I have considered only physical man; let us now try to look at him from the metaphysical and moral side.

In every animal, I see only an ingenious machine to which nature has given the senses to maintain its own strength and to protect itself, up to a certain point, from all that tends to disturb it or to destroy it. I perceive precisely the same things in the human machine, with the difference that, whereas nature alone does everything in the operations of the beast, man cooperates in his own as a free agent. The one chooses or rejects through instinct, and the other through a free act; this means that the beast cannot deviate from the rule prescribed for it, even when it would be advantageous to do so, and that man often deviates from his own rule to his detriment. Thus, a pigeon would die of hunger near a dish filled with the choicest meats, and a cat on a heap of fruit or grain, although either could very well live on the food that it disdains, if it had only thought of trying it; thus, dissolute men give themselves over to excesses, which bring on fever and death, because the mind depraves the senses and the will still speaks when nature is silent.

Every animal has ideas because it has senses; it even combines its ideas up to a certain point, and, in this regard, man differs from beasts only in degree. Some philosophers have even claimed that there is a greater difference between one man and another than between a certain man and a certain beast; it is, therefore, not so much the understanding which constitutes the specific difference between man and the animals as his capacity as a free agent. Nature commands every animal and the beast obeys. Man feels the same impulsion, but he knows that he is free to acquiesce or to resist; and it is particularly in the consciousness of this liberty that the spirituality of his soul is displayed, for physics in some way explains the mechanism of the senses and the formation of ideas, but, in the power of willing, or rather of choosing, and in the consciousness of this power, there are only purely mental acts, which cannot be explained by the laws of mechanics.

But even if the difficulties that surround all these issues left some room for raising questions about this difference between man and animal, there is another very specific quality which distinguishes one from the other and about which there can be no debate; this is the faculty of self-improvement, a faculty which, with the aid of circumstances, successively develops all the others and is inherent in us, as much in the species as in the individual, whereas an animal is, at the end of a few months, what it will be all its life, and its species, at the end of a thousand years, what it was the first year of that thousand. Why is man alone prone to becoming an imbecile? Is it not that he thus returns to his original state and that, whereas the beast, which has acquired nothing and which has nothing more to lose, is always left with its instinct, man, losing once again by old age or other accidents all that his *perfectibility* had enabled him to acquire, thus sinks even lower than the beast? It would be sad for us if we were forced to admit that this distinctive and almost unlimited faculty is the source of all the misfortunes of man; that this faculty, in the course of time, draws him out of that original condition in which he would have spent tranquil and innocent days; and that this faculty, by causing his knowledge and his errors, his vices and virtues to flourish over the centuries, makes him, in the long run, a tyrant over himself and over nature.[3] It would be dreadful to be obligated

---

3. [Note IX] A famous author, calculating the good and evil in human life and comparing the two sums, found that the latter surpassed the former by far, and that, all things considered, life was, for man, a rather poor gift. I am not surprised by his conclusion; he based all his arguments on the constitution of civil man. If he had gone back to natural man, it is likely that he would have obtained very different results, that he would have perceived that man has scarcely any weaknesses other than those he has given himself, and that nature would have been justified. It is not without difficulty that we have succeeded in making ourselves so unhappy. When we consider, on the one hand, the vast labors of men, the many sciences thoroughly studied, the many arts invented, the many forces utilized, the chasms filled, the mountains razed, the rocks broken up, the rivers made navigable, the lands cleared, the lakes dug out, the swamps drained, the enormous buildings raised on earth, the seas covered with ships and sailors; and when we inquire, on the other, with a little thought into the real advantages which have resulted from all of that for the happiness of the human species, we can only be struck by the astonishing disproportion that prevails among these things and deplore the blindness of man, who, in order to feed his foolish pride and I know not what vain admiration for himself, runs eagerly after all the miseries to which he is prone, and from which beneficent nature had taken care to protect him.

Men are wicked—sad and continual experience dispenses with the need for proof; however, I believe I have demonstrated that man is naturally good. What, then, can have depraved him to this extent, if not the changes that have arisen in his constitution, the progress he has made, and the knowledge that he has acquired? Let people admire human society as much as they wish; it will be no less true that society necessarily brings men to hate each other in the degree that their interests conflict, to render to each other apparent services, and, in fact, to do every imaginable harm to each other. What can be thought of dealings in which the reason of each private individual dictates maxims to him that are directly contrary to those which public reason preaches to the society as a whole, and in which each profits from the misfortune of others? There is perhaps no well-to-do man whose avid heirs, and often his own children, do not secretly wish for his death; no ship at sea whose destruction would not be good news to some merchant; no business establishment that a dishonest debtor would not like to see burned along with all the papers it contains; no people that does not rejoice in the disasters of its neighbors. Thus it is that we find our advantage in the misfortunes of our fellow men, and that one person's loss almost always creates another's prosperity, but what is still more dangerous is that public calamities become the expectation and hope of countless private individuals. Some wish for illnesses, others for death, others for war, others for famine; I have seen dreadful men weep with sorrow at the prospect of a fertile year, and the great and deadly fire of London, which cost the life or property of so many unfortunates, made the fortune of perhaps more than ten thousand persons. I know that Montaigne blames the Athenian Demades for having had a worker punished who, by selling coffins at a very high price, gained much from the death of the citizens. But since Montaigne advances the argument that everyone should be punished, it evidently confirms my own.[a] Therefore, let us penetrate beyond our frivolous demonstrations of good will to what goes on in the depth of human hearts, and let us reflect upon what the state of things must be where all men are forced to cherish and destroy each other at the same time, and where they are born enemies by duty and swindlers by interest. If someone answers to me that society is constituted in such a way that each man gains by serving others, I shall reply that this would be very well if he did not gain still more by harming them. There is no profit, however legitimate, that is not surpassed by one that can be made illegally, and the wrong done to one's neighbor is always more lucrative than the good turns. It is, therefore, no longer a question of anything other than finding ways of being assured of acting with impunity, and it is to this end that the powerful use all their strength and the weak all their guile.

Once he has eaten, savage man is at peace with all nature and the friend of all his fellows. What if a dispute sometimes arises over his meal? He never comes to blows without first having compared the difficulty of winning with that of finding his subsistence elsewhere; and since pride is not involved in the quarrel, it ends with a few blows of the fist; the victor eats, the vanquished goes off to seek his fortune, and all is peaceful. But for man in society, there are very different concerns; there is, in the first place, the matter of providing for the necessities and then for the superfluities; next come the luxuries, then immense riches, and then subjects and slaves; he does not have a moment of respite. What is most remarkable is that the less natural and urgent his needs, the more his passions grow, and, what is worse, his power to satisfy them, so that after lengthy prosperity, after having swallowed up many treasures and having destroyed many men, my hero will end by slaughtering everything until he is the sole master of the universe. Such is, in brief, the moral picture, if not of human life, at least of the secret aspirations in the heart of every civilized man.

Compare with an open mind the condition of civil man with that of savage man, and inquire, if you can, into the extent to which—beyond his wickedness, his needs, and his miseries—the former has opened new doors to sorrow and death. If you consider the mental anguish that consumes us, the violent passions that drain and distress us, the excessive work with which the poor are burdened, and the still more dangerous laxity to which the rich give themselves up, so that the poor die from their needs and the rich from their excesses; if you think of the monstrous mixtures of foods, their pernicious seasonings, the spoiled foodstuffs, the adulterated drugs, the dishonesty of those who sell them, the errors of those who administer them, the poison in the vessels in which they are prepared; if you pay attention to the epidemics generated by the bad air in crowds of men gathered together, to those caused by the refinement of our way of living, to going back and forth from inside our houses into the open air, to the use of clothing put on or taken off with too little care, and to all the concerns that our excessive sensuality has turned into needs, which cost us our life or health if we neglect them or deprive ourselves of them; if you take into account the fires and earthquakes which, by engulfing or turning entire cities upside down, cause the inhabitants to perish by the thousands; in a word, if you add up the dangers that all these causes continually bring down upon our heads, you will be conscious of how dearly nature makes us pay for the contempt in which we have held its lessons.

I shall not repeat here what I have said elsewhere about war, but just once, I wish knowledgeable people would be willing or even daring enough to give the public details about the atrocities committed in armies by the suppliers of rations and hospitals; we would see that their not overly secret manoeuvres, which make even the most brilliant armies ineffectual, cause more soldiers to perish than are cut down by enemy swords; it is no less astonishing to calculate the number of men swallowed up every year by the sea, or by hunger, scurvy, pirates, fire, or shipwrecks. Clearly, we must also credit to established ownership and, consequently, to society, assassinations, poisonings, highway robbery, and even the punishments for these crimes, punishments necessary to prevent greater evils, but which, for the murder of one man, cost the lives of two or even more, and actually double the real loss to the human species. How many shameful means of preventing human births and outwitting nature are there? Either by those coarse and depraved tastes which insult its most charming handiwork, tastes unknown to savages and animals, and which arise in civilized countries only in corrupted imaginations; or by those secret abortions, the consequences worthy of debauchery and depraved honor; or by the exposure or murder of countless infants, victims of their parents' poverty or the barbarous shame of their mothers; or, finally, by the mutilation of those unfortunates, a part of whose existence and entire posterity are sacrificed to vain whims, or what is still worse, to the brutal jealousy of a few men, a mutilation which, in this last case, doubly outrages nature, both by the treatment given to those who endure it and by the use to which they are destined.[b]

What if I undertook to show the human species attacked at the time of its origin and even in the most holy of all its bonds, in which no one any longer dares to listen to nature except after having consulted fortune, and in which civil disorder confuses virtues with vices, continence becomes a criminal precaution, and the refusal to grant one's fellow man his life becomes an act of humanity?

But without tearing the veil which conceals so many horrors, let us be content with identifying the ill for which others must supply the remedy.

To all that, let us add the many unhealthy trades which shorten a man's days or destroy his constitution, such as working in mines, preparing various metals and minerals, especially lead, copper, mercury, cobalt, arsenic, and realgar, and those other perilous trades which daily cost the lives of many workers, including roofers, carpenters, masons, and those working at other careers; let all these things be combined, I say, and it will be possible to see in the establishment and perfection of societies the reasons for the diminution of the species observed by more than one philosopher.

Luxury, which is impossible to prevent among men who are greedy for their own conveniences and for the consideration of others, soon completes the harm begun by societies, and under the pretext of supporting the poor, who need not have been created, it impoverishes all the rest, and sooner or later depopulates the state.

Luxury is a remedy much worse than the evil it claims to cure; or rather, it is itself the worst of all the evils in any state whether large or small, which, in order to maintain the throngs of valets and wretches that it has created, overwhelms and ruins the ploughman and the citizen, like those scorching winds of the Midi, which, covering the grass and shrubs with ravenous insects, deprive useful animals of their subsistence and carry famine and death into all the places where they are felt.

From society and from the luxury it engenders arise the liberal and mechanical arts, commerce, letters, and all those useless things that industry makes flourish and that enrich and ruin states. The reason for this destruction is very simple. It is easy to see that, by nature, agriculture must be the least lucrative of all the arts, because the use of its products is the most indispensable for all men, and its price must be proportionate to the means of the poorest. From the same principle it is possible to derive the rule that, in general, the arts are lucrative in an inverse ratio to their utility and that the most necessary must finally become the most neglected. From this we see what to think of the true advantages of industry and the actual results of its progress.

Such are the tangible causes of all the misery into which opulence finally hurls the most admired nations. To the degree that industry and the arts spread and flourish, the scorned farmer, burdened with the taxes necessary for supporting luxury and condemned to spend his life between work and hunger, abandons his fields to go into the cities and seek the bread that he ought to be bringing there. The more the capitals strike the stupid eyes of the people as admirable, the more necessary it is to bemoan seeing the countryside abandoned, land lying fallow, and roads inundated with unfortunate citizens who have become beggars or thieves, and are destined one day to end their misery on the wheel or a dungheap. It is thus that the state, growing rich on one hand, grows weak and becomes depopulated on the other, and that the most powerful monarchies, after much labor to make themselves affluent and uninhabited, end by becoming the prey of poor nations, which succumb to the deadly temptation to invade them, and which, in their turn, grow rich and weak, until they are themselves invaded and destroyed by still others.

Let someone please explain to us just once what could have produced those waves of barbarians who inundated Europe, Asia, and Africa for so many centuries? Did they owe this prodigious population to the vigor of their arts, to the wisdom of their laws, to the excellence of their organization? Let our scientists kindly tell us why, instead of multiplying to this degree, these savage and brutal men, lacking in knowledge, restraint, and education, did not all slaughter each other at every opportunity, in quarreling over their grazing land or hunting places? Let them explain to us how these wretched men even had the audacity to look straight into the eyes of people as clever as we were, with such fine military discipline, such fine codes, such wise laws? Finally, why, since society has been perfected in the northern countries, and since so much trouble has been taken to teach men their mutual obligations and the art of living together agreeably and peacefully, do we no longer see the like of those multitudes of men that were produced in the past? I am very afraid that someone will at last take it into his head to tell me that all those grand things, namely the arts, the sciences, and the laws, have been very wisely invented by men as a salutary pestilence to prevent the excessive multiplication of the species, lest this world which is destined to us might at last become too small for its inhabitants.

What then? Is it necessary to destroy societies, to annihilate yours and mine, and to return to living in the forests with the bears? An inference in the manner of my adversaries that I would rather anticipate than allow them the shame of drawing it. O you, to whom the celestial voice has not made itself heard and who acknowledge no other destiny for your species than to live out this short life in peace; you who can leave your deadly achievements, your restless minds, your corrupted hearts, and your unbridled passions in the midst of cities, reclaim—since it depends on you—your ancient and original innocence; go into the woods to lose from sight and memory the crimes of your contemporaries, and do not fear that you will debase your species by renouncing its knowledge in order to renounce its vices. As for men like me, whose passions have forever destroyed their original simplicity, who can no longer subsist on grass and acorns nor do without laws and leaders; those who were honored through their first father with super-natural lessons; those who will see the justification of a precept which is unimportant in itself and inexplicable within every other system in the intention of giving to human actions in the beginning a morality that they had only acquired over a long period of time; those, in a word, who are convinced that the divine voice called the entire human species to the enlightenment and happiness of the celestial intelligences; all those, through practicing the virtues they commit themselves to follow as they learn to recognize them, will strive to deserve the eternal reward they should expect from them; they will respect the sacred bonds of the societies to which they belong; they will love their fellow men and serve them with all their power; they will scrupulously obey the laws and the men who are their authors and ministers; they will honor above all the good and wise princes who know how to

to praise as a beneficient being the one who first suggested to the inhabitant of the banks of the Orinoco how to use those boards he binds to his children's temples, which insure them of at least a part of their imbecility and original happiness.

Left by nature to instinct alone, or rather, compensated for the instincts he may lack by faculties capable first of replacing them and then of raising him far above nature, savage man will, therefore, begin with purely animal functions. Perception and feeling will be his first state, which he will hold in common with all the animals. Willing and not willing, desiring and fearing will be the first and almost the only operations of his soul, until new circumstances cause it to undergo new developments.

Whatever the moralists may say about it, human understanding owes much to the passions, which, it is commonly agreed, also owe much to the understanding. By the activity of the passions, our reason is perfected; we seek knowledge only because we desire enjoyment, and it is impossible to conceive why a person who has neither desires nor fears would take the trouble to reason. The passions, in their turn, find their origin in our needs and owe their progress to our knowledge, for things can be desired or feared only on the basis of ideas that we can form about them or through the simple impulsion of nature, and savage man, bereft of every sort of enlightenment, experiences only passions of this

---

prevent, cure, or palliate the throng of abuses and evils always ready to overwhelm us; they will stir the zeal of these worthy leaders by showing them without fear and flattery the grandeur of their task and the rigor of their duty. But they will not have any less contempt for a constitution which can be maintained only with the help of so many respectable people who are more often sought than found, and from which, despite all their pains, there always arise more real calamities than apparent advantages.[c] [Rousseau's Note]

a. Michel de Montaigne (1533–92), *Essays*, I.i. 22.

b. But are there not a thousand cases still more frequent and more dangerous in which paternal rights openly offend humanity? How many talents have been buried and how many inclinations forced by the imprudent constraint of fathers! How many men who die wretched and dishonored in a profession for which they had no taste would distinguish themselves in a suitable one! How many happy but unequal marriages have been broken up or troubled, and how many chaste spouses dishonored by these class distinctions which always contradict the order of nature! How many other strange unions have been created by interest and disavowed by love and reason! How many truly honest and virtuous spouses keep each other in agony for having been poorly matched? How many unfortunate young victims of their parents' avarice plunge into vice or pass their sad days in tears and groan under the burden of indissoluble bonds that the heart rejects and gold alone has created! Sometimes fortunate are those whose very courage and virtue have snatched them from life before barba-

rous violence forces them to spend it in crime or despair. Forgive me, forever deplorable father and mother. I embitter your sorrows with reluctance, but may they serve as an eternal and terrible example to anyone who dares, even in the name of nature, to violate the most sacred of her rights!

I have spoken only of those malformed bonds which are the work of our civil order; does anyone think that those over which love and sympathy have presided are themselves free from disadvantages? [Rousseau's note, 1782.]

c. In the final paragraph of this note, which Rousseau added at the last minute, when the work was in press, he faces the question of what should be done to cope with the misery which he has explained and described. His answer here, though much more colored by resigned acceptance than the one offered in *On Social Contract*, proceeds from many of the same premisses. In both works Rousseau denies the possibility of returning to the asocial state of nature. In both he acknowledges that the corruption caused by social life dooms any attempt to improve conditions, though in *On Social Contract* he adopts a somewhat more hopeful stance than the critical resignation suggested here. Both works thus view the problem of reform from the same perspective, graphically delineated by Rousseau in his *Letter to Philopolis*, which responds to one of the numerous critics of the *Discourse on Inequality*: "Society is as natural to the human species as decrepitude is to individuals, and arts, laws, and governments are as necessary for peoples as crutches are necessary for old men," necessary, but not legitimate, unl... they meet the requirements *On Social Contract* describes.

last kind; his desires do not exceed his physical needs.[4] The only goods he knows in the universe are food, a female, and sleep; the only evils he fears are pain and hunger; I say pain, and not death, for an animal will never know what it is to die, and knowledge of death and its terrors is one of the first acquisitions that man made in leaving the animal state.

It would be easy for me, if it were necessary, to support this opinion with facts and to show that in all the nations of the world the progress of the mind has been precisely proportionate to the needs the peoples had received from nature or to those to which circumstances had subjected them and, consequently, to the passions which induced them to provide for those needs. I would show the arts springing up in Egypt and spreading with the overflowing of the Nile; I would follow their progress among the Greeks, where they were seen to germinate, grow, and rise to the heavens among the sands and rocks of Attica without being able to take root on the fertile banks of the Eurotas; I would observe that, in general, the peoples of the North are more industrious than those of the South because they can afford even less not to be so, as if nature thus wanted to equalize things by endowing minds with the fertility it refuses the earth.

But without taking recourse to the uncertain testimonies of history, who does not see that everything seems to remove savage man from the temptation and means to cease being what he is? His imagination depicts nothing for him; his heart demands nothing of him. His moderate needs are so easily satisfied, and he is so far from the level of knowledge necessary for wanting to acquire greater knowledge, that he can have neither foresight nor curiosity. The spectacle of nature becomes unimportant to him, by dint of becoming familiar. There is always the same order, there are always the same revolutions; he does not have the mind to wonder at the greatest marvels, nor can we seek within him the philosophy that man needs in order to know how to examine at some point what he has seen every day. His soul, which nothing can agitate, is wholly given over to the sentiment of its present existence, with no idea of the future, however near it may be, and his plans, as limited as his views, hardly extend to the end of the day. Such is the Carib's degree of foresight even today; he sells his cotton bed in the morning and comes weeping to buy it back in the evening, having failed to foresee that he would need it for the next night.

The more we ponder this subject, the greater the distance between pure sensations and simple knowledge seems to us, and it is impossible to conceive how a man, through his own strength alone, without the help of communication, and without the goad of necessity, could have

---

4. [Note XI] That seems most obvious to me, and I cannot conceive how our philosophers can establish the origin of all those passions they attribute to natural man. Except for the bare physical necessities that nature itself demands, all our other needs have arisen only through habit, before which they were not needs, or through our desires, and one does not desire what one is not in a position to know. From this it follows that nothing could be as tranquil as the soul or as limited as the mind of savage man, who desires only the things that he knows and knows only the things he has the power to possess or are easy to acquire [Rousseau's note].

bridged so great a gap. How many centuries may have elapsed before men were in a position to see any fire other than that from the heavens? How many different chances did they need to learn the most common uses of this element? How often did they let it die out before they acquired the art of reproducing it? And how often may each of these secrets have died with the one who had discovered it? What shall we say about agriculture, an art which demands so much labor and foresight, which depends on other arts, which could very obviously be practiced only in a society that has at least begun, and which is not so much used to procure foods from the earth, which could provide them plentifully without cultivation, as to force it to produce foods that are more to our taste? But let us suppose that men had multiplied to such an extent that the natural produce would no longer have sufficed to feed them, a supposition which, it may be said in passing, would reveal a great advantage for the human species in this way of living. Let us suppose that without forges and workshops, the tools for tilling had fallen from the heavens into the hands of the savages; that these men had vanquished the mortal hatred they all feel towards continuous labor; that they had learned to foresee their needs so far in advance that they had guessed how the earth must be cultivated, grains sown, and trees planted; that they had discovered the art of milling grain and fermenting grapes. These are all things that they must have been taught by the gods, since it is impossible to conceive how they could have learned them on their own. After that, who would be the man mad enough to torment himself by cultivating a field which will be despoiled by the first comer, man or beast, for whom this crop is suitable; and how could each man resolve to spend his life at hard labor, the reward from which is all the more necessary to him the more certain he is of not reaping it? In a word, how could this situation lead men to cultivate the land as long as it is not parceled out among them, that is to say, as long as the state of nature has not been abolished?

Even if we wish to suppose a savage man as skillful in the art of thinking as our philosophers make him out to be; even if we should, following their example, make him out to be a philosopher himself, discovering on his own the most sublime truths, creating for himself, by chains of highly abstract reasoning, maxims of justice and reason derived from the love of order in general or the known will of his Creator; in a word, even if we suppose his mind to be as intelligent and enlightened as it actually is dull and stupid, what use would the species make of all this metaphysics, which could not be communicated and which would perish with the individual who had invented it? What progress could the human race make scattered in the woods among the animals? And to what degree could men mutually perfect and enlighten each other, who, having neither a fixed domicile nor any need of one another, would perhaps meet scarcely twice in their lives, without knowing each other and without speaking to each other.

Let us bear in mind how many ideas we owe to the use of speech, how far grammar trains and facilitates the operations of the mind; and let us bear in mind the unbelievable efforts and the infinite time that the first invention of languages must have cost; let us join these reflections to the preceding ones, and we shall judge how many thousands of centuries must have been necessary for the successive development of the operations of which the human mind was capable.

Permit me, for a moment, to consider the obstacles to the origin of languages. I could content myself with citing or repeating here the research that the Abbé de Condillac has done on this subject, which fully confirms my opinion, and which perhaps even inspired my first ideas about it. But since the way in which this philosopher resolves the objections that he himself raises about the origin of established signs shows that he has assumed what I bring into question, namely, a kind of society already established among the inventors of language, I believe that in referring to his thoughts on this matter, I should add my own in order to discuss the same difficulties in light of my own subject. The first one that comes to mind is to imagine how languages could have been necessary, for since men had no dealings with each other, and no need of any, it is impossible to understand the necessity for inventing languages or even how they became possible, if they were not indispensable. I could well say, like many others, that languages were born in the domestic intercourse between fathers, mothers, and children, but, aside from the fact that this would not resolve the difficulties, it would be repeating the mistake of those who, in reasoning about the state of nature, transfer to it ideas that they have acquired in society; they always see the family gathered together in the same dwelling, with its members maintaining among themselves a union as intimate and permanent as the kind that exists among us, in which a great many common interests unite them. Nevertheless, the fact remains that in this primitive state, having neither houses nor huts nor property of any kind, each person took shelter at random, and often for only one night; males and females united fortuitously, according to chance encounters, opportunity, and desire, without any great need for the power of speech to express what they had to say to each other; they parted from each other with the same ease. At first, the mother nursed her children for her own sake, and, later, when habit had endeared them to her, she nourished them for their own; as soon as they were strong enough to seek their own food, they were not long in leaving her, and since there was almost no other way of finding each other again except by keeping each other in sight, they soon reached the point of not even recognizing each other. Observe further that since the child has to explain all his needs and, consequently, has more to say to the mother than the mother to the child, it must be the child who makes the greatest efforts to invent language, and that the language he uses must be largely of his own making; this would bring into being as many languages as there are individuals to speak them; the wandering, vagabond life, which gives no idiom the time to become consistent, contributes to this multiplication, for to say that the mother teaches the child the words he must use to ask her for this thing or that clearly shows how existing languages are taught, but not how they arose.

Let us suppose that this first difficulty has been overcome. Let us, for a moment, cross over the immense distance which must have separated the pure state of nature from the need for languages; and, assuming them to be necessary, let us try to discover how they might have begun to arise. Here we encounter a new difficulty, worse still than the preceding one, for, if men needed speech to learn how to think, they needed still more to know how to think in order to discover the art of speaking; and even if we understood how vocal sounds were taken as the conventional expressions of our ideas, it would still remain for us to discover what the conventional expressions may have been for ideas that, having no tangible objects, could not be indicated either by gesture or by voice. For this reason, we are scarcely able to formulate tenable conjectures concerning the birth of this art of communicating our thoughts and establishing intercourse between minds, a sublime art which is already very far from its origins, but which the philosopher sees as still being at such a prodigious distance from its perfection that there is no man bold enough to affirm that it will ever reach it, even if the revolutions time necessarily brings about were suspended in its favor, even if prejudice left the academies or stood silent before them, and even if they were able to devote themselves to this thorny problem for entire centuries without interruption.

Man's first language, the most universal, the most energetic, and the only one he needed before it became necessary to persuade an assembly of men, is the cry of nature. Since this cry was wrenched from him only by a kind of instinct in pressing circumstances to beg for help in great dangers, or for relief from violent ills, it was not of great use in the ordinary course of life, where more moderate feelings prevail. When the ideas of men began to spread and multiply, and when closer communication was established among them, they sought more numerous signs and a more extensive language. They multiplied vocal inflections and combined them with gestures, which are more expressive by nature and whose meaning depends less on a prior agreement. They therefore expressed visible and moving objects by means of gestures and audible ones by means of imitative sounds, but since a gesture indicates scarcely anything but objects which are present or easily described and actions which are visible, and since its use is not universal, because darkness or the interposition of a body renders it useless, and since it requires rather than arouses attention, men finally thought of substituting vocal articulations, which, without having the same relationship to certain ideas, are better adapted to represent them all as conventional signs. Such a substitution could only be made by common consent and in a way rather difficult to put into practice for men whose crude organs had as yet no training, and still more difficult to conceive in itself, since that unanimous agreement must have been motivated in some way, and since the power of speech appears to have been quite necessary in order to establish the use of speech.

It must be assumed that the first words men used had, in their mind, a much broader meaning than do those used in languages that are already formed, and that, ignorant of the division of discourse into its constituent parts, they at first gave each word the meaning of a whole sentence. When they began to distinguish subject from predicate, and verb from noun, which was no mean effort of genius, substantives were at first only so many proper nouns; the infinitive[5] was the only verb tense; and, any notion of adjectives must have developed only with considerable difficulty, because every adjective is an abstract word, and abstractions are irksome and rather unnatural operations of the mind.

At first, each object was given a particular name, without regard to genus and species, which these first founders were not in a position to distinguish, and all individual things presented themselves to their minds in isolation, as they are in the spectacle of nature. If one oak tree was called A, another was called B,[6] so that the more limited their knowledge, the more extensive their dictionary must have become. The burden of all this nomenclature could not be easily eliminated, for in order to arrange beings according to common and generic denominations, it was necessary to know their properties and differences; observations and definitions were necessary, that is to say, far more natural history and metaphysics than the men of those times could have possessed.

Moreover, general ideas can be introduced into the mind only with the help of words, and the understanding grasps them only by means of sentences. This is one of the reasons why animals can neither formulate such ideas nor ever acquire the perfectibility that depends upon them. When a monkey moves unhesitatingly from one nut to another, does anyone think that he has the general idea of this type of fruit and that he compares its archetype with these two individual nuts? Undoubtedly not, but the sight of one of those nuts recalls to his memory the sensations he received from the other, and his eyes, modified in a certain way, announce to his sense of taste the modification it is about to receive. Every general idea is purely intellectual; if the imagination is involved at all, the idea immediately becomes particular. Try to draw for yourself the image of a tree in general, and you will never succeed in doing it; in spite of yourself, you must see it as small or large, sparse or bushy, light or dark, and if you could see in it nothing but what is found in every tree, this image would no longer resemble a tree at all. Purely abstract beings are perceived in the same way, or are conceived only by means of discourse. The definition alone of a triangle gives you the true idea of it. As soon as you picture one in your mind, it is a particular triangle and not another, and you cannot avoid making its lines perceptible or its plane colored. It is therefore necessary to utter sentences; it is then necessary to speak to have general ideas, for as soon as the imagination ceases working, the mind progresses no further without the help of dis-

---

5. The present infinitive [Rousseau's note, 1782].
6. For the first idea inferred from two things is that they are not the same, and it often takes a long time to observe what they have in common [Rousseau's note, 1782].

course. If therefore the first inventors of speech could give names only to the ideas they already had, it follows that the first substantives could never have been anything but proper nouns.

But when, by means I cannot conceive, our new grammarians began to extend their ideas and to generalize their words, the ignorance of the inventors must have subjected this method to very strict limitations; and just as they had at first gone too far in multiplying the names of individual things, for lack of any knowledge of the genera and species, they later created too few of them for having failed to consider beings in all their differences. Extending the divisions far enough would have required more experience and knowledge than they could have had and more research and labor than they were willing to expend on it. Now if even at present, new species are discovered every day that until now had escaped all our observations, just imagine how many of them have remained hidden from men who judged things only on first appearance! As for the primary classes and the most general notions, it is superfluous to add that these too must have escaped them. How, for example, would they have imagined or understood the words "matter," "mind," "substance," "mode," "figure," and "movement," when our philosophers, who have been using them for such a long time, have themselves great difficulty in understanding them, and when, since the ideas attached to these words are purely metaphysical, they found no models for them in nature?

I must stop with these first steps, and I beg my judges to suspend their reading here to consider, concerning the invention of physical substantives alone, that is, the easiest part of the language to invent, the distance it still had to go until it could express all the thoughts of men, assume a constant form, be spoken in public, and have an influence upon society. I beg them to consider how much time and knowledge were necessary to discover numbers, abstract words, aorists, and all the tenses of verbs, particles, syntax, the linking of sentences, reasoning, and formulating all the logic of discourse. As for myself, frightened by the increasing difficulties and convinced of the nearly certain impossibility that languages could arise and be established by purely human means, I leave to anyone who will undertake it the discussion of this difficult problem: which was more necessary, a previously established society for the invention of languages, or a previously invented language for the establishment of society?

Whatever the origin of language may be, it is easy to see from the lack of care nature has taken to bring men together through mutual needs or to facilitate their use of speech how little it has prepared them to be sociable, and how little it has contributed to all they have done to establish social bonds. Indeed, it is impossible to imagine why, in that primitive state, a man would sooner need another man than a monkey or a wolf its fellow creature, or, assuming he had this need, what motive could commit the other to provide for it, or even, in this last case, how they could agree among themselves on the conditions. I know that we are told over and over again that nothing could have been so miserable as man in the state of nature, and if it is true, as I believe I have proved, that he could have had the desire and the opportunity to leave that state only after many centuries, this would be a complaint to lodge against nature and not against the one whom nature had thus constituted. But, if I really understand this term *miserable*, it is a word which has no meaning or which signifies only a painful privation and the suffering of body or soul. Now, I would like someone to explain to me what kind of misery there can be for a free being, whose heart is at peace and whose body is healthy. I ask which one, civil or natural life, is most subject to becoming unbearable for those who enjoy it? Around us, we see almost no one but people who complain of their existence, even some who deprive themselves of it insofar as it is in them, and divine and human laws together scarcely suffice to put a stop to this disorder. I ask if anyone has ever heard it said that a free savage has so much as dreamed of complaining about life and of killing himself? Let us therefore judge, with less pride, the side on which true misery lies. Nothing, on the contrary, would have been so miserable as savage man dazzled by knowledge, tormented by passions, and reasoning about a state different from his own. A very wise providence determined that his potential faculties were to develop only with the opportunities to exercise them, so that they might be neither superfluous and burdensome to him, before they were needed, nor overdue and useless when they were needed. He had in instinct alone all that he needed to live in the state of nature; he has in cultivated reason only what he needs to live in society.

It appears at first that men in that state, lacking among themselves any kind of moral relationship or any known duties, could be neither good nor evil and had neither vices nor virtues, unless, taking these words in a physical sense, we call vices the qualities in the individual that can be injurious to his own preservation and virtues those which can contribute to it, in which case, it would be necessary to call the most virtuous the one who least resists the simple impulses of nature. But without deviating from the ordinary sense of the words, it is appropriate to suspend our judgment of such a situation and to distrust our prejudices, until, with scales in hand, we have investigated whether there are more virtues than vices among civilized men; or whether their virtues are more advantageous than their vices are deadly; or whether the progress of their knowledge sufficiently compensates them for the harm they do to each other as they learn of the good they ought to do for each other; or whether they would not be, all things considered, in a happier situation, having neither harm to fear nor good to hope from anyone, rather than being subject to total dependence and being obligated to receive everything from those who are not obligated to give them anything.[7]

Above all, let us not conclude with Hobbes that for want of any idea of goodness, man is naturally evil; that he is vicious because he does not

7. Rousseau draws up this balance sheet in his own ninth note (see pp. 17–18). His conclusion there should be compared with the one he draws in *On* *Social Contract,* Book I, chapter 8, where he weighs the merits of the state of nature against those of life in a legitimate state.

know virtue; that he always refuses his fellow creatures any services he does not believe he owes them; or that, by virtue of the right he properly claims to the things he needs, he foolishly imagines himself to be the sole owner of the entire universe. Hobbes very clearly saw the flaw in all modern definitions of natural right, but the inferences that he draws from his own demonstrate that he takes it in a sense which is no less false. Reasoning upon the principles that he established, this author ought to have said that the state of nature, being the one in which our concern for self-preservation is least prejudicial to that of others, was, consequently, the best suited to peace and the most fitting for the human race. He said exactly the opposite, as a result of having inappropriately included in savage man's concern for self-preservation the need to satisfy a multitude of passions which are the handiwork of society, and which have made laws necessary. An evil man, he said, is a robust child; it remains to be seen whether savage man is a robust child. Even if we were to grant this to him, what would he conclude from it? That if, when he is robust, this man was as dependent on others as when he is weak, there is no sort of excess towards which he would not be inclined; that he would beat his mother when she was too slow in giving him her breast; that he would strangle one of his young brothers when he was inconvenienced by him; that he would bite another's leg, when he was struck or disturbed by him. But being robust and being dependent are, in the state of nature, two contradictory suppositions; man is weak when he is dependent, and he is emancipated before he becomes robust. Hobbes did not see that the same cause that prevents savages from using their reason, as our jurists claim they do, also prevents them from abusing their faculties, as Hobbes himself claims they do, so that it could be said that savages are not wicked precisely because they do not know what it is to be good, for it is neither the development of knowledge nor the restraint of law, but the calm of the passions and ignorance of vice which prevent them from doing evil: *tanto plus in illis proficit vitiorum ignoratio, quam in his cognitio virtutis.*[8] There is, moreover, another principle that Hobbes did not perceive and which, having been bestowed on man to moderate, under certain circumstances, the ferocity of his self-love, or before its birth, the desire for self-preservation,[9] tempers the

---

8. Justin (3rd century A.D.) *Histories*, II.ii.15. "Among them [the Scythians], ignorance of the vices has been much more profitable than knowledge of the virtues among those others [the Greeks]."

9. [Note XV] Self-love and self-esteem must not be confused; they are two very different passions by nature and in their effects.* Self-esteem is a natural sentiment which inclines every animal to look after its own preservation and which, being guided in man by reason and modified by compassion, produces humanity and virtue. Self-love is only a relative, artificial sentiment born in society, which leads each individual to place greater value on himself than on anyone else, which inspires all the evils that men do to one another, and which is the real source of honor.

With this firmly in mind, I say that in our original state, in the true state of nature, self-love did not exist, for, since each man individually looks upon himself as the only witness to his actions, as the only being in the universe who takes an interest in him, and as the only judge of his own merit, a sentiment which originates in comparisons that he is not capable of making cannot possibly spring up in his soul; for the same reason, this man cannot feel either hate or the desire for revenge, passions which can arise only from the judgment that one has been offended; and, since it is the contempt or the intention to do harm and not the injury itself which constitutes the offense, men who know neither how to appraise each other nor to compare themselves with one other can do a great deal of

ardor he feels for his well-being with an innate repugnance toward seeing his fellow man suffer. I do not believe I have to fear any contradiction in granting to man the only natural virtue which the most excessive detractor of human virtues has been forced to recognize. I am speaking of compassion, a disposition fitting for beings as weak and subject to as many ills as we are, a virtue all the more universal and all the more useful to man, since it precedes the use of any kind of reflection within him, and so natural that the beasts themselves sometimes give perceptible signs of it. Without speaking of the tenderness of mothers for their young and of the perils they brave to protect them, we observe everyday the repugnance of horses to trample a living body under foot; and an animal does not, without some uneasiness, pass close by a dead member of its species; there are even some which give them a kind of burial; and the sorrowful lowing of cattle entering a slaughterhouse bespeaks their impression of the horrible spectacle which confronts them. We see with pleasure the author of the *Fable of the Bees* forced to recognize man as a compassionate and sensitive being and to depart from his cold and subtle style, in the example he gives, in order to offer us the pathetic image of a confined man who beholds a wild beast outside snatching a child from his mother's breast, crushing his weak limbs in its murderous teeth, and tearing his palpitating entrails apart with its claws.[1] What frightful agitation will not be felt by this witness of an event in which he takes no personal interest? What anguish will he not suffer at this sight, being unable to give any help to the fainting mother and the dying child?

Such is the pure movement of nature, prior to all reflection; such is the force of natural compassion, which the most depraved moral habits can destroy only with difficulty, since we see everyday in our theaters the kind of man who is moved and cries over the misfortunes of an unfortunate, but who, if he were in the tyrant's place, would even increase his enemy's torments. Mandeville strongly sensed that despite all their ethics, men would never have been anything but monsters, if nature had not given them compassion to sustain their reason, but he did not see that from this quality alone stem all the social virtues he wants to dispute in men. Indeed, what are generosity, clemency, humanity, if not compassion applied to the weak, to the guilty, or to the human species in general? Benevolence and even friendship are, rightly speaking, the products of constant compassion fixed upon a particular object, for, is to desire that someone not suffer anything other than to desire

violence to each other's feelings, when they gain some advantage from it, without ever offending each other. In a word, each man, considering his fellow men almost as he would animals of another species, can steal prey from the weaker or give his up to the stronger, without viewing these acts of pillage as anything but natural events, without the least impulse of insolence or spite, and without any passion other than the joy or sadness of failure or success [Rousseau's note].

*The French terms *amour-propre* and *amour de soi-même* are not easily translated into English. We

have chosen to translate the term *amour-propre* as self-love, which, in Rousseau, has the negative connotation of the kind of pride that only a civilized man feels for himself. *Amour de soi-même*, translated as self-esteem, refers to the legitimate interest a man takes in his own preservation.

1. In *The Fable of the Bees: or, Private Vices, Public Benefits* (1714), Bernard Mandeville anticipates the argument of later *laissez-faire* economists that leaving people free to pursue their particular, selfish interests is the best way to achieve the public good.

that he be happy? Even if it were true that commiseration is only a sentiment that puts us in the place of the person who suffers, a feeling that is obscure and intense in savage man, well-developed but weak in civilized man, how would this idea affect the truth of what I say other than to give it greater force? Indeed, commiseration will be all the more energetic the more intimately the onlooking animal identifies with the suffering animal. Now, it is evident that this identification must have been infinitely closer in the state of nature than in the state of reasoning. It is reason that engenders self-love, and it is reflection that strengthens it; it is reason that turns man back on himself and that separates him from all that annoys and afflicts him. It is philosophy that isolates him; it is philosophy that allows him to say privately, at the sight of a suffering man: "Perish if you will, I am safe." No longer can anything but dangers to the entire society trouble the tranquil sleep of the philosopher and tear him from his bed. His fellow man may have his throat slit with impunity under his window; the philosopher has only to put his hands over his ears and argue with himself a little to prevent nature, which rebels within him, from making him identify with the one who is being murdered. Savage man does not have this admirable talent; and for want of wisdom and reason, he is always seen surrendering heedlessly to the first sentiment of humanity. In riots, in street fights, the populace gathers and the prudent man withdraws; it is the rabble, the women of the marketplace, who separate the combatants and who prevent honest people from slitting each other's throats.

It is, therefore, very certain that compassion is a natural sentiment, which, by moderating the activity of self-esteem in each individual, contributes to the mutual preservation of the whole species. It carries us without thinking to the aid of those whom we see suffering; in the state of nature it takes the place of laws, moral habits, and virtue, with the advantage that no one is tempted to disobey its gentle voice; it will deter any robust savage from depriving a weak child or an infirm old man of the subsistence he has with great difficulty acquired, if he himself hopes to be able to find his own elsewhere. Instead of that sublime maxim of rational justice, *Do unto others as you would have them do unto you*, it inspires in all men that other maxim of natural goodness, much less perfect but perhaps more useful than the preceding one: *Do what is good for you with the least possible harm to others*. It is, in a word, in this natural sentiment rather than in any subtle arguments that we must seek the cause of the repugnance every man would feel in doing evil, even independently of the maxims of education. Although it may be possible for Socrates and minds of that stamp to acquire virtue through reason, the human race would have ceased to exist long ago, if its preservation had depended only upon the reasoning of those who compose it.

With such inactive passions and such salutary restraint, men, who were wild rather than evil and more careful to protect themselves from the harm that might be done to them than tempted to do any to others, were not subject to very dangerous quarrels. Since they had no kind of dealings with each other; since they knew, consequently, neither vanity nor consideration, nor esteem nor contempt; since they had not the least notion of yours and mine nor any real idea of justice; since they regarded the violence that they might endure as a wrong that was easily redressed and not as an injury that must be punished; and since they did not even dream of vengeance, unless it was perhaps unconsciously and on the spot, like the dog who bites the stone that is thrown at him, their disputes would rarely have had bloody consequences had they not had a subject more sensitive than food. But I see that another more dangerous subject remains for me to discuss.

Among the passions that stir the heart of man, there is an ardent, impetuous one which makes one sex necessary to the other, a terrible passion which braves all dangers, overcomes all obstacles, and which, in its fury, seems calculated to destroy the human race, which it is destined to preserve. What will become of men, prey to this unbridled and brutal rage, without modesty, without restraint, and fighting every day over the objects of their love at the price of their lives?

It must be admitted in the first place that the more violent the passions, the more necessary the laws to contain them, but, apart from the fact that the disorders and crimes they cause among us daily demonstrate well enough the insufficiency of the laws in this regard, it would still be well to examine whether these disorders were not born with the laws themselves, for, in that case, even if the laws were capable of quelling such disorders, the very least that ought to be required of them is that they put a stop to an evil that would not exist without them.

Let us begin by distinguishing the moral from the physical in the sentiment of love. The physical is that general desire which leads one sex to unite with the other; the moral is what gives rise to this desire and fixes it exclusively upon a single object, or at least gives it a greater degree of energy for this preferred object. Now, it is easy to see that the moral aspect of love is an artificial sentiment, born of social custom and celebrated by women with much care and cleverness to establish their ascendancy and to make dominant the sex that should obey. This sentiment, being founded on certain notions of merit or beauty that a savage is not in a position to have, and upon comparisons that he is not in a position to make, must mean almost nothing to him, for, just as his mind cannot form abstract ideas of regularity and proportion, so his heart is not susceptible to the sentiments of admiration and love, which, even without being perceived, arise from the application of these ideas; he listens solely to the temperament he has received from nature and not to the taste he has not been able to acquire, and any woman is good for him.

Limited to what is physical in love, and fortunate enough to be ignorant of those preferences that inflame this sentiment and increase its difficulties, men must feel the ardors of their temperament less frequently and less sharply, and must, consequently, have fewer and less cruel disputes among themselves. Imagination, which wreaks so much havoc among us, does not speak to savage hearts; each peacefully awaits the impulsion of nature, yields to it involuntarily, with more pleasure than fury, and, once the need is satisfied, all desire is extinguished.

It is, therefore, incontestable that love itself, like all the other passions, has acquired only in society that impetuous ardor which often makes it fatal to men, and it is all the more ridiculous to portray savages constantly slaughtering each other to satisfy their brutality, since this opinion is directly contrary to experience, and since the Caribs, among all existing people who have, up to now, deviated least from the state of nature, are in fact the most peaceful in their loves and the least subject to jealousy, although they live in a scorching climate, which always seems to cause these passions to grow more active.

With regard to the inferences that might be drawn in several species of animals from the fights between the males which bloody our farmyards or which make our forests resound with their cries in the springtime as they fight over the females, it is necessary to begin by excluding all species in which nature has obviously established relations other than those among us in the comparative strength of the sexes. Thus, cockfights have no implications for the human species. In species where proportion is better observed, these fights can be caused only by the scarcity of females as compared to the number of males, or the periods of exclusion during which the female constantly refuses the advances of the male, which amounts to the same thing, for if each female tolerates the male only during two months of the year, it is the same as if the number of females were reduced by five sixths. Now, neither of these two cases is applicable to the human species, in which the number of females generally exceeds that of the males and in which, even among the savages, females have never been observed to have periods of heat and exclusion, like those of other species. Moreover, since among several of these animals the entire species comes into heat at the same time, there comes a terrible moment of universal ardor, tumult, disorder, and fighting, a moment which does not occur in the human species, in which love is never periodic. It cannot, therefore, be concluded from the fights of certain animals over the possession of females that the same thing would happen to man in the state of nature, and even if this conclusion could be drawn, since these dissensions do not destroy the other species, it must at least be presumed that they would not be more deadly to ours, and it is very apparent that they would raise less havoc in the state of nature than in society, especially in the countries where, since moral habits still count for something, the jealousy of lovers and the vengeance of husbands daily cause duels, murders, and even worse; where the duty of eternal fidelity serves only to create adulterers; and where even the laws of continence and honor necessarily spread debauchery and multiply abortions.

Let us conclude that, wandering in the forests, without industry, without speech, without shelter, without war, and without ties, with no need of his fellow men, nor any desire to harm them, perhaps without ever even recognizing anyone individually, savage man, self-sufficient and subject to few passions, had only the sentiments and knowledge appropriate to that state; that he felt only his true needs and looked only at what he believed he had an interest in seeing; and that his intelligence made no more progress than his vanity. If by chance he made some discovery, he was all the less able to communicate it, because he did not even recognize his own children. Art perished with the inventor; there was neither education nor progress; the generations multiplied uselessly; and since each generation always started out from the same point, centuries passed by in all the crudeness of the early epochs; the species was already old, and man remained ever a child.

If I have dwelled so long upon the supposition of this primitive condition, it is because, having ancient errors and inveterate prejudices to destroy, I thought that I ought to dig down to the roots and show in the picture of the true state of nature how far even natural inequality is from having as much reality and influence in this state as our writers claim.

Indeed, it is easy to see that among the differences that distinguish men, several pass for natural that are uniquely the work of habit and the various modes of living that men adopt in society. Thus, a robust or delicate temperament, the strength or weakness which depend upon it, often come more from the harsh or effeminate manner in which one has been raised than from the original constitution of the body. It is the same with strength of mind, for not only does education produce a difference between cultivated minds and those which are not, but it increases that which exists among the former in proportion to their cultivation, for if a giant and a dwarf walk on the same road, each step they take will give a new advantage to the giant. Now if the prodigious diversity of the kinds of education and the ways of living that prevails in the different orders of the civil state is compared with the simplicity and uniformity of animal and savage life, in which all nourish themselves on the same foods, live in the same manner, and do exactly the same things, it will be understood how much less the difference from man to man must be in the state of nature than in society, and how much natural inequality must increase in the human species through the inequality of social institutions.[2]

But even if nature shows as many preferences in the distribution of its gifts as is claimed, what advantage would the most favored gain from them to the detriment of others, in a state of things that would admit of almost no kind of relationship among men? Where there is no love, of what use is beauty? What will wit mean to people who do not speak, and guile to those who have no dealings with others? I constantly hear it repeated that the strongest will oppress the weak, but let someone explain to me what is meant by this word oppression. Some will dominate by violence, others will moan, being enslaved by all their own

2. Here the clear boundary between natural and social inequality drawn by Rousseau at the very beginning of the *Discourse on Inequality* begins to disappear; on pp. 41–42 below, it is almost obliterated.

whims. That is precisely what I observe among us, but I do not see how it could be said of savage men, to whom one would have great difficulty even explaining what servitude and domination are. One man might well seize the fruits another has gathered, the game he has killed, the cave which serves him as shelter, but how will he ever succeed in making himself obeyed, and what chains of dependence could there be among men who possess nothing? If someone chases me from one tree, I am free to go to another; if someone bothers me in one place, who will prevent me from going elsewhere? Is there a man with strength sufficiently superior to mine, and, in addition, depraved, lazy, and ferocious enough to force me to provide for his subsistence while he remains idle? He must resolve not to lose sight of me for a single instant, to keep me very carefully bound while he is asleep, for fear I may escape or kill him; that is to say, he is obliged to expose himself voluntarily to a difficulty much greater than the one he wants to avoid and the one he causes for me. After all this, what if he momentarily relaxes his vigilance? What if an unforeseen noise makes him turn his head? I take twenty steps into the forest, my chains are broken, and he never in his life sees me again.

Without uselessly prolonging these details, I must make everyone see that since the bonds of servitude are formed merely from the mutual dependence of men and from the reciprocal needs that unite them, it is impossible to enslave a man without first having put him in the position of being unable to do without another person. Since this situation did not exist in the state of nature, it leaves everyone free of the yoke and makes the law of the strongest useless.

After having proved that inequality is scarcely perceptible in the state of nature, and that its influence there is of almost no account, it remains for me to show its origin and progress in the successive developments of the human mind. After having shown that *perfectibility*, the social virtues, and the other faculties that natural man had received potentially could never develop on their own, that to do so they needed the fortuitous concurrence of several extraneous causes which might never have arisen, and without which man would have remained eternally in his original condition, it remains for me to bring together and to consider the different accidents that could have improved human reason while corrupting the species, made a being wicked while making him sociable, and, finally, from so distant a beginning, brought man and the world to the point where we now see them.

I acknowledge that since the events I have to describe could have happened in various ways, I can make up my mind only through conjectures, but, besides the fact that these conjectures become reasons, when they are the most probable that can be derived from the nature of things and the sole means of discovering the truth, the consequences that I want to deduce from mine will not for that reason be conjectural, since, on the basis of the principles I have just established, no other system could be formulated which would not furnish me with the same results and from which I could not draw the same conclusions.

This will excuse me from developing my reflections on the manner in which the lapse of time compensates for the small degree of probability in the events; on the surprising power of very trivial causes, when they operate constantly; on the impossibility, on the one hand, of destroying certain hypotheses, though, on the other, they cannot be given the same degree of certainty as facts; on how two facts, given as real, are to be linked by a series of intermediary facts that are unknown or regarded as such, and how it is within the province of history, when it exists, to supply the facts that link them, or within the province of philosophy, when history is absent, to establish similar facts that may link them; and finally, on how the similarity of events reduces the facts to a much smaller number of different classes than is commonly imagined. It suffices for me to offer these matters for the consideration of my judges; it suffices for me to have arranged things so that the average reader need not consider them.

Second Part

The first man who, having fenced off a plot of land, thought of saying "This is mine" and found people simple enough to believe him was the real founder of civil society. How many crimes, wars, murders, how many miseries and horrors might the human race have been spared by the one who, upon pulling up the stakes or filling in the ditch, had shouted to his fellow men, "Beware of listening to this imposter; you are lost, if you forget that the fruits of the earth belong to all and that the earth belongs to no one." But by that time, things had very probably already come to the point where they could no longer go on as they were, for this idea of property, depending upon many prior ideas which could only have arisen successively, did not suddenly take shape in the human mind. It was necessary to make much progress, to acquire considerable ingenuity and knowledge, and to transmit and increase them from age to age, before arriving at this last stage of the state of nature.[3] Let us, therefore, go further back into the matter, and let us endeavor to recount from a single point of view that slow succession of events and learning in the most natural order.

Man's first sentiment was that of his own existence, his first concern was for his own preservation. The products of the earth furnished him with all the help he needed; instinct led him to make use of them. Hunger and the other appetites made him experience, by turns, various ways of living, but there was one that invited him to perpetuate his species, and this blind inclination, devoid of any sentiment of the heart, produced only a purely animal act. Once the need was satisfied, the two sexes no longer recognized each other, and even the child no longer meant anything to the mother, as soon as he could do without her.

Such was the condition of nascent man; such was the life of an animal

---

3. Note that for Rousseau the state of nature has stages, the last of which includes many aspects of social life.

limited at first to pure sensation, scarcely profiting from the gifts that nature offered him, much less dreaming of wresting anything from it. But he had to learn to surmount the difficulties which soon arose—the height of trees, which prevented him from reaching their fruits, the competition of animals, who were seeking to feed on these fruits, or the ferocity of those for whom he served as prey; everything obliged him to apply himself to physical exercise; he had to make himself agile, swift of foot, vigorous in combat. Natural arms, such as the branches of trees and stones, were soon discovered at hand. He learned to surmount nature's obstacles, to combat other animals when necessary, to contend even with other men for his subsistence, or to compensate himself for what he had to yield to the stronger.

As the human race spread, difficulties multiplied along with men. Differences in soils, climates, and seasons could force them to make changes in their ways of living. Barren years, long hard winters, scorching summers that consume everything demanded new skills from them. Along the sea shores and the river banks they invented the hook and line and became fishermen and eaters of fish. In the forests, they made bows and arrows, and became hunters and warriors; in cold countries, they clothed themselves with the skins of beasts that they had slain; lightning, a volcano, or some happy accident acquainted them with fire, a new resource against the harshness of winter. They learned to preserve this element, then to reproduce it, and, finally, to use it to prepare the meats that they had previously devoured raw.

The repeated use of things different from himself and from each other must naturally have engendered in man's mind the perceptions of certain relations. Those relations that we express with the words large, small, strong, weak, fast, slow, fearful, bold, and other similar ideas, compared when necessary and almost without thinking about it, finally produced in him some kind of reflection, or rather, an involuntary prudence that indicated the precautions most necessary for his safety.

The new knowledge that resulted from this development increased his superiority over the other animals by making him aware of it. He practiced setting traps for them; he misled them in a thousand ways; and, although several surpassed him in strength at combat or in swiftness of foot, he became, in time, the master of those that could serve him and the scourge of those that could harm him. Thus, the first glance he cast upon himself produced in him the first impulse of pride; thus, still hardly knowing how to make distinctions of rank and considering himself in the first rank as a member of his own species, he prepared himself from afar to lay claim to first rank as an individual.[4]

Although his fellow men were not for him what they are for us, and although he had scarcely more dealings with them than with the other animals, they were not forgotten in his observations. The similarities that time could make him perceive among them, his female and him-

4. See also the account on p. 11 above of how men are affected by comparing themselves to animals in the absence of the difficulties which Rousseau here begins to describe.

self, made him identify those he did not perceive, and, seeing that all
men behaved as he himself would have done under similar circumstances, he concluded that their way of thinking and feeling was entirely
consistent with his own, and this important truth, firmly established in
his mind, made him follow, by an intuition as sure as dialectic and more
quick, the best rules of conduct appropriate for him to observe toward
them for his own advantage and safety.

Taught by experience that love of well-being is the sole motive of
human actions, he found himself in a position to distinguish the rare
occasions when common interest could make him rely on the assistance
of his fellow men, and those still rarer occasions when competition could
make him distrust them. In the first case, he united with them in a herd
or at the very most in some sort of free association, which did not obligate anyone and which lasted only as long as the passing need that had
created it. In the second, each sought his own advantage, either by open
force, if he believed he could, or by cleverness and cunning if he felt
himself the weakest.

In that way, men were able imperceptibly to acquire some crude idea
of mutual commitments and of the advantage of fulfilling them, but
only as far as present and palpable interest could demand, for foresight
meant nothing to them, and far from being interested in a distant future,
they hardly thought of the next day. If it was a matter of catching a deer,
each certainly felt strongly that for this purpose he ought to remain faithfully at his post, but if a hare happened to pass within reach of one of
them, it must not be doubted that he pursued it without scruple, and
that, having caught his prey, he troubled himself very little about having
caused his companions to miss theirs.

It is easy to understand that such intercourse did not require a language much more refined than that of crows or monkeys, which gather
together in nearly the same way. Inarticulate cries, many gestures, and
some imitative noises must have composed the universal language for a
long period of time; by adding to these a few articulated and conventional sounds, the establishment of which, as I have already said, is not
very easily explained, men in each region produced particular languages, but crude, imperfect ones, somewhat like those spoken by various savage nations today. I am traveling across multitudes of centuries
like a beam of light, forced on by time which is passing, by the abundance of things I have to say, and by the almost imperceptible progress
at the beginnings of things, for the more slowly events followed one
another, the more rapidly they can be described.

These first improvements finally put men within reach of making more
rapid ones. The more their minds were enlightened, the more industrious they became. Soon, ceasing to fall asleep under the first tree or to
withdraw into caves, they discovered a kind of hatchet made of hard,
sharp stones, which served for cutting wood, digging the earth, and making huts from branches, which they afterwards thought of coating with
clay and mud. This was the epoch of a first revolution, which brought

about the establishment of the family and the distinction between families, and which introduced a sort of property, which was perhaps the origin of many quarrels and fights. Nevertheless, since the stronger were probably the first to build themselves lodgings they felt capable of defending, it is to be presumed that the weak found it quicker and safer to imitate them than to attempt to dislodge them, and, as for those who already had huts, each must rarely have sought to appropriate that of his neighbor, less because it did not belong to him than because it was useless to him, and because he could not seize it without exposing himself to a very lively fight with the family who was occupying it.

The first developments of the heart were the effects of a new situation which united husbands and wives, fathers, and children in a common dwelling; the habit of living together gave rise to the sweetest sentiments known to men, conjugal love and paternal love. Each family became a small society all the more united because reciprocal affection and liberty were its only bonds, and, at that time, the first difference was established in the manner of living of the two sexes, who, until then, had had but one. Women became more sedentary and accustomed themselves to tending the hut and the children, while the men went out to seek their common subsistence. Through living a slightly softer life, the two sexes also began to lose something of their ferocity and vigor, but if each one separately became less fit for combatting wild animals, it was easier, on the other hand, to assemble together in order to resist them.

In this new state, with a simple and solitary life, very limited needs, and the tools that they had invented to meet them, men, enjoying very great leisure, used it to procure for themselves various kinds of conveniences unknown to their forefathers, and this was the first yoke that they unwittingly imposed upon themselves and the first source of evil they prepared for their descendants, for, besides the fact that they thus continued to soften both body and mind, and that these conveniences lost almost all their pleasantness through habit and, at the same time, degenerated into real needs, being deprived of them became much more cruel than possessing them was sweet, and people were unhappy to lose them without being happy to possess them.[5]

Here we catch a slightly better glimpse of how the use of speech was established or imperceptibly improved in the bosom of each family, and we may make further conjectures on how various particular causes could have made language spread and accelerated its progress by making it more and more necessary. Great floods or earthquakes surrounded inhabited districts with water or precipices; upheavals on the globe detached and divided portions of the continent into islands. It is conceivable that a common idiom could have taken shape sooner among men brought

5. The first source of the human misery which Rousseau diagnoses in this *Discourse* is identified here as the acquisition of material goods beyond what were needed for survival under primitive conditions. Readers should ask whether Rousseau assigns causes to this acquisition and just how much he emphasizes it in comparison with the other sources of human misery he describes in the following pages. Note particularly that on p. 38, Rousseau calls the quest for public esteem "the first step toward . . . vice."

together and forced to live together in this way than among those who roamed freely in the forests on the mainland. Thus it is very possible that after their first attempts at navigation, some islanders brought the use of speech among us, and it is at least very probable that society and languages were born on islands and were perfected there before being known on the mainland.

Everything begins to take on a new appearance. Roaming about the woods up to this time, men, having taken to a more settled way of life, slowly come together, unite in various bands, and, finally, in each region, form a particular nation, united by moral habits and character, not by regulations and laws but by the same kind of life and food and by the common influence of climate. In the end, permanent proximity cannot fail to engender some bond between different families. Young people of different sexes live in neighboring huts, the short-lived intercourse required by nature soon leads to another kind, made no less sweet and more permanent by mutual frequentation. People become accustomed to considering different objects and to making comparisons; imperceptibly, they acquire ideas of merit and beauty which produce feelings of preference. By virtue of seeing each other, they can no longer do without seeing each other again. A sweet and tender sentiment steals into their souls and, with the least opposition, becomes an impetuous fury. Jealousy awakens with love, discord triumphs, and the gentlest of the passions receives sacrifices of human blood.

As ideas and feelings succeed one another, and as the mind and heart are trained, the human species continues to be domesticated, contacts increase, and bonds are tightened. People became used to assembling in front of their huts or around a large tree. Song and dance, true children of love and leisure, became the amusement, or rather the occupation of idle men and women gathered together. Each one began to consider the others and to want to be considered in return, and public esteem came to have a value. Anyone who sang or danced the best, who was the most handsome, the strongest, the most skillful, or the most eloquent became the most highly regarded, and this was the first step toward inequality and, at the same time, toward vice. From these first preferences vanity and contempt were born on the one hand, and shame and envy on the other; and the fermentation caused by these new leavens finally produced compounds fatal to happiness and innocence.

As soon as men had begun to appraise each other and the idea of esteem was formulated in their minds, each claimed a right to it, and it was no longer possible to deny it to anyone with impunity. In that way, the first duties of civility arose, even among savages, and in that way, every intentional wrong became an open insult, because along with the injury which resulted from it, the offended party saw in it a contempt for his person, which was often more unbearable than the injury itself. Thus, as each person punished the contempt shown him by others in proportion to the degree to which he valued himself, vengeance became terrible, and men bloodthirsty and cruel. This is precisely the stage most of the savage peoples known to us have reached, and without having sufficiently distinguished between ideas and having observed how far these peoples already were from the first state of nature, some have hastened to conclude that man is naturally cruel and that he needs civil regulations to make him gentler, although nothing is so gentle as man in his primitive state, where, placed by nature at an equal distance from the stupidity of brutes and the fatal enlightenment of civil man, and limited equally by instinct and reason to protecting himself from whatever threatens him, he is restrained by natural compassion from harming anyone himself, and nothing leads him to do so, even after he himself has been harmed. For, according to the axiom of the wise Locke, *there can be no injury, where there is no property.*[6]

But it must be noted that, once society had been established and relations had already developed among men, they needed qualities different from the ones they owed to their primitive constitution; that since morality was beginning to be introduced into human actions, and since each man, prior to the existence of laws, was the sole judge and avenger of the offenses committed against him, the goodness suitable to the pure state of nature was no longer suitable to nascent society; that punishments had to become more severe as the opportunities to offend became more frequent; and that the terror of revenge had to replace the restraint of laws. Thus, although men had become less patient, and natural compassion had already undergone some deterioration, this period of the development of human faculties, maintaining a happy medium between the indolence of the primitive state and the petulant activity of our self-love, must have been the happiest and most enduring epoch. The more we reflect upon it, the more we realize that this state was the least subject to revolutions, the best for man, and that he must have left it only by some fatal accident which for the common good should never have happened. The example of savages, most of whom have been found at this stage, seems to confirm that the human race was made to remain there always; that this state is the true youth of the world; and that all the subsequent advances have apparently been so many steps towards the perfection of the individual, and, in fact, towards the decrepitude of the species.[7]

As long as men remained content with their rustic huts, as long as they confined themselves to sewing their clothing of skins with thorns or fish bones, to adorning themselves with feathers and shells, to painting their bodies with different colors, to improving or embellishing their

6. *Essay Concerning Human Understanding,* IV.iii.18. Rousseau uses Pierre Coste's translation of Locke, but he substitutes the word *d'injure* for *de l'injustice* in the phrase "il ne sauroit y avoir *de l'injustice* où il n'y a point de propriété." Rousseau may have altered Locke's quotation, since he is not speaking, at this point, of the legal possession of property, which is one of the benefits of civil society. See pp. 36–37 above.

7. Note that Rousseau considers life in a very sim-

ple society as morally superior on balance to life in "the pure state of nature," where there is no society at all. It is this passage which caused Rousseau's depiction of life in the state of nature to be associated with the concept of the noble savage, although Rousseau himself had no illusions about the savages discovered in the Americas, and considered the idea of nobility to be a product of civilized reason.

bows and arrows, to carving a few fishing boats or a few crude musical instruments with sharp stones, in a word, as long as they applied themselves only to tasks that a single man could accomplish and only to arts that did not need the cooperation of several hands, they lived free, healthy, good, and happy lives, insofar as their nature permitted, and continued to enjoy among themselves the pleasures of independent intercourse. But from the moment any one man needed help from another, and as soon as they perceived that it was useful for one man to have provisions for two, equality disappeared, property was introduced, work became necessary, and vast forests were changed into pleasant fields, which had to be watered with human sweat and in which slavery and misery were soon seen to spring up and grow with the crops.

Metallurgy and agriculture were the two arts whose invention produced this great revolution. For the poet, it is gold and silver, but, for the philosopher, it is iron and wheat that civilized men and ruined the human race; both were, consequently, unknown to the savages of America who for that reason have always remained as they were; other peoples even seem to have remained barbarians as long as they practiced just one of these arts without the other; and perhaps one of the best reasons why Europe has been, if not sooner, at least more constantly and more highly civilized than the other parts of the world is that it is both the most abundant in iron and the most fruitful in wheat.

It is very difficult to guess how men came to know and to use iron, for it is impossible to believe that, by themselves, they thought of drawing raw material from the mine and giving it the preparations necessary to start melting it before knowing what the results would be. From another point of view, this discovery can even less plausibly be attributed to some accidental fire, because mines are formed only in arid places, stripped of both trees and plants, so that it could be said that nature had taken precautions to conceal this fatal secret from us. There remains, therefore, only the extraordinary circumstance of some volcano which, by belching forth molten metallic materials, might have given observers the idea of imitating this operation of nature. Still, it is necessary to presume in them the great courage and foresight necessary to undertake such a difficult task and to envisage, from such a distant prospect, the advantages that they could derive from it, which scarcely seems possible, except in minds already much more developed than theirs must have been.

As for agriculture, its principle was known long before the practice was established, and it is scarcely possible that men, constantly engaged in obtaining their subsistence from trees and plants, would readily imagine nature's means of growing plants; rather, their industry probably turned in that direction only very late, either because trees, which along with hunting and fishing supplied their food, did not need their care, or for want of knowing how to use wheat, or for want of tools for cultivating it, or for want of foresight concerning their future needs, or, finally, for want of the means to prevent others from appropriating the fruit of their labor. Once they had become more industrious, it is possible to believe that they began by cultivating a few vegetables or roots around their huts with sharp stones and pointed sticks, long before knowing how to prepare wheat and having the implements necessary for cultivation on a large scale, without mentioning the fact that in order to devote oneself to this occupation and to sow the land, one must resolve to lose something at first in order to gain a great deal in the future, a precaution very far removed from savage man's turn of mind, since, as I have said, he finds it very difficult, in the morning, to think of his needs for the evening.

The invention of the other arts was, therefore, necessary to force the human race to apply itself to that of agriculture. As soon as some men were needed to smelt and forge iron, other men were needed to feed them. The more the number of workers happened to increase, the fewer the hands employed in supplying the common subsistence, without there being fewer mouths to consume it, and since some needed foodstuffs in exchange for their iron, the others finally discovered the secret of using iron to increase the supply of foodstuffs. Thus, on the one hand, tilling and agriculture were born, and, on the other, the art of working metals and multiplying their uses.

From the cultivation of lands necessarily followed their division, and from property, once recognized, the first rules of justice, for, in order to render to each his own, each must be able to possess something. Moreover, as men began to project their plans into the future, and as all saw themselves with some property to lose, there was not one of them who did not have to fear reprisals against himself for the wrongs he might do to others. This origin is all the more natural as it is impossible to conceive of the idea of property arising from any source other than manual labor, for it is not apparent what else a man can give, besides his own labor, to appropriate things that he has not made. Labor alone gives the farmer a right to the produce of the ground he has tilled and, consequently, a right to the land, at least until the harvest, and thus from year to year, that which constitutes continuous possession is easily transformed into property. When the ancients, says Grotius, gave Ceres the epithet of legislatrix and the name of Thesmaphoria to a festival celebrated in her honor, they made it understood in that way that the division of lands produced a new kind of right, that is, the right of property, which is different from the one which results from natural law.

Things in this state might have remained equal, if talents had been equal, and if, for example, the use of iron and the consumption of foodstuffs had always been in exact balance, but since there was nothing to maintain this balance, it was soon broken; the strongest did more work; the most skillful turned his to better advantage; the most ingenious found ways to curtail his work; the farmer needed more iron, or the blacksmith more wheat; and, by working equally, one earned a great deal, while the other had barely enough to live on. Thus, natural inequality spreads imperceptibly along with contrived inequality, and the differences among men, developed by differences in circumstances, make themselves more obvious, more permanent in their effects, and begin, in the same proportion, to influence the fate of individuals.

Things having reached this point, it is easy to imagine the rest. I shall not stop to describe the successive invention of the other arts, the progress of languages, the testing and use of talents, the inequality of fortunes, the use or abuse of wealth, or all of the details that follow upon these and that everyone can easily supply for himself. I shall limit myself only to taking a look at the human species placed in this new order of things.

Behold, then, all our faculties developed, memory and imagination in play, self-love aroused, reason made active, and the mind having almost reached the limit of the perfection to which it is susceptible. Behold all the natural qualities put into action, the rank and fate of each man established, not only upon the amount of his property and his power to serve or to harm, but also upon mind, beauty, strength, or skill, upon merit or talents, and since these qualities were the only ones capable of attracting consideration, it soon became necessary to possess them or to affect them; it was necessarily to one's advantage to seem to be other than what one was in fact. To be and to appear became two completely different things, and from this distinction sprang imposing ostentation, deceptive cunning, and all the vices which follow in their train. From yet another perspective, behold man as free and independent as he formerly was, subjugated, so to speak, by a multitude of new needs to all of nature, and especially to his fellowmen, whose slave he becomes, in a sense, even in becoming their master; rich, he needs their services; poor, he needs their help, and even being of average wealth does not enable him to do without them. He must, therefore, constantly seek to interest them in his fate, and make them find it profitable, either actually or apparently, to work for it. This makes him deceitful and crafty with some, imperious and harsh with the others, and makes it necessary for him to abuse all those whom he needs, when he cannot make himself feared by them, and when he does not find it in his interest to serve them in a useful way. Finally, consuming ambition, the zeal to elevate their relative fortune, less out of true need than to set themselves above others, inspires in all men a base inclination to harm each other, a secret jealousy, all the more dangerous as it often assumes the mask of benevolence in order to strike its blow in greater safety; in a word, competition and rivalry on the one hand, conflicts of interest on the other, and always the hidden desire to profit at the expense of others—all these evils are the first effects of property and the inseparable consequences of nascent inequality.[8]

Before signs to represent wealth had been invented, it could scarcely consist of anything but land and livestock, the only real goods men can possess. Now, when inheritances had increased in number and extent

---

8. At the very beginning of the second part of this *Discourse*, Rousseau makes private property the principal cause of misery. Although his depiction of the role of property is extremely dramatic, he does not think it is the first, let alone a sufficient cause, of the deceit, competition, and dependence which compose the human misery this paragraph describes.

to the point that they covered the entire earth and were all contiguous to one another, none could be enlarged any longer except at the expense of others, and the supernumeraries, whom weakness or indolence had prevented from acquiring anything in their turn, became poor without having lost anything, because, although everything was changing around them, they alone had not changed and were obliged to receive or to steal their subsistence from the hand of the rich, and from that point domination and servitude, or violence and pillage, according to the different characters of the rich and the poor, began to arise. The rich, for their part, had scarcely become acquainted with the pleasure of domination, before they began to disdain all others, and, using their former slaves to subdue new ones, they thought of nothing but subjugating and enslaving their neighbors, like those hungry wolves which, having once tasted human flesh, reject all other food, and no longer want anything but men to devour.

In this way, since the most powerful or the most miserable made of their strength or their needs a kind of right to the possessions of others, equivalent, in their opinion, to the right of property, equality was destroyed and followed by the most frightful disorder. In this way, the usurpations of the rich, the brigandage of the poor, the unbridled passions of all, stifling natural compassion and the still feeble voice of justice, made men avaricious, ambitious, and wicked. Between the right of the strongest and the right of the first occupant arose a perpetual conflict which came to an end only in fights and murders. Nascent society made way for the most horrible state of war; the human race, wretched and debased, no longer able to retrace its steps or to renounce its unfortunate acquisitions, and working only toward its shame by abusing the faculties that honor it, brought itself to the brink of ruin.

> *Attonitus novitate mali, divesque miserque,*
> *Effugere optat opes, et quae modo voverat, odit.*[9]

It is impossible that men did not at last reflect upon such a miserable situation and upon the calamities that overwhelmed them. The rich, above all, must soon have felt how disadvantageous for themselves was a state of perpetual war, in which they alone bore all the costs and in which, although all risked their lives, they alone risked their property. Furthermore, however they might disguise their usurpations, the rich were well aware that they were established only upon a precarious and irregular right, and that, having been acquired only by force, they could be taken away from them by force without their having any grounds for complaint. Even those whom industry and ingenuity alone had made rich could scarcely found their property on better titles. They would say in vain: "I built this wall; I earned this piece of ground through my

---

9. Ovid, *Metamorphoses*, XI. 127–28. "Shocked by the newness of the ill, rich, and yet wretched, he seeks to run away from his wealth and hates what he once prayed for." Rousseau refers to the unbearable situation in which Midas found himself after Bacchus granted his wish that everything he touches turn to gold.

labor." Others could respond: "Who gave you the boundary lines; and on what basis do you claim the right to be paid at our expense for work that we did not impose upon you? Are you not aware that vast numbers of your brothers perish or suffer from needing what you have in excess, and that you needed the express and unanimous consent of the human race to appropriate anything from the common subsistence that went beyond your own?" Lacking reasons valid enough to justify himself and strength sufficient to defend himself, easily able to overwhelm an individual but overwhelmed himself by bandits, alone against all, and, on account of mutual jealousies, unable to join forces with his equals against enemies united by the common hope of plunder, the rich man, pressed on by necessity, finally conceived the most carefully thought out plan that ever entered the human mind; this was to use in his favor the very forces of those who were attacking him, to make his adversaries into his defenders, to inspire them with other maxims and to give them other institutions, which were as favorable to him as natural law was opposed.

To this end, after having shown his neighbors the horror of a situation which armed them against each other, which made their possessions as burdensome as their needs, and in which no one found safety either in poverty or in wealth, he easily invented plausible reasons for leading them to his goal. "Let us unite," he said to them, "to protect the weak from oppression, to restrain the ambitious, and to assure each person of the possession of what belongs to him; let us institute rules of justice and peace to which all are obligated to conform, that favor no one in particular, and that in some way make amends for the caprices of fortune by subjecting equally the powerful and the weak to mutual duties. In a word, instead of turning our forces against ourselves, let us assemble them into a supreme power which governs us according to wise laws, protects and defends all the members of the association, repulses common enemies, and maintains us in an eternal concord."

Far fewer words than these were needed to win over crude, easily seduced men who had, furthermore, too many difficulties to clear up among themselves to be able to do without arbitrators and too much avarice and ambition to be able to do without masters for long. All ran headlong into their chains, hoping to ensure their liberty, for, along with enough reason to be conscious of the advantages of political institutions, they did not have enough experience to foresee their dangers; those most capable of anticipating the abuses were precisely those who counted on profiting from them, and even the wise saw the necessity of resolving to sacrifice one part of their liberty to preserve the rest, just as a wounded man has his arm cut off to save the rest of his body.

Such was, or must have been, the origin of society and laws, which gave new fetters to the weak and new powers to the rich, irretrievably destroyed natural liberty, established forever the law of property and inequality, made clever usurpation into an irrevocable right, and, for the benefit of a few ambitious individuals, henceforth subjected the whole human race to labor, servitude, and misery.[1] It is easy to see how the establishment of a single society made that of all the others indispensable, and how, to make headway against united forces, it was necessary to unite in turn. Multiplying or spreading rapidly, societies soon covered the entire surface of the earth, and it was no longer possible to find a single corner in the universe where a person could throw off the yoke and pull his head out from under the often ill-guided sword that he saw hanging perpetually over it. Once civil law had thus become the common rule among citizens, the law of nature retained a place only between the various societies, where, under the name of the law of nations, it was tempered by certain tacit conventions to make relations possible and to take the place of natural commiseration, which, having lost between one society and another nearly all the power that it had between one man and another, no longer dwells in any but a few great cosmopolitan souls, who break through the imaginary barriers which separate peoples, and who, in their benevolence, embrace the whole human race, after the example of the sovereign being who created them.

Remaining thus in the state of nature in relation to each other, political bodies soon felt the effects of the disadvantages that had forced individuals to leave it, and among these great bodies, this state became still more deadly than it had been formerly among the individuals who composed them. This was the origin of the national wars, battles, murders, reprisals that make nature shudder and shock reason, and of all those horrible prejudices that place the honor of shedding human blood in the ranks of the virtues. The most decent people learned to count among their duties that of slaughtering their fellow men; men were finally seen massacring each other by the thousands without knowing why; and there were more murders committed in a single day of combat and more horrors in the taking of a single town, than had been committed in the state of nature over the whole face of the earth during entire centuries. Such are the first effects one perceives of the division of the human race into different societies. Let us come back to their beginnings.

I know that some writers have ascribed other origins to political societies, such as the conquests of the most powerful, or the association of the weak, and the choice among these causes is immaterial to what I wish to establish. Nevertheless, the one I have just set forth seems to me the most natural for the following reasons:[2] (1) Because, in the first case, since the right of conquest is not a right and could not be the basis of any other, the conquerer and the conquered peoples always remain in a state of war towards each other, unless the nation, restored to complete

---

1. The social contract just presented as a remedy to the state of war is condemned here as a failure and a moral abomination. In *On Social Contract*, Rousseau will prescribe a more promising political arrangement to remedy the difficulties described here as arising from the conflicts engendered by social life.

2. Changing the focus of his essay, Rousseau turns here from analysis of the causes of human misery to a discussion, which continues episodically to p. 54, of the standards for deciding whether or not a government is legitimate. The same topic is more systematically considered in *On Social Contract*, Book I, chapters 2–5.

freedom, voluntarily chooses its conquerer as its leader. Until then, whatever capitulations may have been made, since they have been founded only upon violence, and since they are, therefore, *ipso facto* null and void, there can be, according to this hypothesis, neither true society nor body politic, nor any law other than the law of the strongest. (2) Because, in the second case, the words *strong* and *weak* are equivocal, for, in the interval which exists between the establishment of the right of property or of first occupancy and that of political governments, the meaning of these terms is better rendered by the words *poor* and *rich*, because, in fact, before the creation of the laws, a man had no other means of subjecting his equals than by attacking their property or by giving them some part of his own. (3) Because, since the poor had nothing to lose but their liberty, it would have been great folly for them to rid themselves voluntarily of the only good that remained to them in order to receive nothing in exchange; because, since the rich were, on the contrary, vulnerable, so to speak, in every part of their wealth, it was much easier to harm them, and they consequently had to take more precautions in order to protect themselves; and because, in short, it is reasonable to believe that a thing has been invented by those to whom it it useful rather than by those whom it wrongs.

In its beginnings, government had no constant and regular form. The lack of wisdom and experience allowed men to perceive only present disadvantages, and they thought of finding remedies for the others only as they arose. Despite all the efforts of the wisest legislators, the political state remained ever imperfect, because it was little more than the handiwork of chance, and since it was poorly begun, time, in revealing its defects and suggesting remedies, could never correct the defects in the constitution. It was continually patched up, whereas it would have been necessary to begin by clearing the area and discarding all the old materials, just as Lycurgus had done in Sparta, in order afterwards to raise a solid edifice.[3] At first, society consisted only of a few general conventions which all private individuals had committed themselves to observe, and which the community guaranteed for each one of them. Experience must have shown how weak such a constitution was and how easy it was for lawbreakers to avoid conviction or punishment for offenses of which the public alone was to be witness and judge; the law must have been evaded in a thousand ways; disadvantages and disorders must have multiplied continually for people finally to have thought of confiding to individuals the dangerous trust of public authority and of committing to magistrates the task of enforcing obedience to the decisions of the people, for to say that leaders were chosen before the confederation was formed and that ministers of the laws existed before the laws themselves

3. The Spartan solution to the problem of human misery, which creates public spirited citizens by means of wholesale psychosocial transformation, was attractive to Rousseau. He thought it had worked in Sparta, but doubted that, owing to corruption, it could be applied in modern times. Other texts in this edition which elaborate his hopes for the Spartan solution include the chapter on the lawgiver in *On Social Contract*, Book II, chapter 7, and section II of *On Political Economy*, on establishing the reign of virtue.

is an assumption that may not be seriously debated.

It would not be any more reasonable to believe that peoples first of all threw themselves, unconditionally and forever, into the arms of an absolute master, and that the first means of providing for their common security devised by proud and untamed men was to rush headlong into slavery. Why indeed did they give themselves superiors if it was not to defend themselves against oppression and to protect their property, their liberties, and their lives, which are, so to speak, the constituent elements of their being? Now, in the relations between one man and another, since the worst that can happen is for one man to find himself at the other's mercy, would it not have been contrary to common sense to begin by transferring into the hands of a leader the only things they needed his help to preserve? What equivalent could he have offered them for the concession of so precious a right, and, if he had dared to require it under the pretext of defending them, would he not immediately have received the answer of the fable: "What more can the enemy do to us?" It is therefore incontestable, and it is the fundamental maxim of all political right, that peoples have given themselves leaders to protect their liberty and not to enslave themselves. "If we have a prince," said Pliny to Trajan, "it is so that he may preserve us from having a master."[4]

Political theorists engage in the same sophistry about the love of liberty as philosophers do about the state of nature; by the things they see, they judge very different things which they have not seen, and they attribute to men a natural inclination towards servitude on account of the patience with which those they have before their eyes endure theirs, without thinking that it is the same for liberty as for innocence and virtue, the value of which is felt only insofar as one enjoys them himself, and the taste for which is lost as soon as one has lost them. "I know the delights of your country," Brasidas used to say to a satrap who was comparing life in Sparta to that in Persepolis, "but you cannot know the pleasures of mine."[5]

Just as an untamed race horse tosses his mane and tail, paws the earth, and struggles impetuously at the mere approach of the bit, while a broken horse patiently suffers even the crop and spurs, so savage man will not bend his neck to the yoke that civilized man carries without a murmur, and he prefers the stormiest liberty to tranquil subservience. Man's natural disposition for or against servitude must not, therefore, be judged by the debasement of enslaved peoples, but by the wonders that all free peoples have wrought to save themselves from oppression. I know that the former are continually praising the peace and repose they enjoy in their chains, and that *miserrimam servitutem pacem appellant.*[6] But when I see the others sacrificing pleasure, repose, wealth, power, and life itself

---

4. Pliny the Younger (c. 61–114), *Panegyricus*, LV. 7.

5. This remark was actually made by Boulis and Sperthias to the satrap Hydarnes in Herodotus VII. 135 and reported by Plutarch in *Apophthegmata Laconica* 235 F.

6. Tacitus (c. 55– c.114), *Histories*, IV. xvii. "The most wretched servitude they call peace." In the passage from which Rousseau quotes, the Roman historian describes Civilis' efforts to foment rebellion among the Gauls against Rome.

for the preservation of this sole good, which is so disdained by those who have lost it; when I see animals who are born free and abhor captivity dash their brains out against the bars of their prison; when I see multitudes of completely naked savages scorn the sensual pleasures of Europeans and brave hunger, fire, the sword, and death merely to preserve their independence, I feel that it is not for slaves to argue about liberty.

As for paternal authority, from which some writers have derived absolute government and all society, it suffices to note, without having recourse to the contrary proofs of Locke and Sidney, that nothing on earth is further from the ferocious spirit of despotism than the gentleness of that authority which looks more to the advantage of the one who obeys than to the benefit of the one who commands; that by the law of nature the father is master of the child only as long as the child needs his help; that beyond this point they become equals; and that the son, then perfectly independent of the father, owes him only respect and not obedience, for gratitude is clearly a duty that should be owed, but not a right that can be demanded. Instead of saying that civil society is derived from paternal power, it should have been said, on the contrary, that this power draws its principle strength from civil society. An individual was acknowledged the father of several only as long as they remained assembled around him; the father's goods, of which he is really the master, are the bonds which keep the children dependent upon him, and he need not give them a share in his estate except insofar as they clearly deserve it by their constant deference to his wishes. Now, subjects are far from having some similar favor to expect from their despot, since they belong to him in their own right, they and all they possess, or at least he claims this to be the case, and they are reduced to receive as a favor whatever he leaves them of their own property; he is just when he robs them; he is merciful when he allows them to live.

By continuing in this way to examine facts in light of right, we would find no more solidity than truth in the voluntary establishment of tyranny; and it would be difficult to prove the validity of a contract which would be binding on only one of the parties, in which everything would be given to one side and nothing to the other, and which would work only to the detriment of the one who commits himself. This odious system is, even today, very far from being that of wise and good monarchs, and especially of the kings of France, as can be seen in various passages from their edicts and particularly in the following passage from a famous document, published in 1667 in the name and by the orders of Louis XIV. *Let it not be said, therefore, that the sovereign is not subject to the laws of his state, since the contrary is a true proposition of the law of nations, which flattery has sometimes attacked, but which good princes, as divine protectors of their states, have always defended. How much more legitimate it is to say with the wise Plato that perfect happiness in a kingdom is for a prince to be obeyed by his subjects, for the prince to obey the law, and for the law to be just and always directed to the public good.*[7] I shall not stop to inquire whether, since liberty is the noblest of man's faculties, we degrade our nature by lowering ourselves to the level of beasts, which are slaves of instinct, and offend even the Author of our being by renouncing without reservation the most precious of all His gifts by agreeing to commit all the crimes He has forbidden to us in order to please a savage or insane master, and whether this sublime craftsman would be angrier to see His finest handiwork destroyed than to see it dishonored. I shall disregard, if you like, the authority of Barbeyrac, who, following Locke, declares clearly that no one can sell his liberty to the point of subjecting himself to an arbitrary power, which treats him according to its fancy. "For," he adds, "this would be to sell his own life, of which he is not master."[8] I shall ask only by what right those who were not afraid to debase themselves to this degree could have subjected their posterity to the same ignominy and renounced on its behalf assets that it does not owe to their liberality and without which life itself is a burden to all who are worthy of it?

Pufendorf says that just as one transfers his property to another by agreements and contracts, he can also divest himself of his liberty in someone else's favor. This, it seems to me, is a very bad argument, for, in the first place, the property I alienate becomes something entirely foreign to me, and its abuse is unimportant to me, but it does matter to me that my liberty should not be abused, and, without making myself guilty of the evil I shall be forced to do, I cannot leave myself open to becoming the instrument of crime. Moreover, since the right of property is only a matter of convention and human institution, every man can dispose of what he possesses as he pleases, but it is not the same for the essential gifts of nature, such as life and liberty, which everyone is permitted to enjoy and of which, it is at least doubtful that one has the right to divest oneself. By ridding himself of the one, a person degrades his being; by ridding himself of the other, he destroys it insofar as he can; and, since no temporal good can compensate for the loss of either one, renouncing them at any price whatsoever would be an offense against both nature and reason. But even if liberty could be alienated like property, there would be a very great difference for the children, who come into possession of the father's property only by transmission of his right, in view of the fact that liberty is a gift that they derive from nature in their capacity as men, and their parents had no right to deprive them of it. It follows that just as it was necessary to do violence to nature to establish slavery, so it was necessary to change nature to perpetuate this right; and the jurists who have gravely pronounced that the child of a

7. A *Treatise on the Rights of the Most Christian Queen over Various States of the Spanish Monarchy*. This anonymous work was published to support Louis XIV's claim to territory in the Netherlands, which then was under Spanish jurisdiction. In the quoted passage, the Sun King is trying to justify his impending invasion of the Nether-lands as legally authorized, even though he was notorious for putting himself above the law. In citing this text, Rousseau is therefore obliquely denouncing royal absolutism.

8. This quotation is from Jean Barbeyrac's translation of Samuel Pufendorf's *The Law of Nature and Nations* (1706), VII. 7. 6, note 6.

slave would be born a slave have, in other words, decided that a man would not be born a man.

It therefore appears certain to me not only that governments did not have their foundation in arbitrary power, which is only their corruption, their extreme limit, and which finally brings them back to the law of the strongest alone, for which they were at first the remedy, but also that, even if they had begun in this manner, this power, being illegitimate by its nature, could not have served as a basis for the laws of society, nor, consequently, for instituted inequality.

Without presently entering into the research which is yet to be done upon the nature of the fundamental pact underlying every government, I limit myself, in following common opinion, to considering here the establishment of the body politic as a real contract between the people and the leaders that it chooses for itself, a contract by which the two parties obligate themselves to observe laws which are stipulated in it and which form the bonds of their union.[9] Since the people have united all their wills into a single one with respect to social relations, all the articles by which this will is explained become so many fundamental laws, which obligate all the members of the state without exception, and one of which regulates the choice and power of the magistrates charged with watching over the execution of the others. This power extends to everything that can maintain the constitution, without going so far as to change it. To it are joined honors which make the laws and their ministers respectable, and, for the latter, personal prerogatives which compensate them for the painful efforts a good administration costs. The magistrate, for his part, is obligated to use the power entrusted to him only according to the intention of his constituents, to maintain each person in the peaceful enjoyment of what belongs to him, and to prefer on every occasion the public utility to his own interest.

Before experience had shown, or knowledge of the human heart had made it possible to foresee the inevitable abuses of such a constitution, it must have seemed all the better, because those who were charged with seeing to its preservation were themselves most interested in it, for magistracy and its rights are established only upon the fundamental laws, and as soon as these were destroyed, magistrates would cease to be legitimate; people would no longer be bound to obey them; and, since it would not have been the magistrates but the laws which had constituted the essence of the state, everyone would by right recover his natural liberty.

If ever we reflected upon it attentively, this would be confirmed by new arguments, and we would see from examining the nature of the contract that it could not be irrevocable, for, if there were no superior power to guarantee the fidelity of the contracting parties or to force them

9. In this paragraph and the eight which follow, Rousseau raises many of the questions about how a legitimate state must be organized which he answers definitively in *On Social Contract*. The answers he offers here are sketchy, tentative, and significantly different from those he finally advanced.

to fulfill their reciprocal commitments, these parties would remain the sole judges of their own cases, and each of them would always have the right to renounce the contract, as soon as he found that the other was violating its terms or that they had ceased to suit him. It seems that the right to abdicate may be founded upon this principle. Now, let us consider, as we have been doing, only what is established by man. If the magistrate, who has all the power in his hands and who appropriates for himself all the advantages of the contract, still had the right to renounce authority, the people, who pay for all the leaders' mistakes, should with all the more reason, have the right to renounce their dependence. But the frightful dissensions, the endless disorders that this dangerous power would necessarily produce, show more than anything else how greatly human governments needed a basis more solid than that of reason alone, and how necessary it was to public tranquility for divine will to intervene in order to lend to sovereign authority a sacred and inviolable character, which deprived the subjects of the deadly right of disposing of it. Even if religion had done only this one good for men, it would be enough to oblige them all to cherish and adopt it, even with all its abuses, since it saves even more blood than fanaticism has ever shed. But let us follow the thread of our hypothesis.

The various forms of governments owe their origins to the greater or lesser differences which existed among private individuals at the moment of their founding. If there was one man preeminent in power, virtue, wealth, or influence, he alone was elected magistrate, and the state became monarchical; if several who were equal in most respects prevailed over all the others, they were jointly elected, and there was an aristocracy; those whose fortunes or talents were less disproportionate and who were the least removed from the state of nature held the supreme administration in common and formed a democracy. Time proved which of these forms was most advantageous to men. Some remained solely subject to laws; others soon obeyed masters. Citizens tried to protect their liberty; subjects thought only of taking it away from their neighbors, since they could not allow others to enjoy a good which they no longer enjoyed themselves. In a word, on one side there were riches and conquests, and on the other happiness and virtue.

In these various governments, all magistracies were at first elective, and when wealth did not prevail, preference was accorded to merit, which provides a natural ascendancy, and to age, which provides experience in business and composure in deliberations. The elders of the Hebrews, the gerontes of Sparta, the senate of Rome, and the very etymology of our word *seigneur* show how greatly old age was once respected. The more often elections went to men of advanced age, the more frequent they became, and the more the resulting difficulties made themselves felt; intrigues sprang up, factions formed, parties became embittered, civil wars were kindled; the blood of citizens was at length sacrificed to the alleged happiness of the state, and men were on the verge of sinking back into the anarchy of earlier times. Ambitious leading citizens profited from these circumstances to perpetuate their offices within their families; the people, already accustomed to dependence, tranquillity, and the conveniences of life, and already incapable of breaking its chains, consented to increase its servitude in order to secure its tranquillity; and the leaders, having become hereditary, thus became accustomed to regarding their magistracy as a family possession, and themselves as the proprietors of the state of which they were at first only the officers; to calling their fellow citizens their slaves; to counting them like cattle among the things that belonged to them; and to calling themselves the equals of the gods and kings.

If we follow the progress of inequality in these various revolutions, we shall find that the establishment of law and the right of property was its first stage, the institution of magistracy the second, and the transformation of legitimate power into arbitrary power the third and last. Accordingly, the condition of rich and poor was authorized by the first epoch; that of powerful and weak by the second; and, by the third, that of master and slave, which is the final degree of inequality and the stage to which all the others lead, until new revolutions dissolve the government entirely or bring it closer to legitimacy.

To understand the necessity of this progress, we must give less consideration to the motives for establishing the body politic than to the form it assumes when it acts and to the disadvantages that form entails, for the vices that make social institutions necessary are the same ones that make their abuse inevitable, and, since, with the sole exception of Sparta, where the laws were primarily concerned with the education of children and the need for additional laws was practically eliminated by the customs Lycurgus established, laws, which are in general weaker than the passions, restrain men without changing them, it would be easy to prove that every government which always functioned according to the aim of its founding, without becoming corrupted or impaired, would have been established unnecessarily, and that a country in which no one evaded the laws or abused the magistracy, would need neither laws nor magistrates.

Political distinctions necessarily lead to civil distinctions. The growing inequality between the people and its leaders soon makes itself felt among private individuals, and, there, it is modified in a thousand ways according to passions, talents, and circumstances. The magistrate cannot usurp illegitimate power without fashioning his own creatures to whom he is forced to yield some part of it. Besides, citizens only allow themselves to be oppressed to the degree that they are carried away by blind ambition, and since they pay more attention to what is below them than to what is above, domination becomes dearer to them than independence, and they consent to wear chains so that they may in turn give them to others. It is very difficult to reduce to obedience anyone who does not seek to command, nor would the most adroit politician succeed in subjecting men who wanted only to be free, but inequality spreads without difficulty among cowardly and ambitious souls, who are always ready to run the risks of fortune, and almost indifferent about whether they command or serve, depending on what is most advantageous to them. Thus, there must have come a time when the eyes of the people were so bewitched that their leaders had only to say to the least of men: "Be great, you and all your posterity," and he immediately appeared great in everyone's eyes as well as in his own, and his descendants were still more exalted the further they stood from him; the more remote and uncertain the cause, the greater its effects became; the more idlers one could count in a family, the more illustrious it became.

If this were the place to go into detail,[1] I would easily explain how, even without the involvement of government, inequality of influence and authority becomes inevitable among private individuals[2] as soon as, united in the same society, they are forced to compare themselves to each other, and to take into account the differences that they find in their habitual dealings with each other. These differences are of several kinds, but, since wealth, nobility or rank, power, and personal merit are, in general, the principal distinctions by which one is judged in society, I would prove that the harmony or conflict among these different forces is the surest indication of whether a state is well or badly constituted; I would show that among these four kinds of inequality, the personal qualities are the origin of all the others, and that wealth is the one to which they are all reduced in the end, because, being the most immediately useful to a person's well-being and the easiest to transmit, it is easily used to purchase all the rest. This observation makes possible a rather exact assessment of the extent to which each people is removed from its original institution, and of its progress towards the extreme limits of corruption. I would point out how this universal desire for reputation, honors, and preference, which consumes us all, exercises and holds up our talents and strengths to comparison; how it excites and multiplies

1. This paragraph succinctly draws together many of the observations Rousseau made earlier in this *Discourse* about how misery arises from the mere fact of social life.

2. [Note XIX] Distributive justice would itself be opposed to this rigorous equality of the state of nature, even if it were practicable in civil society, and since all the members of the state owe it services proportionate to their talents and strengths, citizens must in their turn be distinguished and favored in proportion to their services. It is in this sense that we must understand a passage from Socrates in which he praises the early Athenians for having known how to distinguish which of the two kinds of equality was the most advantageous, one of which consisted in dividing the same advantages equally among all citizens, and the other in distributing them according to the merit of each. These clever politicians, adds the orator, banishing that unjust equality which makes no distinction between the wicked and the good, cling tenaciously to that which rewards and punishes each according to his merit. But, in the first place, there has never existed a society, however corrupt it might have become, where no distinction was made between the wicked and the good, and in the matter of morality, where the law cannot establish standards exact enough to serve as rules for the magistrate, it very wisely forbids him to judge persons by allowing him to judge only actions, in order not to leave the rank or destiny of citizens to his discretion. Only moral habits as pure as those of the ancient Romans could tolerate Censors, and similar tribunals would soon have thrown everything among us into confusion. It is for public esteem to establish the difference between the wicked and the good; the magistrate is strictly the judge of the law, but the people is the veritable judge of moral habits; it is an honest and even enlightened judge in this respect, a judge which is occasionally deceived but never corrupted. The ranks of citizens should, therefore, be regulated, not according to their personal merit, for this would mean leaving the magistrates with the means of applying the law in an almost arbitrary fashion, but according to the actual services they render to the state, which are open to a more exact assessment [Rousseau's note].

our passions; and how, by making all men competitors, rivals, or, rather, enemies, it daily causes defeats, successes, and disasters of all kinds, by making so many aspirants take part in the same contest. I would show that to this eagerness to be talked about, to this craze to distinguish ourselves, which almost always keeps us in turmoil, we owe what is best and worst among men—our vices and our virtues, our errors and our sciences, our conquerors and our philosophers—that is to say, a multitude of bad things as compared to few good ones. Finally, I would prove that if we see a handful of rich and powerful men at the pinnacle of greatness and fortune, while the crowd grovels in obscurity and misery, it is because the former esteem the things they possess only insofar as others are deprived of them, and because, without any change in their condition, they would cease being happy if the people ceased being miserable.

But these details alone would furnish the material for a considerable work which would weigh the advantages and disadvantages of every government in relation to the rights of the state of nature, and which would unmask all the different faces behind which inequality has appeared up to now and may appear in future centuries, according to the nature of those governments and the revolutions that time will necessarily bring about. We would see the multitude oppressed from within as a consequence of the very precautions that it had taken against what menaced it from without; we would see oppression constantly growing without it ever being possible for the oppressed to know what its limits might be or what legitimate means they would have left to check its progress. We would see citizens' rights and national liberties dying out little by little, and the complaints of the weak treated as seditious murmurs. We would see politics restricting the honor of defending the common cause to a mercenary segment of the people; we would see, as a result, taxes made necessary and the disheartened farmer quitting his field even during peacetime, leaving his plow to gird on the sword. We would see the bizarre and deadly rules of the code of honor arise; we would sooner or later see the homeland's defenders become its enemies, constantly keeping their swords drawn against their fellow citizens; and there would come a time when they would be heard saying to the oppressor of their country:

> *Pectore si fratris gladium juguloque parentis*
> *Condere me jubeas, gravidaeque in viscera partu*
> *Conjugis, invita peragam tamen omnia dextra.*[3]

3. Lucan (39–65) *On the Civil War* (often called *Pharsalia*), I. 376–78.

> If you order me to sink my sword
> in my brother's breast, or in my father's throat
> or even in the unborn child in my pregnant wife's womb,
> I shall do it all, even if my right hand is unwilling.

This historical epic deals with Julius Caesar's struggle against the Senatorial party of Rome, including such figures as Pompey and Cato, who are the real heroes of the work, fighting for their principles.

From the extreme inequality of conditions and fortunes, from the diversity of passions and talents, from the useless or pernicious arts, and from the frivolous sciences would spring a host of prejudices, equally contrary to reason, happiness, and virtue; we would see leaders stirring up everything that can weaken an assembly of men by disuniting them; everything that can give society an air of apparent harmony and sow in it the seeds of real division; everything that can inspire mistrust and mutual hatred in the different orders through setting their rights and interests into opposition, and, consequently, fortifying the power that contains them all.

From the midst of this disorder and these revolutions despotism, gradually raising its hideous head and devouring all that it had perceived to be good and sound in every part of the state, would finally succeed in trampling the laws and people underfoot and in establishing itself upon the ruins of the republic. The times that would precede this last change would be times of trouble and calamities, but, in the end, everything would be swallowed up by the monster, and peoples would no longer have leaders or laws but only tyrants. From this moment, morality and virtue would also cease to be a matter of concern, for wherever despotism reigns, *cui ex honesto nulla est spes*,[4] it admits no other master; as soon as it speaks, neither integrity nor duty is considered, and the blindest obedience is the only virtue left to slaves.

Here is the final stage of inequality and the extreme point that closes the circle and touches the point from which we set out. Here, all private individuals become equals once again, because they are nothing, and once subjects have no law other than the will of the master and the master no other guide than his passions, notions of good and principles of justice vanish once more. Everything here is reduced to the law of the strongest alone, and, consequently, to a new state of nature that differs from the one with which we began in the sense that the former was the pure state of nature and this last is the fruit of excessive corruption. There is, nevertheless, very little difference between these two states, and the contract of government is so completely dissolved by despotism that the despot is master only as long as he is the strongest, and, as soon as he can be driven out, he has no cause to protest against the violence. The riot which ends with the strangling or dethroning of a sultan is as legal an act as those by which, the day before, he disposed of the lives and property of his subjects. Force alone maintained him, and force alone overthrows him. Thus, all things happen in accordance with the natural order, and whatever the outcome of these short and frequent revolutions may be, no one can complain of the injustice of others, but only of his own imprudence or misfortune.[5]

4. Tacitus, *Annals*, V.iii. ". . . in which there is no hope afforded by honesty."
5. Note Rousseau's bleak appraisal of the prospects for revolution as a way to escape the miseries of modern social life. Revolutions, he here suggests, are both continual and unproductive. But compare p. 52, where he offers hope that revolution might bring government "closer to legitimacy," and *On Social Contract*, Book II, chapter 8, where a few salutary revolutions are mentioned.

Thus, in discovering and following the lost and forgotten paths that must have led man from the natural to the civil state, in reestablishing, along with the intermediate positions I have just noted, those which the pressures of time have made me suppress or which imagination has not suggested to me, any attentive reader cannot but be struck by the vast distance that separates these two states. In this slow succession of events, he will see the solution to endless moral and political problems that philosophers cannot resolve. He will sense that since the human race of one era is not the human race of another, Diogenes could not find a man, because he sought among his contemporaries the man of a time which no longer existed. Cato, he will say, perished with Rome and liberty, because he was out of place in his century, and the greatest of men did nothing but astonish a world he would have governed five hundred years earlier. In short, he will explain how the soul and human passions, deteriorating imperceptibly, change in nature, so to speak; why the objects of our needs and pleasures change in the long run; why the original man vanished by degrees; and why society offers nothing more to the sage's eyes than an assemblage of unnatural men and artificial passions which are the handiwork of all these new relations and have no real foundation in nature. What reflection teaches us about that, observation confirms perfectly: savage man and civilized man differ so much in the depths of their hearts and in their inclinations that what constitutes the supreme happiness of one would reduce the other to despair. The former breathes only peace and liberty; he wants only to live and to remain at leisure, and even the Stoic's ataraxia falls far short of his profound indifference to every other object. The always active citizen, on the contrary, sweats, struggles, torments himself constantly to seek out still more laborious occupations. He toils until death; he even hurries toward it to enable himself to live, or he renounces life to acquire immortality. He pays court to the great whom he hates and to the wealthy whom he holds in contempt; he spares nothing to gain the honor of serving them; he proudly boasts of his own baseness and of their protection, and, proud of his slavery, he speaks with disdain of those who do not have the honor of sharing in it. What a spectacle for a Carib is the arduous labor coveted by a European minister! How many cruel deaths would this indolent savage not prefer to the horrors of such a life, which is seldom even tempered by the pleasure of doing good? But for him to understand the purpose of so many concerns, the words *power* and *reputation* would have to possess some meaning in his mind, and he would have to learn that there are men who set some value upon the attention of the rest of the universe, and who know how to be happy and content with themselves on the testimony of others rather than on their own. Such is, in fact, the real cause of all these differences: savage man lives within himself; social man knows only how to live beyond himself in the opinion of others, and it is, so to speak, from their judgment alone that he derives the sentiment of his own existence. It is not my purpose to show how so much indifference towards good and evil could grow out of such a disposition along with such fine moralistic discourses; or to show how, once everything is reduced to appearances, all becomes artificial and deceitful—honor, friendship, and virtue, and often even vice itself, of which men finally discover the secret of boasting, to show, in a word, how, always asking others what we are and never daring to question ourselves in the midst of so much philosophy, humanity, and civility and so many sublime maxims, we have only a deceptive and frivolous outward appearance, honor without virtue, reason without wisdom, and pleasure without happiness. It suffices for me to have proved that this is not the original state of man, and that it is only the spirit of society and the inequality it engenders, which thus transform and corrupt all our natural inclinations.

I have endeavored to lay bare the origin and progress of inequality and the establishment and abuse of political societies, insofar as these things can be deduced from the nature of man by the light of reason alone and independently of the sacred dogmas which give the sanction of divine right to sovereign authority. It follows from this account that inequality, which was almost nonexistent in the state of nature, owes its strength and growth to the development of our faculties and the progress of the human mind and finally becomes permanent and legitimate with the establishment of property and laws. It follows, furthermore, that moral inequality, authorized by positive law alone, is contrary to natural right whenever it is not proportionate to physical inequality—a distinction which adequately determines what should be thought in this regard about the kind of inequality which is prevalent among all civilized peoples—since it is manifestly contrary to the law of nature, however it is defined, for a child to command an old man, for a fool to lead a wise man, and for a handful of men to abound in superfluities, while the starving multitude lacks the bare necessities.

Discourse on Political Economy

The *Discourse on Political Economy* was published in 1755 as an article in the fifth volume of Diderot's *Encyclopédie*. In this essay Rousseau begins to face the question posed by the *Discourse on Inequality* of how in the corrupt modern world a legitimate state might be established. The answer he proposes here is less complete and systematic than the one he offered seven years later in *On Social Contract*. Nevertheless, much of the conceptual framework on which he henceforth built is elaborated in this *Discourse*. Some essential points of substance, such as the need for legal probity, public spirit, and economic equality, are more fully elaborated here than in his later work. The vision of a legitimate state that Rousseau presents here is remarkable above all for its celebration of austere Spartan virtue, a theme which, while present, is eclipsed in *On Social Contract* by his concern with basic principles. Thus, the *Discourse on Political Economy* serves not only as a natural entry into Rousseau's finished system, but also helps to flesh that system out.

Discourse on Political Economy†

ECONOMY, or ŒCONOMY (Moral and Political). This term is derived from οἶχος and νόμος, the Greek words for house and law, and originally signified only the wise and legitimate government of the household for the good of the whole family. The meaning of this term has since been extended to the government of the great family which constitutes the state. In order to distinguish between these two meanings, the latter is called *general* or *political economy*, and the former, *domestic* or *private economy*. This article is concerned only with the first of these. On *domestic economy, see* FATHER OF THE FAMILY.[1]

Even if the state and the family were as closely related as some authors maintain, it would not, on that account, follow that the rules of conduct appropriate for one of these two societies would also be suitable for the other; they differ too greatly in size to be administered in the same way, and there will always be an enormous difference between domestic government, where the father can see everything for himself, and civil government, where the leader sees almost nothing save through the eyes of

---

† None of the 1782 additions has been included.
1. This reference, like several in this essay, is to another article in the *Encyclopédie*, where the *Political Economy* was first published. Rousseau

presented his own ideas about how households should be managed in his novel, *La Nouvelle Héloise*, published in 1761. See 5.2–3 and 6.10.

others. For things to become equal in this respect, the talents, the force, and all the faculties of the father would have to increase in proportion to the size of the family, and the soul of a powerful monarch would have to be to the soul of an ordinary man what the size of his empire is to the inheritance of a private individual.

But how could the government of the state be like that of the family whose foundation is so different? Since the father is physically stronger than his children, paternal power may reasonably be thought of as something established by nature for as long as his help is necessary to them. In the great family whose members are all naturally equal, political authority, being purely arbitrary in the way it is established, can be founded only upon agreements, and the magistrate can command others only by virtue of the laws. The duties of the father are dictated to him by natural feelings, and in a manner that rarely permits him to disobey them. Leaders do not have a similar guide and are not really obligated toward the people to do anything except what they have promised to do, and what the people has a right to demand that they do. Another even more important difference is that, since the children have nothing but what they receive from the father, it is obvious that all property rights belong to him, or emanate from him; it is quite the contrary in the great family, where the general administration is established only to insure private property which is antecedent to it. The principal purpose of the work of the entire household is to preserve and increase the father's patrimony, so that he may one day divide it among his children without impoverishing them, whereas the wealth of the public treasury is only a means, often very poorly understood, of maintaining private individuals in peace and prosperity. In a word, the small family is destined to die out and one day to be dissolved into several other similar families, and whereas the great family is created to endure forever in the same condition, the small one must increase in order to multiply. And not only is it enough for the great family to maintain itself, but it can easily be proved that any increase does it more harm than good.

For several reasons derived from the nature of things, it is the father who should be in command.[2] First, the authority between the father and the mother should not be equal, but the government must be unified, and in every division of opinion, there must be one dominant voice which decides. Secondly, however slight we may suppose the indispositions peculiar to the woman, since they always cause her to be inactive for a certain period, this is a sufficient reason for excluding her from this primacy, for when the balance is perfect, a straw is enough to tip the scales. Moreover, the husband should have the right to oversee the conduct of his wife, because it is important for him to make certain that the children he is forced to acknowledge and raise belong to no one but

2. Rousseau's support for paternal rule within families is not easy to reconcile with his insistence on political equality for all citizens here and in *On Social Contract*. Readers should ask whether the distinctions Rousseau draws here between domestic and political conditions are robust enough to justify his conclusion that, though citizens should participate in legislative politics as equals, in families the father should command.

himself. Thirdly, the children should obey the father, initially out of necessity and afterwards out of gratitude. After having their needs satisfied by him for half of their lives, they ought to devote the other half to providing for his. Fourthly, the servants also owe him their services in exchange for the livelihood that he gives them, although they may break their agreement as soon as it ceases to be appropriate. I say nothing of slavery, because it is contrary to nature and because no law can authorize it.

There is nothing of this kind in political society. Far from the leader having any natural interest in the happiness of private individuals, it is not uncommon for him to seek his own happiness in their misery. If the magistracy is hereditary, a child is often in command of men; if it is elective, a thousand inconveniences arise in the elections, and, in either case, all the advantages of paternity are lost. If you have but one leader, you are at the discretion of a master who has no reason to love you; if you have several, you must endure both their tyranny and their quarrels. In a word, abuses are inevitable and their consequences disastrous in every society in which the public interest and the laws have no natural force and are constantly attacked by the personal interest and the passions of the leader and the members.

Although the functions of the father of a family and the chief magistrate should lead to the same goal, their paths are so different, their duties and rights so distinct, that one cannot confuse them without forming false ideas about the fundamental laws of society and without falling into errors fatal to the human race. In fact, if nature's voice is the best advice a father can listen to in fulfilling his duties, it is, for the magistrate, nothing but a false guide which constantly works to divert him from fulfilling his own, and which sooner or later leads to his downfall or to that of the state, unless he is restrained by the most sublime virtue. The only precaution necessary for the father of a family is to protect himself from depravity and to prevent his natural inclinations from becoming corrupted, but these are the very inclinations that corrupt the magistrate. To do good, the former has only to consult his heart; the latter becomes a traitor the moment he listens to his own. Even his reason should be suspect to him, and he should follow no other guide than public reason, which is the law. Thus, nature has created a multitude of good fathers in families, but it is doubtful that, since the creation of the world, human wisdom has ever produced ten men capable of governing their fellows.

From all that I have just set forth, it follows that *public economy* is correctly distinguished from *private economy*, and that since the state has nothing in common with the family but the obligation of their respective leaders to make each of them happy, the same rules of conduct could not suit them both. I thought these few lines would suffice to destroy the odious system that Sir Robert Filmer tried to establish in a work entitled *Patriarcha*, to which two famous men have done too much honor by writing books to refute it.[3] Besides, this error is very old, since Aristotle himself thought it appropriate to combat it with arguments that one can find in the first book of his *Politics*.

Again I ask my readers to distinguish carefully between *public economy* about which I am to speak and which I call government, and the supreme authority, which I call *sovereignty*, a distinction which lies in the fact that the one has the right to legislate and in certain cases to obligate the very body of the nation, while the other has only executive power and can only obligate private individuals.[4] *See* Politics and Sovereignty.

Permit me for a moment to use a common comparison, inaccurate in many respects but suited to making myself better understood.

The body politic, taken individually, can be considered as an organized, living body and similar to that of a man. The sovereign power represents the head; the laws and customs are the brain, the center of the nervous system and seat of the understanding, the will, and the senses, of which the judges and magistrates are the organs; commerce, industry, and agriculture are the mouth and stomach which prepare the common subsistence; public finances are the blood that a wise *economy*, performing the functions of the heart, sends back to distribute nourishment and life throughout the body; the citizens are the body and members which make the machine move, live, and work, and which cannot be injured in any way without a painful sensation being transmitted right to the brain, if the animal is in a state of good health.

The life of both together is the *self* common to the whole, the reciprocal sensibility and the internal connection between all the parts. What if this communication ceases, the formal unity disappears, and the contiguous parts are only related to one another by their juxtaposition? The man is dead, or the state is dissolved.

The body politic is, therefore, also a moral being which has a will, and this general will, which always tends toward the conservation and welfare of the whole and of each part, and which is the source of the laws, is, for all the members of the state, in their relations to one other and to the state, the rule of what is just and unjust, a truth—just to mention it in passing—which shows how ludicrous it is for so many writers to have treated as theft the shrewdness prescribed to the children of Sparta for earning their frugal meals, as if all that the law decrees could fail to be legitimate.[5] *See under the word* Right the source of this

3. Filmer had defended absolute monarchy as arising from domestic patriarchy. For more on Filmer see below, *On Social Contract*, Book I, chapter 2, note 1. The refuters are John Locke (1632–1704) and Algernon Sidney (1622–83).
4. Rousseau here somewhat elliptically limits the political scope of the present work. Questions of public or political economy, he says, must be decided by an executive, not a legislative agency. Hence the economic issues he is about to raise are treated as matters to be decided by those who apply

rather than make the law.
5. In Sparta, which Rousseau considered a legitimate state, children were allowed to steal their meals, provided they were not caught in the act.
    Rousseau begins in this paragraph to draw a distinction between the particular and the general will. His treatment of this matter here is more extensive than any he provides in *On Social Contract* and helps to explain why in that work he makes obedience to the general will the touchstone of political legitimacy.

great and luminous principle, from which this article develops.

It is important to note that this rule of justice, which is unerring with respect to all citizens, may be faulty with respect to foreigners, and the reason for this is obvious. The will of the state, although general in relation to its members, is no longer so in relation to other states and their members, but becomes for them a particular and individual will, which has its rule of justice in the law of nature. This enters equally into the principle already established, for the great city of the world then becomes the body politic, whose law of nature is always the general will, and whose states and various peoples are merely individual members.

From these same distinctions, applied to each political society and its members, are derived the most universal and certain rules by which to judge a government good or bad, and, in general, the morality of all human actions.

Every political society is composed of other smaller societies of different kinds, each of which has its own interests and guiding principles, but these societies, which everyone perceives, because they have an external and authorized form, are not the only ones which actually exist in the state; all private individuals united by a common interest make up as many other permanent or transitory societies, whose force is no less real for being less apparent, and whose various relationships, when they are carefully observed, provide true knowledge of moral habits. It is all these tacit or formal associations which, through the influence of their own wills, modify in so many ways the manifestations of the public will. The will of these particular societies always has two relations: for the members of the association, it is a general will; for the great society it is a particular will, which is quite often found to be just in the first respect and corrupt in the second. A certain person may be a devout priest, or a brave soldier, or a zealous professional, and yet a bad citizen; a certain decision may be advantageous to the small community and very pernicious to the great one. It is true that since particular societies are always subordinate to those which contain them, the latter ought to be obeyed rather than the former, and the duties of the citizen take precedence over those of the senator, and those of the man over those of the citizen, but, unfortunately, personal interest is always found in an inverse ratio to duty, and it increases in proportion as the association becomes narrower and the commitment less sacred. This is invincible proof that the most general will is also always the most just, and that the voice of the people is indeed the voice of God.

It does not therefore follow that public decisions are always equitable; they may not be so in matters concerning foreign affairs; I have stated the reason for this. Thus, it is not impossible for a well-governed republic to wage an unjust war. Nor is it any more impossible for the council of a democracy to pass evil decrees and condemn the innocent, but this will never happen unless the people is seduced by private interests, which a few clever men with authority and eloquence have been able to substitute for its own. In such a case, public deliberation will be one thing and the general will another. Let no one cite Athenian democracy as an objection, because Athens was not really a democracy, but a very tryannical aristocracy, governed by learned men and orators. Examine carefully what happens in any decision whatever, and you will see that the general will is always for the common good, but that a secret schism often develops, a tacit confederation, which causes the natural disposition of the assembly to be circumvented for the sake of private purposes. In that case, the social body is actually divided into other bodies, whose members acquire a general will which is good and just with regard to these new bodies, but bad and unjust with regard to the whole from which each of them has been severed.

We see that with the aid of these principles it is very easy to explain the apparent contradictions which can be observed in the conduct of so many men who are scrupulous and honorable in certain respects and deceitful and unscrupulous in others, trampling underfoot their most sacred duties, and remaining faithful to the death to commitments which are often unlawful. Thus, the most corrupt men always pay some sort of homage to the public trust; thus (as is noted in the article on RIGHT), even thieves, who are enemies of virtue in the great society, revere its semblance in their dens.

In establishing the general will as the first principle of public *economy* and the fundamental rule of government, I have not thought it necessary to inquire seriously whether the magistrates belong to the people or the people to the magistrates, and whether, in public affairs, one should consider the good of the state or that of its leaders. This question has long been decided one way in practice and another in theory; and, in general, it would be sheer folly to hope that those who are in fact masters will prefer another interest to their own. It would, therefore, be appropriate further to subdivide public *economy* into popular and tyrannical types. The former is that of every state in which unity of interest and will reigns between the people and the leaders; the latter necessarily will exist wherever the government and the people have different interests and, consequently, opposing wills. The maxims of government are inscribed at length in the archives of history and in Machiavelli's satires.[6] The maxims of the people are found only in the writing of philosophers who dare to proclaim the rights of humanity.

I. The first and the most important maxim of legitimate or popular government, in other words, of a government whose aim is the good of the people, is therefore, as I have said, to follow the general will in all things, but, to follow it, it is necessary to know it, and, above all, to distinguish it clearly from the particular will, starting with oneself. This distinction is always extremely difficult to make, and only the most sublime virtue is capable of shedding sufficient light on it. Since it is nec-

6. Rousseau thought that behind Machiavelli's praise for amoral statecraft in *The Prince* lay ironic condemnation. He elaborates this view of *The Prince* in *On Social Contract*, Book III, chapter 6, note 1. By calling *The Prince* a satire, Rousseau reconciled it with the republican principles he so admired in Machiavelli's *Discourses*.

essary to be free in order to will, another difficulty no less great is t͜ insure both public liberty and governmental authority. Inquire into the motives that have brought men, united by their mutual needs in the great society, to unite themselves more closely by means of civil societies, and you will find no other motive than that of insuring the property, life, and liberty of each member through the protection of all. But how can men be forced to defend the liberty of any one among them without infringing on the liberty of others? And how can public needs be met without doing some damage to the private property of those who are forced to contribute to them? Whatever the sophistry with which one may color all this, it is certain that I am no longer free if my will can be constrained, and that I am no longer the master of my property, if someone else can get his hands on it. This difficulty, which must have seemed insurmountable, was overcome along with the first by the most sublime of all human institutions, or rather, by a celestial inspiration, which taught man to imitate here on earth the immutable decrees of the divinity. By what inconceivable art could anyone have found the means to subjugate men in order to make them free? To use the property, the labor, even the lives of all its members in the service of the state without constraining them and without consulting them? To enchain their wills with their own consent? To make that consent more important than their refusal, and to force them to punish themselves when they do what they did not want to do? How can it be that they obey when no one commands, that they serve when there are no masters, and that they are much more free, in fact, because, under apparent subjugation, no one loses any of his liberty except what could be harmful to the liberty of another? These marvels are the handiwork of the law. It is to the law alone that men owe justice and liberty. It is this salutary tool of the will of all which reestablishes natural equality on a legal basis among men. It is this celestial voice which dictates the precepts of public reason to each citizen, and teaches him to act in accordance with the maxims of his own judgment and not to be in contradiction with himself. It is through this voice alone that leaders should speak when they give commands, for, no sooner does a man claim, independently of the laws, to subject another to his private will, than he leaves the civil state and confronts the other man in the pure state of nature, where obedience is never prescribed except by necessity.

The leader's most pressing concern, as well as his essential duty, is, therefore, to oversee the observance of the laws of which he is the minister and upon which all his authority is founded.[7] If he must make others observe the laws, he should, with even greater reason, observe them himself, as the one who enjoys all their protection. For his example is of such force that even if the people were willing to permit him to break free from the yoke of the law, he ought to beware of taking advan-

---

7. This is Rousseau's first answer to the vexing problem posed at the beginning of this section concerning what administrators must do in order to follow the general will. One thing they must do is scrupulously obey and apply enacted law.

tage of so dangerous a prerogative, one which others would in turn soon try to usurp and often to his detriment. At bottom, since all society's commitments are reciprocal by nature, it is impossible to put oneself above the law without renouncing its advantages, and no one owes anything to anybody who claims to owe nothing to anyone else. For the same reason, no immunity from the law will ever be granted on any grounds whatsoever in a well-regulated government. Even the citizens who deserve well of their country should be rewarded with honors but never with privileges, for the republic is on the brink of ruin, as soon as someone thinks that it is perfectly acceptable not to obey the laws. But if ever the nobility or the military or any other order in the state were to adopt such a guiding principle, all would be irretrievably lost.

The power of the laws depends even more on their own wisdom than on the severity of their ministers, and the public will draws its greatest weight from the reason which dictated it. For this reason, Plato considers it a very important precaution always to place at the beginning of edicts a well-reasoned preamble which proves them to be just and useful. In fact, the first of the laws is to respect the laws; severity of punishments is merely a vain expedient conceived by small minds to substitute terror for the respect they cannot obtain. It has continually been observed that the countries in which corporal punishments are the most terrible are also those in which they are the most frequent; thus, the cruelty of penalties is scarcely indicative of anything but the multitude of lawbreakers, and, by punishing all with equal severity, the guilty are forced to commit crimes to escape punishment for their mistakes.

But although government is not master of the law, it is no small thing to be its guarantor and to possess a thousand ways of making it loved.[8] The talent for ruling consists in this alone. When one has force in hand, there is no art in making everyone tremble, and not even much in winning men's hearts, for experience has long since taught the people to attach great importance to all the harm its leaders avoid doing to it and to worship them when they do not hate it. An imbecile who is obeyed can, like anyone else, punish serious crimes; the true statesman knows how to prevent them; he extends his respectable dominion over wills even more than over actions. If he could arrange for everyone to do good, he would have nothing more to do himself, and the masterpiece of his labors would be to be able to remain at rest. It is certain, at least, that the greatest talent of leaders is to disguise their power in order to make it less odious, and to manage the state so peaceably that it seems to need no leaders.

I conclude, therefore, that just as the lawgiver's first duty is to make the laws conform to the general will, the first rule of public *economy* is that the administration should conform to the laws. This will suffice even to prevent the state from being badly governed, if the lawgiver has

8. Rousseau now gives a second response to the question of what administrators must do to follow the general will. They must influence the citizenry, in ways which Rousseau goes on to describe both in this work and in *On Social Contract*, so that it resolutely seeks the public good.

provided, as he should have, for everything that is required by the locality, climate, soil, moral habits, environment, and all the relationships
characteristic of the people he had to institute. This is not to say that
endless administrative and *economic* details are not left to the wisdom of
the government, but it always has two infallible guides for conducting
itself correctly on these occasions: one is the spirit of the law which
should be used in deciding cases that the law could not foresee; the other
is the general will, the source and supplement of all the laws, which
should always be consulted when they fail. How, someone will ask me,
can the general will be known in cases in which it has not expressed
itself? Must the whole nation be assembled at every unforeseen event?
It will be all the less necessary to do so, because it is by no means certain
that its decision would be the expression of the general will, because this
means is impracticable for a large people, and because it is rarely necessary when the government is well intentioned, for the leaders know
very well that the general will is always on the side most favorable to the
public interest, that is to say, the most equitable, so that it is necessary
merely to be just to be assured of following the general will.[9] Often,
when the general will is too openly flouted, it makes itself known despite
the terrible restraint of public authority. I look as close at hand as possible for examples that may be followed in such a case. In China, the
unfailing maxim of the prince is to side against his officials in all disputes
that arise between them and the people. Is bread expensive in one province? Its administrator is put in prison. Does a riot break out in another?
Its governor is dismissed, and every mandarin answers with his head for
all the wrongdoing in his department. This is not to say that there is no
examination of the affair later on in a regular trial, but long experience
has thus caused the verdict to be anticipated. There is rarely any injustice to remedy, and the emperor, persuaded that a public outcry never
arises without reason, always discerns amid the seditious cries he punishes some just grievances that he redresses.

It is no small matter to have made peace and order reign throughout
the republic; it is no small matter that the state is tranquil and the law
respected, but if one does nothing more, there will be more appearance
than reality in all this, and the government will have difficulty making
itself obeyed, if it limits itself to obedience. If it is good to know how to
make use of men as they are, it is better still to make them into what
one needs them to be; the most absolute authority is that which pene-
trates a man's inner being and is exerted no less on his will than on his
actions. Certainly, people are, in the long run, what the government

9. Up to this point Rousseau has said nothing about
how to enact the laws which administrators are to
apply. Although questions of legislative procedure
and organization are outside the scope of the *Political Economy*, Rousseau nevertheless alludes now
to the problem which preoccupies him in *On Social
Contract* of how to make sure that the laws which
administrators apply express the general will. In
On Social Contract Rousseau relies on the institutions of direct democracy to assure that legislation serves the public. Laws must be discussed and
passed by an assembly of the citizens. Here, however, by assigning much lawmaking to administrators, he shows a trust in their legislative integrity
which had given way to deep suspicion by the time
he returned to this question in *On Social Contract*.

makes of them: warriors, citizens, men when it wishes; rabble and riffraff when it pleases. And every prince who holds his subjects in contempt dishonors himself by showing that he did not know how to make them worthy of esteem. Form men, therefore, if you want to command men; if you want the laws to be obeyed, make them loved, so that to make men do what they should, it is enough to make them think they should do it. That was the great art of ancient governments, in those distant times when philosophers gave laws to peoples and used their authority only to make them wise and happy. This gave rise to so many sumptuary laws, so many regulations concerning moral habits, so many public maxims which were accepted or rejected with the greatest care. Even tyrants did not forget this important part of administration, and they took as much care in corrupting the moral habits of their slaves as did the magistrates in correcting those of their fellow citizens. But our modern governments, which believe that they have done everything there is to do when they have raised money, never even imagine that it is necessary or possible to go that far.

II. The second essential rule of public *economy* is no less important than the first. Do you want the general will to be carried out? Make certain that all particular wills are in accord with it, and, since virtue is only this conformity of the particular will with the general, to say the same thing in a word, make virtue reign.[1]

If political writers were less blinded by their ambition, they would see how impossible it is for any establishment whatever to operate in the spirit of its origins, unless it is guided by the law of duty: they would be aware that the mainstay of public authority lies in the hearts of the citizens, and that nothing can take the place of moral habits in the maintenance of the government. Not only is it good and upright men alone who know how to administer the laws, but, fundamentally, it is only honest people who know how to obey them. Anyone who succeeds in tolerating remorse will have no trouble enduring torture, a less severe and continual punishment, from which there is at least the hope of escape, and whatever precautions are taken, those who only await impunity to do wrong hardly lack the means of evading the law or escaping the penalty. In this case, since all private interests join forces against the general interest, which is no longer that of any individual, public vices have greater power to enervate the laws than the laws have to keep vices in check, and the corruption of the people and its leaders finally spreads to the government itself, however wise it may be. The worst of all abuses is to appear to obey the laws while, in truth, breaking them with safety. Before long, the best laws become the most baneful; it would be a hundred times better for them not to exist; this would still be a resource when no others remain. In such a situation, it is useless to pile edicts upon edicts

1. Much of what is distinctive in this *Discourse* to Rousseau's conception of political legitimacy is contained in this section, which shows how to create the civic virtue that is a precondition to the successful operation of his legitimate state. He suggests three means for creating civic virtue: state protection for personal safety, economic equality, and public education.

and regulations upon regulations. All that serves only to introduce other abuses without correcting the original ones. The more you multiply the laws, the more contemptible you make them, and all the supervisors you appoint are only new lawbreakers destined to share the plunder with the veterans or to do their own looting. Soon, the price of virtue becomes that of brigandage. The most vile men become the most reputable; the greater they are, the more contemptible they are; their infamy is manifest in their dignities, and they are dishonored by their honors. If they buy the votes of the leaders or the protection of women, it is only to sell justice, duty, and the state in their turn; and the people which fails to see that its own vices are the principal cause of its misfortunes murmurs and cries out, groaning: "All my misfortunes come only from those I pay to protect me from things of that sort."

At such times, the voice of duty no longer speaks in men's hearts, and leaders are forced to substitute the cry of terror, or the lure of an apparent interest by which they deceive their creatures. At such times, they must take recourse to all the contemptible little tricks they call *rules of state* and *cabinet secrets*. Whatever vigor is left in the government is used by its members to ruin and supplant each other, while business is neglected or transacted only to the degree that personal interest demands and directs. In short, the entire skill of these great politicians is so to bewitch the eyes of those they need that each one may believe he is working for his own interest while only working for *theirs*; I say theirs if indeed the true interest of the leaders is to annihilate their peoples in order to subjugate them and to destroy their own property in order to ensure their possession of it.

But when citizens love their duty, and those entrusted with public authority sincerely apply themselves to fostering this love through their example and their efforts, all difficulties vanish, and administration becomes so easy that it can dispense with that dark art whose very darkness is its only mystery. Those great minds, so dangerous and so admired, all those grand ministers whose glory is inseparable from the misfortunes of the people are no longer missed; public moral habits supplant the genius of leaders; and the longer virtue reigns, the less need there is for talents. Ambition itself is better served by duty than by usurpation. Convinced that its leaders work only toward its happiness, the people spares them, through its deference, from working to strengthen their power: and history shows us in a thousand ways that the authority the people accords to those it loves and by whom it is loved is a hundred times more absolute than all the tyranny of usurpers. This does not mean that the government ought to fear using its power, but that it should use it only in a legitimate manner. History affords countless examples of ambitious or pusillanimous leaders who were ruined by their softness or pride, but no examples of leaders who fared badly merely by being equitable. But moderation should not be confused with negligence, nor gentleness with weakness. To be just, one must be severe: tolerating wickedness, when one has the right and power to repress it, is being wicked oneself.

It is not enough to say to citizens: be good. They must be taught to be so, and example itself, which is in this respect the first lesson, is not the only means that must be used. Love of the homeland is the most effective, for, as I have already said, every man is virtuous when his particular will is wholly in conformity with the general will, and we willingly want what is wanted by the people we love.

It seems that the feeling for humanity is dissipated and weakened by being extended over the whole earth, and that we cannot be moved by calamities in Tartary or Japan, as we are by those of a European people. Interest and commiseration must be limited and compressed in some way to make them active. Now, since this inclination in us can be useful only to those with whom we have to live, it is good that the humanity concentrated among fellow citizens acquires new force within them through the habit of seeing each other and through the common interest which unites them. It is certain that the greatest marvels of virtue have been produced by love for the homeland. Its combination of the force of self-love with all the beauty of virtue gives this sweet and lively sentiment an energy that, without disfiguring it, makes it the most heroic of all the passions. This is the passion that produced so many immortal actions whose brilliance bedazzles our feeble eyes and so many great men whose old style virtues pass for fables, now that love of one's homeland is the object of derision. We should not be surprised. The raptures of tender hearts seem to be quite fanciful to anyone who has not felt them, and the love for one's homeland, a hundred times more lively and delightful than the love for a mistress, likewise cannot be conceived except through being experienced, but it is easy to observe in all the hearts it inflames and in all the actions it inspires, that fiery and sublime ardor apart from which the purest virtue cannot shine. Let us dare to compare Socrates himself to Cato.[2] One was more the philosopher, and the other more the citizen. Athens was already lost, and Socrates had no other homeland than the whole world; Cato always carried his homeland in the depths of his heart; he lived for it alone and could not outlive it. The virtue of Socrates is that of the wisest of men, but compared with Caesar and Pompey, Cato seems a god among mortals. The one teaches a few private individuals, combats the sophists, and dies for the truth; the other defends the state, liberty, and the laws against the conquerers of the world, and finally departs from the earth when he no longer sees a homeland to serve. A worthy student of Socrates would be the most virtuous of his contemporaries; a worthy emulator of Cato would be the greatest. The virtue of the first would bring him happiness; the second would seek his happiness in that of others. We should be taught by one and led by the other, and that alone should determine our preference,

2. Cato of Utica, or Cato the Younger (95–46 B.C.), the strict and uncompromising heir of the ideals of his great-grandfather, Cato the Censor, or Cato the Elder (234 B.C.–149 B.C.), was, like his worthy ancestor, venerated for his integrity and devotion to Roman republican virtues. Called "the conscience of Rome" by Livy, the historian of the Republic, he was an ally of Cicero, who supported Pompey and Scipio against Julius Caesar. When both were defeated, he realized Caesar would conquer Rome and he committed suicide at Utica in 46 B.C.

for a people consisting of wise men has never been created, but it is not impossible to make a people happy.

Do we want peoples to be virtuous? If so, let us begin by making them love their homeland. But how will they come to love it, if their homeland means nothing more to them than it does to foreigners, and if it grants to them only what it cannot refuse to anyone? It would be worse still, if they did not even enjoy the benefit of public safety there, and if their property, lives, or liberty were left to the discretion of powerful men, without it being possible or permissible for them to dare to appeal to the laws. In such a case, being subjected to the duties of the civil state, without enjoying even the rights of the state of nature and without being able to use their force to defend themselves, they would, consequently, be in the worst condition in which free men can find themselves, and the word *homeland*, for them, could only have an odious or absurd meaning. There is no reason to believe that a person can injure or cut off an arm without any sensation of pain being carried to his head, and it is no more believable that the general will would authorize any member of the state, whoever he might be, to harm or destroy another than that the fingers of a man in possession of his reason would go and put out his eyes. The safety of the individual is so closely bound up with the public confederation that, without the respect one owes to human weakness, this agreement would rightfully be dissolved if a single citizen who could have been helped perished inside the state, if a single one were wrongly kept in prison, or if a single court case were lost through an obvious injustice, for, once fundamental agreements are violated, it is no longer apparent what right or what interest could hold the people in the social union, unless it is restrained by force alone, which brings about the dissolution of the civil state.

In fact, is it not the commitment of the body of the nation to provide for the protection of the least of its members with as much care as for that of all the others? And is the good of one citizen any less the common cause than the good of the entire state? Suppose someone tells us that it is right for one person alone to perish for all. I shall admire this precept when it comes from the mouth of a worthy and virtuous patriot who willingly and out of duty gives up his life for his country's sake. But if this means that the government is permitted to sacrifice one innocent person for the good of the multitude, I hold this maxim to be one of the most execrable that tyranny has ever invented, the most false that can be proposed, the most dangerous that can be accepted, and the most directly contrary to the fundamental laws of society. Far from it being the case that one person should die for all, all have committed their property and their lives to the defense of each one of them, so that individual weakness is always protected by public power and each member by the entire state. After making the assumption that one individual after another has been cut off from the body of the people, press the partisans of this maxim to explain more clearly what they mean by *the body of the state*, and you will see that they will finally reduce it to a small number of men who are not the people but the officers of the people, and who, having obligated themselves by a personal oath to perish themselves for the good of the people, claim to prove thereby that the people should perish for them.

What if someone wants to find examples of the protection that the state owes its members and of the respect it owes their persons? These examples should be sought only among the most illustrious and courageous nations of the earth, and there are scarcely any but free peoples among whom the worth of a man is known. It is well known how perplexed the entire republic of Sparta found itself, when the question of punishing a guilty citizen arose. In Macedonia, a human life was a matter of such importance, that for all his grandeur, that powerful monarch Alexander would not have dared put a Macedonian criminal to death in cold blood unless the accused had appeared to defend himself before his fellow citizens and had been condemned by them. But the Romans distinguished themselves above all the peoples of the earth by the regard of their government for private individuals and by its scrupulous attention to respecting the inviolable rights of all members of the state. There was nothing among them as sacred as the life of ordinary citizens; no less than the assembly of the entire people was necessary to condemn one of them. Neither the senate itself nor the consuls in all their majesty had the right to do this, and, among the most powerful people in the world, the crime and punishment of a citizen was a public sorrow; so harsh did it seem to shed blood for any crime, whatever it might be, that by the Porcian Law [the *Lex Portia*], the death penalty was commuted to that of exile for all those who would be willing to endure the loss of such a sweet homeland. Everything in Rome and in the armies bespoke that love fellow citizens felt for each other, and that respect for the Roman name which aroused the courage and inspired the virtue of anyone who had the honor of bearing it. The cap of a citizen delivered from slavery, the civic crown of one who had saved the life of another were looked upon with the greatest pleasure amid the pomp of triumphs, and it is worth noting that of the crowns with which one honors noble actions in wartime, only the civic crown and the crown of triumphant generals were made of grass and leaves; all the others were merely gold. Thus it was that Rome was virtuous and became mistress of the world. Ambitious leaders! A shepherd governs his dogs and his flocks and is the least of men. If it is ever a fine thing to command, it is when those who obey us can honor us. Therefore, respect your fellow citizens, and you will make yourselves worthy of respect; respect liberty, and your power will increase daily; never exceed your rights, and before long they will be boundless.

Let the homeland, therefore, prove itself the common mother of its citizens; let the advantages they enjoy in their country endear it to them; let the government leave them a sufficient share in public administration so that they feel at home; and let the laws be, in their eyes, merely the guarantees of public liberty. These rights, as fine as they are, belong to all men, but without appearing to attack them directly, the bad will of leaders easily reduces their effect to nothing. The law that is abused at the same time serves the powerful as an offensive weapon and as a shield against the weak, and the pretext of public good is always the most dangerous scourge of the people. What is most necessary and perhaps most difficult in government is strict integrity in doing justice to all, and, above all, in protecting the poor against the tyranny of the rich. The greatest harm has already been done, when there are poor people to defend and rich ones to keep in check. The full force of the laws falls only upon those of moderate means; the laws are equally powerless against the treasures of the rich and the destitution of the poor; the first eludes them, the second escapes them; one tears the web apart and the other slips through.

It is, therefore, one of the most important concerns of government to prevent extreme inequality of fortunes, not by taking wealth away from those who possess it but by depriving everyone of the means of accumulating it, and not by building poorhouses but by protecting citizens from becoming impoverished.[3] Men unequally distributed over the territory and crowded into one place while others become underpopulated; arts of pure pleasure and pure industry favored above useful and difficult trades; agriculture sacrificed to commerce; the tax collector made necessary by the poor administration of state funds; and, finally, venality pushed to such extremes that esteem is reckoned in gold coins, and virtues themselves are sold for money. These are the most tangible causes of extreme wealth and poverty, the substitution of private interests for the public interest, the mutual hatred of citizens, their indifference to the common cause, the corruption of the people, and the weakening of all the workings of government. Such ills are consequently difficult to cure when they make themselves felt, but a wise administration should prevent them in order to maintain, along with good moral habits, respect for the laws, love for the homeland, and the vigor of the general will.

But all these precautions will be inadequate if one goes no further. I end this part of public *economy*, where I should have begun. The homeland cannot subsist without liberty, nor liberty without virtue, nor virtue without citizens; you will have everything, if you train citizens; without that, you will only have malicious slaves, beginning with the leaders of the state. Now, training citizens is not just a day's work, and turning them into men requires that they be educated as children. Suppose someone tells me that anyone who has men to govern should not seek outside their nature a perfection of which they are incapable; that he should not wish to destroy the passions within them; and that the execution of such a plan would not be any more desirable than it is possible. I will agree all the more with this, because a man without passions would certainly be a very bad citizen, but it must also be agreed that even if men cannot be taught to love nothing, it is possible to teach them to love one object rather than another, and what is truly beautiful rather

3. Rough equality of wealth is here identified as the goal of an economic policy conducive to civic virtue. Rousseau describes this policy in the next section.

than what is deformed. If, for example, they are trained early enough never to consider their own persons except in terms of their relations with the body of the state, and not to perceive of their own existence, so to speak, except as a part of that of the state, they may finally succeed in identifying themselves in some way with this greater whole, in feeling themselves members of the homeland, in loving it with that exquisite sentiment which every isolated man feels only for himself, in perpetually lifting up their souls toward this great objective, and thus in transforming into a sublime virtue that dangerous disposition from which all our vices arise. Not only does philosophy demonstrate the possibility of these new directions, but history furnishes countless striking examples of them; if they are so rare among us, it is because no one is concerned about whether or not there are any citizens, and still less does anyone think of going about it soon enough to train them. It is too late to change our natural inclinations, once they have taken their course, and habit has reinforced self-love; it is too late to draw us outside of ourselves, once the *human self* centered in our hearts has been given over to that contemptible activity which absorbs all virtue and constitutes the lives of petty souls. How could love for the homeland grow amid so many other passions which stifle it? And what remains for fellow citizens of a heart already divided between avarice, a mistress, and vanity?

It is from the first moment of life that we must learn how to deserve to live, and, as we share in the rights of citizenship by being born, we must begin to discharge our duties at the moment of our birth. If there are laws for the period of adulthood, there should be laws for the period of childhood which teach us to obey others; and, just as each man's reason cannot be left the sole arbiter of his duties, so the education of children can all the less be abandoned to the knowledge and prejudices of their fathers, because it is a matter of greater importance to the state than to their fathers; for, according to the natural course of things, the father's death often robs him of the final fruits of this education, but the homeland sooner or later feels its effects; the state remains, and the family dies out. If the public authority, by taking the place of fathers and assuming this important function, acquires their rights by fulfilling their duties, the fathers have all the less reason to complain about it, because, in this regard, they are doing absolutely nothing but changing a name, and because they will hold in common, as citizens, the same authority over their children as they exercised separately as *fathers*, and will be obeyed no less well while speaking in the name of the law than they were while speaking in the name of nature. Public education, under the rules prescribed by the government and under the magistrates established by the sovereign, is, therefore, one of the fundamental principles of popular or legitimate government.[4] If children are brought up in common in the bosom of equality, if they are steeped in the laws of the state

4. Rousseau's espousal of public education—carried out by officials outside the home—is difficult to reconcile with his backing at the beginning of this *Discourse* (see pp. 59–60) for domestic patriarchy. Fathers who are legally forbidden to educate their children are barred from a decisive means of ruling over them.

and the precepts of the general will, if they are taught to respect them above all things, if they are surrounded by examples and objects which constantly remind them of the tender mother who nourishes them, of the love she bears for them, of the inestimable benefits they receive from her, and of what they owe her in return, let us not doubt that they will thus learn to love each other as brothers, never willing anything but what society wills, substituting the actions of men and citizens for the vain and empty prattle of sophists, and one day becoming the defenders and fathers of the homeland whose children they will have been for so long.

I shall not discuss the magistrates destined to preside over this education, which is certainly the state's most important business. It is obvious that if such tokens of public confidence were accorded lightly, if this sublime function were not, for those who had worthily fulfilled all the others, the reward for their labor, the sweet and honorable repose of their old age, and the culmination of all honors, the entire enterprise would be useless and the education unsuccessful; for, wherever the lesson is not sustained by authority and the precept by example, instruction remains fruitless and virtue itself loses credit in the mouth of one who does not practice it. But let illustrious warriors bent under the weight of their laurels preach courage, let honest magistrates who have turned grey wearing the purple and sitting on the bench teach justice, and, in this way, they will both train virtuous successors for themselves and transmit from age to age to the generations that follow the experience and talents of leaders, the courage and virtue of citizens, and the rivalry common to all of living and dying for their homeland.

I know of only three peoples who practiced public education in the past, namely, the Cretans, the Lacedemonians, and the ancient Persians. Among all three, it had the greatest success, and, among the last two, it worked wonders. Once the world was divided into nations too large to be well governed, this method was no longer practicable, and other reasons which the reader can easily see have also prevented its ever being attempted by any modern people.[5] It is a very remarkable thing that the Romans were able to do without it, but for five hundred years, Rome was a continual miracle that the world cannot hope to see again. The virtue of the Romans, engendered by the horror of tyranny and the crimes of tyrants as well as by an innate love for the homeland, made all their houses into as many schools for citizens, and the unlimited power of fathers over their children placed so much severity in the private order that the father, more feared than the magistrates, was, in his domestic tribunal, the censor of moral habits and the avenger of the laws.

Thus, an attentive and well-intentioned government, constantly trying to maintain or restore love for the homeland and good moral habits

5. Note the pessimism implicit in these remarks about the prospects for establishing a legitimate state. Rousseau's doubts about the practicality of his project are stronger and more numerous in *On Social Contract*.

among the people, forestalls from afar the evils which sooner or later result from the indifference of citizens towards the fate of the republic, and contains within strict limits that personal interest which so isolates private individuals that the state is weakened by their power and has nothing to hope for from their good will. Wherever a people loves its country, respects its laws and lives simply, little else remains to be done to make it happy, and in public administration where fortune plays a lesser role than in the fate of private individuals, wisdom is so close to happiness that these two ends are combined.

III. It is not enough to have citizens and to protect them; it is also necessary to consider their subsistence, and providing for the public needs is an obvious consequence of the general will and the third essential duty of government.[6] This duty is clearly not to fill the granaries of private individuals and exempt them from working, but to maintain abundance so much within their reach that to acquire it labor is always necessary and never useless. It also extends to all the activities involved in the management of the treasury and the expenditures of public administration. Thus, after having discussed general *economy* in relation to the government of persons, it remains for us to consider it in relation to the administration of property.

This part offers no fewer difficulties to surmount or contradictions to resolve than the preceding one. Certainly, the right of property is the most sacred of all the citizens' rights and more important in certain respects than liberty itself, either because it puts a greater value on the preservation of life, or because, with goods being easier to usurp and more difficult to defend than one's person, more respect must be given to what can more easily be stolen, or, finally, because property is the true foundation of civil society and the true guarantee of the citizens' commitments. For if persons had no responsibility for their possessions, nothing would be so easy as evading one's duties and scorning the laws. On the other hand, it is no less certain that the maintenance of the state and the government incurs costs and expenses, and, as anyone who grants the end cannot deny the means, it follows that the members of society should contribute some of their assets to its upkeep. Besides, it is difficult to make the property of private individuals secure on the one hand, without attacking it on another, and it is impossible for all the regulations concerning inheritances, wills, and contracts not to restrict the citizens in certain respects regarding the disposition of their own wealth and, consequently, regarding their right of property.

But besides what I have said above about the harmony which reigns between the authority of the law and the liberty of the citizen, there is,

---

6. The rest of this *Discourse* considers economic policy, especially questions of public finance. Political values are the controlling factor in this discussion. Rousseau's concern to prevent or forestall the corruption which would preclude establishing a legitimate state leads him to set aside efficiency and growth, to which most economists are devoted, in favor of equality, simplicity, and self-sufficiency as the values which the economy should serve. The picture of a well-ordered economy which Rousseau paints here, as well as in *On Social Contract* and in his writings on Corsica and Poland, thus differs markedly in its rustic austerity from that painted by modern economists, whether socialist or laissez-faire.

with respect to the disposition of possessions an important observation to be made, which surmounts many of these difficulties. As Pufendorf has shown, the right of property does not by nature extend beyond the life of the owner, and the instant a man dies, his wealth no longer belongs to him.[7] Thus, prescribing to him the conditions under which he can dispose of it is, at bottom, less a seeming impairment of his right than a real extension of it.

In general, although the laws which regulate the power of private individuals to dispose of their own possessions can be enacted only by the sovereign, the spirit of these laws, which the government should follow in applying them, is that, from father to son and from relation to relation, a family's possessions should go outside of it and be alienated as little as possible. There is an obvious reason for this in favor of children, to whom the right of property would be quite useless, if their father left them nothing, and who, moreover, having often contributed by their own work to the acquisition of their father's property, share as individuals in his right to it. But another more remote and no less important reason is that nothing is more deadly to moral habits and to the republic than continual changes of rank and fortune among the citizens, changes which are the proof and origin of a thousand disorders, which disturb and confuse everything, and by which those who are brought up for one thing find themselves destined for another; neither those who rise nor those who fall are able to acquire the precepts or knowledge fitting for their new condition, much less perform its duties.[8] I shall proceed to the matter of public finance.

If the people governed itself and there were no intermediary between the administration of the state and the citizens, they would only have to assess themselves on certain occasions, in proportion to the public needs and the abilities of individuals, and since no person would ever lose sight of how the funds would be collected and used, neither fraud nor abuse could slip into their handling. The state would never be encumbered with debts, nor the people overburdened with taxes, or, at least, certainty about how the taxes were used would console the people for the severity of the tax. But things cannot be carried on in this manner; and however limited a state is in size, civil society is always too large in number to be governed by all the members. Public monies must necessarily pass through the hands of the leaders, all of whom have, besides the interest of the state, their own private interests, which are not the last to be heeded. The people, for its part, perceiving the leaders' greed and their extravagant spending, rather than the public needs, complains about seeing itself deprived of the necessities in order to furnish others with superfluities; and once these maneuvers have embittered it to a certain extent, the most honest administration could not succeed in restoring confidence. In that case, if contributions are voluntary, they produce noth-

---

7. Samuel Pufendorf (1632–94), *De jure naturae et gentium* (1672, *The Law of Nature and of Nations*), IV.10. 4.

8. Rousseau's aversion to social mobility sometimes, as here, is so intense that he sounds like an opponent of equal opportunity.

ing; if they are compulsory, they are illegitimate; and the difficulty of a just and wise *economy* lies in this cruel alternative of allowing the state to perish or attacking the sacred right of property, which upholds it.

The first thing the founder of a republic should do after the establishment of laws is to find sufficient assets to support the magistrates and other officers and all public expenditures. These resources are called *oerarium* or *fisc*, if they are in the form of money, or *public domain*, if they are in the form of land, and the latter is far preferable to the former for reasons that are easy to see. Anyone who has reflected long enough upon this matter can hardly be of any other opinion than that of Bodin, who views public domain as the most honest and secure of all the means of providing for the needs of the state;[9] and it is worthwhile to note that Romulus' first concern in the division of lands was to set aside a third of them for this use. I acknowledge that it is possible for the proceeds from poorly administered public property to amount to nothing, but it is not in the actual nature of public property to be poorly administered.

Prior to any appropriation of these resources, they should be earmarked or approved by the assembly of the people or the estates of the country, which should then determine their use. After this solemn ceremony, which makes these resources inalienable, their very nature changes, so to speak, and their revenues become so sacred that diverting the least thing to the detriment of its intended purpose is not only the most infamous of all thefts but a crime of high treason. It is a great disgrace for Rome that the integrity of the quaestor Cato was a matter for discussion, and that an emperor, upon rewarding the talent of a singer with a few coins, needed to add that this money came from his family's fortune and not from the state's treasury. But if there are few men like Galba, where will we find men like Cato?[1] And when vice is no longer dishonorable, what leaders will be scrupulous enough first to refrain from putting their hands on the public revenues left to their discretion, and eventually from deceiving themselves by pretending to confuse their vain and scandalous dissipations with the glory of the state, and the means of expanding their authority with those of increasing the power of the state? It is above all in this delicate aspect of administration that virtue is the only effective instrument, and that the integrity of the magistrate is the only restraint capable of containing his greed. The ledgers and all the accounts of managers serve less to disclose their dishonesty than to conceal it, and prudence is never as quick to imagine new precautions as knavery is to elude them. Therefore, abandon account books and papers, and put finances back into faithful hands: only then will they be faithfully managed.

9. Jean Bodin (1530–96), *Six Books on the Commonwealth* (1576), 6.2.
1. See *Discourse on Political Economy*, note 2, p. 69. Western tradition holds up both Catos as exemplars of republican virtue. Both served as quaestors, or financial administrators, whose integrity and honesty were above reproach. Like

wise, Servius Sulpicius Galba (5 B.C.–A.D.69), who served as Roman emperor from June 68 to January 69, succeeding Nero, had a reputation as a strict impartial military leader who became an unpopular emperor, because he disliked lavish display and failed to reward certain officials by robbing the public treasury.

Once public resources are established, the leaders of the state are rightfully the administrators of them, for this administration is a part of government that is always essential, though not always equally so; its influence increases in proportion as the influence of other sources of power diminishes, and it can be said that a government has reached the final stage of corruption, when nothing is left of its sinews but money. Now, since all governments constantly tend to grow weaker, this reason is enough to show why no state can subsist if its revenues do not constantly increase.

The first inkling of the necessity of this increase is also the first sign of internal disorder in the state, and the wise administrator, while thinking about how to find money to meet the present need, does not neglect to inquire into the remote causes of this new need, just as a sailor, upon seeing the water filling his ship, does not forget, while setting the pumps in motion, to seek out and plug the leak.

From this rule is derived the most important maxim in financial administration, which is to take far greater pains to prevent needs than to raise revenues; whatever diligence one can exercise, the relief which comes only after ills have arisen and more slowly, always leaves the state in distress. While one thinks of a remedy for one difficulty, another is already making itself felt, and the remedies themselves produce new difficulties, so that, at last, the nation is burdened with debts, the people are downtrodden, the government loses all its vigor and spends a great deal of money to do very little. I believe that the marvels of the governments of antiquity, which did more with their parsimony than ours do with their great treasuries, were a result of this great, well-established maxim, and perhaps this maxim is the source of the popular meaning of the word *economy*, which is understood to mean the wise use of what one has rather than the means of acquiring what one does not have.

Leaving aside the public domain, which yields returns to the state in proportion to the integrity of those who govern it, if anyone had a sufficiently thorough knowledge of the total strength of the general administration, especially when it is limited to legitimate means, he would be astonished by the resources leaders have for anticipating all public needs, without putting a hand on the possessions of private individuals. Since they are masters of all the commerce in the state, nothing is so easy for them as to manage it in such a way that everything is provided for, often without even appearing to have had a hand in it. The distribution of commodities, money, and merchandise in just proportions, as indicated by times and places, is the true secret of finances and the source of wealth, provided that administrators know how to carry their plans far enough and take a present and apparent loss on one occasion in order to realize immense profits in the distant future. When we see a government paying duties rather than receiving them for exporting grain in years of plenty and importing it in years of scarcity, we need to have such facts before our eyes to believe them, and we would have classified them with works of fiction, if they had occurred long ago. Let us suppose that the establishment of public warehouses was proposed to prevent famine in bad years. How many countries would make the maintenance of such a useful establishment serve as a pretext for new taxes? In Geneva, these granaries, established and maintained by a wise administration, are a public resource in bad years and the state's principal source of revenue at all times. *Alit et ditat*[2] is the just and noble inscription which can be read on the facade of the building. To explain here the economic system of good government, I have often turned my eyes to that of this republic and felt content to find in my own homeland the example of wisdom and happiness that I would like to see prevail in every country.

If one examines how the needs of a state grow, one will find that this often happens in much the same way as with private individuals—less from real necessity than from an increase in useless desires—and that expenses are often increased only as a pretext for raising revenues, so that the state would sometimes gain from not being rich, and its apparent wealth is fundamentally more burdensome than poverty itself would be. One can hope, it is true, to keep the peoples in stricter dependence, by giving them with one hand what has been taken away from them with the other, and this was the policy Joseph used with the Egyptians, but this vain sophistry is all the more deadly to the state to the degree that money no longer returns to the same hands from which it came, and that such principles merely serve to enrich idlers with spoils taken from productive men.

The taste for conquest is one of the most obvious and dangerous causes of this increase in needs. This taste, often engendered by a different kind of ambition than the one it seems to proclaim, is not always what it appears to be, and its real motive is not so much the apparent desire to make the nation larger as the hidden desire to increase the internal authority of its leaders with the help of an increase in the number of troops and through the diversions that are created in the minds of the citizens by wartime objectives.

What is certain, at the very least, is that nothing is as oppressed or miserable as peoples who conquer, and that even their successes serve only to increase their miseries. Even if history did not teach us this, reason would suffice to show us that the larger the state is, the heavier and more burdensome in proportion its expenditures become, for every province must pay its share of the expenses of the general administration, and, beyond that, each must spend the same amount for its own particular administration as it would if it were independent. Add to this the fact that all fortunes are made in one place and consumed in another; this soon destroys the equilibrium of production and consumption, and impoverishes much of the countryside to enrich a single town.

Another cause for the increase in public needs results from the preceding one. A time may come when citizens, no longer considering themselves to have an interest in the common cause, would cease to be

2. Nourish and make wealthy.

defenders of the homeland, and when magistrates would rather command mercenaries than free men, if only, in due course, to use the former to subjugate the latter more effectively. Such was the condition of Rome at the end of the Republic and under the emperors, for all the victories of the early Romans, like those of Alexander, had been won by brave citizens, who knew how, when necessary, to shed their blood for their homeland, but who never sold it out. Marius was the first who, in the Jugurthine War, dishonored the legions by introducing freedmen, vagabonds, and other mercenaries into them.[3] Having become enemies of the very people they were charged with making happy, tyrants established regular troops, ostensibly to keep foreigners in check, but actually to oppress the inhabitants. In order to raise these troops, farmers had to be taken from the land; their absence not only decreased the quality of foodstuffs, but their upkeep introduced taxes which increased the price of food. This first disorder caused the peoples to complain; to subdue them, the number of troops had to be increased, and so, as a result, did their misery, and the more their despair grew, the more imperative it was to keep on increasing the troops still more to ward off its effects. On the other hand, these mercenaries, whose worth could be reckoned by the price at which they sold themselves, were proud of their debasement, held in contempt the laws which protected them as well as their brothers whose bread they ate, and believed it a greater honor to be Caesar's henchmen than Rome's defenders; and, given over to blind obedience, they kept their daggers raised against their fellow citizens, ready at the first sign to cut their throats. It would not be difficult to show that this was one of the principal causes of the downfall of the Roman Empire.

The invention of artillery and fortifications has, in our times, forced the princes of Europe to reestablish the use of regular troops to protect their fortified positions, but with even more legitimate motives, it is to be feared that the effect will be equally deadly. It will be no less necessary to depopulate the countryside to raise armies and garrisons; it will be no less necessary to oppress the peoples to maintain them, and these dangerous establishments have, for some time, been growing so rapidly all over our region that only the imminent depopulation of Europe, and, sooner or later, the ruin of the peoples who inhabit it can be foreseen.

Be that as it may, it should be noted that such institutions necessarily subvert the true economic system, which derives the principal revenue of the state from the public domain, and leave only the troublesome resource of subsidies and taxes, which remain for me to discuss.

It should be remembered here that the foundation of the social pact is property, and its first condition is that each person should be maintained in the peaceful possession of what belongs to him. It is true that by the same treaty each person, at least tacitly, obligates himself to be

---

3. Gaius Marius (157–86 B.C.) was a Roman statesman first elected consul in 107 B.C. and a famous military commander who rose through the ranks. Owing to his ability, Rome won the difficult campaign against Jugurtha, king of Numidia. He was backed by his soldiers in the political struggles of the time and rewarded them with bonuses of land or money.

assessed for a contribution to the public needs, but since this commitment cannot harm the fundamental law, and presupposes that the taxpayers acknowledge the evidence of need, it is clear that in order to be legitimate, this assessment should be voluntary; it should not arise from a particular will, as if it were necessary to have the consent of each citizen, who should pay only what he pleases, which would be directly contrary to the spirit of the confederation, but from a general will by a majority of votes on the basis of a proportional scale that leaves nothing arbitrary in the rate of taxation.

This truth that taxes can only be legitimately established through the consent of the people or its representatives has been generally recognized by all the philosophers and jurists who have acquired some reputation in matters of political right, including Bodin himself.[4] If some have established seemingly contrary maxims, quite aside from the fact that it is easy to see the private motives that have induced them to do so, they attach so many conditions and restrictions to them, that it all comes down, at bottom, to exactly the same thing. For whether the people can refuse or whether the sovereign should not demand is immaterial with respect to right, and if it is only a question of force, it is totally useless to examine what is or is not legitimate.

Taxes levied on the people are of two kinds: some are property taxes and are collected on things; and the others are personal taxes and are paid by the head. Both are called *taxes* or *subsidies*. When the people fixes the amount it pays, it is called a *subsidy*; when it pays the entire amount assessed at a fixed rate of taxation, it is then called a *tax*. In the book *The Spirit of the Laws*, a head tax is found to be more appropriate to servitude and a property tax more suited to liberty.[5] This would be incontestable if the shares paid by head were equal, for nothing would be more disproportionate than such a tax, and the spirit of liberty consists, above all, in exactly observed proportions. But if the head tax is exactly proportionate to the means of private individuals, as the tax in France known as the *capitation* could be and which is, thus, both real and personal, it is the most equitable, and, consequently, the best suited to free men. These proportions seem, at first, very easy to observe, because being relative to each person's position in the world, the indications are always public, but besides the fact that the elements of greed, influence, and fraud may leave no traces, all the elements that should enter into these calculations are rarely taken into account. First, one should consider the relationships of quantities, according to which, all things being equal, anyone who has ten times more wealth than another should pay

4. Here and in the preceding paragraph, Rousseau oversteps his definition of political economy by touching on a legislative rather than an administrative matter. Tax laws, we are told, must be enacted by majority vote, though who must vote—the citizens or their representatives—is left unclear. In *On Social Contract*, the procedure for enacting tax laws is more precise: like all legislative decisions, those concerning taxes must be made in public assembly by all the citizens. Rousseau's fear of taxes as a resource with which rulers will oppress subjects, already evident in this *Discourse*, is so much stronger in *On Social Contract* that he there (Book III, chapter 15) recommends doing without taxes and replacing them with enforced labor and contributions in kind.

5. Montesquieu, *The Spirit of the Laws*, X. iii. 15.

ten times more than the poorer one. Secondly, one should consider the relationship of use, that is, the distinction between what is necessary and what is superfluous. Anyone who has only the bare necessities should not pay anything at all; the taxation of anyone who has more than he needs, can, when the occasion demands, be extended to the amount that exceeds the necessities.[6] To this he will reply that, given his rank, what would be superfluous for a man of inferior status is a necessity for him, but this is a lie, for, just like a cowherd, a man of high standing has two legs and only one belly. Moreover, these alleged necessities of life are so far from being necessary to his rank that if he knew how to renounce them for some praiseworthy cause, he would only be the more respected for it. The people would prostrate themselves before a minister who went to council on foot, because he had sold his carriages when the state had a pressing need. Finally, the law does not prescribe magnificence for anyone, and the proprieties are never grounds for going against right.

A third relationship that is never taken into account, although it should always be considered first of all, is that of the benefits everyone derives from the social confederation, which provides powerful protection for the immense possessions of the rich and scarcely allows a poor wretch to enjoy the cottage he has built with his own hands. Are not all the advantages of society for the powerful and rich? Are not all lucrative positions filled by them alone? Are not all privileges and exemptions reserved for them? And is not public authority completely in their favor? When a man of high standing robs his creditors or cheats in other ways, is he not always certain of impunity? Are not the beatings he administers and the acts of violence he commits, even the murders and assassinations he is guilty of, hushed up and no longer even mentioned after six months? If this same man is robbed, the entire police force is immediately on the move, and woe to the innocent persons he suspects. What if he has to pass through a dangerous area? He has escorts through the countryside. What if the axle of his carriage happens to break? Everyone rushes to his aid. What if someone is making noise outside his door? He says one word and everyone is silent. What if the crowd inconveniences him? He makes a gesture and everyone moves aside. What if a cart driver gets in his way? His men are ready to knock him senseless. And better that fifty honest pedestrians going about their business be run over than that a lazy scoundrel in his carriage be delayed. All this respect costs him not a penny; it is the rich man's right, and not what he buys with his wealth. How different is the picture of the poor man! The more humanity owes him, the more society refuses him. All doors are closed to him, even when he has the right to open them; and if sometimes he obtains justice, it is with greater difficulty than another would have in obtaining a pardon. If there is unpleasant work to be done or a militia

---

6. Rousseau starts off by backing taxation proportionate to income and wealth. But by urging that those who can afford only the necessities of life pay no tax at all, he winds up advocating progressive taxation, which takes a larger percentage of income and wealth from the rich than from the poor.

to be raised, he is the one who is given preference; he always bears, besides his own burden, the one from which his richer neighbor has the influence to have himself exempted. When the slightest accident befalls him, everyone avoids him. If his humble cart overturns, I count him fortunate if, far from being helped by anyone, he avoids the insults of the rude servants of some young duke who is passing by. In short, all free assistance is denied him when he needs it, precisely because he has nothing with which to pay for it; but if a poor man has the misfortune of having an honest soul, a beautiful daughter, and a powerful neighbor, I consider him a man lost.

Another no less important consideration is that the losses of poor men are much less easy to offset than those of the rich, and that the difficulty of acquiring wealth always increases in proportion to need. Nothing is created from nothing; that is as true in business as it is in physics; money is the seed of money, and the first ten francs are sometimes more difficult to earn than the second million. But there is still more. Everything that the poor man spends is forever lost to him, and remains in or returns to the hands of the rich, and since taxes sooner or later pass into the hands of the very men who share in the government, or to those who are closely connected to it, they have, even in paying their share of taxes, a palpable interest in increasing them.

Let us summarize in a few words the social pact between the two estates: *You need me, for I am rich and you are poor; let us make an agreement between us: I shall permit you to have the honor of serving me on the condition that you give me what little you have left in return for the trouble I shall be taking to command you.*

If all these things are carefully worked out, we will find that in order to levy taxes in an equitable and truly proportionate way, the tax rates should not only be determined in proportion to the assets of taxpayers, but in a proportion consisting in the difference between their conditions and the superfluity of their possessions. This important and very difficult calculation is carried on everyday by multitudes of honest clerks who know arithmetic, but a Plato or a Montesquieu would not have dared undertake it without trembling and imploring heaven for enlightenment and integrity.[7]

*   *   *

7. The last five pages of this *Discourse*, omitted here, consider in detail the kinds of taxes that should be assessed. Rousseau opposes taxes on land or grain as detrimental to agriculture; and he favors taxes on luxuries as conducive to equality of wealth.

On Social Contract
or
Principles of Political Right

On Social Contract, published in 1762, systematically sets out Rousseau's views, which he had been elaborating for at least eight years, on how a legitimate state should be established, organized, and run. What marks a state as legitimate for Rousseau, thus giving it a right to unqualified obedience, is its guarantee to all its members of the freedom to enact their own laws. The institutional device which Rousseau relies on to allow this freedom is direct democracy. If those who are subject to a state's jurisdiction assemble together to make its laws, that state is legitimate, since all of its members then have a direct and equal legislative voice. Rousseau's main task in *On Social Contract* is to vindicate the tight connection between direct democracy and legislative freedom by identifying the numerous contextual requirements and institutional conditions which a direct democracy must meet, if its members are indeed to be self-legislating.

By the time one reaches the end of *On Social Contract*, it becomes obvious that only in rare and difficult cases does Rousseau believe the citizens of a direct democracy can be the authors of their laws. Society must be small, isolated, homogeneous, and egalitarian. A superhuman lawgiver must launch the state by endowing it with sound principles. Political institutions, meticulously divided into legislative and executive, must be in exquisite balance. No state has ever met these demanding requirements, nor is it likely that a state ever will. Rousseau's bleak assessment of the prospects for legitimate democracy is bound to distress those of us who are inspired by his vision of citizens as lawmakers, assembled together to decide their own fates. One of the best reasons to read *On Social Contract* is for help in deciding whether that vision should be abandoned, adjusted, or intrepidly sought.

On Social Contract or Principles of Political Right

—foederis aequas
Dicamus leges.
Aeneid XI[1]

1. Rousseau cites Virgil's *Aeneid*, XI. 436, where, after the funeral rites and mourning for his son Pallas, King Latinus, finding himself without allies, proposes to end the violence by drawing up an equitable treaty ("Let us make equitable treaty terms"), so that both Latins and Trojans may live in peace as citizens in Italy.

Foreword

This little treatise is extracted from a more extensive work, undertaken in the past without having considered my strength, and long since abandoned. Of the various fragments that might have been taken from what was completed, this is the most important and seemed to me the least unworthy of being offered to the public. The rest no longer exists.

Book I

I wish to discover if, in the civil order, there can be any legitimate and fixed rule of administration, taking men as they are and laws as they can be.[2] I shall, in this inquiry, always strive to reconcile what right permits with what interest prescribes, so that justice and utility may not be divided.

I broach the subject without giving proof of its importance. I shall be asked if I am a prince or a lawmaker, since I am writing on politics. I answer that I am neither, and that this is precisely why I am writing on politics. If I were a prince or a lawmaker, I would not waste my time talking about what ought to be done; I would either do it or remain silent.

I was born the citizen of a free state and a member of the sovereign, and, however feeble an influence my voice may have in public affairs, my right to vote on them suffices to make it my duty to inform myself on such matters. I am always happy, whenever I reflect upon the nature of government, to find in my inquiries new reasons for loving that of my own country!

CHAPTER 1 THE SUBJECT OF THIS FIRST BOOK

Man is born free, and everywhere he is in chains.[3] Anyone who thinks himself the master of others is no less a slave than they. How has this change come about? I do not know. What can make it legitimate? I believe I can resolve this question.

If I were to consider only force and its effects, I would say that as long as a people is compelled to obey and does so, it does well; as soon as it can shake off the yoke and does so, it does even better, for, either this people, in recovering its liberty by the same right as the one by which it was stolen, is entitled to regain it, or no one was entitled to take it away. But the social order is a sacred right which serves as the basis of all the others. Yet, this right is not derived from nature; it is, therefore, founded

2. Rousseau is not concerned with the administrative function of government, as the phrase "rule of administration" might suggest. His subject is basic constitutional arrangements.

3. This sentence distills two of Rousseau's claims in the *Discourse on Inequality* that social life robs us of our natural freedom, and that this loss is irreversible. Rousseau will argue in the eighth chapter

of this book that in a just society a new sort of freedom is attained. In the present chapter and the three that follow, he rejects four traditional tests for a state's legitimacy. Neither familial descent, nor physical prowess, nor military success, nor ownership of slaves gives a ruler the right to be obeyed.

upon agreements. It is a question of knowing what these agreements are. Before coming to that, however, I must prove what I have just asserted.

CHAPTER 2 ON THE FIRST SOCIETIES

The oldest of all societies and the only natural one is that of the family. Even so, the children remain bound to their father only as long as they need him to survive. As soon as this need ceases to exist, the natural bond is dissolved. The children, free from having to obey their father, and the father, free from having to care for his children, return all alike to a state of independence. If they continue to remain united, they do so not naturally but voluntarily, and the family itself is maintained only by agreement.

This common liberty is a consequence of man's nature. His first law is to see to his own preservation; his first concerns are those he owes to himself, and, as soon as he reaches the age of reason, being then the sole judge of the proper means of preserving himself, he thereby becomes his own master.

The family, therefore, is, if you will, the first model for political societies: the leader is like the father and the people like his children; and all, having been born free and equal, alienate their liberty only for their own advantage. The main difference is that, in the family, the father's love for his children repays him for the care he provides them, whereas in the state, the pleasure of commanding replaces a love that the leader does not feel for his peoples.

Grotius denies that all human power is established for the benefit of those who are governed; he cites slavery as an example.[4] His most usual manner of arguing is always to establish rights on the basis of fact.[5] It is possible to argue in a more consistent manner, but not in one more favorable to tyrants.

It is therefore uncertain, according to Grotius, whether the human race belongs to a hundred men or so, or whether these hundred men or so belong to the human race, and, all through his book, he appears to lean towards the first view; this is also Hobbes's opinion. Thus, we find the human race divided into herds of cattle, each with a leader who keeps watch over it in order to devour it.

Just as the herdsman is superior by nature to his herd, so the shepherds of men, who are their leaders, are superior by nature to their peoples. In Philo's account, the emperor Caligula reasoned in this manner and concluded appropriately enough for this analogy that either kings were gods or that peoples were beasts.[6]

---

4. Hugo Grotius (1583–1645) was a Dutch jurist and statesman. Rousseau refers here and elsewhere to his *De jure belli ac pacis* (On the Law of War and Peace), first published in 1625.

5. "Scholarly research in public law is often only the history of former abuses; and anyone who takes the trouble to study it too deeply is misguidedly obstinate." (*Treatise on the Interests of France in Relation to Her Neighbors* by the Marquis d'Argenson, printed at Rey publishers in Amsterdam). This is precisely what Grotius did* [Rousseau's note, with 1782 correction].

*All of Rousseau's notes to *On Social Contract* have been included. His additions to the 1782 edition are also indicated by date.

6. Philo Judaeus (25 B.C.–A.D. 54) was a Jewish philosopher from Alexandria, who offered his readers an outsider's view of Rome.

Caligula's reasoning comes down to that of Hobbes and Grotius.[7] Before any of them, Aristotle also had said that men are not naturally equal but that some are born to be slaves and others to be masters.[8]

Aristotle was right, but he mistook the effect for the cause. Every man born into slavery is born to be a slave; nothing is more certain. Slaves lose everything in their chains, even the desire to escape from them; they love their servitude as Ulysses's companions loved their brutishness.[9] If there are, therefore, slaves by nature, it is because there have been slaves against nature. Force created the first slaves; their cowardice has perpetuated their condition.

I have said nothing of King Adam or Emperor Noah, father of three great monarchs who divided the world among themselves, as did the children of Saturn, with whom they have been compared. I hope that my moderation will be appreciated, for, being the direct descendant of one of these princes, and perhaps of the eldest branch, how do I know whether I might not find myself the legitimate king of the human race through a verification of titles? Be that as it may, it cannot be denied that Adam was sovereign of the world, just as Robinson was of his island, as long as he was its only inhabitant, and what was most agreeable about this empire was that the monarch, secure on his throne, had nothing to fear from rebellions, wars, or conspirators.[1]

CHAPTER 3 ON THE RIGHT OF THE STRONGEST

The strongest man is never strong enough to remain forever the master, unless he transforms his might into right and obedience into duty. Hence, the right of the strongest, a right that is ostensibly understood ironically and actually established as a principle. But will anyone ever explain this word to us? Force is a physical power; I do not see what kind of morality can result from its effects. Yielding to force is an act of necessity, not of will; it is, at most, an act of prudence. In what sense could this be a duty?

Let us suppose for a moment that this alleged right exists. I say that nothing but inexplicable nonsense results from it, for as soon as might makes right, the effect changes along with the cause; any new force that overcomes the first also inherits its rights. As soon as it becomes possible to disobey with impunity, it is possible to disobey legitimately; and since the strongest is always in the right, it is only a question of behaving so that one may be the strongest. But what kind of right is one which perishes when the force behind it ceases to exist? If force makes it necessary to obey, it is no longer necessary to obey out of a sense of duty; if a person is no longer forced to obey, he is no longer obligated to do so.

7. Rousseau is a bit short with Hobbes, who thought men equal in the important sense that they are equally able to harm one another.

8. See Aristotle's (384–322 B.C.) discussion of slavery in *Politics* 1. 4–8, where he claims some men are slaves by nature.

9. See a short treatise by Plutarch entitled: *That Beasts Employ Reason* [Rousseau's note].

1. Rousseau is pointedly satirizing the doctrine of the divine right of kings espoused by royalists like Sir Robert Filmer, author of *Patriarcha, or the Natural Power of Kings* (London 1680), in which he defends absolute monarchy by tracing royal authority back to the domestic absolutism of Noah and Adam.

We can see, therefore, that this word right adds nothing to force; in this context, it means nothing at all.

Obey the powers that be. If that means to yield to force, the precept is good but superfluous; I answer that it will never be violated. All power comes from God,[2] I admit, but every illness comes from him as well. Is this to say that calling a doctor is forbidden? If a thief surprises me in a corner of the woods, I am forced to give him my purse, but am I, in conscience, obligated to give it to him when I could hide it? For, after all, the pistol in his hand is also a kind of power.

Let us agree, therefore, that might does not make right, and that we are obligated to obey only legitimate powers. Thus, my original question always recurs.[3]

CHAPTER 4 ON SLAVERY[4]

Since no individual has natural authority over his fellow man, and since force creates no rights, agreements remain the basis of all legitimate authority among men.

If a private individual, says Grotius, can alienate his liberty and make himself the slave of a master, why could not an entire people alienate its liberty and make itself the subject of a king? There are a good many equivocal words in this statement which need explanation, but let us confine ourselves to the word *alienate*. To alienate means to give or to sell. Now, a man who makes himself another's slave does not give himself; at the very least, he sells himself for his subsistence, but for what purpose does a people sell itself? Far from furnishing his subjects with their subsistence, a king only derives his own from them, and, according to Rabelais, a king does not live on little. Do subjects, then, give up their persons on condition that their property will also be taken? I do not see what they have left to keep.

It will be said that the despot guarantees his subjects civil tranquillity.[5] That may be, but what do they gain by that, if the wars which his ambition brings upon them, his insatiable greed, and the vexations of his administration devastate them more than their own dissensions? What do they gain, if that very tranquillity is one of their miseries? Living in dungeons is also tranquil: is that enough to make them appealing? The Greeks confined in the Cyclop's cave lived tranquilly there while awaiting their turn to be devoured.[6]

To say that a man gives himself for nothing is to say something absurd and inconceivable; such an act is illegitimate and invalid, if only because

---

2. See Romans 13:1 and Paul's discussion of the secular government of Rome.
3. This question concerns the characteristics of a legitimate state, one that deserves to be obeyed.
4. The purpose of this chapter is less to attack slavery than to dispose of the argument, advanced above all by Grotius, that people who voluntarily agree to obey a state ought to obey it, even if it deprives them of their freedom.

5. Rousseau disputes Hobbes's claims that an unlimited government is the best means of achieving domestic peace, and that such peace is the principle aim of the social contract.
6. Locke also develops this theme in *Two Treatises of Government*, II. xix. 228; both arguments are inspired by the Polyphemus episode in Book IX of Homer's *Odyssey*.

anyone who does such a thing is not in his right mind. To say the same thing of an entire people is to suppose a nation of madmen: madness does not make right.

Even if each individual could alienate himself, he cannot alienate his children, for they are born men and free; their liberty belongs to them, and no one has the right to dispose of it but they themselves. Before they reach the age of reason, the father can, in their name, stipulate conditions for their preservation and well-being, but he cannot give them to someone else irrevocably and unconditionally, since such a gift is contrary to nature's ends and exceeds the rights of fatherhood. In order, then, for an arbitrary government to be legitimate, the people in each generation would have to be free to accept or reject it, but, then, this government would no longer be arbitrary.

To renounce one's liberty is to renounce one's humanity, the rights of humanity and even its duties. No compensation is possible for someone who renounces everything. Such a renunciation is incompatible with man's nature, and to strip him of all freedom of will is to strip his actions of all morality.[7] In short, an agreement that stipulates absolute authority on one hand and unlimited obedience on the other is vain and contradictory. Is it not clear that one is not committed in any way to a person from whom one has the right to demand everything, and does not this single condition, this lack of equality or mutual obligation, suggest the meaninglessness of such an act? For, since all that he has belongs to me, what rights would my slave have against me, and, since his rights are mine, what sense is there in this idea that I have a right against myself?

Grotius and the others find in war another origin for this supposed right of slavery. Since the victor, according to them, has the right to kill the vanquished, the latter can buy back his life at the cost of his liberty, an agreement all the more legitimate because it is advantageous to both parties.

But it is clear that this supposed right to kill the vanquished in no way results from the state of war. If only because, living in their original state of independence, they lack the constant intercourse necessary to constitute either a state of peace or a state of war, men are not naturally enemies. It is the relation of things and not of men that constitutes war; and since the state of war cannot arise from simple personal relations, but only from proprietary relations, private war, that is, the war of man against man, cannot exist either in the state of nature, where there is no established property, or in the social state, where everything is under the authority of the laws.

Individual combats, duels, and encounters are acts that do not constitute a state of war, and, with regard to those private wars authorized by

---

7. Rousseau here grounds his argument against unlimited government on his commitment to the value of moral responsibility. Unlimited government is illegitimate because, by depriving us of freedom, it deprives us of the responsibility for our acts, and, hence, of our very humanity. This same commitment to moral responsibility will be central to his defense of direct democracy.

the Establishments of Louis IX, king of France, and suspended by the Peace of God, they are abuses of feudal government, an absurd system if ever there was one, contrary to the principles of natural right and to every good political organization.

War is not, therefore, a relation of man to man but a relation of state to state, in which individuals are enemies only by accident, not as men or even as citizens,[8] but as soldiers, not as members of the homeland, but as its defenders. In short, the enemies of each state can only be other states and not men, inasmuch as true relations cannot be established between things of different natures.

This principle is even in conformity with the general maxims established in every age and with the invariable practice of all civilized peoples. Declarations of war are warnings not so much to the powers that be as to their subjects. Whether a king, a private individual, or a people, the foreigner who robs, kills, or detains the subjects without declaring war on the prince is not an enemy but a brigand. Even in open war, a just prince rightly takes possession of all that belongs to the public in the enemy country, but he respects the person and property of private individuals; he respects the rights upon which his own are founded. Since the purpose of war is the destruction of the enemy state, one has the right to kill its defenders as long as they bear arms, but as soon as they lay them down and surrender, ceasing to be enemies or instruments of the enemy, they become once again simply men, and no one has any further right over their lives. Sometimes it is possible to kill the state without killing a single one of its members, but war confers no right except that which is necessary to its purpose. These principles are not those of Grotius; they are not founded upon the authority of poets, but they are derived from the nature of things and are founded upon reason.

With regard to the right of conquest, it has no foundation other than the law of the strongest. If war does not give the victor the right to slaughter the vanquished, this right, which he does not actually possess, cannot be the basis of a right to enslave them. We have the right to kill the enemy only when we cannot enslave him; the right to enslave him does not, therefore, come from the right to kill him; it is, then, an unjust exchange to make him purchase his life, over which no one has any right, at the price of his liberty. In establishing the right of life and death upon the right of slavery, and the right of slavery upon the right of life and death, are we not clearly arguing in a vicious circle?

8. The Romans, who have understood and respected the right of war better than any nation in the world, carried their scruples so far in this regard that no citizen was permitted to serve as a volunteer without having expressly enlisted against the enemy, and specifically against such and such an enemy. When a legion in which Cato the Younger [Cato the Elder's son], took up his first arms under Popillius was formed anew, Cato the Elder wrote to Popillius that, if he was willing for his son to continue to serve under him, he would have to make him swear a new military oath, because, once the first was annulled, he could no longer bear arms against the enemy. And the same Cato wrote to his son to take care not to present himself for combat until he had taken this new oath. I know that some will oppose my argument with the example of the siege of Clusium and other particular cases, but I am citing laws, customs. The Romans are the ones who have less often transgressed their laws than other nations; and they are the only ones who have had such fine ones [Rousseau's note, 1782].

Even assuming this terrible right to kill everyone, I say that a slave created by war or a conquered people is under no obligation of any sort toward a master, except to obey him as long as force makes it necessary. In taking the equivalent of a man's life, the victor has not really spared him anything: instead of killing him for no good purpose, he has killed him profitably. So far is he, therefore, from having acquired any authority over this slave other than that created by force, that the state of war subsists between them as before; their relationship is indeed the result of it, and the custom of the right of war presupposes no peace treaty. They have made an agreement, it is true, but far from putting an end to the state of war, this agreement presupposes its continuation.

Thus, however we view the matter, the right of slavery is invalid, not only because it is illegitimate but also because it is absurd and meaningless. These words, *slavery* and *right*, are contradictory; they are mutually exclusive. Whether spoken by one man to another or by one man to an entire people, the following statement will always be equally nonsensical: *I am making an agreement with you wholly at your expense and wholly for my benefit, which I shall observe as long as I please and which you will observe as long as I please.*

CHAPTER 5 THAT WE MUST ALWAYS GO BACK TO A FIRST AGREEMENT [9]

Even if I were to grant all that I have so far refuted, the supporters of despotism would not find their cause any further advanced. There will always be a great difference between subduing a multitude and governing a society. Where isolated individuals are successively enslaved by a single man, whatever their number may be, I see there only a master and his slaves, not a people and its leader; it is an aggregation, if you will, but not an association; in it, there is neither public good nor body politic. Even if such a man had enslaved half the world, he is still only a private individual; his interest, separate from that of the others, is still only a private interest. If this same man happens to die, his empire is left broken up and disunited after him, just as an oak disintegrates and falls into a heap of ashes after it has been consumed by fire.

A people, says Grotius, can give itself to a king. According to Grotius, a people is therefore a people before giving itself to a king. That gift is in itself a civil act; it presupposes a public decision. Therefore, before examining the act by which a people elects a king, it would be good to examine the act by which a people becomes a people, for, since this act is necessarily prior to the other, it is the true foundation of society. [1]

Indeed, if there were no prior agreement, why, unless the election were unanimous, would the minority have an obligation to submit to

9. The previous three chapters have refuted some standard views of what makes a state legitimate. In this chapter, Rousseau introduces his contractualist claim that in a legitimate state, obedience is based on free and rational agreement.

1. In this paragraph, Rousseau announces a theme that grows in importance as he proceeds. It is the relations among the members of society, rather than their relations to officials, that are crucial for the legitimacy of a state.

the choice of the majority, and why do a hundred men who want a master have the right to vote on behalf of ten who do not? The law of majority rule is itself established by agreement and presupposes unanimity on at least one occasion.

CHAPTER 6 ON THE SOCIAL PACT

I assume men to have reached the point at which the obstacles to their preservation in the state of nature have a resistance greater than the forces each individual can use to maintain himself in that state.[2] At this point, that primitive state could no longer subsist, and the human species would perish if it did not change its way of living.

Now, since men cannot engender new forces but merely unite and direct the existing ones, they have no other means of preserving themselves than to form by aggregation a sum of forces that can overcome this resistance, bring them into play by means of a single motive power, and make them act in concert.

This sum of forces can arise only from the cooperation of several men, but since each man's strength and liberty are the primary instruments of self-preservation, how will he commit them without harming himself and without neglecting the care he owes himself? This difficulty, in relation to my subject, can be set forth in these terms:

"To find a form of association that defends and protects the person and possessions of each associate with all the common strength, and by means of which each person, joining forces with all, nevertheless obeys only himself and remains as free as before." Such is the fundamental problem to which the social contract furnishes the solution.

The clauses of this contract are so determined by the nature of the act that the slightest modification would render them null and void, so that, although they have never perhaps been formally enunciated, they are everywhere the same, everywhere tacitly admitted and recognized, until the social pact is violated, and each person regains his original rights and recovers his natural liberty, losing the civil liberty for which he renounced it.[3]

Rightly understood, these clauses can all be reduced to one alone, namely, the total alienation of each associate with all his rights to the whole community.[4] For, in the first place, since each person gives himself entirely, the condition is equal for all, and since the condition is equal for all, no one has an interest in making it burdensome for the others.

2. The dire conflict to which Rousseau alludes here is described in the *Discourse on Inequality* as arising from the competition engendered by social life. Rousseau's concern in that work is to show how existing states control this struggle by depriving subjects of their freedom. In this case, however, his aim is prescriptive: to show how a state should be organized to make its subjects free as well as safe.

3. Note that for Rousseau what makes a state legitimate is not that its subjects expressly agree to the terms of this contract, but that it abides by these terms, whether they expressly agree to them or not.

4. Taken alone, this sentence makes Rousseau sound like a partisan of intolerable tyranny, but the elaboration of this sentence in this and the next two paragraphs shows that he envisages nothing sinister when he calls for total alienation to the community. The community to which we should submit turns out to be a democratic community of equals in whose operation each has an equal and effective share. Cf. below, Book II, chapter 4.

Furthermore, since the alienation is made without reservation, the union is as perfect as it can be, and no associate has anything more to claim. For, if some rights were left to private individuals, and there were no common superior who could decide between them and the public, each person, being in some respects his own judge, would soon claim to be so in every instance; the state of nature would subsist, and the association would necessarily become tyrannical or ineffectual.

Finally, each person, in giving himself to all, gives himself to no one, and as there are no associates over whom he does not acquire the same right as he concedes to them over himself, he gains the equivalent of all that he loses and more force to preserve what he has.

If, then, we eliminate whatever is not essential to the social pact, we shall find that it can be reduced to the following terms: *Each of us puts his person and all his power in common under the supreme control of the general will, and, as a body, we receive each member as an indivisible part of the whole.*[5]

In place of the private person of each contracting party, this act of association at once produces a collective and artificial body, composed of as many members as the assembly has votes, which receives from this same act its unity, its collective self, its life, and its will. This public person, which is thus formed by the union of all the other persons, formerly took the name of *city*[6] and now takes that of *republic* or *body politic*, and its members call it a *state* when it is passive, a *sovereign* when it is active, and a *power* when comparing it to others of its kind. As for the associates, they collectively take the name of the *people*, and, individually, they are called *citizens*, when they participate in the sovereign authority, and *subjects* when they are subject to the laws of the state. But these terms are often confused and mistaken for one another; it is enough to know how to distinguish them when they are used with absolute precision.

CHAPTER 7 ON THE SOVEREIGN

This formula shows that the act of association includes a reciprocal commitment between the public and the private individuals composing it, and that each individual, contracting, so to speak, with himself, finds

---

5. Ought we obey the general will, as Rousseau recommends? No answer is possible until we learn more about the nature of the general will and about how to know what it prescribes. Much of Book II of *On Social Contract*, as well as chapters one to three of Book IV, give the information needed for an intelligent response.

6. The true meaning of this word has been almost entirely effaced among the moderns; most take a town for a city, and a townsman for a citizen. They do not know that houses make the town but that citizens make the city. This same error formerly cost the Carthaginians dearly. I have not read that the title of *cives* has ever been given to the subject of any prince, not even formerly to the Macedonians, nor, in our times, to the English, although

they are nearer liberty than all the rest. Only the French construe this term *citizen* quite loosely, because they have no real idea of its meaning, as we can see in their dictionaries; otherwise, they would, by usurping this word, fall into the crime of high treason; among them, this name expresses a virtue and not a right. When Bodin endeavored to speak of our citizens and townsmen, he committed a gross blunder, by mistaking the former for the latter. Mr. D'Alembert was not mistaken, and, in his article *Geneva*, properly distinguished the four orders of men (even five, counting simple strangers) in our town, of which two alone compose the Republic. No other French author, as far as I know, has understood the real meaning of the word *citizen* [Rousseau's note].

himself committed in two ways: namely, towards private individuals as a member of the sovereign, and towards the sovereign as a member of the state. But the maxim of civil law that no one is bound by commitments made to himself cannot be applied here, for there is a great difference between being obligated to oneself and being obligated to a whole of which one is a part.

It should further be noted that the public decision which can obligate all the subjects toward the sovereign, because of the two different relationships in which each of them is envisaged, cannot, for the opposite reason, obligate the sovereign towards itself, and that, consequently, it is contrary to the nature of the body politic for the sovereign to impose upon itself a law that it cannot break. Since the sovereign can only be considered in one and the same relationship, it is then in the position of a private individual contracting with himself; hence, we see that there is not, nor can there be, any kind of fundamental law binding on the body of the people, not even the social contract.[7] This does not mean that this body cannot perfectly well commit itself towards others in anything that does not violate this contract, for, with regard to foreigners, it becomes a single being, an individual.

But, the body politic or sovereign, deriving its being only from the sanctity of the contract, can never obligate itself, even towards others, in anything that violates this original act, such as alienating some portion of itself or submitting to another sovereign. To violate the act by which it exists would be to annihilate itself, and that which is nothing produces nothing.

As soon as this multitude is thus united in one body, no one can offend any of its members without attacking the body, much less offend the body without the members feeling the effects. Thus, duty and interest equally obligate the two contracting parties to help each other, and the same men must seek to unite, in this double relationship, all the advantages that depend upon it.

Now, the sovereign, formed solely by the private individuals who compose it, neither has nor can have any interest contrary to theirs; consequently, the sovereign power has no need to give a guarantee to the subjects, because it is impossible for the body to want to harm all its members, and we shall see hereafter that it cannot harm any one of them as an individual. Merely by virtue of its special nature, the sovereign is always everything that it should be.[8]

---

7. No state is legitimate for Rousseau unless its citizens have the right not only to make, but also to change or repeal, *all* of its laws, including those, such as a constitution or bill of rights, which limit and direct it. By giving citizens control of all legislation, Rousseau exposes himself to the charge of showing reckless disregard for political stability. This was one aspect of his doctrine that led Rousseau's native Geneva to condemn *On Social Contract* as "destructive of all governments." Yet, much of the work, above all the second half of Book III, is devoted to showing how the kind of direct democracy Rousseau deems legitimate can be preserved. Although he insists on granting citizens an unlimited right to legislate, Rousseau encourages them to exercise this right with care and moderation.

8. The last declaration in this paragraph is bound to astonish the reader who has yet to be told very much about the nature of Rousseau's sovereign or about the general will which it expresses. The next book of *On Social Contract* gives reasons why the laws and policies of a democratic state that meets his criteria for legitimacy are sure to serve the common interest.

But this is not true of the subjects in relation to the sovereign, which, despite the common interest, could not rely upon their commitments, unless it found the means of insuring their fidelity.

Indeed, each individual can, as a man, have a particular will contrary to or different from the general will he has as a citizen. His private interest may speak to him quite differently from the common interest; his absolute and naturally independent existence may make him envision what he owes to the common cause as a gratuitous contribution, the loss of which will be less harmful to others than its payment is burdensome to him, and, considering the artificial person that constitutes the state as an imaginary being because it is not a man, he would enjoy the rights of a citizen without wanting to fulfill the duties of a subject, an injustice that would bring about the ruin of the body politic, were it to spread.

In order, therefore, that the social pact may not be an empty formula, it tacitly includes the commitment, which alone can give force to the others, that anyone who refuses to obey the general will shall be compelled to do so by the entire body; this means nothing else than that he will be forced to be free, for such is the condition which, by giving each citizen to the homeland, protects him against all personal dependence, a condition which determines the workings of the political machine, and which alone renders legitimate civil commitments, which would otherwise be absurd, tyrannical, and subject to the most enormous abuses.[9]

CHAPTER 8 ON THE CIVIL STATE

This passage from the state of nature to the civil state produces a most remarkable change in man, by substituting justice for instinct in his conduct, and giving his actions the morality they previously lacked. Only when the voice of duty succeeds physical impulse and right succeeds appetite does man, who had until then considered only himself, find himself compelled to act on different principles and to consult his reason before listening to his inclinations. Although in this state he denies himself several of the advantages he owes to nature, he gains others so great—his faculties are exercised and developed, his ideas are extended, his feelings are ennobled, his whole soul is so uplifted—that if the abuses of this new condition did not often degrade him beneath the condition from which he emerged, he would constantly have to bless the happy moment that tore him away from it forever, and made a stupid and shortsighted animal into an intelligent being and a man.

Let us reduce this entire balance to terms that can easily be compared. What man loses by the social contract is his natural liberty and an

9. It is easy to see why a recalcitrant citizen in Rousseau's legitimate democracy may be rightfully forced to obey a law. Since all laws in such a democracy serve the common interest, anyone who breaks one takes unfair advantage of his fellow citizens. What is less obvious is why the coercion imposed on the lawbreaker makes him free. It does so because it protects him from dependence on the arbitrary wills of other individuals and preserves his opportunity to enjoy the civil and moral liberty which the next chapter describes.

unlimited right to everything that tempts him and to everything he can take; what he gains is civil liberty and the ownership of everything he possesses. In order to avoid being mistaken about these compensations, we must carefully distinguish between natural liberty, which is limited only by the strength of the individual, and civil liberty, which is limited by the general will, and between possession, which is only the result of force or the right of the first occupant, and ownership, which can be based only on a real title.

Besides the preceding, another benefit which can be counted among the attainments of the civil state is moral liberty, which alone makes man truly his own master, for impulsion by appetite alone is slavery, and obedience to the law that one has prescribed for oneself is liberty. But I have already said too much on this point, and the philosophical meaning of the word *liberty* is not part of my subject here. [1]

CHAPTER 9 ON REAL ESTATE

At the moment the community is formed, each member gives himself to it, just as he is at the time, himself and all his forces, which include the goods he possesses. It is not that by this act what one possesses changes in nature by changing hands and becomes property in the hands of the sovereign, but, just as the forces of the city are incomparably greater than those of a private individual, public possession is also, in point of fact, stronger and more irrevocable, without being more legitimate, at least for foreigners. For, with regard to its members, the state is master of all their possessions through the social contract, which serves as the basis of all rights within the state, but, with regard to other powers, it is master only through the right of first occupancy which it derives from private individuals.

The right of first occupancy, although more real than the right of the strongest, becomes a true right only after the establishment of the right of property. Every man naturally has a right to everything he needs, but the positive act that makes him the owner of a piece of property excludes him from all the rest. Once he has his share, he must limit himself to it, and he has no other claim against the community. That is why the right of first occupancy, which is so weak in the state of nature, deserves the respect of every civilized man. In this right, we respect not so much what belongs to others as what does not belong to us.

In general, to sanction the right of first occupancy to any piece of land

---

1. This chapter enumerates the values to which Rousseau appeals in arguing for the merits of a democratic community of equals. Besides the morality and rationality mentioned in the first paragraph, which Rousseau seems to attribute more to social life in general than to a specially democratic way of life, the other, more specifically democratic values are civil liberty, the freedom from government to do anything not prohibited by laws which serve the common interest, and moral liberty, the freedom to make and follow one's own rules. Kant, for whom self-legislation is so central to morality, revered Rousseau as the Newton of the moral universe.

The contrast in this chapter between the advantages of life in the natural and civil states should be compared to the similar one at the end of Book II, chapter 4, and the quite different assessment of the two ways of life in the *Discourse on Inequality*. (See the *Second Discourse*, pp. 25–26, and the ninth note to this discourse, pp. 17–18.)

whatever, the following conditions are necessary: first, this land must not yet be inhabited by anyone; secondly, one must occupy only the area one needs to subsist; thirdly, one must take possession of it not by a vain ceremony but by labor and cultivation, the only sign of ownership that, in the absence of legal titles, should be respected by others.

Indeed, in granting the right of first occupancy to need and labor, are we not taking it as far as it can go? Is it not possible to establish limits to this right? Will it suffice to set foot on a piece of the common ground to claim all at once to be master of it? Will it suffice to have the strength to throw other men off it momentarily to take away forever their right to come back to it? How can a man or a people seize a vast territory and deprive the entire human race of it other than by a punishable usurpation, since such an act robs the remaining men of the dwelling place and food that nature gives them in common? When Nuñez Balboa, standing on the shore, took possession of the South Seas and all of South America in the name of the crown of Castille, was that enough to dispossess all the inhabitants and to exclude all the princes of the world? On such a footing, these ceremonies multiplied vainly enough, and the Catholic King had only to take immediate possession of the entire universe from his chambers, afterwards eliminating from his empire what was previously possessed by other princes.

It is easily understood how the adjoining properties of private individuals are united and become public territory, and how the right of sovereignty, extending from the subjects to the land they occupy, becomes at once real and personal; this places the landowners in greater dependency, and makes their strength itself the guarantee of their fidelity. Ancient monarchs do not appear to have been well aware of this advantage, for, only calling themselves kings of the Persians, the Scythians, the Macedonians, they seemed to regard themselves as leaders of men rather than as masters of countries. Today's monarchs more cleverly call themselves kings of France, Spain, England, etc. By thus holding the land, they are quite sure of holding its inhabitants.

What is remarkable about this alienation is that far from robbing private individuals by accepting their property, the community only assures them of legitimate possession, and changes usurpation into a genuine right and possession into ownership. Therefore, since owners are considered depositaries of the public wealth, and since their rights are respected by all members of the state and upheld against foreigners with all its forces, they have, so to speak, acquired everything that they have given up by a transfer that is advantageous to the public and still more so to themselves. This paradox is easily explained by the distinction between the rights that the sovereign and the owner have to the same piece of land, as we shall see hereafter.[2]

2. The alienation of possessions described in this chapter is an aspect of the benign total alienation mentioned above in the sixth chapter. The community to which individuals alienate their possessions, being a democratic community of equals, assures a safe, fair allocation of public as well as private property. Private property has an important place in Rousseau's legitimate state, provided that, as he insists in his own note to this chapter (p. 98), it is not too unequally distributed. See also Book II, chapter 11 and On Political Economy, (pp. 75–83).

It may also happen that men begin to unite before posse anything, and that, after appropriating land enough for all, they use ɩt in
common or divide it among themselves either equally or according to
proportions established by the sovereign. In whatever way this acquisition is made, the right of each individual to his own piece of land is
always subordinate to the community's right to everything, without which
there would be neither solidity in the social bond nor real power in the
exercise of sovereignty.

I shall end this chapter and this book with a remark that ought to serve
as the basis of the whole social system; instead of destroying natural
equality, the fundamental pact, on the contrary, substitutes a moral and
legitimate equality for whatever physical equality nature had been able
to impose among men, and, although they may be unequal in strength
or in genius, they all become equal through agreements and law.[3]

END OF THE FIRST BOOK

Book II

CHAPTER 1 THAT SOVEREIGNTY IS INALIENABLE

The first and foremost consequence of the principles established above
is that the general will alone can direct the forces of the state in accordance with the end for which it was instituted, that is, the common good,
for, if the opposition of private interests has made the establishment of
societies necessary, the agreement of these same interests has made it
possible. It is what these different interests hold in common that forms
the social bond, and if there were not some point of agreement among
them, no society could exist. Indeed, it is solely on the basis of this
common interest that society should be governed.

I say, therefore, that sovereignty, being nothing more than the exercise of the general will, can never be alienated, and that the sovereign,
which is merely a collective being, can only be represented by itself;
power can indeed be transferred but not will.

In fact, if it is not possible for a particular will to agree on some point
with the general will, it is at least impossible for this agreement to be
lasting and constant, for the particular will tends by nature towards partiality and the general will towards equality. It is even more impossible
to have any guarantee of this agreement, even though it should always
exist; this would not be an effect of art but of chance. The sovereign may
well say: "I now will what this man wills, or at least what he says he
wills," but it cannot say, "What this man wills tomorrow, I too shall

---

3. Under bad governments this equality is only
apparent and illusory; it only serves to maintain
the poor man in his misery and the rich man in
his usurpation. Indeed, the laws are always useful
to those who have possessions and harmful to those
who have nothing; whence it follows that the social
state is advantageous to men only insofar as they
all have something and none of them has too much
[Rousseau's note].

will," since it is absurd for the will to give itself fetters for the future, and since no will can consent to anything that is contrary to the good of the being who wills it. If the people, therefore, simply promises to obey, it dissolves itself by that act and loses what makes it a people; at the moment a master exists, there is no longer a sovereign, and from that moment the body politic is destroyed.

This is not to say that the orders of leaders cannot pass for expressions of the general will, as long as the sovereign, free to oppose them, does not do so. In such a case, the consent of the people must be presumed from universal silence. This will be explained at greater length.[4]

CHAPTER 2 THAT SOVEREIGNTY IS INDIVISIBLE

For the same reason that sovereignty is inalienable, it is indivisible, for the will is general,[5] or it is not; it is the will of the body of the people, or of only a part. In the first case, this declared will is an act of sovereignty and constitutes law; in the second, it is merely a particular will, or an act of magistracy; at the very most it is a decree.

But our political theorists, being unable to divide sovereignty in principle, divide it in its purpose; they divide it into force and will; into legislative power and executive power; into the rights of taxation, justice, and making war; into internal administration and the power of negotiating with foreigners; sometimes they mingle all these parts, and sometimes they separate them. They turn the sovereign into a fantastic being composed as a mosaic of inlaid fragments; it is as if they created man out of several bodies, one of which would provide the eyes, another the arms, another the feet and nothing more. The magicians of Japan, it is said, cut a child into pieces before the eyes of the spectators; then, throwing all the pieces into the air one after another, they make the child fall back to earth alive and completely reassembled. The juggling acts of our political theorists are more or less like this; after having dismembered the social body by a spell worthy of the fair, they reassemble the pieces, we know not how.

This error results from not having formulated an accurate notion of sovereign authority, and from having taken for parts of that authority what were only emanations of it. Thus, for example, the acts of declaring war and making peace have been regarded as acts of sovereignty, but they are not, since each of these acts is not a law, but merely an application of the law, a particular act which determines how the law applies to a particular case, as we shall clearly see when the idea attached to the word *law* has been defined.[6]

By analyzing the other divisions in a similar manner, we would find

4. See Book III, chapter 11 (p. 140).

5. For a will to be general, it is not always necessary for it to be unanimous, but all the votes must be counted; any formal exclusion destroys the generality [Rousseau's note, 1782].

6. See Book II, chapter 6 (p. 106), where Rousseau points to the generality of law as what distinguishes it from other kinds of governmental enactments. Sovereign and legislative authority are thus equivalent for Rousseau.

that whenever we think sovereignty is divided, we are mistaken, and that the rights which are taken to be parts of this sovereignty are always subordinate to it and always presuppose supreme wills which these rights only execute.

It would be impossible to say how much this lack of precision has obscured the determinations of the authors who write on matters of political right, when they have attempted to judge the respective rights of kings and peoples on the basis of the principles they had established. Anyone can see, in Chapters 3 and 4 of the first book of Grotius, how this learned man and his translator Barbeyrac were entangled and hampered by their sophistries, for fear of saying too little or too much in expressing their views, and offending the interests they had to conciliate. Grotius, a refugee in France, discontent with his own country and wishing to pay court to Louis XIII to whom his book is dedicated, spares no pains to deprive the peoples of all their rights and bestow them upon kings in the most artful way possible. This would also have been much to the liking of Barbeyrac, who dedicated his translation to the king of England, George I. But, unfortunately, the expulsion of James II, which he calls abdication, forced him to be on his guard, to equivocate, to be evasive, in order to avoid making William appear to be a usurper.[7] If these two writers had adopted true principles, all these difficulties would have been removed, and they would always have remained consistent, but they would have told the sad truth and paid court only to the people. Indeed, truth does not lead to success, and the people confers neither embassies, professorial chairs, nor pensions.

CHAPTER 3 WHETHER THE GENERAL WILL CAN ERR

It follows from what has gone before that the general will is always in the right and always tends toward the public utility, but it does not follow that the decisions of the people are always equally correct. A person always wills his own good, but he does not always see it; the people is never corrupted, but it is often deceived, and it is only then that it appears to will what is bad.[8]

There is often a great difference between the will of all and the general will; the latter looks only to the common interest; the former looks to the private interest and is only a sum of particular wills, but take away from these same wills the pluses and minuses that cancel each other out,[9] and

---

7. James II was king of England from 1685 to 1688, when he was forced to leave the country during the Glorious Revolution and was replaced by Mary, his Protestant daughter, and her husband, William of Orange, governor of the Netherlands. Parliament imposed conditions in the "Bill of Rights" which limited their authority and that of all their royal successors.

8. Here Rousseau broaches the main difficulty with his view of a legitimate state as radically democratic: the laws enacted in the sovereign assembly of such a state might be unjust and harmful, since they might not express the general will. *On Social*

Contract can be fruitfully read as an attempt to show how a democracy must be organized so that it serves the common good.

9. "Every interest," says the Marquis d'Argenson, "has different principles. The agreement of two particular interests is formed by opposition to that of a third." He might have added that the concurrence of all interests arises in opposition to the interest of each individual. If there were not any different interests, the common interest would hardly exist and would never meet any obstacle; everything would proceed on its own, and politics would cease to be an art [Rousseau's note].

the general will remains as the sum of the differences.

If, when a sufficiently informed people deliberates, the citizens were to have no communication among themselves, the general will would always result from the large number of small differences, and the decision would always be good.[1] But when factions, partial associations, are formed at the expense of the greater one, the will of each of these associations becomes general with respect to its members, and particular with respect to the state; it may then be said that there are no longer as many voters as men, but only as many as there are associations. The differences become less numerous and yield a less general result. Finally, when one of these associations is so large that it prevails over all the others, your result is no longer just a sum of small differences but a single difference; there is, at that point, no longer a general will, and the opinion which prevails is merely a particular one.

It is important, therefore, in order to have a clear enunciation of the general will, that there be no partial association in the state and that each citizen speak only for himself;[2] such was the unique and sublime institution of the great Lycurgus. If there are partial societies, it is necessary to multiply their number and to prevent inequality from existing among them, as Solon, Numa, and Servius did.[3] These precautions are the only good ones for ensuring that the general will is always enlightened, and that the people is not deceived.

CHAPTER 4 ON THE LIMITS OF SOVEREIGN POWER

If the state or city is only an artificial body whose life consists in the union of its members, and if the most important of its concerns is its own preservation, it must have a universal and compelling force in order to move and dispose each part in the manner best suited to the whole. Just as nature gives each man absolute power over all his members, the social pact gives the body politic absolute power over all its own; and it is this same power, under the direction of the general will, which bears, as I have said, the name of sovereignty.

But beyond the public person, we have to consider the private persons who compose it, whose life and liberty are naturally independent of it. It is a question, then, of clearly distinguishing the respective rights of the citizens and the sovereign,[4] and the duties the former have to fulfill as subjects from the natural rights they should enjoy as men.

It is agreed that each person alienates through the social pact only the

1. The "communication" referred to here is not face to face discussion among citizens in the sovereign assembly, but private caucuses of special interest groups.

2. "It is true," says Machiavelli, "that some divisions harm republics while others benefit them. Those which harm them involve factions and partisans. Since a founder of a republic cannot prevent strife from occurring, he can at least see to it that there are no factions" (*History of Florence*, VII. i) [Rousseau's note].

3. Lycurgus (c. 9th century B.C.) was a reformer of Spartan and Solon (?638–?559 B.C.) of Athenian political institutions. The institutions of the Roman Republic, according to tradition, were established by Numa Pompilius (?end of 8th century B.C.) and reorganized by Servius Tullius (?7th century B.C.). Sparta and Republican Rome served Rousseau as inspirations for his vision of democracy.

4. Attentive readers, do not hurry, I beg you, to accuse me here of contradicting myself. I have not been able to avoid it in my terms, given the poverty of language; but wait [Rousseau's note].

part of his power, possessions, and liberty that will be important to the community, but it must also be agreed that the sovereign alone is the judge of what is important.[5]

A citizen owes to the state all the services he can render, as soon as the sovereign asks for them, but the sovereign, on the other hand, cannot impose on the subjects any restraints that are useless to the community, nor can it even want to do so, for, under the law of reason just as under the law of nature, nothing is done without a cause.

The commitments which bind us to the social body are obligatory only because they are mutual, and their nature is such that in fulfilling them we cannot work for others without also working for ourselves. Why is the general will always in the right, and why do all constantly will the happiness of each person, unless it is because there is no one who does not apply this word *each* to himself and who does not think of himself when voting for all? This proves that equality of right and the notion of justice it produces stem from each man's preference for himself, and, consequently, from the nature of man; that the general will, to be truly so, must be general in its object as well as in its essence; that it must come from all to be applied to all; and that it loses its natural rectitude when it tends toward some individual and determinate object, because, in such a case, we have no real principle of equity to guide us in judging what is foreign to us.[6]

Indeed, as soon as it becomes a question of a particular fact or right on a point which has not been settled by a previous and general agreement, the matter becomes arguable. It is a case in which the interested private individuals are one of the parties and the public the other, but in which I see neither the law that should be followed, nor the judge who should give the decision. It would be ridiculous in such a case to want to refer the matter to an express decision of the general will, which can only be the conclusion of one of the parties, and which is, consequently, for the other party, only a foreign, particular will, inclined on this occasion to injustice, and subject to error. Thus, just as a particular will cannot represent the general will, the general will, in turn, changes in nature when it has a particular object, and, as a general will, it cannot pronounce judgment on either a man or a fact. When the people of Athens, for example, named its leaders or reduced them to the ranks, bestowed honors on one, imposed penalties on another, and, by multitudes of particular decrees, exercised all the functions of government indiscriminately, it no longer had, in such cases, a general will properly speaking; it was no longer acting as sovereign but as magistrate. This will

---

5. The fact that the sovereign assembly has unbounded control over each member's fate adds to the urgency of assuring that its decisions are wise and just.

6. One of the means Rousseau counts on most heavily to assure that the sovereign assembly expresses the general will is laid out in this chapter. The enactments passed by the assembly must be general in the sense that they apply equally to all. The assembled citizens would be too tempted to serve private interests, if they could pass enactments for the advantage of particular individuals or groups, rather than the whole community. General rules, on the other hand, have such uncertain benefits and costs for individuals that they cannot readily be crafted so as to advantage particular persons or groups.

seem contrary to prevailing notions, but I must be given time to set forth my own.

It should be understood from the preceding that what makes the will general is not so much the number of voters as the common interest uniting them, for, in this arrangement, each necessarily submits to the conditions he imposes on others, an admirable concurrence of interest and justice, which gives the common decisions an equitable character which is seen to vanish in the discussion of any particular issue for want of a common interest to unite and identify the ruling of the judge with that of the contending party.

From whatever direction we go back to our principle, we always reach the same conclusion, namely, that the social pact establishes such an equality among the citizens that they all commit themselves under the same conditions and should all enjoy the same rights. Thus, by the very nature of the pact, every act of sovereignty, that is to say, every authentic act of the general will, obligates or favors all citizens equally, so that the sovereign knows only the body of the nation and makes no distinctions between any of those who compose it. What in fact is an act of sovereignty? It is not an agreement between a superior and an inferior, but an agreement between the body and each of its members, a legitimate agreement, because it is based upon the social contract; equitable, because it is common to all; useful, because it can have no other purpose than the general good; and reliable, because it is guaranteed by the public force and the supreme power. As long as the subjects are only bound by agreements of this sort, they obey no one but their own will, and to ask how far the respective rights of the sovereign and citizens extend is to ask to what point the latter can commit themselves to each other, one towards all and all towards one.

We can see from this that the sovereign power, wholly absolute, wholly sacred, and wholly inviolable as it is, does not and cannot exceed the limits of the general agreements, and that every man can fully dispose of whatever has been left to him of his goods and liberty through these agreements, so that the sovereign never has a right to burden one subject more than another, because when the matter becomes a private one, its power is no longer competent.

Once these distinctions have been admitted, it is obviously untrue that under the social contract there is any real renunciation on the part of private individuals, since their situation, as a result of this contract, is actually preferable to what it was previously, and, instead of alienating anything, they have only exchanged, to their advantage, an uncertain and precarious existence for another that is better and more secure, natural independence for liberty, the power to harm others for their own safety, and their force, which others could overcome, for a right that the social union makes invincible. Their very lives, which they have dedicated to the state, are continually protected by it, and when they imperil their lives for the defense of the state, what are they then doing but giving back to the state what they have received from it? What are they doing that they were not doing in greater danger and more frequently in the state of nature, when, engaging in inevitable quarrels, they would, at the risk of their lives, defend their means of preserving them. All have to fight if necessary for the homeland, it is true; but then no one ever has to fight for himself. Do we not still gain something by running part of the risks to insure our safety that we would have to run for ourselves as soon as we are deprived of it?

CHAPTER 5 ON THE RIGHT OF LIFE AND DEATH

It may be asked how private individuals, having no right to dispose of their own lives, can transfer to the sovereign the very right they do not possess.[7] This question appears difficult to resolve only because it is poorly posed. Every man has the right to risk his own life in order to preserve it. Has it ever been said that anyone who throws himself out a window to escape a fire is guilty of suicide? Has such a crime ever even been imputed to someone who perishes in a storm, even if he was fully aware of the danger when he embarked?

The social treaty has as its end the preservation of the contracting parties. Anyone who desires the end also desires the means, and these means are inseparable from certain risks, even certain losses. Anyone who desires to preserve his life at the expense of others should also give it up for them when it is necessary. Now, the citizen is no longer the judge of the perils to which the law wants him to expose himself, and when the prince[8] has said to him: "It is expedient for the state that you die," he should die, since it is only on this condition that he has lived in safety up to that time, and since his life is no longer merely a blessing of nature, but a conditional gift of the state.

The death penalty imposed on criminals can be envisaged in nearly the same way; it is to avoid being the victim of an assassin that we consent to die if we become one. Under such an accord, far from disposing of our own lives, we think only of protecting them, and it is not to be presumed, therefore, that any of the contracting parties plans to have himself hanged.

Moreover, every wrongdoer, by attacking society's laws, becomes, through his transgressions, a rebel and a traitor to his country; by violating its laws, he ceases to be one of its members, and he even makes war against it. In such a case, the preservation of the state is inconsistent with his own; and one of the two must perish; and when the guilty one is put to death, it is less as a citizen than as an enemy. The proceedings and judgment are the proof and declaration that he has broken the social treaty, and that he is, consequently, no longer a member of the state. Now, since he has acknowledged himself such, at the very least by his

7. Locke asks this question in *The Second Treatise of Civil Government*, section 23.
8. In Rousseau's technical vocabulary, which he does not explain until Book III, chapter 1, the term *prince* refers not to a sovereign, but to the administrative officials charged by the sovereign assembly with the task of executing legislation.

residence, he must be severed from the state by exile as a violator of the pact, or by death as a public enemy, for such an enemy is not an artificial entity, he is a man, and in such a case, the right of war is to kill the vanquished.

But, it will be said, the condemnation of a criminal is a special act. I agree, but such a condemnation is not a function of the sovereign; it is a right the sovereign can confer without itself being able to exercise it. All my ideas are interconnected, but I cannot set them forth all at once.

Besides, the frequency of corporal punishment is always a sign of weakness or laxity in the government.[9] There is no evildoer who could not be made good for something. Only a person who cannot be preserved without danger can rightfully be put to death, even as an example.

With respect to the right to pardon or to exempt a guilty person from the penalty carried by the law and pronounced by the judge, this is a function of that which is above the judge and the law, that is to say, the sovereign; still, its right in this matter is not very well defined, and the instances in which this right is exercised are very rare. In a well-governed state there are few punishments, not because many pardons are granted, but because there are few criminals; the very multitude of crimes ensures impunity when the state is in decline. Under the Roman Republic, neither the senate nor the consuls ever attempted to grant pardons; even the people did not grant any, although it sometimes revoked its own judgments. Frequent pardons give notice that crimes will soon no longer require any pardon at all, and everyone can see where that leads. But I feel my heart murmuring and holding back my pen; let us leave the discussion of these questions to the just man who has never erred, and who himself has never needed pardoning.

CHAPTER 6 ON LAW

Through the social pact we have given existence and life to the body politic; it is now a question of giving it movement and will through legislation, for the original act by which this body is formed and united in no way determines what it must do to preserve itself.

What is good and consistent with order is so by the nature of things and independently of human conventions. All justice comes from God, and He alone is its source, but if we knew how to receive it from so high a source, we should need neither government nor laws. No doubt there is a universal justice emanating from reason alone, but in order to be admitted among us, this kind of justice must be reciprocal. Considered from a human viewpoint, the laws of justice, for want of natural sanctions, are useless among men; they work only to the advantage of the wicked and the disadvantage of the just; the latter observes these laws with respect to others, although no one observes them with respect to

9. In Book III, chapter 1, Rousseau gives the term *government* a technical meaning as the administrative or executive power, staffed by the officials whom he calls the *prince*.

him. Agreements and laws are therefore necessary for uniting rights to duties and for bringing justice back to its objective. In the state of nature, where everything is held in common, I owe nothing to those to whom I have promised nothing; I recognize as belonging to others only what is of no use to me. It is not so in the civil state, where all rights are fixed by law.

But just what, after all, is a law? As long as people are content to attach only metaphysical ideas to this word, they will continue to argue without understanding each other, and when they have said what a law of nature is, they will have no better idea of what a law of the state is.[1]

I have already said that there is no general will with respect to a particular object.[2] In fact, this particular object is either within the state or outside it. If it is outside, a will that is foreign to the state is not general in relation to it, and if this object is within the state, it is part of it. Just so, a relation between the whole and its part is formed, which makes them two separate beings, one of which is the part and the other of which is the whole minus this same part. But the whole minus a part is not the whole, and as long as this relationship subsists, there is no longer a whole, but only two unequal parts. Hence, it follows that the will of the one is no longer general in relation to the other.

But when the whole people makes rules for the whole people, it is considering only itself, and if a relation is then formed, it is between the whole object from one point of view and the whole object from another point of view with no division of the whole. In this case, the matter about which it makes the rules is, like the will that makes rules, general. This act is what I call a law.

When I say that the object of the laws is always general, I mean that the law considers the subjects as a body and actions in the abstract, never one man as an individual, or a particular action. Thus, the law can decree that there will be privileges, but it cannot give them to particular individuals by name; the law can create several classes of citizens, even determine the qualifications which will give them the right to be in these classes, but it cannot name the specific individuals to be admitted to them; it can establish a monarchical government and hereditary succession, but it cannot elect a king or name a royal family. In short, no function relating to an individual object belongs to the legislative power.[3]

Given this view, it is immediately apparent that it is no longer necessary to ask whose business it is to make laws, since they are acts of the general will; nor whether the prince is above the law, since he is a member of the state; nor whether the law can be unjust, since no one is unjust

---

1. This paragraph is certainly aimed at Montesquieu's definition of law in *The Spirit of the Laws*, I. 1, as "the necessary relations that derive from the nature of things."

2. This was said in chapter 4 of this book, where many of the ideas about law elaborated here were first presented.

3. In this paragraph, Rousseau is struggling to show how legislation can be both fair and effective. Unless laws can apply to classes of individuals such as the sick, the aged, or the poor, their scope is so limited that they cannot effectively serve the public interest, but if laws can apply to classes of individuals, they may treat some unfairly. Clearly, to prohibit the naming of individuals in laws is inadequate to protect groups against legislative discrimination. It is also inadequate to protect individuals, since stratagems can be easily devised to discriminate against individuals without mentioning their names.

towards himself; nor how we can be free and yet subject to the laws, since they are but the record books of our wills.

It can also be seen that, since the law reunites the universality of the will with that of the object, what one man, whoever he may be, orders on his own authority is not a law; even what the sovereign orders with respect to a particular object is not a law, but a decree; it is not an act of sovereignty, but one of magistracy.

I therefore give the name republic to any state ruled by law, no matter what its form of administration, for only then does public interest govern, and the commonwealth really exist. Every legitimate government is republican;[4] I shall explain what government is later on.

Laws are, properly speaking, only the conditions of civil association. The people who are subject to the laws should be their author; defining the conditions of the society is solely a function of those who form the association, but how will they define them? Will it be by common accord, by sudden inspiration? Does the body politic have an organ for declaring its will? Who will give it the foresight necessary to formulate decisions on this basis, and to announce them in advance, or how will it make these decisions in time of need? How would a blind multitude, which often does not know what it wants because it rarely knows what is good for it, carry out on its own as great and difficult an undertaking as that of creating a system of legislation? By itself, the people always wants the good, but does not always see it. The general will is always in the right, but the judgment that guides it is not always enlightened. It must be made to see things as they are, sometimes as they should appear to it; it must be shown the right path that it seeks to protect it from being led astray by particular wills; it must be made to see places and times in relation to one another, taught to weigh the attractions of present and tangible advantages against the danger of remote and hidden ills. Private individuals can see the good they reject; the public wants the good it does not see. All are equally in need of guides. The former must be constrained to bring their wills into conformity with their reason; the latter must be taught to know what it wants. Public enlightenment, then, results in the union of understanding and will within the social body, which gives rise to close cooperation among the parts, and finally, to the greatest strength of the whole. Hence arises the need for a lawgiver.[5]

CHAPTER 7 ON THE LAWGIVER

To discover the rules of society most suitable for nations, it would require a superior intelligence, who saw all the passions of men without feeling any of them; who had no relation to our nature yet knew it thor-

4. I do not mean by this word only an aristocracy or a democracy, but in general every government guided by the general will, which is the law. To be legitimate, the government must not be confused with the sovereign, but must be its minister; then, even monarchy is a republic. This will be clarified in the following book [Rousseau's note].

5. In this transitional paragraph, Rousseau shifts attention in his effort to assure that the sovereign expresses the general will from the internal workings of the legislative assembly to the economic, social, and cultural contexts in which the assembly operates. These contextual matters are his main concern in the remaining pages of this book.

oughly; who was independent of us for happiness, yet truly willing to pay attention to ours; and, finally, who, in preparing for himself a distant glory in the ages to come, could work in one world and reap his rewards in another.[6] It would take gods to give laws to men.

To define the civil or kingly man he seeks in his book *The Statesman*, Plato used the same reasoning with respect to right that Caligula used with respect to facts. But if it is true that a great prince is a rare man, what will be said of a great lawgiver? The former has only to follow the pattern which the latter must propose. The latter is the engineer who invents the machine; the former is merely the worker who sets it up and makes it run. "At the birth of societies," says Montesquieu, "the rulers of republics create the institutions, and afterwards the institutions mold the rulers."[7]

Anyone who dares to undertake the founding of a people should feel himself capable of changing human nature, so to speak, of transforming each individual, who by himself is a perfect and solitary whole, into part of a greater whole from which this individual receives, in a way, his life and his being; of altering the human constitution in order to strengthen it; and of substituting a partial and artificial existence for the physical and independent existence we have all received from nature. He must, in a word, take away man's own forces in order to give him new ones which are alien to him, and which he cannot use without the help of others. The more inactive and impotent these natural forces are, and the greater and more enduring the acquired ones are, the more solid and perfect the institution is as well, so that if each citizen is nothing and can do nothing except through all the others, and if the force acquired by the whole is equal or superior to the sum of the natural forces of all the individuals, it can be said that legislation has reached the highest level of perfection it can attain.

The lawgiver is, in every respect, an extraordinary man in the state. If he should be so by reason of his genius, he is not less so by reason of his position. It is not magistracy; it is not sovereignty. This office, which sets up the republic, does not enter into its constitution; it is a particular and superior function, which has nothing in common with human authority, for, if he who commands men should not enforce the laws, he who enforces the laws should not command men; otherwise, his laws, the ministers of his passions, would often only perpetuate his unjust attitudes; and he could never avoid having the sanctity of his work tainted by private views.[8]

6. A people becomes famous only when its legislation begins to decline. It is not known for how many centuries the institutions of Lycurgus made the happiness of the Spartans possible before they were known to the rest of Greece [Rousseau's note].

7. *Consideration on the Causes of the Roman's Greatness and Decline*, chapter 1.

8. Rousseau gives his lawgiver the almost impossible task of endowing the future members of a legitimate state with the devotion to the public that is needed if their political decisions are to express the general will.

In resorting to a lawgiver as the means to found his system, Rousseau was inspired by examples from ancient history and by Machiavelli's discussion of a founding lawgiver in the *Discourses*.

It is important to remember that Rousseau excludes the lawgiver from any part in the operation of the state he founds. The "laws" he gives are moral habits and basic constitutional arrangements. However unsavory the machinations of the lawgiver may be, they thus do not infringe on the authority of the citizens assembled to legislate.

When Lycurgus gave laws to his homeland, he began by abdicating his kingship. It was the custom of most Greek cities to entrust the establishment of their laws to foreigners. The modern republics of Italy often imitated this practice; that of Geneva did as much and found itself the better for it.[9] During her finest days, Rome saw all the crimes of tyranny reborn in her bosom and saw herself on the verge of perishing for having put legislative authority and sovereign power into the same hands.

Nevertheless, the decemvirs,[1] never arrogated to themselves the right of passing any law merely on their own authority. *Nothing that we propose to you,* they said to the people, *can become law without your consent. Romans, be yourselves the authors of the laws which are to fashion your happiness.*

Anyone who drafts the laws, therefore, has or should have no legislative right, and the people itself cannot, whenever it might wish, divest itself of this incommunicable right, because, according to the fundamental pact, only the general will binds private individuals, and it is never certain that a particular will is in conformity with the general will, until after it has been submitted to the free vote of the people. I have already said this, but it is not useless to repeat it.[2]

Another difficulty merits some attention. The sages who want to speak to the vulgar herd in their own language rather than in the language of the people cannot make themselves understood. Now, there are thousands of ideas that are impossible to translate into the language of the people. Overly general views and overly remote aims are equally beyond its understanding; each individual, appreciating no other plan of government than the one which is relevant to his private interest, finds it difficult to perceive the advantages he is to derive from the continual deprivations that good laws impose. In order for a nascent people to appreciate sound political maxims and follow the fundamental rules of statecraft, the effect would have to become the cause; the social spirit, which should be the product of the way in which the country was founded would have to preside over the founding itself; and, before the creation of the laws, men would have to be what they should become by means of those same laws. Thus, the lawgiver, incapable of appealing either to force or reason, must have recourse to an authority of another order, which can lead without compelling and persuade without convincing.

This is what has forced the fathers of nations in every age to take

9. Those who consider Calvin only as a theologian are poorly acquainted with the breadth of this genius. The drafting of our wise edicts, in which he played a significant role, does him as much honor as his *Institutes*. Whatever revolution time may bring in our religion, as long as the love of country and liberty is not extinct among us, the memory of that great man will never cease to be blessed.* [Rousseau's note].

* John Calvin (1509–64) was a French law student when he was influenced by Luther and turned to theology. Having fled France during one of Francis I's persecutions of heretics, he became a political and religious leader of the Protestant Reformation in Switzerland, especially in Geneva. Rousseau esteemed Calvin not as a theologian who emphasized justification by faith, but as a lawgiver who gave the Church a prominent role in Genevan affairs in order to guide education and morals. This church government censored books, prohibited luxuries and amusements, and emphasized prayer and work.

1. In 451 B.C. a committee of ten men codified Roman law in response to the complaints of the plebeians.

2. Cf. above, p. 106. In chapter 15 of the next Book, Rousseau again insists that every law be ratified by the "people in person".

recourse to divine intervention and to credit the gods with their own wisdom, so that the peoples, bound by the laws of the state as by those of nature, and recognizing the same power in the formation of the city as in the creation of man, might freely obey and docilely bear the yoke of public felicity.

In order to lead by divine authority those who could not be moved by human prudence, the lawgiver places the decisions of this sublime reason, which rises above the understanding of the vulgar herd, in the mouth of the immortals.[3] But it is not the privilege of every man to make the gods speak, or to be believed when he announces himself their interpreter. The lawgiver's greatness of soul is the true miracle that must give proof of his mission. Any man may engrave stone tablets, or buy an oracle, or feign a secret relationship with some divinity, or train a bird to speak in his ear, or find other crude means of deceiving the people. A man who knows only how to accomplish these things might even be able to assemble, by chance, a band of fools, but he will never found an empire, and his extravagant creation will soon perish with him. Vain illusions form a transitory bond; only wisdom can make it lasting. The surviving Jewish laws, those of the child of Ishmael,[4] which for ten centuries have ruled half the world, today still proclaim the greatness of the men who dictated them; and while proud philosophy or blind party spirit see them only as lucky imposters,[5] the true political theorist admires in their institutions the great and powerful genius which presides over enduring establishments.

It is not necessary to conclude from this, along with Warburton,[6] that politics and religion have a common purpose among us, but that, in the origin of nations, one serves as an instrument of the other.

CHAPTER 8 ON THE PEOPLE

Just as the architect, before erecting a great edifice, sounds and tests the ground to see if it can support the weight, so the wise founder does not begin by drafting laws which are simply good in themselves, but first investigates whether or not the people for which he intends them is capable of tolerating them. For this reason, Plato refused to give laws to the Arcadians and the Cyrenians, knowing that these two peoples were rich and could not tolerate equality; for this reason, good laws and wicked men were found together in Crete, because Minos had only disciplined a people with many vices.

3. "Actually," says Machiavelli, "there never existed a person who could give unusual laws to his people without recourse to God, for otherwise such laws would not have been accepted, for the benefits they bring, although evident to a prudent man, are not self-explanatory enough to be evident to others" (*Discourses on Livy*, I. xi) [Rousseau's note].
4. Rousseau is referring to Mohammed. The Arabs were considered the descendants of Ishmael.
5. This sally is aimed at the French *philosophes*,

who Rousseau had more thoroughly denounced in his first major work, *Discourse on the Sciences and the Arts* (1750). The *philosophes* often treated religion as the work of imposters whose goal was to control people by deluding them.
6. Rousseau is referring here to William Warburton (1698–1779), an English theologian who wrote on the problem of the relationship between church and state and engaged in a long polemics against such Enlightenment thinkers as Hume and Voltaire.

A thousand nations have flourished on the earth, which could never have tolerated good laws,[7] and even those which could have done so have only been capable of doing so for a very brief period of their entire existence. Like men, peoples are docile only in their youth; in growing old, they become incorrigible. Once customs are established and prejudices have taken root, trying to reform them is a dangerous and vain undertaking; the people, like the stupid and cowardly patient who trembles at the sight of the doctor, cannot even bear to have someone treat its ills in order to do away with them.

It is true that just as some illnesses unhinge men's minds and erase their memory of the past, so there are, sometimes, in the life of a state, violent epochs when revolutions do to peoples what certain crises do to individuals, when horror of the past takes the place of loss of memory, and when the state, set ablaze by civil wars, is reborn, so to speak, from its ashes and, issuing from the arms of death, regains the vigor of its youth. This was the case with Sparta in the time of Lycurgus, Rome, after the Tarquins,[8] and, in our times, Holland and Switzerland, after the expulsion of their tyrants.

But such events are rare; they are exceptions whose explanation is always found in the particular constitution of the state in question. They cannot even happen twice to the same people, for a people can make itself free as long as it is still barbarous, but it can no longer do so when its mainspring is worn out. Public disturbances may then destroy it, but revolutions cannot reestablish it, and, as soon as its chains are broken, it falls apart and ceases to exist. Henceforth, it needs a master, not a liberator. Free peoples, remember this maxim: liberty can be acquired, but never recovered.[9]

Youth is not infancy. There is for nations, as for men, a time of youth, or if you wish, maturity, that must be awaited before they are subjected to laws, but the maturity of a people is not always easy to recognize, and if it is assumed prematurely, the effort will fail. One people is tractable at birth; another is not so at the end of ten centuries. The Russians will never be truly civilized, because they have been subjected to law and order too soon. Peter had a genius for imitation; he did not have true genius, which creates and makes everything anew. Some of the things he did were good, but most were untimely. He saw that his people was barbarous, but did not see that it was not ripe for civilizing; he attempted to bring it under law and order when it needed only to be trained. He attempted to make Germans or Englishmen out of his subjects, when he should have begun by making them into Russians; he prevented them from ever becoming what they could have been, by

7. Note that earthly flourishing is not an index of legitimacy for Rousseau.
8. The Tarquins, early Etruscan kings of Rome, were tyrants thrown out by Lucius Junius Brutus.
9. In these paragraphs Rousseau gives free reign to his historical pessimism and to his doubts about the merit of reform and revolution. Before a legit-

imate state can be founded, the times must be ripe; and such times, which usually occur at the beginning of a people's history, if they occur at all, are exceedingly rare and evanescent. Since Rousseau thinks that neither reform nor revolution can succeed except at such times, he normally supports established institutions.

persuading them that they were something they were not.[1] In this same way, a French tutor molds his pupil to shine for a moment during his childhood, and, then, never to amount to anything. The Russian Empire will attempt to subjugate Europe, and will itself be subjugated. The Tartars, its subjects or its neighbors, will become its masters and ours. To me, this revolution seems certain. All the kings of Europe are working together to hasten its coming.

CHAPTER 9 CONTINUED

Just as nature has set limits to the stature of a well-formed man, past which it creates only giants or dwarfs, so there are limits to the size of a well-constituted state, so that it may be neither too large to be well governed, nor too small to endure on its own. In every political body, there is a maximum strength, which it cannot exceed, and from which growth often makes it deviate. The more the social bond is stretched, the more slack it grows, and, a small state is generally stronger in proportion to its size than a large one.

A thousand arguments demonstrate this maxim. First, administration becomes more difficult over great distances, just as a weight becomes heavier at the end of a longer lever. It also becomes more burdensome as the number of levels multiplies, for, in the first place, each city has its own administration paid for by the people; each district has its own, again paid for by the people; next each province; then the larger scale governments, the satrapies[2] and vice-royalties, each always paid for more dearly than the one below it, and always at the expense of the unfortunate people; finally comes the supreme administration which crushes all the rest. So many additional charges continually exhaust the resources of the subjects; far from being better governed by all these different orders, they are less so than if they had but a single one over them. In the meantime, there remain scarcely any resources for emergencies, and when the state must take recourse to these, it is always on the brink of ruin.

That is not all. Not only is the government less vigorous and swift in enforcing the laws, preventing nuisances, correcting abuses, and forestalling seditious enterprises that may develop in distant places, but the people has less affection for its leaders whom it never sees, for its homeland, which, in its eyes, seems like the whole world, and for its fellow citizens, most of whom are strangers to each other. The same laws cannot be appropriate for so many diverse provinces, which have different moral habits as well as contrasting climates and cannot all tolerate the same form of government. Different laws only engender disorder and

---

1. Peter the Great, Russian tsar from 1682 to 1725, westernized, secularized, and militarized his country. Rousseau's criticism of Peter is also aimed at Voltaire, who had publically lauded Peter for making his subjects into Europeans. Rousseau believed that a chief duty of a founding lawgiver

was to develop his people's distinctive character.
2. The term *satrapies*, which refers to the provinces of ancient Persia, is suggestive of large despotic states or states with complex and antiquated administrative systems.

confusion among peoples which, living under the same leaders and in continual communication with one another, intermarry and, bound by other customs, never know if their heritage is really their own. Talents are buried, virtues unknown, vices unpunished, in this multitude of men unknown to one another and brought together by the seat of the supreme administration in one location. Leaders, overwhelmed by business, see nothing for themselves, and clerks govern the state. Finally, the measures that must be taken to maintain the general authority, which so many distant officials wish either to evade or abuse, completely absorb public concern, so that none is left for the happiness of the people, and scarcely any for its defense in an emergency; and it is thus that a body too large for its constitution collapses and perishes, crushed under its own weight.

On the other hand, the state must give itself a reliable foundation, if it is to be stable enough to withstand the shocks it is certain to sustain and the efforts it will be forced to make to sustain itself, for all peoples have a kind of centrifugal force by which they continually act against each other and tend to expand at the expense of their neighbors, like the vortices of Descartes.[3] Thus the weak ones run the risk of being quickly swallowed up, and scarcely a one can preserve itself, except by putting itself into a kind of equilibrium with all the others, which renders the pressure everywhere nearly equal.

This makes it clear that there are reasons for expansion and reasons for contraction, and it is not the least of the statesman's talents to find between them the proportion most advantageous to the preservation of the state. It can be said in general that the reasons for expansion, being only external and relative, should be subordinated to the reasons for contraction, which are internal and absolute; a healthy and strong constitution is the first thing to be sought, and it is necessary to count more upon the vigor that is born of a good government than upon the resources furnished by a large territory.[4]

Moreover, there have been states so constituted that the need for conquests entered into their very constitution, and in order to maintain themselves, they were forced to expand constantly. Perhaps they congratulated themselves greatly on this happy necessity, which nevertheless revealed to them, along with the limits of their greatness, the inevitable moment of their downfall.

CHAPTER 10 CONTINUED

A body politic can be measured in two ways, that is to say, by the area of its territory, and by the number of its people, and there is a ratio

3. René Descartes (1596–1650), the French philosopher, formulated a theory of vortices, possibly in an effort to reconcile Galileo's new conception of the universe with the views of the Church. Affirming the nonexistence of the void, Descartes held that the universe is entirely composed of vor-tices, or large bodies of whirling matter.
4. The project of establishing a legitimate democracy thus faces geographical difficulties that are almost as insuperable as the historical difficulties raised in the previous chapter.

between these two measurements which will properly define the true size of the state. Men make up the state, and the land sustains them; this ratio is, therefore, that the land suffice to maintain the inhabitants, and that there are as many inhabitants as the land can feed. The *maximum* force of a given number of people is found in this proportion, for, if there is too much land, the protection of it is burdensome, the cultivation inadequate, the produce excessive, and this is the immediate cause of defensive wars; if there is not enough land, the state finds itself at the mercy of its neighbors for what it needs, and this is the immediate cause of offensive wars. Every people whose position gives it no alternative but that between commerce or war is weak in itself; it depends upon its neighbors; it depends on events; its existence can never be anything but uncertain and short. It subjugates others and changes its situation, or it is subjugated and ceases to exist. It can preserve its liberty only by virtue of being small or large.

A fixed ratio between the area of land and the number of men that are mutually sufficient cannot be expressed mathematically, as much because of the differences that exist in the quality of the land, the degree of its fertility, the nature of its produce, and the influence of its climates, as because of the noticeable differences in the temperaments of its inhabitants, some of whom consume little in a fertile country, and others a great deal in a more barren one. It is also necessary to take note of the greater or lesser fecundity of the women, the attributes of the country that are more or less favorable to population, and the number of people whom the lawgiver can hope to unite there by means of the laws he establishes, for he must base his judgment not on what he sees, but on what he foresees, nor should he dwell so much upon the present state of the population as upon the state it should naturally attain. Finally, there are countless occasions on which particular accidents of locality require or permit the inclusion of more land than seems necessary. Thus, the population will spread out a great deal in a mountainous country, where the natural products, namely, woods and pastures, require less work, where experience teaches us that the women are more fecund than in the plains, and where a sizeable piece of sloping ground affords only a small area of level ground, the only area that need be counted on for vegetation. On the contrary, the population may contract along the seashore, even on nearly barren rocks and sand, because fishing can to a large extent compensate for the produce of the land, because men must be more closely gathered together to repulse pirates, and because it is easier, furthermore, to rescue the country from the burden of overpopulation by means of colonies.

To these conditions for the founding of a people must be added one which can take the place of no other, but without which they are all useless: that is, the enjoyment of peace and abundance; for the time at which a state is being organized, like that when a batallion is being formed, is the moment when the body is least capable of resistance and easiest to destroy. Resistance would be more successful during a time of absolute disorder than during a moment of unrest, when each is concerned with his own position and not with the danger. If war, famine, or sedition arises in this time of crisis, the state will inevitably be overthrown.

Governments have often been established during such turbulent times, but then these are the very governments that destroy the state. Usurpers always bring on or choose these moments of public unrest to have enacted, with the help of public panic, destructive laws that the people would never deliberately adopt. The choice of the moment for instituting a government is one of the surest characteristics by which the work of the lawgiver can be distinguished from that of the tyrant.

What kind of a people is, then, fit for legislation? The one which finds itself already bound together by some common origin, interest, or agreement but has not yet born the true yoke of law; the one that has no deeply rooted customs or superstitions; the one that has no fear of being overcome by sudden invasion and, without entering into its neighbors' quarrels, is also able to resist each of them alone, or to make use of one to repulse the other; the one in which each member can be known by all, and in which no one is compelled to place on one man a burden too great for him to bear; the one that can do without other peoples and that all other peoples can do without;[5] the one that is neither rich nor poor but can be self-sufficient; and, finally, the one that combines the stability of an ancient people with the docility of a new one. What makes the work of the lawgiver difficult is not so much what must be established as what must be destroyed; and what makes success so rare is the impossibility of finding the simplicity of nature combined with the needs of society. All these conditions, it is true, are rarely produced together. Thus, few well-constituted states are to be seen.

There is still one country in Europe fit for legislation, that is, the island of Corsica. The valor and persistence with which that brave people was able to recover and defend its liberty indeed makes it deserve to have some wise man teach it how to preserve its liberty. I have a certain premonition that this small island will one day astonish Europe.[6]

CHAPTER 11 ON THE VARIOUS SYSTEMS OF LEGISLATION

If we inquire into exactly what constitutes the greatest good of all, which should be the end of every system of legislation, we shall find that it comes down to these two principal objectives, *liberty* and *equality*.

---

5. If one of two neighboring peoples could not do without the other, this would be a very difficult situation for the former and a very dangerous one for the latter. Every wise nation will, in such cases, endeavor very quickly to deliver the other from this dependence. The republic of Thlascala, an enclave within the empire of Mexico, preferred to do without salt rather than to buy if from the Mexicans or even to accept it free of charge. The wise Thlascalans saw a trap hidden beneath such generosity.

They kept themselves free, and this small state, enclosed within that great empire, was finally the instrument of its downfall [Rousseau's note].

6. Although Rousseau's gloom about the prospects for establishing a legitimate state led him to hope only in Corsica, the Corsicans were greatly cheered by his confidence in their troubled island and asked him to suggest a constitution. Rousseau agreed but never completed his *Constitutional Project for Corsica*.

Liberty, because all private dependence is only so much force taken away from the body of the state; equality, because liberty cannot continue to exist without it.[7]

I have already said[8] what civil liberty is; with regard to equality, the word should not be understood to mean that the degrees of power and wealth are absolutely the same, but that power should fall short of all violence and never be exercised except by virtue of rank and law, and that, with regard to wealth, no citizen should be rich enough to be able to buy another, and none poor enough to be forced to sell himself, which presupposes moderation in wealth and influence on the part of the upper classes, and moderation in avarice and covetousness on the part of the lower classes.[9]

Such equality, they say, is a chimera of speculation which cannot exist in practice. But if abuse is inevitable, does it follow that it should not at least be regulated? Precisely because the force of things always tends to destroy equality, the force of legislation should always tend to uphold it.

But these general objectives of the foundation of every good political system must be modified in each country by the relations which arise as much from the local situation as from the character of the inhabitants, and, on the basis of these relations, each people must be assigned a particular method of establishing laws that is the best, not perhaps in itself, but for the state for which it is intended. For example, is the soil barren and unproductive, or the country too crowded for its inhabitants? Turn towards industry and arts, and exchange what they produce for the commodities you lack. Or, on the other hand, do you live on rich plains and fertile hillsides? Do you lack inhabitants in areas with good land? Give all your attention to agriculture, which causes men to multiply, and drive out the arts, which would only make you succeed in depopulating the countryside by gathering its few inhabitants together in a few locations.[1] Or do you live on a long and accessible coast? Cover the sea with ships, and cultivate commerce and navigation; you will have a brilliant and short existence. Does the sea along your coasts wash over nothing but almost inaccessible rocks? Remain barbarians and fish eaters; you will live more tranquilly, perhaps better, and surely more happily. In short, beyond the principles common to all, each people has within itself some cause which orders it in a particular way, and makes its legislation appropriate for it alone. Thus, in times past, the Hebrews, and recently, the Arabs, have taken religion as their principal objective, the

---

7. Note that Rousseau sets a higher value on liberty than on equality, whose task is to serve as a means to liberty.
8. Cf. Book I, chapter 8.
9. Do you then wish to give the state stability? Bring the two extremes as closely together as possible; allow neither rich men nor beggars. These two conditions, naturally inseparable, are equally deadly to the common good; from the one spring supporters of tyranny, and from the other tyrants; it is always

between them that the traffic in public liberty is carried on; one group buys it and the other sells it [Rousseau's note].
1. Any branch of foreign commerce, says the Marquis d'Argenson, serves but little purpose for the state in general; it can enrich a few private individuals, even a few towns, but the whole nation gains nothing from it, and the nation is not better off for it [Rousseau's note].

Athenians letters, Carthage and Tyre commerce, Rhodes seafaring, Sparta war, and Rome virtue. The author of *The Spirit of the Laws* has shown through a host of examples the skill by which the lawgiver directs the foundation of the political system towards each of these objectives.

The constitution of a state becomes truly strong and lasting when the conventions are observed in such a way that natural relations and the laws are always in agreement on the same points, and that the latter only serve to insure, accompany, and amend, so to speak, the former. But if the lawgiver is mistaken in his objective and adopts a principle different from the one which arises from the nature of things, if one principle tends toward servitude and the other toward liberty, if one tends towards wealth and the other towards population growth, if one tends towards peace and the other towards conquest, then the laws will be imperceptibly weakened, the constitution will deteriorate, and the state will not cease being in turmoil until it is changed or destroyed, and invincible nature has regained her dominion.[2]

CHAPTER 12 DIVISION OF THE LAWS

To bring order to the whole, or to give the best possible form to the commonwealth, there are various relations to consider. First, there is the action of the entire body upon itself, that is, the relation of the whole to the whole, or of the sovereign to the state, and this relation is composed of the relations among intermediate terms, as we shall see later on.[3]

The laws which regulate this relation bear the name of political laws, and they are also called fundamental laws, with good reason if they are wise, for, if there is, in each state, only one good way of ordering it, the people that has founded it should hold on to it, but if the established order is bad, why would anyone take the laws that prevent it from being good to be fundamental? Nevertheless, whatever the circumstances, a people is always free to change its laws, even the best ones, for, if it wishes to harm itself, who has the right to prevent it from doing so?

The second relation is that of the members to each other or to the body as a whole, and this relation should be as small as possible in the first respect and as great as possible in the second, so that each citizen will be perfectly independent from all the others and extremely dependent on the city; this is always done by the same means, for only the force of the state makes its members free. It is from this second relation that civil laws arise.

It is possible to consider a third kind of relation between the individual and the law, namely, the relation of disobedience to its penalty, and this

2. With the characteristically bleak remarks in this chapter concerning economic and social structure, Rousseau ends the survey, begun in chapter 7, of the conditions which the lawgiver must find or make before he can hope to found a legitimate state.

3. We see this in Book III, chapter 1, where the most important intermediate term turns out to be *government*—the administrative agency that applies legislation.

gives rise to the establishment of criminal laws, which, at bottom, are less a particular kind of law than the sanction of all the others.

To these three kinds of laws is added a fourth, the most important of all, which is engraved in neither marble nor bronze, but in the hearts of the citizens; which forms the true constitution of the state; which acquires new vigor every day; which, when other laws grow old or die out, gives them new life or takes their place, preserves a people in the spirit of its origins, and imperceptibly substitutes the force of habit for that of authority. I am speaking of moral habits, customs, and, above all, of opinion, a part of the law unknown to our political theorists, but upon which, nonetheless, the success of all the other laws depends, the part with which the great lawgiver concerns himself in secret, while he appears to limit himself to particular regulations that are only the sides of the arch, of which moral habits, slower to arise, form at length the unshakable keystone.

Among these various classes, the political laws, which determine the form of the government, are the only ones relevant to my subject.[4]

END OF THE SECOND BOOK

Book III

Before speaking of the various forms of government, let us try to determine the precise meaning of this word, which has still not been very well explained.

CHAPTER 1 ON GOVERNMENT IN GENERAL

I warn the reader that this chapter must be read carefully, and that I lack the skill to make myself clear to anyone who is unwilling to be attentive.

Every free action has two causes which combine to produce it: one mental, namely the will that determines the act, and the other physical, namely, the power that executes it. When I walk towards an object, I must first will to go towards it, and, in the second place, my feet must take me there. If a paralyzed man wills to run, and if an able bodied man wills not to run, both of them will remain where they are. The body politic has the same motive powers; force and will are likewise distinguished within it; the former under the name of *executive power*, and the latter under the name of *legislative power*. Nothing is or ought to be done in the body politic without their concurrence.

We have seen that legislative power belongs to the people, and can only belong to it alone. It is easy to see, on the contrary, from the principles previously established, that executive power cannot belong to the general public in its legislative or sovereign capacity, because this power

4. This chapter opens the way from Rousseau's discussion of how to establish a legitimate state to   his discussion of how its political institutions should be designed.

consists only of particular acts which fall outside the province of the law, and, consequently, outside that of the sovereign, all of whose acts can be nothing other than laws.[5]

An appropriate agent is, therefore, needed to unite public power and put it into operation under the guidance of the general will, to assist in the communication between state and sovereign, and to do, in a way, for the public person, what the union of soul and body does for a man. This is the reason for having a government in the state, and it is inappropriately confused with the sovereign, of which it is only the minister.

What, then, is government? An intermediate body established between the subjects and the sovereign for their mutual dealings, charged with the execution of the laws and with the maintenance of liberty, both civil and political.

The members of this body are called magistrates or *kings*, that is to say, *governors*; and the body as a whole bears the name of *prince*.[6] Thus, those who claim that the act by which a people subjects itself to leaders is not a contract are quite right. Government is absolutely nothing more than a commission, a post in which leaders, as ordinary officers of the sovereign, exercise in its name the power which it has entrusted to them and which it can limit, modify, and take back whenever it pleases, since the alienation of such a right is incompatible with the nature of the social body and contrary to the purpose of the association.

I therefore call the legitimate exercise of executive power *government* or supreme administration, and the man or body charged with that administration, the *prince* or magistrate.[7]

Within government are found intermediate forces whose relationships make up that of the whole to the whole or of the sovereign to the state. This latter relationship can be represented as that between the extremes of a continuous proportion whose proportional mean is the government. The government receives from the sovereign the orders it gives the people, and for the state to be in proper equilibrium, there must be, once adjustments are made, equality between the product or power of the government taken in itself and the product or power of the citizens, who are sovereigns on the one hand and subjects on the other.[8]

5. Cf. Book II, pp. 99 and 106.

6. It is for this reason that in Venice the title of Most Serene Prince is given to the Collegio even when the Doge does not attend* [Rousseau's note].

*The government of Venice had the form of a pyramid: from the Great Council at its base, it moved upwards through the Senate, the Collegio, and the Signoria to the Doge at the apex. A body called the Council of Ten functioned outside the constitutional pattern and had extraordinary powers in emergencies.

7. As indicated in note 9 on p. 105, Rousseau gives the term *government* a technical meaning quite different from its meaning in everyday speech. In reading Book III, which deals mainly with government, one must be careful to remember that when Rousseau talks about government he is referring not to the political system as a whole, but to one of its parts: the administrative agency whose task is to apply popularly enacted law.

8. In Book I, chapter 6, Rousseau called the citizens of his ideal democracy sovereign in their capacity as law-makers, and subjects in their capacity as obeyers of the law. Here he shows how the administrative agency that he calls government serves as an intermediary between the two aspects of citizenship. As lawmakers, the citizens give general rules to their government, as law-obeyers, they receive its particular directives. The government, since it mediates between the citizens' two capacities, is crucial for keeping the political system balanced. If it is too strong, it will usurp legislative authority; and if too weak, it will be unable to apply the law effectively. Rousseau devotes most of what follows in this and the next chapter to explaining how much power the government should have. The gist of his message, extracted from the mathematics in which it is embedded, is that the more numerous the citizens, the stronger their government must be.

Moreover, it would be difficult to alter any of the three terms without instantly breaking up the proportion. If the sovereign wishes to govern, or if the magistrate wishes to make laws, or if the subjects refuse to obey, disorder follows upon order, force and will no longer act in concert, and the state thus dissolves and falls into despotism or anarchy. Finally, just as there is only one proportional mean between each relationship, there is no more than one good government possible in a state. But since countless events can change the relationships of a people, not only can different governments be good for different peoples, but they may be good for the same people at different times.

In trying to give some idea of the various relationships that can occur between these two extremes, I shall take the number of people as an example, since it is a relationship which is easily expressed.

Let us suppose that the state is composed of ten thousand citizens. The sovereign can only be considered collectively and as a body, but each private person in his capacity as a subject is considered as an individual. Thus, the sovereign is to the subject as ten thousand is to one; that is, each member of the state has as his share only one ten-thousandth of the sovereign authority, although he is totally in subjection to it. If the people is composed of one hundred thousand men, the condition of the subjects remains unchanged, and each bears equally the entire dominion of the laws, while his vote, reduced to one hundred thousandth, has ten times less influence in their drafting. Thus, since the subject always remains a single individual, the ratio between the sovereign and the subject increases with the number of citizens. Whence it follows that the more the state expands, the more liberty is diminished.

When I say that the ratio increases, I mean that it moves farther away from equality. Thus, the greater the ratio in the geometric sense, the less a relationship there is in the ordinary sense; in the former, the ratio, considered in terms of quantity, is measured by the quotient and, in the latter, the relationship, considered in terms of identity, is estimated by similarity.

Now, the less the particular wills relate to the general will, that is, the less moral habits relate to laws, the more the repressive force must be increased. Therefore, to be effective, the government must be relatively stronger in proportion as the people is more numerous.

On the other hand, since the enlargement of the state offers those entrusted with public authority greater temptations to abuse their power and greater means to do so, the more force the government must have to restrain the people, and the more the sovereign, in its turn, must have to restrain the government. I am speaking here not of absolute power but of the relative strength of the different parts of the state.

It follows from this double ratio that the continuous proportion between the sovereign, the prince and the people is not an arbitrary idea but a necessary consequence of the nature of the body politic. It follows further that since one of the extremes, namely the people as subject, is fixed and represented by the number one, whenever the doubled ratio increases or decreases, the simple ratio likewise increases or decreases, and that, as a consequence, the middle term is changed. This shows that there is no unique and absolute form of government, but that there can be as many governments different in nature as there are states different in size.

If, in holding this system up to ridicule, someone were to say that in order to find this proportional mean and give form to the body of the government, it is only necessary, according to me, to derive the square root of the number of the people, I should respond that I am only taking that number here as an example; that the ratios of which I am speaking are not measured only by the number of men, but, more generally, by the quantity of action, which is produced by the combination of a multitude of causes; and that, moreover, if I momentarily borrow mathematical terms to express myself in fewer words, I have still not overlooked the fact that moral quantities cannot be expressed with mathematical precision.

The government is, on a small scale, what the body politic, which includes it, is on a large scale. It is an artificial entity endowed with certain faculties, active like the sovereign, passive like the state; and it can be broken down into other similar relations, which consequently give rise to a new proportion, and within it to still another, in accordance with the order of magistrates, until we reach an indivisible middle term, that is a single leader or supreme magistrate, who can be represented in the middle of this progression, as the number one between the series of fractions and that of whole numbers.

Without troubling ourselves over this multiplication of terms, let us be content to consider the government as a new body within the state, distinct from the people and the sovereign, and an intermediary between the two.

The essential difference between these two bodies is that the state exists by itself, and the government exists only through the sovereign. Thus, the dominant will of the prince is, or should be, nothing other than the general will, or the law; its force is only a concentration of the public force; and as soon as it wants to initiate some absolute and independent act on its own, the bond that holds the whole together begins to grow slack. If the prince should finally come to have a particular will more active than that of the sovereign and to use some of the public force which is in its hands in order to obey this particular will, so that there were, so to speak, two sovereigns, one by right and the other in fact, the social union would instantly vanish, and the body politic would be dissolved.

However, in order for the body of the government to have an existence, a real life that distinguishes it from the body of the state, and in order for all its members to be able to act in concert and fulfill the purpose for which it was instituted, it needs a separate *self*, a sensibility in common with its members, a force and a will of its own that tends towards its preservation. This separate existence presupposes assemblies, councils, the power of deliberation and resolution, rights, titles, and privileges that belong exclusively to the prince, and make the position of magistrate the more honorable in proportion as it is more burdensome. The difficulties lie in the manner of arranging this subordinate whole within the whole in such a way that it in no way impairs the general constitution by strengthening its own; that it always distinguishes its particular force, intended for its own preservation, from the public force, intended for the preservation of the state; and, in short, that it is always ready to sacrifice the government to the people rather than the people to the government.

Furthermore, although the artificial body of the government is the handiwork of another artificial body, and has, in a sense, only a borrowed and subordinate life, this does not prevent it from being able to act with more or less vigor or speed, or from enjoying, so to speak, more or less robust health. Finally, without departing directly from the aim for which it was established, it may stray from it more or less, according to the way in which it is constituted.[9]

From all these differences arise the various relationships that the government must have with the body of the state, in accordance with the accidental and particular relationships by which the state itself is modified, for the government that is best in itself will often become the most corrupt, if its relationships are not altered in accordance with the defects of the body politic to which it belongs.

CHAPTER 2 ON THE PRINCIPLE THAT CONSTITUTES THE VARIOUS FORMS OF GOVERNMENT

To set forth the general cause of these differences, it is necessary to distinguish here between the prince and the government, just as I have previously distinguished between the state and the sovereign.

The body of the magistracy can be composed of a greater or smaller number of members. We have said that the ratio of the sovereign to the subjects was all the greater as the people was more numerous, and, by an obvious analogy, we can say as much about the government with respect to the magistrates.

Now, since the total force of the government is always that of the state, it does not vary. Whence it follows that the more of this force it uses on its own members, the less is left to it for acting upon the whole people.

The more numerous the magistrates, therefore, the weaker the government. Since this is a fundamental maxim, let us apply ourselves to clarifying it further.

We can distinguish in the person of the magistrate three essentially

9. In the final paragraphs of this chapter, Rousseau begins to raise a vexing problem that will preoccupy him later in this book. The citizens of a legitimate state should not all serve as administrators, but should establish an executive agency to apply the laws they enact. Yet such an agency, being an organized partial association, perpetually threatens to divert the state from serving the public good. To show how to resist this unavoidable threat is the main purpose of Book III.

different wills. First, there is the private will of the individual, which tends only towards his particular advantage; secondly, there is the common will of the magistrates, which relates solely to the advantage of the prince, and which may be called the corporate will since it is general in relation to the government and particular in relation to the state of which the government forms a part; thirdly, there is the will of the people or the sovereign will, which is general both in relation to the state considered as the whole and to the government considered as part of the whole.

In perfect legislation, the particular or individual will should be nonexistent; the corporate will belonging to the government should be very subordinate; and, as a consequence, the general or sovereign will should always be dominant and the sole guide of all the others.

According to the natural order, on the contrary, these different wills become more active to the degree that they are concentrated. Thus, the general will is always the weakest, the corporate will is in second place, and the particular will is the first of them all, so that, in the government, each member is first himself, then a magistrate, and then a citizen, a gradation directly opposed to the one required by the social order.

Granting this, let us suppose that the whole government is in the hands of a single man. In such a case, the particular will and the corporate will are perfectly united, and the latter is, consequently, at the highest degree of intensity possible. Now, since the use of force is dependent upon the degree of will, and since the absolute force of the government does not vary, it follows that the most active government is that of a single man.

Let us, on the contrary, unite the government with the legislative authority; let us make the sovereign the prince, and all the citizens as many magistrates. Then, the corporate will, merged with the general will, can be no more active than the latter, and leaves to the particular will its full force. Thus, the government, still having the same absolute force, will have its minimum relative force or activity.

These relationships are incontestable, and other considerations serve further to confirm them. We can see, for example, that each magistrate is more active within his particular group than each citizen within his own, and that, consequently, the particular will has much more influence on the acts of the government than on those of the sovereign, for each magistrate is nearly always charged with some function of government, whereas each citizen, taken separately, exercises no function of sovereignty. Besides, the more the state expands, the more its real force increases, even though it does not increase in direct proportion to its size, but when the state remains the same size, it is useless to increase the number of magistrates; the government does not thereby acquire any greater real force, because this real force is that of the state, whose size remains unchanged. Thus the relative force or activity of the government diminishes, without any increase in its absolute or real force.

It is also certain that business is carried on more slowly as more people are put in charge of it; by granting too much to prudence, they grant too little to fortune; opportunity is often missed, and the fruits of deliberation are often lost through constantly deliberating.

I have just proved that the government grows slack in proportion as magistrates multiply, and I have previously proved that the more numerous the people, the more repressive force must increase. Whence it follows that the ratio of magistrates to government should be the inverse of the ratio of subjects to sovereign; that is to say, the larger the state becomes, the more the government should shrink, so that the number of leaders diminishes as the number of people increases.

Moreover, I am speaking here only of the relative force of the government and not of its rectitude, for, on the contrary, the more numerous the magistrates, the more closely the corporate will approximates the general will, whereas, under a single magistrate this same corporate will is, as I have said, merely a particular will. Thus, what may be lost on the one hand can be gained on the other, and the art of the lawgiver is to know how to determine the point at which the force and will of government, which are always in inverse proportion, are combined in the ratio most advantageous to the state.[1]

CHAPTER 3 CLASSIFICATION OF GOVERNMENTS

In the preceding chapter, we have seen why the various kinds or forms of government are distinguished by the number of members who compose them; it remains to be seen, in this chapter, how this classification is made.

In the first place, the sovereign can entrust the government to the whole people or to the majority of the people, so that there are more citizen magistrates than common private citizens. This form of government is given the name of *democracy*.

Or else, it can confine the government to the hands of a small number, so that there are more common citizens than magistrates, and this form bears the name of *aristocracy*.

Finally, it can concentrate the whole government in the hands of a single magistrate from whom all the others derive their power. This third form is the most common, and is called *monarchy*, or royal government.

It must be noted that all these forms, or at least the first two, can exist in varying degrees and even have a rather broad range, for democracy can include the entire people or be confined to half. Aristocracy, in its turn, can be indeterminately confined to any number of people from half down to the smallest number. Even royalty admits of some division. Sparta always had two kings, in accordance with its constitution, and, in the Roman Empire, there were as many as eight emperors at one time, without it being possible to say that the empire was divided. Thus,

---

1. Here Rousseau charges the founding lawgiver with still another task: to design a government that is small enough to take effective action and large enough to resist private temptations to misapply the law.

there is a point at which each form of government merges with the next, and it is apparent that within these three classifications alone, government can actually have as many different forms as the state has citizens.

There is more. Since this same government can, in certain respects, be subdivided into different parts, one part administered in one way, and one in another, these three forms in combination may result in a multitude of mixed forms, each of which can be multiplied by all the simple forms.

In every age, there has been a good deal of debate over the best form of government, without the consideration that each of them is, in certain cases, the best, and, in others, the worst.

If the number of supreme magistrates in different states should be in inverse proportion to that of citizens, it follows that, in general, democratic government is most suited to small states, aristocracy for those of moderate size, and monarchy for large ones. This rule is derived directly from the principle, but how can we count the multitude of circumstances that can furnish exceptions?

CHAPTER 4 ON DEMOCRACY

Anyone who makes the law knows better than any other how it should be executed and interpreted. It seems, therefore, that no better constitution could be found than the one in which executive and legislative power are joined. But this very arrangement makes such a government inadequate in certain respects, because things that should be distinguished are not, and because the prince and the sovereign, being merely the same person, form, so to speak, only a government without government.

It is not good for the one who makes the laws to execute them or for the body of the people to divert its attention from general objectives and turn it to particular ones. Nothing is more dangerous than the influence of private interests in public affairs, and the abuse of laws by the government is a lesser evil than the corruption of the lawmaker which is the inevitable result of pursuing particular views. In such a case, the state is altered in substance, and all reform becomes impossible. A people that would never abuse government would never abuse independence; a people that would always govern well would not need to be governed.

Taking the term in the strict sense, true democracy has never existed, and never will. It is contrary to the natural order for the majority to govern and the minority to be governed. It is impossible to imagine that the people would constantly remain assembled to attend to public affairs, and it is evident that it could not establish committees to do so without changing the form of administration.

Indeed, I believe I can lay down as a principle the idea that when the functions of government are divided among several tribunals, the least numerous sooner or later acquire the greatest authority, if only because the ease of expediting their business naturally brings them to this point.

Besides, how many things that are difficult to combine does this form of government presuppose? First, a very small state where the people can easily assemble and where each citizen can easily know all the others. Secondly, great simplicity of moral habits which prevents business matters from multiplying and thorny debates from arising. Next, great equality of ranks and fortunes, without which equality of rights and authority could not subsist for long. Finally, little or no luxury, for luxury either results from wealth or makes it necessary; it corrupts both the rich and the poor, the former by possession and the other by covetousness; it sells the homeland to indolence and vanity; it deprives the state of all its citizens by enslaving some to others and all to public opinion.

That is why a celebrated author has identified virtue as the principle of the republic, for all these conditions could not subsist without virtue. But for want of having made the necessary distinctions, this lofty genius often lacked precision and sometimes clarity, and he did not see that since sovereign authority is everywhere the same, the same principle should have a place in every well-constituted state, to a greater or lesser degree, it is true, as required by the form of government.[2]

Let us add that there is no government so subject to civil wars and domestic unrest as democratic or popular government, because there is none that so strongly and continually tends to change in form, or which demands more vigilance and courage to be maintained in its own. Under this type of constitution above all, the citizen should arm himself with strength and constancy, and say each day of his life, from the bottom of his heart, what a virtuous palatine[3] said in the Diet of Poland: *Malo periculosam libertatem quam quietum servitium.*[4]

If there were a people of gods, it would govern itself democratically. So perfect a government is not suited to men.[5]

CHAPTER 5 ON ARISTOCRACY

We have here two very distinct artificial entities, namely, the government and the sovereign, and, consequently, two general wills, one in relation to all the citizens, the other solely for the members of the administration. Thus, although the government may regulate its internal policy as it wishes, it can never speak to the people except in the

---

2. The celebrated author is Montesquieu (*The Spirit of the Laws*, III. 3), who singled out virtue in the sense of public spirit as the motivating "principle" that must sway citizens in a democracy. In his chapters on the lawgiver and his tasks, Rousseau showed his agreement with Montesquieu on the need for public spirit as a democratic citizen's chief motive. His quarrel with Montesquieu in this paragraph arises from his belief that Montesquieu confines the need for public spirit to democracies in which the citizens both make and apply the law. Rousseau finds need of public spirit wherever citizens legislate, even if they do not administer directly.

3. The Palatine of Posnania, father of the king of Poland, duke of Lorraine [Rousseau's note].
4. "I prefer dangerous liberty to peaceful servitude."
5. Readers who lose sight of what Rousseau means by the term government are bound to misconstrue this dictum. The most that it rules out as unattainable is a state democratically administered. Rousseau may not even go this far. In chapter 12 of this book, and in footnote 3 on p. 138, while discussing the Roman Republic, he comes close to calling its government democratic. See also footnote 5 on p. 154.

name of the sovereign, that is to say, in the name of the people itself, a fact that must never be forgotten.

The first societies governed themselves aristocratically. The heads of families deliberated among themselves about public affairs; young people deferred willingly to the authority of experience. Whence the terms *priests, elders, senate, gerontes.* In our own times, the savages of North America still govern themselves in this way, and are very well governed.

But to the extent that social inequality came to prevail over natural inequality, wealth or power[6] was preferred to age, and aristocracy became elective. Finally, the power transmitted along with wealth from fathers to children created patrician families, and made government hereditary, and there were sometimes senators who were only twenty years old.

There are, therefore, three kinds of aristocracy: natural, elective, and hereditary. The first is suited only to simple peoples; the third is the worst of all governments. The second is the best; it is aristocracy properly so-called.

Besides the advantage of distinguishing between the two powers of sovereignty and government, aristocracy has the advantage of choosing its members; for, in popular government, all citizens are born magistrates, but this kind of aristocracy limits them to a small number, and they become magistrates only through election,[7] a means by which integrity, knowledge, experience, and all the other reasons for public preference and esteem become so many new guarantees of being wisely governed.

Furthermore, assemblies are more easily convened, business is more thoroughly discussed and expedited in a more orderly and diligent fashion, and the prestige of the state is better sustained abroad by venerable senators than by a despised or unknown multitude.

In a word, it is the best and most natural arrangement for the wisest to govern the multitude, when it is certain that they will govern for its benefit and not their own; it is unnecessary to multiply jurisdictions uselessly, or to do with twenty thousand men what one hundred well-chosen men can do still better. But it must be noted that the corporate interest begins by becoming less inclined to direct the public force in accordance with the requirements of the general will, and that another inevitable tendency removes a portion of executive power from the jurisdiction of the laws.

With regard to specific circumstances, a state should neither be so small nor a people so simple and upright that the execution of the laws follows immediately from the public will, as in a good democracy. Nor should a nation be so large that the leaders, who are scattered about in

---

6. It is clear that, among the ancients, the word *optimates* did not mean the best but the most powerful [Rousseau's note].

7. It is very important to regulate by laws the procedure for the election of magistrates, for, if it is abandoned to the will of the prince, it is impossible to avoid falling into hereditary aristocracy as

happened in the republics of Venice and Berne. Accordingly, the first has been in a state of disintegration for a long time, but the second is maintained by the extreme wisdom of its Senate; it is a very honorable and very dangerous exception [Rousseau's note].

order to govern it, can each act as sovereign in his own region, and begin by making themselves independent in order finally to become masters.

But if aristocracy requires somewhat fewer virtues than popular government, it also requires others that are proper to it, such as moderation among the rich and contentment among the poor, for it seems that rigorous equality would be out of place in an aristocracy; it was not so much as even observed in Sparta.

Besides, if this form entails a certain inequality of wealth, it does so in order that the administration of public affairs may generally be entrusted to those who are best able to devote all their time to it, but not, as Aristotle claims, in order that the wealthy may always be given preference.[8] On the contrary, it is essential that an opposite choice should occasionally teach the people that more important reasons for preference can be found in a man's personal merits than in his wealth.

CHAPTER 6 ON MONARCHY

So far we have considered the prince as an artificial and collective entity, united by the force of the laws, and entrusted with executive power in the state. We have now to consider this power concentrated in the hands of a natural person, a real man, who alone has the right to dispose of it in accordance with the laws. Such a person is called a monarch or king.

This form of administration is completely in contrast with the other forms, in which a collective being represents an individual. Here, an individual represents a collective being, so that the artificial unity constituting the prince is at the same time a physical unity, and all the faculties that the law unites with so much difficulty in the other kinds are found naturally united in this one.

Thus, the will of the people, the will of the prince, the public force of the state, and the particular force of the government, all respond to the same motive power; all the springs of the machine are in the same hands, everything moves toward the same goal, there are no opposing movements that are mutually destructive, and it is impossible to imagine another constitution in which so little effort produces so much action. Archimedes, seated quietly on the shore and effortlessly launching a great vessel, represents in my mind a skillful monarch governing his vast estates from his study, and making everything move while himself appearing to be motionless.

But if there is no form of government which has more vigor, there is also none in which the particular will holds greater sway and more easily dominates the others; everything moves toward the same end, it is true, but this end is not that of public happiness, and the very force of the administration constantly works to the detriment of the state.

Kings want to be absolute rulers, and from afar men cry out to them

---

8. In *Politics* III. vi, Aristotle in fact denies that wealth in an aristocracy gives a right to public office.

that the best way to be so is to make themselves loved by their peoples. This is a fine maxim, and even, in certain respects, very true. Unfortunately, it will always be an object of ridicule in royal courts. The power that comes from the peoples' love is undoubtedly the greatest, but it is precarious and conditional; princes will never be content with it. The best kings want to be able to be wicked if it pleases them, without ceasing to be masters. A political sermonizer will find it useless to tell them that since the force of the people is theirs, it is in their best interest for the people to be prosperous, numerous, and formidable; kings know perfectly well that this is untrue. It is in their personal interest, first of all, for the people to be weak, miserable, and wholly unable to resist them. I acknowledge that if the subjects were always perfectly submissive, it would then be in the prince's interest for the people to be powerful, so that this power, being his own, would make him formidable in his neighbors' eyes, but since this interest is only secondary and subordinate, and since power and perfect submissiveness are incompatible, princes naturally always give preference to the maxim that is most immediately useful to them. This is what Samuel forcefully pointed out to the Hebrews;[9] this is what Machiavelli has clearly demonstrated. Under the pretext of advising kings, he gave excellent advice to the people. Machiavelli's *Prince* is the handbook of republicans.[1]

By examining general relationships, we have found that monarchy is suited only to large states, and our findings are confirmed in an examination of monarchy itself. The larger the number of public administrators, the smaller the ratio between the prince and the subjects becomes and the nearer it approaches equality, so that this ratio becomes a ratio of one to one, or absolute equality in a democracy. This same ratio increases in proportion as the government contracts, and it reaches its *maximum* when the government is in the hands of one man alone. Then, there is too great a distance between the prince and the people, and the state lacks a tight bond. In order to create it, there must therefore be intermediate orders in the state. There must be princes, lords, and noblemen to fill them. Now, none of this is suitable for a small state, which would be ruined by all these social differences.

But if it is difficult to govern a large state, it is much more difficult for one man to govern it alone, and everyone knows what happens when the king relies on deputies.

Monarchical government has one essential and inevitable defect that will always make it rank below republican government; in a republic, the public voice almost never elevates to the highest offices any but enlightened and capable men, who fill their offices honorably, whereas,

9. I Samuel 8:10–18. In this passage, Samuel reports God's response to those asking Him for a king.

1. Machiavelli was an honest man and a good citizen, but, attached to the house of the Medici, he was forced during the oppression of his homeland to conceal his love for liberty. The mere choice of his execrable hero sufficiently manifests his secret intention, and the comparison of the maxims in his book *The Prince* to those in his *Discourses* and his *History of Florence* demonstrates that this profound political theorist has until now had only superficial or corrupt readers. The court of Rome strictly prohibited his book: I really believe it is that court he depicts most clearly [Rousseau's note, 1782].

in monarchies, those who succeed are most often only petty bunglers, rascals, and schemers, whose petty talents enable them to attain important positions at court, in which they immediately display their incompetence to the public. The people makes fewer mistakes in its choices than the prince, and a man of true merit is almost as rare in a royal ministry as a fool at the head of a republican government. Thus, when, by some happy chance, one of those men born to govern takes the helm in a monarchy that has nearly been destroyed by those crowds of fine managers, everyone is quite surprised by the resources he finds, and his coming marks an era in the history of the country.

In order for a monarchical state to be well governed, its greatness or size must be commensurate with the abilities of the one who governs. It is easier to conquer than to rule. With a long enough lever, it is possible to shake the world with a single finger, but it requires the shoulders of Hercules to hold it up. If a state is the least bit too large, the prince is almost always too small. On the contrary, when the state happens to be too small for its leader, which is very rare, it is still poorly governed, because the leader, who is always in pursuit of his great schemes, forgets the interests of the people and makes them no less wretched by abusing his great talents than a leader who is limited by the lack of such talents. A kingdom should expand or contract, so to speak, with each reign, according to the capability of the prince, but a state with a senate, whose talents are less variable, can have stable boundaries, and an administration that is no less efficient.

The most obvious disadvantage of the government of one man alone is the lack of that continuous line of succession which, in the other two forms of government, creates an unbroken bond. With one king dead, another is needed; elections leave dangerous intervals; they are stormy; and unless the citizens have a disinterestedness and an integrity that monarchical government seldom allows, intrigue and corruption ensue. It is difficult for the one to whom the state has been sold to resist selling it in turn and recouping the money the strong have extorted from him by taking it from the weak. Sooner or later, everything becomes corrupt under such an administration, and then the peace enjoyed under kings is worse than the disorder of the interregna.

What has been done to prevent these ills? In certain families, crowns have been made hereditary, and an order of succession has been established to prevent any debate upon the death of kings. That is to say, the disadvantages of elections have been replaced by those of regencies; apparent tranquillity has been favored over wise administration; and the risk of having children, monsters, or imbeciles for leaders is preferred to arguing over the choice of good kings. What has not been taken into consideration is that, by exposing ourselves thus to the risks of hereditary monarchy, we place almost all the odds against ourselves. What a sensible answer Dionysius the Younger gave when his father, reproaching him for a shameful action, asked "Have I set such an example for you?" "Ah," replied the son, "your father was not king!"

When a man is brought up to command others, everything conspires to deprive him of reason and a sense of justice. Great pains are taken, it is said, to teach young princes the art of ruling; it appears that this training is of no benefit to them. It would be better to begin by teaching them the art of obeying. The greatest kings history has known were not brought up to rule; ruling is a skill that is even less thoroughly mastered after it has been too well learned, and one that is better acquired by obeying than by commanding. *Nam utilissimus idem ac brevissimus bonarum malarumque rerum delectus, cogitare quid aut nolueris sub alio principe aut volueris.* [2]

One consequence of this lack of coherence is the inconstancy of the royal form of government, which is sometimes directed according to one plan and sometimes according to another, depending upon the character of the ruling prince or of the people who rule for him, and which cannot for long possess a fixed objective or consistent management; this variability, which causes the state to drift from maxim to maxim and from project to project, does not occur in the other forms of government, in which the prince is always the same. Thus, we may see generally that if there is more cunning in a court, there is more wisdom in a senate, and that republics pursue their ends through more consistent and coherent policies, whereas any revolution in a royal ministry produces one in the state, since the maxim common to all ministers and to almost all kings is to take the course opposite from that of their predecessor in everything.

From this same incoherence comes the solution to a sophism that is very familiar to royalist political theorists. This sophism not only involves comparing civil government to domestic government and the prince to the father of a family, an error which has already been refuted, but also generously giving this magistrate all the virtues he should have and always assuming that the prince is what he should be, an assumption which supports the notion that royal government is obviously preferable to any other, because it is unquestionably the strongest, and because it needs only a corporate will that is more in conformity with the general will in order to be the best as well.

But if, according to Plato,[3] the individual who is a king by nature is so rare, how often will nature and fortune conspire to crown him, and if royal education necessarily corrupts those who receive it, what is to be expected of a succession of men brought up to rule? It is surely, therefore, willful self-deception to confuse the royal form of government with that of a good king. In order to see what this form of government is in reality, it must be considered as it is under incompetent or wicked princes, for either they are incompetent or wicked when they reach the throne, or else the throne makes them so.

These difficulties have not escaped the notice of our authors, but they

2. Tacitus: *Histories* L. I.* [Rousseau's note].
*Rousseau refers to Tacitus, *Histories*, I.16: "For the most useful and shortest way of distinguishing between good and evil is to ask yourself what you would or would not have wished to happen if someone else were king."
3. In *Civili* [*The Statesman*; Rousseau's note].

are not troubled by them. The remedy, they say, is to obey without a murmur. God in his wrath grants us bad kings, and they must be borne as punishments from heaven.[4] Undoubtedly, this is an edifying discourse, but I wonder if it might not be more appropriate in a pulpit than in a book on political theory. What is to be said of a physician who promises miracles, and whose only skill is to exhort the sick to patience? It is well known that when there is a bad government it must be endured; the question is how to find a good one.

CHAPTER 7 ON MIXED GOVERNMENTS

Strictly speaking, there is no such thing as a simple form of government. A single leader must have subordinate magistrates; a popular government must have a leader. Thus, in the division of executive power, there is always a gradation from the greater number to the smaller, with the difference that the greater number is sometimes dependent upon the smaller, and sometimes the smaller on the greater.

At times, the division is equal, either when the constituent parts are mutually dependent, as in the government of England, or when the authority of each part is independent but imperfect, as in Poland. This latter form is bad, because there is no unity in the government, and the state lacks cohesion.

Which is better, a simple or mixed form of government? This is a question vigorously debated among political theorists, and one to which I must give the same reply that I have previously given to questions about all forms of government.

In itself, the simple form of government is the best, solely because it is simple. But when the executive power is not sufficiently dependent on the legislative, that is, when there is a greater ratio between the prince and the sovereign than between the people and the prince, this lack of proportion must be remedied by dividing the government, for then all its parts have no less authority over the subjects, and their division makes all of them together less powerful in relation to the sovereign.

The very same disadvantage can also be prevented by establishing magistrates, who, leaving the government undivided, serve only to balance the two powers and to maintain their respective rights. In that case, the government is not mixed; it is limited.

The opposite kind of disadvantage can be remedied by similar means, and when the government is too lax, tribunals can be set up to strengthen it. This is usually done in all democracies.[5] In the first case, the government is divided in order to weaken it, and, in the second, to strengthen

---

4. Advocates of royal absolutism, such as Bossuet, who were influential in Rousseau's time, used the theological argument being derided here. Readers must not be misled by the savagery of Rousseau's attack on monarchic government into thinking that he regards it as incorrigibly illegitimate. For a somewhat more nuanced assessment of mon-archy, in cases where it is the established regime, see the final lines of Rousseau's ninth note (note 3 on p. 19), to the *Discourse on Inequality*.

5. Note the implication in this remark that, contrary to what was suggested in Chapter 4 of this book, a democratic government may be workable, provided it is equipped with the proper safeguards.

it, for the *maximums* of strength and weakness are both found in simple forms of government, whereas mixed forms result in an average strength.

CHAPTER 8 THAT NOT ALL FORMS OF GOVERNMENT ARE SUITED
TO EVERY COUNTRY

Since liberty is not the fruit of every climate, it is not within the reach of all peoples. The more one ponders this principle established by Montesquieu, the more one feels it to be true. The more one contests it, the more opportunities there are to establish it with new proofs.[6]

In all the governments of the world, the public person[7] consumes, but produces nothing. What, then, is the source of the substance it consumes? It is the labor of its members. The surplus of private individuals produces public necessities. Whence it follows that the civil state can subsist only as long as men's labor produces more than they need.

Now this surplus is not the same in every country in the world. In several it is large, in others moderate, in others nonexistent, and in still others there is a deficit. This ratio depends on the fertility of the climate, the kind of labor the land requires, the nature of its products, the force of its inhabitants, the greater or lesser level of consumption necessary for them, and several other similar ratios of which it is composed.

On the other hand, not all governments are of the same nature; they are more or less voracious, and the differences are based upon this additional principle, namely, that the further public contributions are removed from their source, the more burdensome they are. The measurement of this burden should not be based upon the amount of taxes but upon the path they must travel in order to return to the hands from which they came; when this circulation is prompt and well established, it matters little whether the payments are small or large; the people is always rich and finances are always in good condition. On the contrary, however little the people gives, when this small amount does not return, it is soon exhausted by continual giving; the state is never rich, and the people is always poverty-stricken.

It follows from the above that the more the distance between the people and the government increases, the more burdensome taxes become. Thus, in a democracy, the people is the least burdened; in an aristocracy, it is more so; and in monarchy, it bears the greatest weight. Monarchy, therefore, is suited only to opulent nations, aristocracy to states as moderate in wealth as in size, and democracy to states that are small and poor.

In fact, the more we reflect on this, the more we find in it the difference between free states and monarchies; in the former, everything is used for the common utility; in the latter, public and private forces have

6. Rousseau is inspired in this chapter by Montesquieu's concern, most evident in Book XVII of *The Spirit of the Laws*, with climatic constraints on political liberty. Rousseau's discussion touches somewhat uncertainly both on how climate affects the form of government and on how it affects the locus of sovereignty.

7. Rousseau explains what he means by this term at the end of chapter 6 of Book I.

a reciprocal relationship; and as one increases, the other grows weak. In short, instead of governing subjects in order to make them happy, despotism makes them miserable in order to govern them.

Thus, in every climate, there are natural conditions which make it possible to determine the form of government the vigor of the climate requires and even the kind of inhabitants it must have. Unproductive and barren areas where the product is not worth the labor should remain uncultivated and uninhabited, or be populated only by savages. Areas where men's labor yields no more than the bare necessities should be inhabited by barbarous peoples; in such places, any polity would be impossible. Areas where labor yields a moderate surplus are suited to free peoples; those where the abundant and fertile soil produces much in return for little labor need the monarchical form of government, in order to consume the excessive surplus of the subjects through the luxury of the prince, for it is better that this surplus be absorbed by the government than dissipated by private individuals. There are exceptions, I know, but these very exceptions prove the rule, in that sooner or later they produce revolutions which bring things back within the order of nature.

Let us always distinguish general laws from particular cases that may modify their effect. Even if the entire South of France were covered with republics and the entire North with despotic states, it would be no less true that the effects of climate make despotism suited to hot countries, barbarism to cold countries, and good polity to intermediate regions. I understand further, that even if the principle is granted, its application may be disputed. It may be said that there are cold countries that are very fertile and southern ones that are quite barren. But this poses a difficulty only for those who do not examine every aspect of the matter. As I have already said, it is necessary to take into account labor, forces, consumption, etc.

Let us suppose that of two equal plots of land one produces five units and the other ten. If the inhabitants of the first consume four units and those of the second nine, the surplus from the first yield will be one fifth and that from the second one tenth. Since the ratio of these two surpluses will then be the inverse of that of their yields, the plot of land that produces only five units will yield a surplus double that of the plot that produces ten.

But there is no question of a double yield, and I do not believe that anyone even dares, as a general rule, to equate the fertility of cold countries with that of hot countries. Nevertheless, let us admit such equality exists; let us weigh, if you will, England against Sicily, and Poland against Egypt. Farther south we shall have Africa and the Indies; farther north, we shall have nothing at all. To achieve this equality of yield, what difference in cultivation is needed? In Sicily, one has only to scratch the earth; in England what pains one must take to till it! Now, where more hands are needed to produce the same yield, the surplus must necessarily be smaller.

Consider also that the same number of men consumes much less in hot countries. The climate requires moderation for good health. Europeans who want to live there just as they do at home all perish from dysentery and indigestion. "We are," says Chardin, "carnivorous beasts, wolves, in comparison to the Asians. Some attribute the sobriety of the Persians to the fact that their land is less cultivated, but I myself believe, on the contrary, that their land is less abundant in foodstuffs because the inhabitants need less. If their frugality," he continues, "were an effect of the poverty of the land, only the poor would eat little, whereas generally everyone does so, and people would eat more or less in each province according to the fertility of the region, whereas, the same sobriety is found throughout the kingdom. They are very well satisfied with their way of life, saying that one need only look at their complexion to recognize how far it excels that of the Christians. Indeed, the complexion of the Persians is smooth; they have fair, delicate, and glossy skin, whereas the complexion of their Armenian subjects, who live in the European manner, is coarse and blotchy, and their bodies are fat and heavy."[8]

The nearer one comes to the equator, the less people live on. They eat almost no meat; rice, corn, couscous, millet, and cassava are their usual foods. In the Indies, there are millions of men whose sustenance costs less than a penny a day. Even in Europe, we see appreciable differences in appetite between the peoples of the North and those of the South. A Spaniard could live for a week on the dinner of a German. In countries where people are more voracious, luxury also turns towards edible things. In England, it appears on a table laden with meats; in Italy, you are treated to sugar and flowers.

Luxury in clothing reveals similar differences. In climates where changes of season are sudden and violent, people have better and simpler clothes; in those where people dress only to adorn themselves, glamour is more sought after than utility, and clothes themselves are a luxury there. In Naples, you will always see men in gold-embroidered jackets and no stockings walking in the Posilippo quarter. The same is true of buildings; everything is devoted to magnificence when there is no need to fear harm from the weather. In Paris or London, people want to be housed warmly and comfortably. In Madrid, they have superb drawing-rooms, but no windows that close, and people sleep in rat holes.

Foods are much more substantial and tasty in hot countries; this is a third difference and it cannot fail to influence the second. Why are so many vegetables eaten in Italy? Because they are good, nutritious, and excellent in flavor. In France, where they are raised with nothing but water, they are not nutritious and count for almost nothing as food. Yet, they occupy no less land, and cost at least as much effort to cultivate. Experience proves that the wheat of Barbary, inferior in other respects to that of France, yields far more flour, and that the wheat of France, in turn, yields more than that of the North. From this it may be inferred

8. Jean Chardin (1643–1713), *Voyage en Perse et aux Indes orientals* (4 vols., 1735), III. 76. 83–84.   Chardin had started out for India in 1665 but remained in Persia for six years.

that a similar gradation in the same direction is generally observed from the equator to the pole. Now, is it not a distinct disadvantage to obtain less food from an equal amount of produce?

To all these different considerations, I can add another, which follows from them, and strengthens them; that is, hot countries have less need of inhabitants than cold countries, and yet could feed more; this produces a double surplus that is always to the advantage of despotism. The larger the area occupied by the same number of inhabitants, the more difficult it is for them to revolt, because they cannot consult among themselves either promptly or secretly, and it is always easy for the government to get wind of their plans and cut off communications. But the closer together a numerous people comes, the less the government can usurp from the sovereign; the leaders deliberate as safely in their chambers as the prince in his council, and the crowd assembles as rapidly in public squares as troops in their quarters. The advantage of a tyrannical government lies, therefore, in acting over great distances. With the points of support it establishes for itself, its force, like that of levers, increases with distance.[9] That of the people, on the contrary, operates only when it is concentrated; as it spreads, it evaporates and is lost, just as gunpowder scattered on the ground only ignites grain by grain. The least populated countries are therefore the best suited to tyranny: wild beasts reign only in deserts.

CHAPTER 9 ON THE SIGNS OF GOOD GOVERNMENT

When it is asked, therefore, what is absolutely the best kind of government, the question being raised is as insoluble as it is indeterminate; or, if you wish, there are as many right answers as there are possible combinations in the absolute and relative positions of peoples.

But if it is asked what signs can show us whether a given people is well or poorly governed, that is another matter, and the question, being one of fact, could be resolved.

It is not resolved, however, because each person wishes to do so in his own way. The subject praises public tranquillity, the citizen individual liberty; the one prefers the safety of possessions, the other that of persons; the one insists that the best government is the most severe, the other maintains that it is the most gentle; the former wants crimes to be punished, and the latter wants them prevented; the one thinks it is fine to be feared by his neighbors, the other prefers to be ignored by them; the one is content when money circulates, the other demands that the people have bread. Even if there were agreement on these and similar points, would any progress have been made? Since moral quantities cannot be

9. This does not contradict what I said previously [Book II, chapter 9] about the disadvantages of large states, for it was a question there of the authority of the government over its members, and here it is a question of its power over subjects. Its scattered members serve as its fulcrum for acting from a distance on the people, but it has no fulcrum for acting directly upon these members themselves. Thus, in one case, the length of the lever is the cause of its weakness, and in the other of its strength [Rousseau's note].

precisely measured, even if there were agreement about the signs of good government, how could there be any agreement about the manner of assessing them?

As for me, I am always astonished that people fail to recognize such a simple sign, or that they have the bad faith not to agree to it. What is the aim of political association? It is the preservation and prosperity of its members. And what is the surest sign that they are safe and prosperous? It is their number and their population.[1] Do not, therefore, go elsewhere to seek this much disputed sign. All things being equal in other respects, the government under which the citizens increase and multiply the most without foreign aid, without naturalizations, and without colonies is unquestionably the best; the one under which a people diminishes and dies out is the worst. Statisticians, it is now up to you; count, measure, compare.[2]

CHAPTER 10 ON THE ABUSE OF GOVERNMENT, AND ITS TENDENCY TO DEGENERATE

Just as the particular will acts constantly against the general will, so government mounts a continual effort against sovereignty. The greater this effort becomes, the more the constitution deteriorates, and as there is here no other corporate will to resist that of the prince and to balance it, the prince is sooner or later bound to oppress the sovereign and break the social treaty. That is the inherent and unavoidable vice which, from the birth of the body politic, relentlessly tends to destroy it, just as old age and death destroy the human body.

There are two general processes by which a government degenerates:

---

1. Notice that Rousseau regards population and not wealth as the index of prosperity.

2. The centuries which merit preference for bringing prosperity to the human race must be judged by the same principles. Those in which arts and letters have been seen to flourish have been too greatly admired by some who did not fathom the secret purpose of their cultivation or consider their deadly effect: "*idque apud imperitos humanitas vocabatur, cum pars servitutis esset.*"[a] Shall we never perceive in the maxims of books the crude interest that makes their authors speak? No! Whatever they may say, when a country is becoming depopulated, despite its brilliance, it is not true that all is going well, and the fact that a poet has a private income of 100,000 francs is not enough to make his age the best of all. It is less necessary to pay attention to the apparent calm and tranquillity of leaders than to the welfare of whole nations, especially the most populous states. Hail devastates a few cantons, but it rarely causes famine. Riots and civil wars greatly frighten leaders, but they do not cause the people's real misfortunes, which may even abate while they argue over who will tyrannize them. Their real prosperity or adversity is a product of their permanent condition. When all remain crushed under the yoke, it is then that everything declines; it is then that the leaders destroy

the peoples at their ease: "*ubi solitudinem faciunt, pacem appellant.*"[b] When the quarrels of the great agitated the kingdom of France, and the coadjutor of Paris carried a dagger in his pocket to Parlement, that did not prevent a great many of the French people from living happily in free and honest tranquillity. Long ago, Greece flourished in the midst of the cruelest wars; blood ran in torrents, and yet the whole country was filled with men. It seemed, said Machiavelli, that amid murders, proscriptions, and civil wars, our republic only became more powerful; the virtue of its citizens, their moral habits, and their independence did more to strengthen it than all its dissensions did to weaken it. A little agitation provides the driving force in men's souls, and what really makes the species prosper is not so much peace as liberty[c] [Rousseau's note].

[a] Tacitus, *Agricola* 31: "And that [i.e., the refinement of Roman life] was called civilization among the inexperienced, although it was part of servitude."

[b] Tacitus, *Agricola* 30: "Where they create a desert, they call it peace."

[c] Rousseau's reference to Machiavelli is an adaptation of a passage in the Preface to *The History of Florence.*

namely, when it contracts, or when the state dissolves.

The government contracts when it passes from the many to the few, that is, from democracy to aristocracy, and from aristocracy to monarchy. That is its natural tendency.[3] If it moved backward from the few to the many, it could be said that it grows slack, but this reverse progression is impossible.

Indeed, government never changes its form unless its worn-out mainspring leaves it too weakened to conserve the form it has. Now if it grew more slack by extending itself, its force would be reduced to nothing at all, and it would be even less likely to subsist. It is, therefore, necessary to refit and tighten the mainspring to the degree that it is giving way, otherwise, the state it sustains would fall into ruins.

The dissolution of the state can come about in two ways.

First, it occurs when the prince no longer administers the state in accordance with the laws and usurps sovereign power. A remarkable change then comes about: it is not the government but the state that contracts. I mean that the state as a whole dissolves and another forms within it, composed solely of the members of the government, and to the rest of the people, it is no longer anything more than their master and tyrant. Thus, the instant the government usurps sovereignty, the social pact is broken, and all the common citizens, rightfully returning to their natural liberty, are forced but not obligated to obey.

The same thing also happens when the members of the government

---

3. The slow formation and progress of the Republic of Venice in its lagoons offers a notable example of this sequence of events; and it is quite astonishing that, after more than twelve hundred years, the Venetians seem still to be only in the second stage, which began with the *Serrar di Consiglio*[a] in 1198. As for the ancient dukes for whom they are reproached, whatever the *Squittinio della libertà veneta*[b] may say, it has been proved that they were not their sovereigns.

Without fail, the example of the Roman Republic will be raised as an objection, which, it will be said, followed a completely opposite course of development, passing from monarchy to aristocracy, and from aristocracy to democracy. I am very far from thinking about it in this way.

The first constitution of Romulus was a mixed government that promptly degenerated into despotism. As a result of particular causes, the state perished before its time just as a newborn child dies before having attained manhood. The expulsion of the Tarquins was the true epoch of the birth of the Republic. But it did not at first take on a constant form, because failure to abolish the patriciate left only half of the work done. For in this way, since hereditary aristocracy, which is the worst of all forms of legitimate administration, remained in conflict with democracy, a form of government that is always fluctuating and uncertain, it was not fixed, as Machiavelli has proved, until the establishment of the tribunes; only then was there true government and real democracy. In fact the people was then not only sovereign but also magistrate

and judge; the Senate was only a subordinate tribunal whose purpose was to moderate and concentrate the government; and the Consuls themselves, although patricians, chief magistrates, and generals with absolute authority in war, were, in Rome, only presidents of the people.

From that time on, the government was also seen to follow its natural inclination and to tend strongly towards aristocracy. Since the patriciate was being abolished, as if by itself, the aristocracy was no longer in the body of patricians as it is in Venice and Genoa, but in the body of the Senate, which was composed of patricians and plebeians, and even in the body of the Tribunes when they began to usurp active power. For words do not affect things and when the people has leaders who govern for it, whatever name these leaders bear, the government is always an aristocracy.

From the abuse of aristocracy sprang the civil wars and the triumvirate. Sulla, Julius Caesar, and Augustus became in fact real monarchs, and, finally, under the despotism of Tiberius, the state was dissolved. Roman history does not, therefore, belie my principle; it confirms it [Rousseau's note].
[a]The "Serrata," or closing of the council, is usually dated as 1297 and was a reorganization of the Grand Council by the Doge Pietro Gradenigo which guaranteed aristocratic control by limiting membership to the noble families in the "Libro d'oro."
[b]Published in 1612, this anonymous work advocated monarchical rule by divine right for the Republic of Venice.

separately usurp the power they should exercise only as a body, which is no less an infraction of the laws and produces even greater disorder. At that point, there are, so to speak, as many princes as magistrates, and the state, no less divided than the government, perishes or changes in form.

When the state dissolves, the abuse of government, whatever form it takes, is given the common name of *anarchy*. To distinguish further, democracy degenerates into *ochlocracy*, aristocracy into *oligarchy*; I would add that monarchy degenerates into *tyranny*, but this last word is equivocal and requires some explanation.

In the ordinary sense, a tyrant is a king who governs with violence and without regard for justice and laws. In the strict sense, a tyrant is a private individual who arrogates royal authority to himself without having any right to it. This is how the Greeks understood the word tyrant; they applied it indifferently to good and bad princes whose authority was not legitimate.[4] Thus, *tyrant* and *usurper* are two perfectly synonymous terms.

In order to give different names to different things, I call the usurper of royal authority a *tyrant*, and the usurper of sovereign power a *despot*. The tyrant is the one who takes control in opposition to the laws in order to govern according to the laws; the despot is the one who places himself above the laws themselves. Thus, the tyrant cannot be a despot, but the despot is always a tyrant.

CHAPTER 11 ON THE DEATH OF THE BODY POLITIC

Such is the natural and inevitable tendency of the best constituted governments. If Sparta and Rome have perished, what state can hope to endure forever? If we wish to form an enduring political system, let us not therefore dream of making it eternal. To succeed, we must not attempt the impossible, nor should we flatter ourselves that we may give the work of men a stability that human things do not allow.

The body politic, as well as the body of a man, begins to die from the moment of its birth and bears within itself the causes of its destruction. But each of these bodies may have a constitution that is more or less robust and suited to preserve it for a longer or shorter period of time. A man's constitution is the work of nature, that of the state is the work of art. It is not for men to prolong their lives, but it is for them to prolong that of the state insofar as that is possible, by giving it the best constitution it can have. The best constituted state will also come to an end, but

---

4. "*Omnes enim et habentur et dicuntur tyranni, qui potestate utuntur perpetua in ea civitate quae libertate usa est.*"[a] It is true that Aristotle[b] distinguishes between the tyrant and the king, on the ground that the former governs for his own benefit, and the latter only for the benefit of his subjects, but, besides the fact that all Greek authors have generally taken the word *tyrant* in a different sense, especially as it appears in Xenophon's *Hiero*, it would follow from Aristotle's distinction that, since the beginning of the world, there has not yet been a single king [Rousseau's note].

[a] Cornelius Nepos, *Life of Militades*, viii: "For all are considered and said to be tyrants who possess perpetual power in a city that has once been free."

[b] See *Nicomachean Ethics*, VIII. 10.

much later than any other, if no unforeseen accident causes its downfall prematurely.

The animating principle of political life lies in sovereign authority. Legislative power is the heart of the state, executive power is the brain, which sets all the parts in motion. When the brain is stricken with paralysis, the individual may remain alive. A man may remain an imbecile and live, but as soon as the heart ceases to function, the animal is dead.

It is not through laws that the state subsists; it is through legislative power.[5] Yesterday's law is not binding today, but silence is presumed to mean tacit consent, and the sovereign supposedly gives constant confirmation to the laws it does not repeal while able to do so. All that it has once declared to be its will is always its will, unless it revokes its declaration.

Why then are ancient laws held in such great respect? It is precisely because they are ancient. We are to believe that only their excellence could have preserved them for so long a time; if the sovereign had not always found them to be salutary, it would have revoked them a thousand times. That is why, far from growing weak, the laws continually acquire new strength in every well-constituted state; the prejudice in favor of antiquity each day renders them more venerable; yet, wherever laws grow weak as they grow older, this proves that legislative power no longer exists and that the state no longer lives.

CHAPTER 12 HOW SOVEREIGN AUTHORITY IS MAINTAINED

The sovereign, having no force other than legislative power, acts only through laws, and since laws are the only authentic acts of the general will, the sovereign can act only when the people is assembled. "The people assembled!" it will be said. "What a chimera!" Today it is a chimera, but it was not so two thousand years ago. Has human nature changed?

The limits of the possible in moral matters are less narrow than we think. Our weaknesses, our vices, our prejudices make them so. Base souls do not believe in great men; vile slaves smile with a mocking air at the word liberty.

In light of what has been done, let us consider what can be done; I shall not speak of the ancient republics of Greece, but the Roman Republic was, it seems to me, a large state, and the city of Rome a big city. The last census showed four hundred thousand citizens bearing arms in Rome, and the last census of the empire more than four million citizens, not counting subjects, foreigners, women, children, or slaves.

It is possible to imagine how many difficulties there were in calling the immense population of this capital and its environs to assemble so

5. At this point Rousseau connects his just completed analysis of executive agency as necessary but lethal for a democratic state with his earlier analysis of direct legislation by all citizens as what makes that state legitimate. The remainder of this book is devoted to showing how executive agency and a directly legislating citizenry can be least destructively combined.

frequently. Yet, few weeks went by without the Roman people being called to assemble, and even several times a week. Not only did it exercise the rights of sovereignty, but some of the rights of government. It handled certain matters, it tried certain cases, and in the public square, this whole people acted in the role of magistrates almost as often as in that of citizens.

By going back to the early days of nations, we would find that most ancient governments, even monarchies such as those of the Macedonians and the Franks, had similar councils. Be that as it may, one incontestable fact answers all objections. Arguing from the actual to the possible seems sound to me.

CHAPTER 13 CONTINUED

It is not enough for the assembled people to have determined the constitution of the state at one point by sanctioning a body of laws; it is not enough for it to have established a perpetual government or to have once and for all made provision for the election of magistrates. In addition to the special assemblies that emergencies can require, there must be some scheduled periodically that nothing can abolish or prorogue, so that on the appointed day, the people is rightfully convened by law, without needing any other formal convocation.

But aside from these assemblies, which are made legal by their date alone, any assembly of the people that has not been convoked by the magistrates appointed for that purpose and in accordance with the prescribed procedures must be held as illegitimate and all that is done there as invalid, because the order to assemble should itself emanate from the law.

As for whether legitimate assemblies should occur more or less frequently, this depends on so many considerations that no precise rules can be given about it. It can only be said that, in general, the stronger a government is, the more frequently the sovereign should show itself.

I will be told that this may be good for a single town, but what is to be done when the state includes several of them? Will sovereign authority be divided, or is it to be concentrated in a single town to which all the rest are subjugated?

I answer that neither one nor the other should be done. In the first place, sovereign authority is a simple whole, and it cannot be divided without being destroyed. In the second, no town, any more than a nation, can be legitimately subjected to another, because the essence of the body politic lies in the reconciliation of obedience and liberty, and because the words *subject* and *sovereign* are true correlatives, whose meanings are combined in the single word citizen.

I answer further that uniting several towns into a single republic is always bad, and that anyone wishing to form such a union should not flatter himself that he has avoided the natural drawbacks. The abuses of large states should not be raised as an objection to someone who is only in favor of small ones. But how can small states be given enough strength to resist large ones? Just as the Greek cities of old resisted the great King, and as Holland and Switzerland have more recently resisted the House of Austria.[6]

Nevertheless, if the state cannot be reduced to the right limits, another possibility still remains; this is to allow no capital, to make the government sit in each town alternately, and also to assemble the estates of the country in each of them in turn.

Populate the territory evenly, extend the same rights everywhere, bring forth abundance and life in every location; in this way, the state will become all at once the strongest and best governed possible. Remember that the walls of towns are only made from the remains of country houses. For every palace I see being built in the capital, I believe I see an entire countryside reduced to rubble.

CHAPTER 14 CONTINUED

The moment the people is legitimately assembled as a sovereign body, all jurisdiction of the government ceases, the executive power is suspended, and the person of the humblest citizen is as sacred and inviolable as that of the foremost magistrate, because wherever a represented person is found, there is no longer any representative. Most of the disorders that arose in the Roman comitia resulted from ignoring or neglecting this rule. The consuls were, on such occasions, only the presiding officers of the people, the tribunes were ordinary speakers,[7] the senate, nothing at all.

These intervals of suspension, during which the prince recognizes or ought to recognize an actual superior, have always been dangerous to it, and these assemblies of the people, which are the shield of the body politic and the bridle on the government, have at all times been the horror of leaders. They therefore spare no efforts, objections, difficulties, or promises to discourage the citizens from holding them. When the latter are greedy, cowardly, irresolute, and fonder of repose than liberty, they do not hold out for long against the redoubled efforts of the government; so it is that, as the resisting force constantly increases, sovereign authority vanishes in the end, and most cities fall and perish before their time.

But between sovereign authority and arbitrary government an intermediate power is sometimes introduced, and it must be discussed.

CHAPTER 15 ON DEPUTIES OR REPRESENTATIVES

As soon as public service ceases to be the principle concern of the citizens, and they prefer to serve with their purses rather than their per-

---

6. At the end of chapter 15 of this book, Rousseau suggests confederation as a means by which small states might obtain the strength they need to defend themselves against aggressors.

7. Almost in the sense given to this word in the English Parliament. The similarity between these posts would have put the consuls and tribunes in conflict, even if all jurisdiction had been suspended [Rousseau's note].

sons, the state is already nearing its ruin. Is it necessary to march into battle? They pay troops and stay at home. Is it necessary to go to the council? They appoint deputies and stay at home. Thanks to laziness and money, they finally have soldiers to enslave the homeland and representatives to sell it.

It is the worry brought on by commerce and the arts, the avid pursuit of profits, softness, and the love of comfort that replaces personal services with money. The citizen gives up part of his profits to increase them at his convenience. Give only money and soon you will have chains. The word *finance* is a term for slaves; it is unknown in the ancient city state. In a truly free state, the citizens do everything with their own hands, and nothing with money. Far from paying to be exempted from their duties, they would pay to fulfill them personally. Far be it from me to accept commonplace ideas; I believe forced labor is less contrary to liberty than taxes.

The better constituted the state, the more public concerns prevail over private ones in the minds of the citizens. There are even many fewer private concerns, because the sum of common happiness furnishes a more considerable portion of each individual's happiness, and there remains less for the individual to seek through his own private efforts. In a well-run republic, everyone rushes to the assemblies; under a bad government no one likes to take a single step to get there, because no one takes any interest in what is being done in them, because everyone sees that the general will cannot prevail, and, finally, because domestic cares are all consuming.[8] Good laws lead to the making of better ones; bad laws bring about worse ones. The state must be counted as lost, as soon as someone says, with regard to the affairs of the state, "What do I care?"

The waning of patriotism, the pursuit of private interests, the vastness of states, conquests, and the abuse of government have suggested the use of deputies or representatives of the people in the nation's assemblies. These are what certain countries dare to call the third estate. Thus, the particular interests of two orders occupy first and second place, and the public interest only the third.[9]

Sovereignty cannot be represented for the same reason that it cannot be alienated; it consists essentially in the general will, and a will cannot be represented: it is either the same will or it is different; there is no middle ground. Deputies of the people, therefore, are not, nor can they be, its representatives, they are merely its agents; they can decide nothing definitively. Any law the people has not ratified in person is invalid;

8. The political apathy that continues to be regarded as democracy's chief bane is here ascribed to three separate but related causes: (1) a belief on the part of citizens that public decisions do not significantly affect their interests, (2) their disgust with the political process for failing to serve the public good, (3) their correlative belief in the predominant significance for satisfying interests of decisions made within the precincts of domestic life.
9. French society before the Revolution was divided into three orders or estates—clergy, nobles, and commoners, composed of direct taxpayers. Each estate sent representatives to a sporadically convened national assembly, called the States General, where the three orders sat and voted separately, so that the third estate of commoners could be easily outvoted by the small minority of nobles and clergy. The animus toward this arrangement expressed here by Rousseau was shared by the French revolutionaries, whose first success was to change the procedures followed by the States General convened in 1789 so that the three orders sat and voted as a single group.

it is not a law. The English people thinks it is a free people; it is greatly mistaken; it is free only during the election of the members of parliament; as soon as they are elected, it is enslaved, it is nothing. The way in which the English people uses the brief moments of its liberty truly makes it deserve to lose that liberty.

The idea of representatives is modern: it comes to us from feudal government, from that iniquitous and absurd type of government which degrades the human race and dishonors the name of man. In ancient republics and even in monarchies, the people never had representatives; the word itself was unknown. It is quite remarkable that in Rome where the tribunes were so sacred, no one ever even imagined that they could usurp the functions of the people, and that in the midst of such a great multitude, they never attempted to pass a single plebiscite on their own authority. The difficulties sometimes caused by the crowd should be judged, nevertheless, by what happened in the time of the Gracchi, when part of the citizens cast their votes from the rooftops.

Where right and liberty mean everything, disadvantages mean nothing. This wise people always kept everything in proper proportions: the Roman people allowed its lictors to do what its tribunes would not have dared to do; it had no fear that its lictors would try to represent it.

To explain, nevertheless, how the tribunes sometimes represented the Roman people, it is enough to understand how the government represents the sovereign. Since the law is merely the declaration of the general will, it is clear that the people cannot be represented in the exercise of legislative power, but it can and should be in that of executive power, which is merely force applied to law. This shows that if the matter were examined closely, it would be found that very few nations have laws. Be that as it may, it is certain that the tribunes, having no share in executive power, could never represent the Roman people by the rights their offices conferred upon them, but only by usurping those of the senate.

Among the Greeks, whatever the people had to do, it did by itself; it was constantly assembled in the public square. The Greeks inhabited a region with a mild climate; they were not greedy; slaves did their work; their greatest concern was their liberty. No longer having the same advantages, how can you preserve the same rights? Your harsher climates increase your needs;[1] six months of the year, the public square is unbearable, your muted tongues cannot make themselves understood in the open air, you set more value on your earnings than on your liberty, and you fear slavery much less than poverty.

What! Is liberty maintained only with the support of servitude? Perhaps so. The two extremes meet. Everything that is not found in nature has its drawbacks, and civil society more than all the rest. There are unfortunate situations in which the liberty of one man can be preserved only at the expense of another man's, and in which the citizen can be

1. To adopt the luxury and softness of the orientals in cold countries indicates a willingness to be given their chains; it means submitting to them with even greater necessity than the orientals themselves [Rousseau's note].

perfectly free only if the slave is completely enslaved. Such was the situation in Sparta. As for you, modern peoples, you have no slaves, but you are slaves; you pay for their liberty with your own. You boast of your preference in vain; I find more cowardice than humanity in it.

I do not mean by all this that it is necessary to have slaves, nor that the right of slavery is legitimate, since I have proved the contrary. I am merely stating the reasons why modern peoples who believe themselves free have representatives, and why ancient peoples had none. Be that as it may, the moment a people gives itself representatives, it is no longer free; it no longer exists.

All things considered, I do not see how the sovereign can possibly continue to exercise its rights among us unless the republic is very small.[2] But if it is very small, will it be subjugated? No! I shall show later on[3] how the external power of a great people can be combined with the easy administration and sound order of a small state.

CHAPTER 16 THAT THE INSTITUTION OF THE GOVERNMENT IS NOT A CONTRACT

Once the legislative power has been well established, there is the problem of establishing the executive power in the same way, for the latter, which operates only by means of particular acts, is essentially different from the former and is, therefore, naturally separate from it. If it were possible for the sovereign, considered as such, to possess executive power, right and fact would be so confused that we would no longer know what is law and what is not, and the body politic thus denatured would soon fall prey to the violence it was instituted to prevent.

Since the citizens are all made equal by the social contract, everyone can prescribe what everyone else should do, whereas no one has the right to require another to do anything he does not do himself. Now it is precisely this right, indispensable for imparting life and movement to the body politic, that the sovereign gives the prince in instituting the government.

Some have claimed that this act of establishment was a contract between the people and the leaders it gives itself, a contract by which the two parties stipulated the conditions under which one party obligates itself to command and the other to obey. It will be granted, I am sure, that this is a strange way of making a contract! But let us see whether or not this opinion is tenable.

First, the supreme authority can no more be modified than alienated; to limit it is to destroy it. It is absurd and contradictory for the sovereign

---

2. Note that Rousseau's reason for severely limiting the size of a legitimate state is not the impracticality of direct legislation in a large state but the loss to citizens of their role as authors of the law. For more on why Rousseau favors small states see Book II, chapter 9.

3. This is what I had meant to do in the sequel to this work, when, in treating external relations, I would have come to the subject of confederations. This is an entirely new subject whose principles have yet to be established [Rousseau's note].

to give itself a superior; to be obligated to obey a master is to be restored to complete liberty.

Furthermore, it stands to reason that this contract between the people and such and such persons would be a particular act. Whence it follows that this contract cannot be a law or an act of sovereignty, and that it would, as a consequence, be illegitimate.

It is also clear that the contracting parties would be subject among themselves only to the law of nature and without any guarantee of their reciprocal commitments, which is repugnant in every way to the civil state. Since anyone who has force in hand is always master of how it is used, the term "contract" could as well be given to the act of a man who would say to another, "I am giving you all my property on condition that you give me back whatever you wish."

There is only one contract in the state; it is that of the association; and that one by itself excludes any other. It would be impossible to imagine any other public contract that would not violate the first one.

CHAPTER 17 ON THE INSTITUTION OF GOVERNMENT

In what terms, therefore, should the act by which the government is instituted be conceived? To begin with, I shall point out that this act is complex, or composed of two others, namely, the establishment of the law, and the execution of the law.

By the first, the sovereign decrees that there shall be a governmental body established in such and such a form, and it is clear that this act is law.

By the second, the people appoints the leaders who will take charge of the established government. Now, since this appointment is a particular act, it is not a second law, but only a consequence of the first and a function of government.

The difficulty is to understand how there can be an act of government before government exists, and how the people, which is only sovereign or subject, can become prince or magistrate under certain circumstances.

Here again, one of those astonishing properties of the body politic, by which it reconciles seemingly contradictory operations, comes to light. For this operation is accomplished by a sudden conversion of sovereignty into democracy, so that, without any perceptible change, and solely through a new relation of all to all, the citizens, having become magistrates, pass from general to particular acts, and from the law to its execution.

This change in relation is not a speculative subtlety without practical examples. It happens every day in the English Parliament, where the lower chamber, on certain occasions, turns itself into a committee of the whole in order better to discuss business, and, thus, from the sovereign court of the preceding moment becomes an ordinary commission, in such a way that it next reports to itself as the House of Commons what it has just settled in the committee of the whole, and once again debates under one title what it has already decided under another.

The advantage peculiar to democratic government is that it can actually be established by a simple act of the general will. After that, the provisional government remains in office, if this is the form adopted, or establishes in the name of the sovereign the government prescribed by law, and everything thus proceeds according to the rules. It is not possible to institute the government in any other legitimate way without renouncing the principles previously established.

CHAPTER 18 THE MEANS OF PREVENTING USURPATIONS OF THE GOVERNMENT

From these clarifications, it follows, in confirmation of Chapter 16, that the act which institutes the government is not a contract but a law, that the trustees of executive power are not the masters of the people but its officials, that it can establish and discharge them whenever it pleases, that for them there is no question of contracting but only of obeying, and that in assuming the functions imposed on them by the state they are merely fulfilling their duty as citizens, without in any way having the right to argue over the conditions.

When it happens, therefore, that the people institutes a hereditary government, whether it is monarchical and within one family, or aristocratic and within one class of citizens, it does not enter into a contract; it gives the administration a provisional form until it chooses to organize it differently.

It is also true that these changes are always dangerous, and that the established government should never be tampered with unless it becomes incompatible with the public good, but this cautious approach is a maxim of politics and not a rule of law, and the state is no more bound to leave civil authority to its leaders than to leave military authority to its generals.

It is also true that it is impossible, in such cases, to be too careful about observing all the formalities required to distinguish a regular and legitimate act from a seditious uproar, and the will of an entire people from the clamor of a faction. Here, above all, nothing must be conceded to the odious case except what cannot be refused on the strictest legal grounds, and the prince must also turn this obligation to its own advantage in order to preserve its power in spite of the people, without incurring the possible charge of usurpation; for by appearing to exercise only its own rights, the prince can very easily extend them, and, on the pretext of preserving public tranquillity, prevent assemblies designed to reestablish sound order; in this way, the prince takes advantage of a silence it prevents from being broken or of irregularities that it makes others commit to assume the consent of those whom fear has silenced and to punish those who dare speak out. Thus, the decemvirs, having first been elected for one year, and then kept in office for a second, tried to perpetuate their power by no longer permitting the comitia to assemble, and by this simple means all governments of the world, once public power has been vested in them, sooner or later usurp sovereign authority.

The periodic assemblies of which I have already spoken are the proper means of preventing or postponing this misfortune, especially when they require no formal convocation, for then the prince cannot prohibit them without openly declaring itself a violator of the laws and an enemy of the state.[4]

These assemblies, whose only purpose is the preservation of the social treaty, should always be opened with two propositions which can never be suppressed, and which come up for the vote separately.

The first: *Does it please the sovereign to preserve the present form of government?*

The second: *Does it please the people to leave the administration in the hands of those who are presently in charge of it?*

I am here assuming what I believe I have demonstrated, namely, that there is no fundamental law in the state that cannot be repealed, not even the social pact, for if all the citizens assembled break this pact by common consent, there can be no doubt that it was broken quite legitimately. Grotius even thinks that each person can renounce the state of which he is a member and recover his natural liberty and his property by leaving the country.[5] Now, it would be absurd to think that all the citizens together could not do what each of them can do separately.

END OF THE THIRD BOOK

Book IV

CHAPTER 1 THAT THE GENERAL WILL IS INDESTRUCTIBLE

As long as several men gathered together consider themselves a single body, they have but one will, which is concerned with their common preservation and the general welfare. Then, all the driving forces of the state are simple and sturdy; its principles are clear and bright; it has no entangled, conflicting interests; the common good is everywhere quite apparent, and only common sense is needed to perceive it. Peace, unity, and equality are the enemies of political subtleties. Simple and upright men are difficult to deceive because of their simplicity; enticements and clever pretexts cannot take them in; they are not even clever enough to

---

4. These periodic assemblies were mentioned in chapters 13 and 14 of this book. It is not too clear what differences in function and in the way they are convened Rousseau envisages between the assemblies he is describing here, which serve to control the government, and the legislative assemblies first described toward the beginning of Book II. But it would be a mistake to conclude from what Rousseau says in this chapter that he would confine the sovereign assembly in a legitimate state to the job of preventing governmental usurpation. Being a legislature, it is much more active.

5. It must be clearly understood that a person may not leave in order to evade his duty and to avoid serving his homeland at the moment it needs him. In such a case, flight would be criminal and punishable; it would no longer be withdrawal but desertion [Rousseau's note].

be duped. When, among the happiest peoples in the world, troops of peasants are seen settling the affairs of state under an oak tree, and always conducting themselves wisely, can we help scorning the refinements of other nations, which make themselves illustrious and miserable with so much art and mystery?

A state so governed needs very few laws, and as it becomes necessary to promulgate new ones, that necessity is universally understood. The first to propose them is only saying what all the others have already felt, and there is no question either of intrigues or of eloquence to secure passage into law of what each has already resolved to do, once he is certain the others will do as he has done.

What misleads thinkers who consider only states which were badly constituted from the beginning is that they are struck by the impossibility of maintaining such an administration. They laugh at the thought of all the foolish things that a clever rascal or an insinuating speaker could make the people of Paris or London believe. They are unaware that Cromwell would have been sentenced to hard labor by the people of Berne and the Duke of Beaufort imprisoned by the Genevans.[6]

But when the social bond begins to grow slack and the state to grow weak, when private interests begin to make themselves felt and small societies begin to influence the larger one, the common interest deteriorates and encounters opponents, unanimity no longer prevails in the voting, the general will is no longer the will of all, contradictory views and arguments arise, and the best advice is not accepted without disputes.

Finally, when the state, on the brink of ruin, subsists only in an empty and illusory form, when the social bond is broken in every heart, and when the meanest interest brazenly flaunts the sacred name of the public good, then the general will becomes mute; everyone, guided by secret motives, expresses opinions no more like those of a citizen than if the state had never existed, and iniquitous decrees, which have no other end than the private interest, are falsely passed under the name of laws.

Does it follow from all this that the general will is annihilated or corrupted? No. It is always constant, incorruptible, and pure, but it is subordinated to other wills that prevail over it. Detaching his interest from the common interest, each man clearly sees that he cannot completely separate the two, but his share of the public misfortunes seems negligible to him compared to the exclusive good he claims to be obtaining for himself. Apart from this private good, he wills the general good in his own interest, just as strongly as anyone else. Even in selling his vote for money, he does not extinguish the general will in himself; he evades it. The error he commits is that of changing the formulation of the question and answering something other than what he is asked, so that instead of saying through his vote *it is advantageous to the state*, he

6. Oliver Cromwell (1599–1658) and the Duke of Beaufort (1616–69) were both leaders of insurrectionary movements in the seventeenth century. Cromwell led the Puritans in the English Civil War which resulted in the execution of Charles I in 1649. François de Vendôme, duke of Beaufort, an ally of the Cardinal de Retz, led the French nobles in the Fronde, a rebellion in 1648 against the young Louis XIV, which Mazarin ruthlessly suppressed.

says *it is advantageous to this man or that party for such and such a motion to pass*. Thus, the rules of procedure in assemblies are not so much intended to uphold the general will as to make certain that it is always questioned and that it always answers.

I could reflect at length here upon the simple right of voting in every act of sovereignty, a right which nothing can take away from the citizens, and upon the right of expressing opinions, of making proposals, of analyzing and discussing, which the government always takes great care to allow only to its members, but this important subject would require a separate treatise, and I cannot say everything in this one.[7]

CHAPTER 2 ON VOTING

It may be seen from the preceding chapter that the manner in which general business matters are treated can give a rather reliable indication of the current condition of the morality and health of the body politic. The more harmony reigns in the assemblies, that is, the closer opinions come to being unanimous, the more dominant, therefore, is the general will, but long debates, dissensions, and tumult proclaim the ascendancy of private interests and the decline of the state.

This seems less obvious when two or more orders enter into its constitution, as in Rome where the patricians and plebeians often disturbed the comitia by their quarrels, even in the finest days of the Republic, but this exception is more apparent than real, for, in that case, owing to an inherent defect in the body politic, there are, so to speak, two states in one; what is not true of the two together is true of each separately. And, indeed, even in the stormiest times, the plebiscites of the people, when the senate did not interfere with them, always passed quietly and by a large majority of votes. Since the citizens had but one interest, the people had but one will.

At the other extremity of the circle, unanimity returns. This occurs when the citizens, having fallen into servitude, no longer have either liberty or will. Then, fear and flattery turn votes into acclamations; there are no longer any deliberations, only worshipping or cursing. Such was the vile way in which the senate expressed its opinions under the emperors. Sometimes that was done with ridiculous precautions: Tacitus observes that during the reign of Otho, the senators, while heaping abuse upon Vitellius, habitually made frightful noises at the same time, so that, if by chance he became the master, he would not be able to learn what each of them had said.[8]

---

7. This chapter recapitulates ideas advanced in Books I and II about how a society must be organized in order to assure that laws enacted by its sovereign assembly express the general will. Here, however, Rousseau puts more emphasis than he did earlier on unanimity and the absence of disagreement as evidence of legitimacy.

In the final paragraph, he assigns so much deliberative activity to the government that he raises doubts about the role of the sovereign assembly in deliberating on proposed legislation. The next chapter, and Book II, chapter 3, more clearly give the assembly the decisive role in legislative deliberation that it needs if citizens are to be the self-directing agents described in Book I, chapter. 8.

8. *Histories*, I. 85.

These diverse considerations give rise to the maxims by which the manner of counting votes and comparing opinions should be regulated, according to whether the general will is more or less easily recognized and the state is more or less in decline.

There is but one law that by its nature requires unanimous consent. This is the social pact, for civil association is the most voluntary act in the world. Since every man is born free and master of himself, no one can, under any pretext whatsoever, subjugate him without his consent. To decide that the son of a slave is born a slave is to decide that he is not born a man.

If there are, therefore, opponents of the social pact at the time it is made, their opposition does not invalidate the contract; it merely prevents them being included in it; they are foreigners among citizens. When the state is instituted, residency implies consent; to inhabit the territory is to submit to the sovereign authority.[9]

Apart from this original contract, the vote of the majority is always binding on all the others; this is a consequence of the contract itself. But it may be asked how a man can be free while he is forced to conform to wills which are not his own. How are the opponents free while they are bound by laws to which they have not consented?

I reply that the question is not properly put. The citizen consents to all the laws, even to those that pass against his will, and even to those which punish him when he dares violate any of them. The unchanging will of all the members of the state is the general will; through it they are citizens and free.[1] When a law is proposed in the assembly of the people, what they are being asked is not precisely whether they approve or reject the proposal, but whether or not it is consistent with the general will that is their own; each expresses his opinion on this point by casting his vote, and the declaration of the general will is derived from the counting of the votes. When, therefore, the opinion contrary to my own prevails, this merely proves that I was mistaken, and that what I considered to be the general will was not so. If my private opinion had prevailed, I would have done something other than what I had willed; it is then that I would not have been free.

This presupposes, it is true, that all the characteristics of the general

---

9. This should always be understood as applying to a free state, for otherwise, family, property, lack of shelter, necessity, or violence can detain an inhabitant in a country against his will, and then his living there no longer by itself implies his consent to the contract or to the violation of the contract* [Rousseau's note].
* Rousseau's note deserves close consideration, because it prevents inferring from the paragraph to which it is appended the notorious conclusion, implied by earlier theorists such as Locke, that once a state of the proper sort has been founded by unanimous agreement, anyone who lives under its jurisdiction gives it his consent, even if it behaves

tyrannically. By specifying in this footnote that residence does not entail consent except in a "free state," Rousseau shifts attention from conditions at the founding of a state to its present mode of operation as what should be considered in deciding on its legitimacy.
1. In Genoa, the word, *libertas* can be read on the front of the prisons and on the fetters of galley-slaves. This application of the motto is fine and just. Indeed, it is only wrong-doers from every level of society who prevent the citizen from being free. In a country where all such people were in the galleys, the most perfect liberty would be enjoyed [Rousseau's note].

will are still in the majority: when they cease to be there, whatever side one takes, liberty no longer exists.[2]

By showing earlier how particular wills replace the general will in public deliberations, I have given a sufficient indication of how this abuse may be prevented; I shall say more about this later. As for the proportion of votes needed to declare the general will, I have also given the principles by which it can be determined. The difference of a single vote breaks a tie, a single opponent puts an end to unanimity, but between unanimity and a tie there are several unequal degrees, at any one of which the required proportion may be fixed in accordance with the condition and needs of the body politic.

Two general rules can serve to regulate these proportions: the first is that the more important and serious the decisions, the closer the prevailing opinion should be to unanimity; the second is that the more hastily the matter under consideration must be decided, the smaller the prescribed majority should be; in decisions that must be reached immediately, a majority of a single vote should suffice. The first of these two rules seems more appropriate for legislation, and the second for administration. Be that as it may, it is a combination of the two that establishes the best proportions for the deciding majority.

CHAPTER III ON ELECTIONS

With regard to the elections of the prince and the magistrates, which are, as I have said, complex acts, there are two ways to proceed; namely, by choice and by lot. Both have been used in various republics, and a highly complicated mixture of the two is still seen today in the election of the Doge of Venice.

Voting by lot, says Montesquieu, *is natural to democracy*. I agree, but why is this so? *Drawing lots*, he continues, *is a method of election that harms no one; it leaves each citizen with a reasonable hope of serving his country*.[3] These are not reasons.

If we are mindful that the election of leaders is a function of government and not of sovereignty, we shall see why drawing lots is in the

---

2. In the two somewhat cryptic preceding paragraphs, Rousseau faces up more forthrightly than anywhere else in *On Social Contract* to the charge that citizens who vote with the minority in a legitimate democracy, being forced to do what they think wrong, lack the freedom that such a democracy is intended to provide. The second of the two paragraphs is crucial for understanding Rousseau's answer to this charge, since it sets a very strict condition that must be met before an outvoted citizen should conclude that his vote against an enacted law was wrong. Unless the majority has "all the characteristics of the general will," the outvoted citizen who is constrained to obey the law he opposed, far from being free, is seriously oppressed. How then does he decide whether the majority has these liberating characteristics? Rousseau never says

explicitly, but the message to be found at many crucial junctures of *On Social Contract* is that in a society organized as envisioned in this work, the majority of the citizens would surely be reliably animated by the public spirit that assures legislation for the common good. Yet even in a society with all of Rousseau's legitimizing traits, it would still be possible, though very unlikely, for a majority to pass a law which failed to express the general will. In that case, a citizen in the minority might still deem his vote wrong on the grounds that, by acceding to the majority, he would best uphold the institutions which enable him to be a self-legislating agent and which conduce most to the common good.

3. *The Spirit of the Laws*, II. 2.

nature of democracy, where administration is so much the better as its acts are less numerous.

In every true democracy, public office is not an advantage but a heavy burden that cannot justly be imposed upon one private individual rather than another. The law alone can impose this burden on the one to whom it falls by lot. For then, since conditions are the same for all, and the choice does not depend upon any human will, there is no particular application to alter the universality of the law.

In an aristocracy, the prince chooses the prince; the government preserves itself, and it is there that voting is appropriate.

The example of the election of the Doge of Venice, far from destroying this distinction, confirms it: this mixed form is suited to a mixed government. For it is a mistake to regard the government of Venice as a true aristocracy. The people has no share whatsoever in the government there; the nobility is itself the people. The multitude of impoverished Barnabites[4] has never come close to holding any public office, and its nobility consists only in the empty title of Excellency and in the right to attend the Grand Council. Since this Grand Council is as numerous as our General Council in Geneva, its illustrious members have no more privileges than our ordinary citizens. It is certain that aside from the extreme disparity between the two republics, the bougeoisie of Geneva corresponds exactly to the Venetian patriciate; our natives and inhabitants correspond to the townsmen and people; and our peasants correspond to the subjects on the mainland. In short, however this Republic is considered, if its size is ignored, its government is no more aristocratic than our own. The main difference is that since we have no lifelong leader, we do not have the same need to draw lots.

Elections by lot would have few drawbacks in a true democracy in which, all things being equal both in morality and talent as well as in maxims and fortunes, it would hardly matter who was chosen. But I have already said that there is no true democracy.

When elections by choice and by lot are combined, the first method should be used to fill positions which require special talents, such as military posts; the second is suited to those in which common sense, justice, and integrity are sufficient, such as judicial offices, because in a well-constituted state, these qualities are common to all the citizens.

Neither drawing lots nor voting has any place in monarchical government. Since the monarch is by law the sole prince and single magistrate, the choice of his lieutenants belongs to him alone. When the Abbé de St. Pierre proposed to multiply the councils of the king of France and to elect their members, he did not see that he was proposing to change the form of government.

It remains for me to speak about the method of casting and recording

---

4. In the seventeenth and eighteenth centuries, the Venetian nobility experienced an increasing gap between the rich and the poor. Barnabites (*barnabotti*) was the name given to this growing class of impoverished nobles, because they lived in or near the parish of San Barnaba. This serious social problem, among others, enervated the Venetian Republic.

votes in the assembly of the people, but perhaps the history of how the Romans arranged these matters will more vividly explain all the rules that I could establish. It will not be unbefitting a judicious reader to see in some detail how public and private affairs were handled in a council of two hundred thousand men.[5]

CHAPTER IV ON THE ROMAN COMITIA

We have no really reliable records from the early days of Rome; there is, in fact, every indication that most of the things reported about them are fables;[6] and, in general, the most instructive part of the annals of a people, that is, the history of its founding, is what we most often lack. Experience teaches us every day the causes that give rise to the revolutions of empires, but since peoples are no longer being created, we have scarcely anything but conjecture to explain how they were once brought into being.

The practices we find established attest that at least they had some origin. Traditions that go back to these origins, those supported by the greatest authorities and confirmed by the strongest arguments, should pass for the most certain. These are the rules I have tried to follow in seeking to discover how the freest and most powerful people on earth exercised its supreme power.

After the founding of Rome, the emerging Republic, that is, the founder's army, composed of Albans, Sabines, and foreigners, was divided into three classes, which from this division took the name of *tribus*. Each of these tribes was subdivided into ten curiae, and each curia into decuriae, at the head of which were placed leaders called *curiones* and *decuriones*.

In addition to this, a body of one hundred cavalrymen or knights, know as a century, was drawn from each tribe: from this it is seen that such divisions, unnecessary in a small market town, had at first only a military purpose. But it appears that an instinct for greatness led the small town of Rome to provide itself in advance with an administrative system befitting the capital of the world.

---

5. Comprising almost a quarter of *On Social Contract*, the next chapters are devoted to Roman political institutions. What they contribute to Rousseau's political theory is a matter for debate. Many thoughtful commentators, such as E. H. Wright, C. E. Vaughan, and Robert Derathé, have dismissed them as trivial padding, irrelevant to Rousseau's argument. Others, such as Michel Launay and Richard Fralin, have considered them to be what Rousseau himself says they are in this paragraph: a source of illustrations for his maxims. The problem with this approach, the reader will discover, is that the Roman political system, as described in what follows, is far from being the simple egalitarian, participatory democracy that Rousseau regards as a legitimate state. Considered historically, in the context of Machiavelli's *Dis-*

courses and the continuing use of the myth of the virtuous Roman Republic, Rousseau's use of Roman examples is understandable if not wholly consonant with his own ideas about democracy. The most appropriate way to consider these chapters is perhaps on a par with Rousseau's writings on Geneva, Poland, and Corsica. Here, as in those works, he can be understood to describe institutions which apply his principles under less than ideal conditions.

6. The name *Rome*, which is claimed to be derived from *Romulus*, is Greek and means *force*; the name *Numa* is also Greek, and means *law*. What is the likelihood that the first two kings of this city bore in advance names so clearly related to what they did? [Rousseau's note.]

One disadvantage soon arose from this initial division. The tribes of the Albans[7] and Sabines[8] always remained the same size, while the tribe of the foreigners[9] constantly grew through their perpetual influx into Rome, and the latter soon surpassed the other two. The remedy that Servius found for this dangerous abuse was to change the division, and, for the division of the races, which he abolished, to substitute one based upon the area of the town occupied by each tribe. Instead of three tribes, he created four, each of which occupied one of the hills of Rome and bore its name. Thus, while remedying an existing inequality, he also prevented it from recurring in the future; and to make this a division not only one of places but also of people, he prohibited the inhabitants of one quarter from moving into another, and so prevented the races from becoming intermingled.

He also doubled the three former centuries of cavalrymen and added to them twelve others, but he still kept the old names, a simple and judicious plan, which enabled him to distinguish the body of knights from that of the people without causing the latter to complain.

To these four urban tribes, Servius added fifteen others, called rural tribes, because they were created from the inhabitants of the country-side, divided into as many districts. Subsequently, the same number of new tribes was created, and the Roman people finally found itself divided into thirty-five tribes, a number which remained fixed until the end of the Republic.

This distinction between the tribes of the town and the tribes of the countryside produced one result worth noting, because there is no other example of it, and because Rome owed to it both the preservation of her moral habits and the growth of her empire. It might be thought that the urban tribes soon arrogated all the power and honors to themselves, and lost no time in downgrading the rural tribes; what happened was quite the reverse. The early Romans' taste for country life is well known. It came to them from the wise founder who linked rural and military labors to liberty, and, so to speak, relegated to the town arts, crafts, intrigue, fortune, and slavery.

Thus, since all the illustrious Romans lived in the country and culti-vated the land, it became customary to seek those who would sustain the Republic only in the countryside. Since this way of life was that of the worthiest patricians, it was honored by all; the simple and hard life of the villagers was preferred to the lax and idle life of the city dwellers of Rome, and someone who would have been only a wretched proletarian in the city became, as a laborer in the fields, a respected citizen. It is not without reason, Varro used to say, that our great-souled ancestors established in the village the nursery of those robust and valiant men who defended them in times of war and fed them in times of peace. Pliny actually says that the rural tribes were honored because of the men who belonged to them, whereas cowards were dishonored by being

---

7. *Ramnenses* [Rousseau's note].   9. *Luceres* [Rousseau's note].
8. *Tatienses* [Rousseau's note].

transferred in disgrace into urban tribes. The Sabine, Appius Claudius, having come to settle in Rome, where honors were heaped upon him, became a member of a rural tribe, which later took his family's name. Finally, the freedmen all joined urban tribes, never rural ones; and there is not, during the entire history of the Republic, a single example of a freedman who attained any public office, even though he had become a citizen.

This was an excellent maxim, but it was carried so far that it finally produced a change and certainly an abuse in the system of administration.

First, the censors, after having for so long arrogated to themselves the right of transferring citizens arbitrarily from one tribe to another, permitted most of them to become members of whatever tribes they chose to join; this permissiveness surely did no good, and deprived the censorship of one of its main sources of vitality. Moreover, since the great and powerful all had themselves inscribed in the rural tribes, and the freedmen who had become citizens remained with the populace in the urban ones, the tribes in general no longer had either a specific locale or territory, but all were so intermixed that it was no longer possible to identify the members of each except by means of the registers, so that the idea of the word tribe became personal rather than territorial in meaning, or rather, became little more than a chimera.

Furthermore, it came about that the tribes of the town, being closer to the meeting places, were often the strongest in the assemblies, and sold the state to those who deigned to buy the votes of the rabble who made them up.

As for the curiae, the founder had created ten in each tribe, and the entire Roman people then contained within the walls of the town was composed of thirty curiae, each with its temples, its gods, its officials, its priests, and its festivals, which were called *compitalia*, and resembled the *Paganalia* which the rural tribes held in later times.

Since the thirty curiae in Servius's new division could not be equally divided among his four tribes, and since he did not want to tamper with their number, the curiae became another division of the inhabitants of Rome, independent of the tribes: but there was no question of having curiae either within the rural tribes or among the people who made them up, because once the tribes had become a purely civil institution, and another system of administration had been introduced for raising troops, Romulus' military divisions were found to be superfluous. Thus, although every citizen was enrolled in a tribe, far from every one was enrolled in a curia.

Servius created still a third division, which bore no relation to the first two and became, through its effects, the most important of all. He divided the entire Roman people into six classes, which he distinguished from each other by property rather than place or person, so that the first classes were filled by the rich, the last by the poor, and those in the middle by men who enjoyed moderate wealth. These six classes were subdivided into one hundred ninety-three other bodies called centuries, and these bodies were distributed in such a way that the first class alone contained more than half of them, and the last contained but one. Thus, it turned out that the class with the smallest number of men had the largest number of centuries, and that the entire last class counted as only one subdivision, although it alone contained more than half the inhabitants of Rome.

To make the significance of this third division less obvious to the people, Servius contrived to give it a military look: he put two centuries of armorers into the second class and two of weapon makers into the fourth. In each class, except the last, he made a distinction between the young and the old, that is, between those who were obligated to bear arms, and those who were exempt by law because of their age; this distinction, more than the one based on wealth, made it necessary to retake the census quite often. Finally, he insisted that the assembly be held on the Campus Martius, and that all those of military age come there with their arms.

The reason he did not make this same distinction between young and old in the last class is that the populace of which it was composed was not accorded the honor of bearing arms for the homeland; a man had to possess a home to acquire the right to defend it; and among those countless beggers who today adorn the armies of kings, there is perhaps not one who would not have been scornfully expelled from a Roman cohort, in a time when soldiers were the defenders of liberty.

In the last class, however, there was still one distinction made between the *proletarians* and those who were called *capite censi*. The former, who were not quite reduced to nothing, at least gave citizens to the state, sometimes even soldiers, in times of pressing need. As for those who had nothing at all and who could only be counted by the head, they were considered entirely worthless, and Marius was the first who deigned to enlist them.

Without deciding here whether this third division was good or bad in itself, I believe I can affirm that it could be made practicable only because of the simple moral habits of the first Romans, their disinterestedness, their taste for agriculture, and their contempt for commerce and the passion for profit. Where is the modern people among whom the devouring greed, the restless spirit, the intrigue, the continual moving about, and the perpetual changes in fortune could allow a similar system to endure for twenty years without overturning the whole state? It must also be duly noted that moral habits along with the censorship, which were stronger than this institution, corrected its defects in Rome, and that any rich man could find himself relegated to the class of the poor, for having too openly flaunted his wealth.

From all this, it is easy to understand why there is scarcely ever any mention of more than five classes, although there were actually six of them. The sixth, which furnished neither soldiers for the army nor voters at the Campus Martius[1] and was of virtually no use to the Republic, scarcely counted for anything.

Such were the different divisions of the Roman people. Let us now look at the effect they had on the assemblies. These assemblies, when legitimately convened, were called *comitia*; they were ordinarily held in the Roman Forum or the Campus Martius, and were separated into *comitia curiata, comitia centuriata*, and *comitia tributa*, according to which of these three divisions was the basis of their organization: the curial assemblies were established by Romulus, the centurial assemblies by Servius, and the tribal assemblies by the tribunes of the people. No law received sanction, nor was any magistrate elected, except in the assemblies, and as there was no citizen who was not enrolled in a curia, a century, or a tribe, it follows that no citizen was excluded from the right to vote, and that the Roman people was truly sovereign by law and in fact.

In order for the comitia, or assemblies, to be convened legitimately and for what was done there to have the force of law, three conditions had to be met: first, the body or magistrate who convened them had to be vested with the authority necessary to do so; secondly, the assembly had to be held on one of the days permitted by law; third, the auguries had to be favorable.

The reason for the first rule needs no explanation. The second is an administrative matter; thus, it was not permissible to hold assemblies on holidays or on market days, when the people from the countryside, coming to Rome on business of their own, did not have time to spend the day in the Forum. By means of the third rule, the Senate kept a proud and restless people in check, and appropriately tempered the passion of seditious tribunes, although the latter found more than one way to free themselves from this constraint.

Laws and the election of leaders were not the only matters submitted to the judgment of the assemblies. Since the Roman people had usurped the most important functions of government, it can be said that the fate of Europe was decided in its assemblies. Their varied aims gave rise to the different forms these assemblies took according to the matters that had to be settled.

To judge these various forms, it suffices to compare them. In establishing the curiae, Romulus's intention was to have the people contain the Senate and the Senate contain the people, while he dominated both equally. By means of this arrangement, he therefore gave the people all the authority of number to balance that of power and wealth, which he left to the patricians. But in the spirit of monarchy, he nevertheless left a greater advantage to the patricians through the influence of their clients upon the voting majority. This admirable institution of patrons and clients

1. I say to *Campus Martius* because it was there that the *comitia centuriata* used to assemble; in the two other forms of assembly, the people used to gather in the *Forum* or elsewhere, and then the *capite censi* had as much influence and authority as the leading citizens [Rousseau's note].

was a masterpiece of politics and humanity, without which the patriciate, so contrary to the spirit of the Republic, could not have survived. Rome alone had the honor of giving the world this fine example, which never led to any abuse, but which has never yet been followed.

Since this same form of curiae continued under all the kings up to Servius, and since the reign of the last Tarquin was not considered legitimate, royal laws were generally referred to as *leges curiatae*.

Under the Republic, the curiae, still confined to the four urban tribes, and including only the populace of Rome, could come to an agreement neither with the Senate which led the patricians, nor with the tribunes, who, though plebeians, led the well-to-do citizens. They therefore fell into disrepute, and their degradation was such that their thirty lictors met to do what the curial assemblies should have done.

The division by centuries was so favorable to the aristocracy that it is not easy to see at first how the Senate ever failed to prevail in the centurial assemblies, by which the consuls, censors, and other curule magistrates were elected. Indeed, of the one hundred ninety-three centuries into which the six classes of the entire Roman people were divided, ninety-eight were included in the first class, and since votes were counted only by centuries, the first class alone had a greater number of votes than all the others. When all its centuries were in agreement, the rest of the votes were not even counted; what the minority had decided passed for a decision of the multitude, and it can be said that in the centurial assemblies business was more often settled by a majority of money than by a majority of votes.

But this extreme authority was tempered in two ways. First, since the tribunes as well as a consistently large number of plebeians usually belonged to the class of the rich, their influence counterbalanced that of the patricians in this first class.

The second way consisted of the following: instead of having the centuries begin the voting according to their numerical order, which would always have meant beginning with the first class, one century was chosen by lot, and it[2] alone proceeded to carry out the elections; after this, all the other centuries were summoned on another day in the order of their rank to repeat the same election, which they ordinarily confirmed. Thus, the authority of example was taken away from rank in order to be given to lot, in accordance with the principle of democracy.

There resulted from this practice yet another advantage: that is, the citizens from the country had time between the two elections to inform themselves on the merit of the conditionally named candidate, so that they could vote with knowledge of the facts. But under the pretext of expediting matters, this practice was finally abolished, and the two elections were held the same day.

The tribal assemblies were, properly speaking, the council of the Roman people. They were convened only by the tribunes; in them, the tribunes

---

2. This century, thus chosen by lot, was called *praerogativa*, because it was the first one asked to vote, and this is the origin of the word *prerogative* [Rousseau's note].

were elected and held their plebiscites. Not only did the Senate have no status in them, but it did not even have the right to attend them, and, since they were forced to obey laws upon which they had not been able to vote, the senators were, in this respect, less free than the humblest citizens. This injustice was entirely ill-contrived and alone sufficed to invalidate the decrees of a body that did not admit all its members. Even if all the patricians had attended these assemblies by virtue of their rights as citizens, they would then have become simply private individuals, and they would hardly have had any real influence upon a system of voting in which votes were recorded by counting heads and in which the humblest proletarian had as much impact as the leader of the senate.

It can be seen, therefore, that aside from the order which resulted from these various arrangements for recording the votes of such a great people, these arrangements are not unimportant in themselves, for each one had effects related to the views which caused it to be preferred.

Without going into any greater detail here, it follows from the previous clarifications that the tribal assemblies were the most favorable to popular government, and the centurial assemblies to aristocracy. As for the curial assemblies, in which the populace of Rome alone formed the majority, they were suited only to promoting tyranny and evil schemes, and consequently had to fall into disrepute, since even those involved in sedition abstained from using a method that left their plans too greatly exposed. It is certain that all the majesty of the Roman people lay only in the centurial assemblies; they alone were complete assemblies, since the curial assemblies excluded the rural tribes, and the tribal assemblies the senate and the patricians.

As for the manner of recording the votes, it was, among the early Romans, as simple as their moral habits, though less simple than in Sparta. Each man cast his vote aloud, and a recorder wrote the votes down one by one; a majority vote in each tribe determined the vote of the tribe; a majority vote among the tribes determined the vote of the people; and the same was true for the curiae and the centuries. This practice was good as long as honesty reigned among the citizens and everyone was ashamed to vote publicly for an unjust proposal or an unworthy cause, but when the people became corrupt and votes were bought and sold, it was agreed that votes should be cast in secret, in order to restrain the buyers through distrust and to give scoundrels the means to avoid being traitors.

I know that Cicero condemns this change and attributes the ruin of the Republic to it in part. But although I feel the weight that Cicero's authority should be given in this matter, I cannot concur in his opinion. I think, on the contrary, that the downfall of the state is accelerated by not making enough changes of this kind. Just as the regimen of healthy people is not right for the sick, so the laws suited to a good people should not be used to govern a corrupt people. Nothing gives better proof of this maxim than the long life of the Venetian Republic, which maintains the semblance of an existence solely because its laws are suited only to wicked men.

Tablets were therefore given to the citizens on which each one could vote without anyone knowing what his opinion was. New formalities were also established for collecting the tablets, counting the votes, comparing the numbers, etc. None of this, however, prevented the honesty of the officials entrusted with these functions[3] from often being suspect. Finally, in order to prevent intrigue and trafficking in votes, edicts were passed, and their sheer number proves how useless they were.

Towards the last days of the Republic, it was often impossible to avoid taking recourse to extraordinary expedients to compensate for the inadequacy of the laws. Sometimes miracles were concocted, but this means, which could deceive the people, could not deceive those who governed it; sometimes an assembly was abruptly convoked before the candidates had time to fashion their intrigues; at other times, a whole session was spent on talk, when it was seen that the people had been won over, and was ready to come to a bad decision. But, in the end, ambition eluded every effort; and what is most unbelievable is that in the midst of so many abuses, this immense people, with the help of its ancient regulations, continued to elect magistrates, pass laws, try cases, and expedite public and private affairs with almost as much ease as the senate itself could have done.

CHAPTER 5 ON THE TRIBUNATE

When an exact proportion cannot be established among the constituent parts of the state, or when unavoidable causes continually alter their relations, then a special magistracy, which is separate from the others, is set up, and it puts each term back into its true relationship with the others, and creates a link or middle term between the prince and the people, or the prince and the sovereign, or, if necessary, both sides at once.

This body, which I shall call the *tribunate*, is the guardian of the laws and the legislative power. It sometimes serves to protect the sovereign against the government, as the tribunes of the people did in Rome; sometimes to uphold the government against the people, as the Council of Ten now does in Venice; and sometimes to maintain equilibrium on both sides, as the ephors did in Sparta.

The tribunate is not a constituent part of the republic, and should have no share in the legislative or executive power, but for that very reason, its own power is greater, for, being able to do nothing, it can prevent everything. It is more sacred and more revered as a defender of the laws than the prince that executes them and the sovereign that enacts them. This is what was clearly apparent in Rome when those proud patricians, who always despised the people as a whole, were forced to bow before an ordinary official of the people, who had neither patronage nor jurisdiction.

A wisely tempered tribunate is the firmest support of a good constitu-

---

3. "Custodes, Diribitores, Rogatores suffragiorum" [Guardians, Distributors, and Collectors of votes; Rousseau's note].

tion, but if it ever has even a little too much force, it disrupts everything. Weakness, however, is not in its nature, and, provided that it is something, it is never less than it needs to be.

It degenerates into tyranny when it usurps the executive power, which it should only moderate, and when it wants to administer the laws that it should only protect. The enormous power of the ephors, which was not dangerous as long as Sparta preserved its moral habits, hastened their corruption once it had begun. The blood of Agis, massacred by those tyrants, was avenged by his successor: the crime and punishment of the ephors hastened equally the downfall of this republic, and after Cleomenes, Sparta no longer amounted to anything. Rome perished in the very same way, and the excessive power of the tribunes, usurped by degrees, finally served, with the help of laws made for the sake of liberty, as a safeguard for the emperors who destroyed it. As for the Council of Ten in Venice, it is a bloody tribunal, a horror to the patricians and people alike, and which, far from proudly protecting the laws, now that they have been debased, serves no purpose other than to strike blows in the dark that no one dares to notice.

Like the government, the tribunate is weakened as the number of its members multiplies. When the tribunes of the Roman people, who at first were two in number and then five, tried to double this number, the senate allowed them to do so, quite certain that it could use some of them to hold the others in check; this was exactly what happened.

The best way to prevent usurpations by such a formidable body, although no government has so far thought of it, would be to avoid making this body permanent, and to fix specific periods during which it would be dispensed with. These periods, which should not be long enough for abuses to become firmly established, can be fixed by law in such a way that they can easily be cut short, if necessary, by a special order.

This method appears to me to have no drawbacks, because, as I have said, the tribunate, which is not a part of the constitution, can be suspended without harming it; and it also seems effective to me because a newly reinstated magistrate starts out not with the power his predecessor had, but with the power given him by law.

CHAPTER 6 ON DICTATORSHIP

The flexibility of laws, which prevents them from being adapted to events, can, in certain cases, make them pernicious, and, in a time of crisis, they can in themselves cause the downfall of the state. The order and slowness of legal procedures require a space of time that circumstances sometimes do not permit. Countless cases for which the lawgiver has made no provision can arise, and a very necessary part of foresight is being aware that one cannot foresee everything.

No one, therefore, should seek to strengthen political institutions to the point of losing the power to suspend their operation. Even Sparta allowed its laws to lie dormant.

But only the greatest dangers can counterbalance the danger of changing the public order, and the sacred power of the laws should never be checked except when the safety of the homeland is at stake. In these rare and obvious cases, public safety is provided for through a special act, which makes the worthiest man responsible for it. This mandate can be given in two ways, according to the nature of the danger.

If increasing the activity of the government is sufficient to remedy the situation, it is concentrated in the hands of one or two of its members. In this way, the authority of the laws is not altered, but merely the form of their administration. If the peril is such that the legal apparatus is an obstacle to protecting the laws, then a supreme leader is named who silences all the laws and momentarily suspends the sovereign authority; in such cases, the general will is not in doubt, and it is evident that the people's primary intention is that the state should not perish. Thus, the suspension of legislative authority does not abolish it; the magistrate who silences it cannot make it speak; he dominates it without being able to represent it. He can do anything except make laws.

The first means was employed by the Roman Senate, when it charged the consuls according to a consecrated formula with providing for the safety of the Republic; the second was employed when one of the two consuls appointed a dictator,[4] a practice for which Alba Longa had established the precedent in Rome.

In the early days of the Republic, the Romans quite often resorted to dictatorship, because the state did not yet have a sufficiently stable basis to be capable of sustaining itself by the strength of its constitution. Since the moral habits of the period made many precautions superfluous that would have been necessary at other times, there was no fear either that a dictator would abuse his authority, or that he would attempt to keep it beyond his term of office. On the contrary, it seemed that such great power was a burden for the one who held it, so quickly did he hasten to rid himself of it, as if taking the place of the laws were too onerous and perilous a position!

Thus, it is not the danger of its being abused but that of its being degraded that evokes criticism of the imprudent use of this supreme office in early times. For while it was squandered on elections, dedications, and the purely formal proceedings, there was reason to fear that it would become less formidable in time of need, and that people would grow accustomed to regarding as an empty title what was only used in empty ceremonies.

Towards the end of the Republic, the Romans, having become more cautious, used the dictatorship sparingly with no more reason than they had used it lavishly in the past. It was easy to see that their fears were ill-founded; that the weakness of the capital then protected it against the magistrates in its midst; that a dictator could, under certain circumstances, defend the public liberty without ever being able to attack it;

---

4. This nomination was made at night and in secret, as if they were ashamed to place a man above the laws [Rousseau's note].

and that Rome's chains would not be forged within Rome itself, but in its armies: the weak resistance Marius offered to Sulla, and Pompey to Caesar, clearly showed what could be expected from internal authority opposed to external force.

This error caused the Romans to make serious mistakes. Such, for example, was the failure to appoint a dictator in the Catiline affair, for, since this was only a question of the city itself, and, at most, of some province in Italy, the dictator, with the unlimited authority the laws gave him, would easily have quelled the conspiracy, which was, in fact, stifled by a concurrence of fortunate accidents that human prudence has no right to expect.

Instead of that, the Senate was content to hand over all its power to the consuls, so that Cicero, in order to take effective action, was forced to exceed this power in a fundamental way, and, although in the first transports of joy, his conduct was approved, he was afterwards justly called to account for the blood of citizens shed in violation of the laws, a reproach which could never have been made against a dictator. But the consul's eloquence led everyone astray, and, though a Roman, he himself, preferring his own glory to his homeland, sought not so much the most legitimate and certain means of saving the state as a way to take all the credit for doing so.[5] Thus, he was justly honored as Rome's liberator, and justly punished as a lawbreaker. However brilliant his recall from exile may have been, it was definitely a free pardon.

Moreover, whatever the way in which this important responsibility is conferred, it is important to limit its duration to a very short term that can never be extended; in the crises that call for it to be established, the state is soon either destroyed or saved, and, once the emergency had passed, dictatorship becomes either tyrannical or useless. In Rome, where the dictators remained in office for only six months, most of them resigned before their term was over. If the term had been longer, they might well have been tempted to extend it, as the Decemvirs did with their term of one year. The dictator had only enough time to meet the need that had led to his election; he had no time to dream up other projects.

CHAPTER 7 ON THE CENSORSHIP

Just as the general will is declared through the law, so public judgment is declared through the censorship; public opinion is the kind of law which the censor administers, and which he applies only to particular cases, after the example of the prince.

Far from being the arbiter of the people's opinion, therefore, the censorial tribunal is only its mouthpiece, and as soon as it deviates from public opinion, its decisions are null and void.

It is useless to distinguish the moral habits of a nation from the objects

5. He could not have predicted what would have happened, had he proposed a dictator, since he did not dare nominate himself and could not make certain that his colleague would nominate him [Rousseau's note].

of its esteem, for all these things proceed from the same principle and are necessarily intermingled. Among all the peoples of the world, it is not nature but opinion which decides their choice of pleasures. Reform men's opinions, and their moral habits will purify themselves. Men always love what is beautiful or what is found to be so, but in making this judgment they make mistakes; the problem, therefore, is to regulate this judgment. Anyone who judges moral habits judges honor, and anyone who judges honor takes his law from opinion.

The opinions of a people spring from its constitution; although the law does not regulate moral habits, legislation gives rise to them; when legislation grows weak, moral habits degenerate, but the judgment of the censors will not then do what the force of law has not done.

It follows from this that the censorship can be useful for preserving moral habits but never for reestablishing them. Establish censors while the laws are still vigorous; as soon as their vigor is lost, all hope is gone; nothing legitimate has any force once the laws no longer have any.

The censorship preserves moral habits by preventing opinions from becoming corrupt, by preserving their rectitude with wise applications, and sometimes even by giving them a fixed form when they are still uncertain. The use of seconds in duels, once all the rage in the kingdom of France, was abolished there merely by these words in one of the king's edicts: *as for those who are cowardly enough to call on seconds.* This judgment, anticipating that of the public, determined the matter once and for all. But when the same edicts tried to declare that it was also an act of cowardice to fight duels—which is quite true, but contrary to common opinion—the public mocked a decision which concerned a matter upon which it had already passed judgment.

I have said elsewhere[6] that since public opinion is not subject to constraint, there should be no vestige of it in the tribunal established to represent it. It is impossible to admire overly much the skill with which this device, entirely lost by modern peoples, was brought into play among the Romans and even better among the Lacedemonians.

When a wicked man introduced a good proposal in the council of Sparta, the Ephors, ignoring it, had the same proposal made by a virtuous citizen. What honor for the one, what disgrace for the other, without either of the two having been praised or blamed! Certain drunkards from Samos[7] defiled the tribunal of the Ephors: the next day, a public edict gave the Samians permission to be rascals. True punishment would have been less severe than such impunity. When Sparta pronounced upon what was or was not decent, Greece did not appeal her judgments.

---

6. In this chapter, I am only pointing out what I have treated at greater length in the *Letter to M. D'Alembert* [Rousseau's note].

7. These were from another island which the delicacy of our language forbids me to name on this occasion* [Rousseau's note, 1782].

* The reference is to a description of the inhabitants of the island of Chios by the moralistic Greek biographer and essayist, Plutarch (c. 46 – c. 120).

CHAPTER 8 ON CIVIL RELIGION

At first men had no kings but the gods, nor any other government but theocracy. They reasoned like Caligula, and, at the time, they reasoned correctly. A lengthy deterioration of feelings and ideas must occur before people can bring themselves to take one of their fellow creatures as their master and flatter themselves that they will be better off.

From the simple fact that a god was placed at the head of every political society, it followed that there were as many gods as peoples. Two peoples, foreign to each other, and nearly always enemies, could not recognize the same master for long; two armies joining battle could not obey the same leader. Thus, national divisions led to polytheism and this in turn led to theological and civil intolerance, which are by nature the same, as will be shown hereafter.

The fanciful notion the Greeks had of rediscovering their gods among barbarous peoples came from the other notion they had of regarding themselves as the natural sovereigns of these peoples. But nowadays scholarship revolving around the identity of gods of different nations seems quite ridiculous, as if Moloch, Saturn, and Cronos could be the same; as if there could be anything in common among imaginary beings with different names!

If it is asked how there came to be no wars of religion in pagan times when every state had its own cult and its own gods, I answer that it was for this very reason that each state, having both its own cult and its own government, did not distinguish between its gods and its laws. Political war was also theological: the provinces of the gods were marked out, so to speak, according to national boundaries. The god of one people had no rights over any other people. The gods of the pagans were not jealous gods; they divided dominion over the world among themselves: even Moses and the Hebrew people sometimes acceded to this view by speaking of the god of Israel. True, they regarded as false the gods of the Canaanites, a proscribed people, doomed to destruction, whose land they were to occupy, but look at how they spoke of the divinities of neighboring peoples they were forbidden to attack! *Is not the possession of what belongs to Chamos your god your just due?* said Jephthah to the Ammonites. *We possess by the same title all the lands our triumphant God has acquired.*[8] This, it seems to me, was a clear acknowledgment of parity between the rights of Chamos and those of the God of Israel.

---

8. *Nonne ea quae possidet Chamos deus tuus, tibi jure debentur.* This is the text of the Vulgate which Father De Carrières has translated as *Ne croyez-vous pas avoir droit de posséder ce qui appartient à Chamos votre Dieu?* I am ignorant of the intent of the Hebrew text, but I see that in the Vulgate Jephthah positively acknowledges the right of the god Chamos, and that the French translator weakened this acknowledgement by inserting a "selon vous" [an "according to you"] which is not in the Latin * [Rousseau's note].

* Judges 11:24. Father De Carrières translated the Latin as follows: "Do you not believe that you have a right to possess what belongs to your god Chamos?" In *The New Oxford Annotated Bible*, the passage reads: "Will you not possess what Chemosh your god gives you to possess?" In Judges 11, Israel, attacked by Sihon, defeats him and takes possession of the land of the Amorites. The gist of the quotation is that a nation may rightfully keep whatever its god gives to it in war.

But when the Jews, while under the domination of the kings of Babylon and later the kings of Syria, wished to remain steadfast in recognizing no other god but their own, this refusal, regarded as rebellion against their conqueror, brought upon them the persecutions we read of in their history and of which we see no other examples before the advent of Christianity.[9]

Since each religion was, therefore, exclusively tied to the laws of the state which prescribed it, there was no other way to convert a people except by enslaving it, nor any other missionaries than conquerors, and since the obligation to change religions was the law imposed on the vanquished, it was necessary to vanquish a people before talking about such a change. Far from men fighting for the gods, it was, as in Homer, the gods who fought for men; each person asked his own god for victory and paid for it with new altars. Before taking a town, the Romans called upon its gods to abandon the place, and when they allowed the Tarentines to keep their angry gods, it was because, at the time, they regarded these gods to be under the domination of their own and forced to pay them homage: they allowed the vanquished to keep their gods as they allowed them to keep their laws. A wreath for the Jupiter of the Capitoline was often the only tribute they imposed.

Finally, when the Romans had spread their religion and their gods along with their empire, and had often themselves adopted those of vanquished peoples by granting to both alike the rights of the city, the peoples of this vast empire gradually found themselves to have multitudes of gods and cults that were nearly the same everywhere; and that is how paganism finally became one and the same religion throughout the known world.

It was under these circumstances that Jesus came to establish a spiritual kingdom on earth, which, by separating the theological from the political system, kept the state from remaining unified, and caused the internal divisions that have never ceased to trouble Christian peoples. Now, since this new idea of an otherworldly kingdom could never have entered the minds of pagans, they always considered the Christians as true rebels who, beneath a mask of hypocritical submissiveness, were only seeking the right moment to make themselves independent and the masters, and cleverly to usurp the authority that they pretended, in their weakness, to respect. This was the cause for the persecutions.

What the pagans had feared happened; then, appearances changed, the humble Christians changed their tune, and this so-called otherworldly kingdom was soon seen, under a visible ruler, to become the most violent despotism on earth.

However, since there have always been civil laws and a prince, this dual power has caused a perpetual jurisdictional conflict, and this has made all good administration impossible in Christian states, and no one

9. The latest evidence shows that the Phocian War, called a *Holy War*, was not a war of religion. Its purpose was to punish sacrileges and not to subdue unbelievers [Rousseau's note].

has ever succeeded in finding out whether he is obligated to obey the master or the priest.

Several peoples, however, even in Europe and its vicinity, have tried to preserve or reestablish the old system, but without success; the spirit of Christianity has won completely. The sacred cult has always remained or again become independent of the sovereign and has lacked necessary connections to the state. Mohammed had very sound views; he organized his political system tightly, and, as long as the form of his government endured under his successors, the caliphs, this government was completely unified, and, for that reason, good. But the Arabs, having become prosperous, literate, polished, soft, and cowardly, were subjugated by barbarians; the division between the two powers then began again; although this division is less apparent among the Moslems than among the Christians, it is there, nevertheless, especially in the sect of Ali, and there are states, such as Persia, where it continually makes itself felt.

Among us, the kings of England have established themselves as heads of the Church, and the czars have done the same, but, with this title, they have made themselves less its masters than its ministers; they have gained not so much the right to change it as the power to maintain it; where they are not legislators, they are only princes. Wherever the clergy constitutes a body,[1] it is master and legislator in its own domain. There are, therefore, two powers, two sovereigns, in England and in Russia, just as there are elsewhere.

Of all the Christian writers, the philosopher Hobbes is the only one who clearly saw the evil and its remedy, who dared to propose the reunification of the two heads of the eagle and the complete restoration of political unity, without which no state or government will ever be well constituted. But he should have seen that the domineering spirit of Christianity was incompatible with his system, and that the interest of the priest would always be stronger than that of the state. It is not so much what is abhorrent and false in his political theory as what is just and true that has made it hated.[2]

I believe that if the historical facts were analyzed from this point of view, it would be easy to refute the opposing sentiments of Bayle and Warburton, one of whom claims that no religion is useful to the body politic, while the other maintains, on the contrary, that Christianity is its firmest support. To the first it could be proved that no state was ever founded without religion as its foundation, and to the second that Chris-

---

1. It should indeed be observed that it is not so much the formal assemblies, like those of France, that bind the clergy into one body, as the communion of the churches. Communion and excommunication are the social pact of the clergy, a pact by means of which it will always be master of peoples and kings. All the priests who belong to the same communion are fellow citizens, although they may be from the opposite ends of the earth. This invention is a political masterpiece. There was nothing similar among pagan priests; thus, they never formed a clerical body [Rousseau's note].

2. Notice, for instance, in a letter written by Grotius to his brother, dated April 11, 1643, what this learned man praises and what he criticizes in the book, *De cive*. It is true that, inclined to being indulgent, he seems to forgive the author the good for the sake of the bad, but not everyone is so merciful [Rousseau's note].

tian law is fundamentally more harmful than useful to the strong constitution of the state. To succeed in making myself understood, I need only give a bit more precision to the unduly vague ideas about religion as they bear upon my subject.

Considered in relation to society, which is either general or particular, religion can also be divided into two kinds, namely, the religion of man and the religion of the citizen. The former, without temples, altars, or rites, limited to the purely inward worship of the supreme God and to the eternal duties of morality, is the pure and simple religion of the Gospel, the true theism, and what might be called natural divine law. The latter, established in a single country, gives it gods, its own tutelary patrons: it has its dogmas, its rites, its outward form of worship prescribed by law; outside the single nation that practices it, this religion considers everything infidel, foreign, barbarous; it extends the duties and rights of man only as far as its altars. Such were all the religions of early peoples, and they may be given the name of civil or positive divine law.

There is a third, more peculiar sort of religion, which, by giving men two sets of laws, two leaders, and two homelands, subjects them to contradictory duties and prevents them from being able to be both devout men and good citizens. Such is the religion of the Lamas, such is that of the Japanese, and such is Roman Christianity. The latter can be called the religion of the priest. It results in a sort of mixed and antisocial code of law that has no name.

Considered from a political standpoint, these three types of religion all have their faults. The third is so obviously bad that it is a waste of time to amuse oneself by proving that it is. Everything that breaks down social unity is worthless: all institutions that place man in contradiction with himself are worthless.

The second is good in the sense that it unites divine worship with love of the laws, and by making the homeland the object of the citizens' adoration, it teaches them that to serve the state is to serve its tutelary god. It is a kind of theocracy in which there should be no other pontiff than the prince, and no other priests than the magistrates. To die for one's country, then, is to be a martyr, to violate the laws is to be impious, and to subject a guilty man to public execration is to condemn him to the wrath of the gods; *sacer estod.*[3]

But it is bad in that, being based upon error and falsehood, it deceives men, makes them credulous and superstitious, and drowns true worship of the divinity in empty ceremonials. It is also bad, when it becomes exclusive and tyrannical and makes a people bloodthirsty and intolerant, so that it breathes only murder and slaughter, and believes that it performs a holy act in killing anyone who does not accept its gods. This puts such a people in a natural state of war with all others, which is very detrimental to its own security.

Thus, what remains is the religion of man or Christianity, not the

3. This expression literally means "let him be sacred," but in Rome it was actually an expression by which an individual could be ostracized and delivered to the judgment of the gods.

Christianity of today but that of the Gospel, which is altogether different. Through this religion which is holy, sublime, and true, men, as children of the same God, all acknowledge each other as brothers, and the society that unites them is not dissolved even by death.

But since this religion has no particular relation to the body politic, it leaves to the laws only the force that they have in themselves, without adding any other force to them, and because of this, one of the chief bonds of particular societies remains ineffective. Furthermore, far from binding the hearts of the citizens to the state, it detaches them from it, as from all earthly things: I know of nothing more contrary to the social spirit.

We are told that a people of true Christians would form the most perfect society imaginable. I see but one great difficulty with this assumption: a society of true Christians would no longer be a society of men.

I would even say that this supposed society, with all its perfection, would neither be the strongest nor the longest lasting. By virtue of being perfect, it would be lacking in unity; its most devastating flaw would lie in its very perfection.

Each man would do his duty; the people would be obedient to the laws, the leaders would be just and moderate, the magistrates would be honest and incorruptible, the soldiers would be scornful of death; there would be neither vanity nor luxury; all that is very fine, but let us look further.

Christianity is a completely spiritual religion, concerned solely with heavenly matters; the Christian's homeland is not of this world. He does his duty, it is true, but he does it with a profound indifference towards the success or failure of his efforts. Provided he has no reason to reproach himself, it matters little to him whether all goes well or badly here below. If the state is flourishing, he hardly dares to enjoy the public happiness; he fears priding himself on his country's glory; if the state is in decline, he blesses the hand of God which weighs heavily on his people.

For a society to be peaceful and for harmony to be maintained, all its citizens without exception would have to be equally good Christians, but if, by misfortune, there is just one ambitious man, just one hypocrite, a Catiline, for example, or a Cromwell, that man will most certainly get the better of his pious compatriots. Christian charity does not readily allow a man to think ill of his neighbor. As soon as the ambitious man has, by some trick, discovered the art of deceiving such citizens and seizing part of the public authority, there will be a man appointed to high office; it is God's will that he be respected; and soon there is a power; it is God's will that it be obeyed; and suppose the man entrusted with this power abuses it; it is the rod with which God punishes his children. People would have scruples about driving out the usurper; it would be necessary to disturb the public tranquillity, to resort to violence, to shed blood; none of this is at all in keeping with Christian meekness; and after all, in this vale of tears, what does it matter whether we are free or in bondage? The essential thing is to get to heaven, and resignation is just one more means of doing so.

What if a foreign war breaks out? The citizens march willingly into combat; not one of them dreams of fleeing; they do their duty, but they have no passion for victory; they know better how to die than how to conquer. What does it matter whether they are the victors or the vanquished? Does not providence know better than they what they need? Just imagine what advantage a proud, impetuous, passionate enemy could take of their stoicism! Set them against those generous peoples consumed by an ardent love of glory and homeland; imagine your Christian republic face to face with Sparta or Rome; the pious Christians will be beaten, crushed, destroyed before having had time to get their bearings, or they will owe their safety only to the contempt that their enemies feel for them. In my opinion, the oath taken by the soldiers of Fabius was a noble one; they did not swear to die or to conquer; they swore to return as victors and kept their oath: never would the Christians have taken an oath like this; they would have believed they were tempting God.

But I am mistaken in speaking of a Christian republic; these two words are mutually exclusive. Christianity preaches nothing but servitude and dependence. Its spirit is too favorable to tyranny for tyranny not always to take advantage of it. True Christians are made to be slaves; they know it and are scarcely moved by it; this short life has too little worth in their eyes.[4]

Christian troops, we are told, are excellent. I deny this. Can anyone show me some that are? As for me, I do not know of any Christian troops. The crusades will be cited. Without disputing the valor of the crusaders, I shall point out that far from being Christians, they were soldiers of the priest, they were citizens of the church; they were fighting for its spiritual home, which the church, we know not how, had made temporal. Rightly understood, this should be accounted as paganism; since the Gospel established no national religion, holy war is impossible among Christians.

Under the pagan emperors, Christian soldiers were brave; all the Christian authors affirm this, and I believe it: there was a rivalry between them and the pagan troops for honor. As soon as the emperors became Christians, this rivalry ceased, and when the cross had driven out the eagle, all Roman valor disappeared.

But leaving political considerations aside, let us return to the question of right, and determine the principles relating to this important point.[5]

---

4. See Machiavelli, *Discourses*, II.2, for a similar argument.

5. Having rejected paganism and Christianity as incompatible with the principles of a legitimate state, Rousseau now presents, as the last point in *On Social Contract*, his view of the appropriate religion. He believes that a legitimate democracy cannot possibly succeed unless its citizens are confirmed in their commitment to the public good by a religious sanction. Yet, the religious doctrine described in the next three paragraphs, being dogmatically affirmed and coercively enforced, is far from obviously compatible with Rousseau's ideal of democratic citizenship. These paragraphs on the civil religion should be read in conjunction with Book II, chapter 7, on the lawgiver, which takes up the issue of religion and politics at its conclusion. Rousseau wrote his first draft of the chapter on civil religion on the back of his draft of the chapter on the lawgiver.

The right which the social pact gives the sovereign over the subjects does not, as I have said, go beyond the limits of public utility.[6] The subjects are not, therefore, accountable to the sovereign for their opinions except insofar as these opinions are of importance to the community. Now, it is of great importance to the state for each citizen to have a religion that makes him love his duties, but the dogmas of this religion interest neither the state nor its members except insofar as these dogmas relate to morality and the duties that anyone who professes it is bound to fulfill towards others. Each one may have, in addition, such opinions as he pleases, without it being the sovereign's business to know them, for since the sovereign has no jurisdiction in the other world, whatever the fate of the subjects may be in the life to come is none of its business, provided they are good citizens in this life.

There is, therefore, a purely civil profession of faith, the articles of which are for the sovereign to determine, not precisely as religious dogmas, but as sentiments of sociability, without which it is impossible to be a good citizen or a faithful subject.[7] Without being able to obligate anyone to believe them, the sovereign can banish from the state anyone who does not believe them; it can banish him not for being impious but for being unsociable, for being incapable of sincerely loving the laws and justice, and of sacrificing his life, if need be, for his duty. If, after having publicly acknowledged these same dogmas, someone behaves as though he does not believe them, let his punishment be death; he has committed the greatest of crimes, he has lied before the laws.

The dogmas of the civil religion should be simple, few in number, and precisely enunciated, without explanations or commentaries. The existence of a powerful, intelligent, beneficent, prescient, and provident divinity, the life to come, the happiness of the just, the punishment of the wicked, the sanctity of the social contract and the laws: these are the positive dogmas. As for negative dogmas, I limit them to one alone: this is intolerance; it is part of the cults we have excluded.

Those who distinguish between civil and theological intolerance are mistaken in my opinion. These two types of intolerance are inseparable. It is impossible to live in peace with people one believes to be damned; to love them would be to hate God who punishes them; it is absolutely necessary either to convert them or to torment them. Wherever theo-

---

6. "In the republic," says the Marquis d'Argenson, "each man is perfectly free with regard to that which does not harm others." This is the invariable limit; it cannot be set any more exactly. I have been unable to deny myself the pleasure of sometimes quoting this manuscript, although it is unknown to the public, in order to honor the memory of an illustrious man who is worthy of respect because, even as a government official, he kept the heart of a true citizen as well as just and sound views on the government of his country [Rousseau's note].

7. In pleading for Catiline,* Caesar tried to establish the dogma of the mortality of the soul. To refute him, Cato and Cicero wasted no time phi-

losophizing; they were content to show that Caesar spoke like a bad citizen and advanced a doctrine pernicious to the state. In fact, that is what the Roman Senate had to judge, and not a theological question [Rousseau's note].

* Catiline (Lucius Sergius Catilina, c. 108 B.C. – 62 B.C.), a Roman aristocrat, had a reputation in his youth for degenerate behavior but came to hold several prestigious political offices. His political life was actively corrupt, and he conspired against the government on several occasions. In 62 B.C., after Catiline failed to win the consulship, his plot to seize the government by force was forestalled by Cicero.

logical intolerance is allowed, it is impossible for it not to have some civil effect,[8] and once it does, the sovereign is no longer sovereign, even in temporal matters: from that time onwards, priests are the true masters; kings are merely their officers.

Now that there is no longer and can no longer be an exclusive national religion, all those which tolerate others must be tolerated, insofar as their dogmas are in no way contrary to the duties of a citizen. But whoever dares say, *outside the church, no salvation*, should be driven from the state, unless the state is the church, and the prince is the pontiff. Such a dogma is good only in a theocratic government, in every other it is pernicious. The reason for which Henry IV is said to have embraced the Roman religion ought to make every honest man, and especially every prince who can reason, leave it.[9]

CHAPTER 9 CONCLUSION

After having set down the true principles of political right and having endeavored to establish the state on that basis, it remains to support the state by means of its foreign relations, which would include the law of nations, commerce, the right of war and conquest, public law, leagues, negotiations, treaties, and so forth. But all that forms a new subject too vast for the limits of my vision; I should always have kept my eyes on things closer at hand.

---

8. Marriage, for example, being a civil contract, has civil effects, without which a society cannot even subsist. Let us suppose then that a clergy reaches the point where it claims for itself alone the right to perform this act, a right which it must necessarily usurp in every intolerant religion. In that case, is it not clear that by making the most of the church's authority at the right moment, it will render that of the prince ineffectual, and the latter will no longer have any subjects except those whom the clergy are willing to give up? Is it not clear that by conducting themselves prudently and standing firm, the clergy alone—master of marrying or not marrying people, according to whether or not they accept this or that doctrine, or whether they admit or reject this or that formula, whether they are more or less devout—will dispose of inheritances, offices, citizens, and the state itself, which cannot endure, if it is no longer composed of anyone but bastards? But, it will be said, there will be appeals on the grounds of abuse, there will be summonses, decrees, and seizures of church property. What a pity! The clergy, if only it has as much good sense as courage, will let this be done and will proceed as usual; it will quietly allow the appeals, the summonses, the decrees, and the seizures, and it will end up by being the master. It is not, it seems to me, a great sacrifice to abandon a part when one is sure of taking possession of the whole [Rousseau's note].

9. Henry IV (1552–1610) was able to claim the throne of France by converting from Calvinism to Catholicism in 1593.

END

BACKGROUNDS

Jean-Jacques Rousseau: A Biographical Sketch*

Rousseau begins his *Confessions* with the declaration: "But I am made unlike anyone I have ever met; I will even venture to say that I am like no one in the whole world. I may be no better, but at least I am different. Whether Nature did well or ill in breaking the mould in which she formed me, is a question which can only be resolved after the reading of my book."[1] Rousseau always perceived himself as "unique" and constantly exercised his independence in ways that astounded, impressed, angered, alienated, and confused his contemporaries and generations of critics that followed.

From the beginning, as Rousseau complains in the *Confessions*, he seemed destined to an unhappy life. His mother died at his birth in 1712, leaving his father disconsolate. Isaac Rousseau was a watchmaker by trade and a socially ambitious artisan. He had married Suzanne Bernard, whose family belonged to the academic elite of Geneva. Jean-Jacques, their second son, was born in the house she had inherited from her uncle, a prominent theologian and scholar. The library in this house provided Rousseau with his early education. Isaac Rousseau favored his younger son and taught him to love reading by giving him novels and Plutarch's *Lives*; he taught the boy to think of his native Geneva as a modern Rome.

Rousseau's irresponsible father, who preferred hunting, dancing, and dueling to watchmaking, eventually had to sell the Bernard house and return to the artisan quarter of Geneva with his two sons. When he was forced to leave Geneva for challenging someone of high social standing, Rousseau's older brother disappeared, and Jean-Jacques, at the age of ten, was sent to live with his mother's brother. When Rousseau was thirteen his uncle apprenticed him to a boorish, insensitive, and cruel engraver who punished him harshly for adolescent pranks. It began an unhappy three years for Jean-Jacques.

In March 1728 Rousseau returned from a walk in the countryside too late to enter the city gates, and rather than face his master's wrath, he fled from Geneva. He sought the society of the noble and wealthy in Piedmont and Savoy. After he converted to Roman Catholicism in Turin, he found shelter with Madame de Warens, who was thirty years old and also a recent convert. He lived with her in Annecy and Chambéry from 1729 until 1742, first as a cherished guest and then as a lover, although he travelled and worked elsewhere on occasion. Madame de Warens' influence was crucial to his intellectual development; she encouraged him to spend much of his time in reading and study, especially after 1735. Unlike many of the great figures of the Enlightenment, Rousseau was self-taught. He kept notebooks full of excerpts on subjects from every

* By Julia Conaway Bondanella.
1. *The Confessions of Jean-Jacques Rousseau*, trans. J. M. Cohen (Baltimore: Penguin, 1953), p. 17.

area of knowledge—science, mathematics, astronomy, music, literature, and others. He read the works of political philosophers such as
Hobbes and Locke, and gained a new appreciation for his birthplace and
the importance of citizenship in Geneva.

Dissatisfied with his relationship with Madame de Warens and her
liaison with another man, Rousseau finally left for Paris in 1742 with
his play *Narcisse* and a new system of musical notation to submit to the
Academy of Sciences. His first years in Paris were discouraging, but he
succeeded in interesting various influential women of Parisian society in
his fate, including the wealthy Madame Dupin. One of them helped
him gain a position as secretary to the Comte de Montaigu, the new
French Ambassador to Venice. He soon became embroiled in a dispute
with the Ambassador and was humiliated and disillusioned at being treated
like a servant. This quarrel, which led to his dismissal, confirmed his
opinion that justice could never be realized in a social system based on
the inequality of status, and it was during this time that he began to
develop the political ideas of *On Social Contract*.

On his return to Paris Rousseau became friends with many of the
philosophes of the French Enlightenment, including Denis Diderot and
Jean Le Rond d'Alembert, co-editors of the *Encyclopédie*. The *philosophes* had been inspired by Newton's theories, which seemed to suggest
the very real possibility of using rational means to discover social and
political laws which would improve earthly life. Assuming that reason
was a tool for discovery in every sphere, these thinkers promoted education, undertook to write an encyclopedia of human knowledge which
would be accessible to the layman, questioned political, religious and
literary rules, advocated tolerance, contested the privileges of aristocrats,
and presumed that science and technology would stimulate material
progress.

In 1746 Rousseau was invited to take a position as secretary for the
Dupins. While serving the Dupin family as a research assistant, he studied various political theorists, including Montesquieu, published works
on music, composed operas and ballets, and wrote plays. He also acquired
a mistress, Thérèse le Vasseur, who worked at the hotel in Paris where
he stayed. She was not one of the beautiful, educated, upper-class women
he admired, but a maid, and he kept her and her family the rest of his
life. At the age of fifty-six, he married Thérèse, after she had borne him
five children, all of whom were sent to an orphanage soon after their
birth.

Eventually, Rousseau received the recognition he desired by winning
the prize offered by the Academy of Dijon for an essay on the question:
"Has the progress of the sciences and arts contributed to the purification
of morals?" Encouraged by Diderot, Rousseau wrote his *Discours sur les
sciences et les arts (Discourse on the Sciences and the Arts*, 1750), which
contrasted the virtuous peoples of antiquity who lived simple lives close
to nature with the refined but corrupt moderns. The polemics provoked
by this essay, which attacked popular Enlightenment values, as well as

his musical success with *Le dévin du village* (*The Village Soothsayer*, 1752), which was played several times at Fontainebleau and the Opéra, ensured his recognition as one of the bright new thinkers of the times.

Although Rousseau felt socially inept and, unlike Voltaire, was not a particularly witty conversationalist, he had the kind of intellect and personal charm that brought him acceptance in the salons and among the *philosophes*. Yet he challenged the ideals of his progressive "enlightened" friends, and became more and more alienated from them. His frequent quarrels with various Enlightenment figures such as Voltaire and Hume also reflect his difficult personality. Apparently, he rarely spoke ill of others, but his behavior was often unpredictable, provocative, or self-destructive. For fear of losing his intellectual integrity as a critic of the rich, he declined to meet with the King, who probably would have offered him a pension. He also resigned another lucrative position, renounced his ideas of acquiring fame and fortune, and helped support himself by copying music.

In these years between 1752 and 1762 Rousseau wrote his most important works. The first was the *Discours sur l'origine de l'inégalité* (*Discourse on Inequality*, 1755), which won Rousseau fame throughout Europe and America. Also published in 1755 was his article *Économie politique* (*Discourse on Political Economy*), which appeared in the fifth volume of the *Encyclopédie*.

While composing these works Rousseau had returned to Geneva. At that time, he converted back to Protestantism in order to resume his rights as a citizen. However, his joy at being in his native city was quickly dissipated because Voltaire, with whom he was on bad terms, had just moved into Les Délices, very near Geneva. Rousseau then decided to move to L'Ermitage (the Hermitage), Madame d'Épinay's[2] country house near Paris, a decision prompted by his dispute with Voltaire and his fear that in Geneva he would not be entirely free to write and publish his works. Between April 1756 and December 1757, Rousseau found great enjoyment in the rural solitude of L'Ermitage. While there he worked on his *Dictionnaire de musique* (*Dictionary of Music*, finally published in 1768 in Paris) and studied the works of the Abbé de Saint-Pierre.[3]

Rousseau left L'Ermitage after a quarrel with Madame d'Épinay, Grimm,[4] and Diderot which stemmed from his infatuation with Sophie d'Houdetot, Madame d'Épinay's sister-in-law. In her he saw Julie, the heroine of his novel *La nouvelle Héloïse* (*The New Heloise*, printed in Holland by Michel Rey in 1761). Rousseau was indiscreet, and Madame d'Houdetot quickly broke off with him, but Rousseau suspected that Diderot had compromised his position, and, feeling betrayed, he

2. Louise-Florence d'Epinay, a wealthy Parisian woman with literary aspirations who befriended Rousseau, was the daughter of an impoverished nobleman. She had married a wealthy financier in 1745. Rousseau enjoyed passing the time at La Chevrette, her château near Montmorency forest.
3. Charles Irenée Castel Saint Pierre (1658–1743) was an astute political and social critic whose works

had a profound effect on Rousseau. His *Projet de paix perpetuelle* (1713) inspired various efforts to achieve universal peace.
4. Frederick Melchior Grimm, an impoverished German baron, came to France as a tutor, where he became a close friend of Rousseau, with whom he shared a passion for music.

denounced Diderot publicly in the Preface to his *Lettre à M. d'Alembert sur les spectacles* (*Letter to D'Alembert*, 1758).

He remained in the Montmorency forest, which had become his "study," for four more years, first in a house he rented in the park at Mont-Louis, and then in the Petit Chateau of the marshal of Luxembourg, another of his patrons. It was at Mont-Louis that he wrote the *Lettre à M. d'Alembert*, in which he considers the effects of entertainment, including theater and actors, on society. Although theater might be suitable for monarchies, he felt, free entertainment such as festivals, dances, games, concerts, and athletic competitions would be more appropriate for republics.

After the immediate and popular reception of his novel, *The New Héloïse*, Rousseau went back to work on *Émile* and the "*Institutions politiques*" ("*Political Institutions*"). *Émile*, published in 1762, presents his theory of domestic education. Having established that civilization has corrupted man's original nature, he depicts the development of a child raised in the country and allowed to grow in accord with "the natural progress of the human heart." The objective of education, says Rousseau, should be to form an independent, well-rounded human being who can engage in any vocation. Recognizing that the child has different needs at different stages of development, Rousseau criticizes earlier theorists for treating children like adults and claims that understanding the psychology of children is crucial to a successful educational system. His conception of education rests on the notion that childhood is akin to the state of nature and that parents should not attempt to socialize their children too early.

Rousseau's other great work of this period was *On Social Contract* (1762) which he extracted from the much larger "*Political Institutions*," a work Rousseau was unable to complete. While *Émile* shows how a few children in a corrupt society can be saved through the ministrations of a tutor, *On Social Contract* suggests that political reform can end corruption itself. Both, however, seek protection for the liberty of individuals.

It was risky at the time to publish such works as *On Social Contract*, and after it was published by Rey in Amsterdam in the spring of 1762, its circulation in France was forbidden. But *Émile* brought a stronger storm of protest. The man who described himself as the only one in France who still believed in God was vigorously attacked by those who defended the purity of the faith. The section on the *Profession de foi du vicaire savoyard* (*Profession of Faith of a Savoyard Priest*), which Rousseau had intended to publish separately, was condemned for its unorthodox and unacceptably subjective view of religion. The Parlement of Paris issued a writ for Rousseau's arrest on June 9, 1762. Likewise, the Genevan Advisory Council condemned both *Émile* and *On Social Contract* on June 19 of the same year. However the French writ was not immediately enforced and Rousseau was able to flee. His ill health and age doubtlessly exacerbated the uncertainty of his situation. He spent the next three years at Motiers in Neuchâtel, then part of Prussia. He defended himself in two works which appeared during this time—July 1762 to

September 1765—and he renounced his Genevan citizenship in 1763 rather than become involved in another quarrel.

Driven from Motiers by a public demonstration, he was then expelled from the Île Saint-Pierre by the authorities in Berne. He returned temporarily to Paris before accepting David Hume's invitation to go to Scotland and England. Although he took offense at some of Hume's efforts to help him, thus managing to return the offense, he stayed almost a year and a half in England, before returning to France in May 1767. There he lived the life of a hunted man, constantly changing his residence and his name over the next three years. In 1770, after receiving assurances that he could live in Paris, he moved into quarters on the rue Platrière but still suffered from feelings of persecution. He spent his time copying music, gathering herbs, and writing.

During this last period in his life, he wrote the unfinished *Projet de constitution pour la Corse* (*Constitutional Project for Corsica*, 1765), and *Considérations sur le gouvernement de Pologne* (*Considerations on the Government of Poland*, 1772). Both works apply the principles he enunciated in *On Social Contract*. Between 1765 and 1775, despite his doubts about being able to finish it, he completed his autobiography, the *Confessions*, as well as *Rousseau, juge de Jean-Jacques* (*Rousseau, Judge of Jean-Jacques*), and *Rêveries d'un promeneur solitaire* (*Reveries of a Solitary Walker*). None of these autobiographical writings was published until after his death, which came unexpectedly on July 2, 1778, in Ermeonville, where he was buried. His body was transferred to the Panthéon during the French Revolution.

Rousseau's death did not put an end to the controversy inspired by his ideas and his personal idiosyncracies. In the first sentence of *Emile*, he formulates the problem which was to preoccupy all his thought: "Nature has created man to be happy and good, but society depraves him and makes him miserable."[5] Inspired by the new science as well as the discoveries of explorers, the *Discourse on Inequality* yielded not only new insights into the effects of social life but also a new method of analyzing such questions which divorced them from tradition and authority. In *Political Economy* and *On Social Contract*, Rousseau's proposals for solving the problems of inequality, which he saw as the primary source of social evil, challenged the assumptions of an age which ranked men on the basis of birth, wealth, and power rather than individual rights or talents. At the same time, he cast doubt upon some cherished Enlightenment values—the faith that reason could solve human problems and that progress was beneficial.

He posed questions about the political and social activities of men which have become part of our intellectual heritage and which have taken new forms in our own times. Rousseau laid the foundations for the modern debate, continued by other visionaries like Marx, on human nature, government, and the real costs of industrial and technological progress.

---

5. Jean-Jacques Rousseau, *Emile*, trans. Allan Bloom (New York: Basic Books, 1979), p. 7.

JEAN-JACQUES ROUSSEAU

Rousseau believed that his contemporaries conspired to misunderstand him and his writings, and the tone of the *Confessions* is deliberately defensive. His relationships with people were difficult, and he depicts himself as a man whose life can be best understood in terms of his feelings: "I easily forget my misfortunes, but I cannot forget my faults, and still less my genuine feelings. The memory of them is too dear ever to be effaced from my heart. I may omit or transpose facts, or make mistakes in dates; but I cannot go wrong about what I have felt, or about what my feelings have led me to do; and these are the chief subjects of my story. The true object of my confessions is to reveal my inner thoughts exactly in all the situations of my life."[1]

From Rousseau's CONFESSIONS

[Rousseau tries in this passage to justify placing his five children in an orphanage. The events date from 1750.]

    * * * Thérèse became pregnant for the third time.[2] Too sincere with myself, too proud in my heart, to be willing to belie my principles by my actions, I began to consider the fate of my children and my relationship with their mother, by reference to the laws of nature, justice, and reason, and of * * * religion.

*　*　*

    If I was mistaken in my conclusions, nothing can be more remarkable than the calm spirit in which I surrendered to them. If I were one of those low-born men, deaf to the gentle voice of Nature, a man in whose breast no real feeling of justice and humanity ever arose, this hardness of heart would have been quite easy to explain. But my warm-heartedness, my acute sensibility, the ease with which I formed friendships, the hold they exercised over me, and the cruel wrench when they had to be broken; my innate goodwill toward my fellow men; my burning love for the great, the true, the beautiful, and the just; my horror of evil in every form, my inability to hate, to hurt, or even to wish to; that softening, that sharp and sweet emotion I feel at the sight of all that is virtuous, generous, and lovable: is it possible that all these can ever dwell in the same soul along with depravity which, quite unscrupulously, tramples the dearest of obligations underfoot? No, I feel, and boldly declare—it is impossible. Never for a moment in his life could Jean-Jacques have been a man without feelings or compassion, an unnatural father. I may have been mistaken, but I could never be callous. If I were to state my reasons, I should say too much. For since they were strong enough to seduce me, they would seduce many others; and I do not wish to expose any young people who may read me to the risk of being misled by the

1. *The Confessions of Jean-Jacques Rousseau*, trans. J. M. Cohen (Baltimore: Penguin, 1953), p. 262.   2. *Ibid.*, pp. 332–34.

same error. I will be content with a general statement that in handing my children over for the State to educate, for lack of means to bring them up myself, by destining them to become workers and peasants instead of adventurers and fortune-hunters, I thought I was acting as a citizen and a father, and looked upon myself as a member of Plato's Republic. More than once since then the regret in my heart has told me that I was wrong. But far from my reason having told me the same story, I have often blessed Heaven for having thus safeguarded them from their father's fate, and from that which would have overtaken them at the moment when I should have been compelled to abandon them. If I had left them to Mme d'Épinay or to Mme de Luxembourg who, out of friendship or generosity, or from some other motive, offered to take charge of them at a later date, would they have been happier, would they have been brought up at least as honest people? I do not know; but I am sure that they would have been led to hate, and perhaps to betray their parents. It is a hundred times better that they have never known them.

My third child, therefore, was taken to the Foundling Hospital like the others, and the next two were disposed of in the same way, for I had five in all. This arrangement seemed so good and sensible and right to me that if I did not boast of it openly it was solely out of regard for their mother. But I told everyone whom I had told of our relationship. * * * In a word, I made no mystery about my conduct, not only because I have never been able to conceal anything from my friends, but because I really saw nothing wrong in it. All things considered, I made the best choice for my children, or what I thought was the best. I could have wished, and still do wish, that I had been brought up and nurtured as they have been.

*   *   *

[Rousseau describes how he came to write his *Discourse on Inequality* in 1753, during the years of his early success in Paris as the author of the prize-winning *Discourse on the Sciences and the Arts* and an opera entitled *The Village Soothsayer.*]

* * * it was in that year, I think, of 1753, that the Dijon Academy proposed "The Inequality of Mankind" as a subject for discussion.[3] I was struck by this great question and surprised at the Academy's daring to propose it. But since they had the courage, I thought that I might be bold enough to discuss it, and set about the task.

In order to think this great matter out at my leisure, I went to Saint-Germain for some seven or eight days with Thérèse and our landlady, who was a decent woman, and a woman friend of hers. I think of this trip as one of the most pleasant in my life. The weather was very fine; those good women undertook all the trouble and expense; Thérèse amused herself in their company, and I, without a care in the world, came in at

3. *Ibid.*, pp. 361–63.

mealtimes and was unrestrainedly gay over table. For all the rest of the day, wandering deep into the forest, I sought and I found the vision of those primitive times, the history of which I proudly traced. I demolished the petty lies of mankind; I dared to strip man's nature naked, to follow the progress of time and trace the things which have distorted it; and by comparing man as he had made himself with man as he is by nature, I showed him in his pretended perfection the true source of his misery. Exalted by these sublime meditations, my soul soared towards the Divinity; and from that height I looked down on my fellow men pursuing the blind path of their prejudices, of their errors, of their misfortunes and their crimes. Then I cried to them in a feeble voice which they could not hear, "Madmen who ceaselessly compain of Nature, learn that all your misfortunes arise from yourselves!"

The outcome of these mediations was the *Essay on Inequality* which Diderot preferred to all my other works. His advice was most useful to me in the writing of it. But nowhere in Europe did it find more than a few readers who understood it, and not one of them chose to speak of it. It had been written to compete for the prize. I sent it in, therefore, though I was certain beforehand that it would not win, for I knew very well that it is not for work of this kind that Academy prizes are founded.

*   *   *

[When Rousseau left Geneva for France, he converted to Catholicism, the religion of his newly adopted country. Then on a visit to Geneva in 1754, he converted back to Protestantism, because he believed that a citizen should accept his country's religion. Rousseau's views on religious truth and the role of religion in the state offended ecclesiastical authorities in France and Geneva at the same time that his belief in God separated him from other Enlightenment thinkers, such as Voltaire. Here, Rousseau reflects on his decisions regarding religion.]

* * * On my arrival in that city [Geneva], I gave myself up to the republican enthusiasm that had led me there, and that enthusiasm was increased by the welcome I received.[4] Fêted and made much of by all classes, I surrendered entirely to patriotic zeal and, ashamed of being excluded from my rights as a citizen by my profession of a faith different from that of my fathers, I decided publicly to return to Protestantism. The Gospel being, in my opinion, the same for all Christians, and the fundamentals of dogma only differing over points that men attempted to explain but were unable to understand, it seemed to me to rest with the Sovereign alone in each country to settle the form of worship and the unintelligible dogma as well. It was, therefore, I thought, the citizens' duty to accept the dogma and follow the cult of their country, both as prescribed by law. My association with the Encyclopaedists, far from shaking my faith, had strengthened it because of my natural aversion for quarreling and for parties. My study of man and the Universe had shown me every-

4. *Ibid.*, pp. 365–66.

where final causes and the intelligence which directed them. My reading of the Bible, particularly of the Gospels, to which I had applied myself for some years, had led me to despise the base and foolish interpretations given to the words of Jesus Christ by persons quite unworthy of understanding them. In a word, philosophy, while attaching me to what was essential in religion, had freed me from the host of petty forms with which men have obscured it. Considering that for a reasonable man there were no two ways of being a Christian, I considered also that everything to do with form and discipline in each country belonged to the province of the law. It followed from this most sensible, social, and peaceable principle, which has brought such cruel persecutions upon me, that since I wished to be a citizen I must become a Protestant and return to the established faith of my country.

* * *

[Here, Rousseau speculates on the motives of his critics and describes the genesis of the political philosophy finally formulated in *On Social Contract*. He had left behind Paris, his critics, and the confusion of society in 1756 to live in the countryside near Paris.]

* * *

Of the various works that I had on the stocks there was one on which I had long meditated and to which I was more attracted than to the others.[5] To it I was anxious to devote the whole of my life, for it would, in my opinion, put the seal on my reputation. This was my *Political Institutions*. It was thirteen or fourteen years since I had conceived the original idea for it, at the time when I was in Venice and had some opportunity of observing the defects in that Republic's highly vaunted constitution. Since then my ideas had been greatly broadened by my study of the history of morals. I had seen that everything is rooted in politics and that, whatever might be attempted, no people would ever be other than the nature of their government made them. So the great question of the best possible government seemed to me to reduce itself to this: "What is the nature of the government best fitted to create the most virtuous, the most enlightened, the wisest, and, in fact, the best people, taking the word 'best' in its highest sense?" I believed that I saw a close relationship between that question and another, very nearly though not quite the same: "What is the government which by its nature always adheres closest to the law?" From which one comes to: "What is the law" and to a chain of questions of that magnitude. I saw that all this was leading me to some great truths which would make for the happiness of the human race, but above all for that of my native land, whose ideas of law and liberty had not seemed to me, on my recent journey, as just or as clear-cut as I could have wished: and I considered this indirect method of teaching them these truths the best calculated to spare the pride of the citizens and to secure me forgiveness for having been able

5. *Ibid.*, pp. 377–79.

to see a little farther in this respect than they.

Although I had been engaged in this work for five or six years, I had not got very far with it. Books of this kind require reflection, leisure, and quiet. Besides, I was working at it, as they say, behind closed doors, and I had preferred not to communicate my plan to anyone, even to Diderot. I was afraid that it would seem too bold for the age and the country in which I was writing, and that my friends' alarm might hinder me in the execution.[6] I did not yet know whether it would be finished in time or in such a manner as to admit of its publication during my lifetime.

I will even admit that as a foreigner living in France I found my position most favourable for truth-telling. For I knew that if I continued, as I intended, to print nothing in the country without licence I need account to nobody for my opinions or for their publication anywhere else. I should have been much less free even at Geneva, where the magistrates would have had the right to censure the contents of my books, wherever they might have been printed. This consideration had played a great part in making me yield to Mme d'Épinay's persuasions and give up my plan of settling in Geneva. I felt, as I have written in *Émile*, short of being an intriguer, if one wishes to devote one's books to the true benefit of one's country, one must write them abroad.

* * *

* * * In the storm that has engulfed me my books have served as a pretext; the attack was against myself. They cared very little about the author, but they wished to destroy Jean-Jacques; and the greatest crime they discovered in my writings was the honour they might bring me. But let us not anticipate. I do not know whether this mystery, which remains one to me, will hereafter be cleared up in my readers' eyes. I only know that if my declared principles really brought down on me the treatment I suffered, it would not have been so long before I was its victim. For that piece of writing in which these principles were most boldly, if not foolhardily, stated appeared to have produced its effect even before my retirement to the Hermitage, without anyone thinking, I will not say of picking a quarrel with me, but even of preventing the works' publication in France, where it sold as openly as in Holland. Afterwards *The New Héloïse* appeared with no greater difficulty and, I venture to say, gained the same applause; and, what may seem almost incredible, the profession of faith of this same Héloïse on her deathbed is identical with that of the Savoyard vicar. All that is challenging in *On Social Contract* had previously appeared in the *Essay on Inequality*; all that is challenging in *Émile* was previously in *Julie*. Now these outspoken passages excited no murmur against the two former works; it was not they, therefore, that created an outcry against the two latter.

6. It was Duclos's wise severity that I particularly feared. As for Diderot, all my talks with him always tended, I do not know why, to make me more satirical and caustic than I was by nature. It was that which deterred me from consulting him on an enterprise in which I meant to employ solely the power of reason, without any vestige of venom or prejudice. The tone which I adopted for this work can be judged by that of *On Social Contract*, which derives from it [Rousseau's Note].

* * *

[Over the years, it became apparent that Rousseau and Voltaire could rarely agree on anything, so different were they in temperament and outlook. Voltaire's dislike for abstract reasoning, his satirical wit, his practical bent, and his emphasis on the tangible were sharply different from Rousseau's abstract ideals, belief in the goodness of man and nature, and his strong emotional and religious feelings. In the following passage, Rousseau ridicules Voltaire's poem on the 1755 earthquake in Lisbon, particularly Voltaire's rejection of the optimistic view that all must be for the best in a world created by a good and benevolent God.]

* * *

Struck by seeing that poor man [Voltaire], weighed down, so to speak, by fame and prosperity, bitterly complaining, nevertheless, against the wretchedness of this life and finding everything invariably bad, I formed the insane plan of bringing him back to himself and proving to him that all was well.[7] Though Voltaire has always appeared to believe in God, he has really only believed in the Devil, because his so-called God is nothing but a malicious being who, according to his belief, only takes pleasure in doing harm. The absurdity of this doctrine leaps to the eye, and it is particularly revolting in a man loaded with every kind of blessing who, living in the lap of luxury, seeks to disillusion his fellow men by a frightening and cruel picture of all the calamities from which he is himself exempt. I who had a better right to count up and weigh the evils of human life examined them impartially and proved to him that there was not one of all those evils that could be blamed on Providence, not one that has not its source rather in the misuse that man has made of his faculties than in Nature herself. * * *

I have never published or even shown these two letters. * * * In the meantime Voltaire has published the reply that he promised me. It is nothing less that his novel *Candide*, of which I cannot speak because I have not read it.

* * *

[By 1760, the relations between the two great men had become even more strained.]

I do not like you sir.[8] You have done me injuries which could not be anything but extremely painful to me—to me, your disciple and admirer. In gratitude for the refuge she gave you, you have ruined the city of Geneva. In gratitude for the praise I have lavished on you when among them, you have alienated my fellow citizens from me. It is you who have made life in my native land unbearable to me. It is you who will cause me to die on foreign soil, deprived of all a dying man's consola-

7. *Ibid.*, p. 399–400. In this passage, Rousseau refers to an exchange of letters with Voltaire in 1756 on the Lisbon earthquake, which marks the beginning of their quarrel.

8. *Ibid.*, pp. 500–501. This excerpt is from a letter written to Voltaire in 1760 and reprinted in the *Confessions.*

tions, and so little honoured as to be thrown into the gutter, whilst all the honors a man can expect will follow you to your grave in *my* country. In fact, I hate you, since you have willed it so; but I hate you as a man better fitted to love you, had you so willed it. Of all the feelings towards you which filled my heart, there remains only that admiration which cannot be denied to your splendid genius, and a love for your writings.

* * *

[Rousseau describes the circumstances in which he completed and published *On Social Contract*.]

* * * I found myself with about a thousand crowns in hand.[9] *Émile*, to which I had settled down in earnest when I finished *Héloïse*, was well advanced, and I expected the profit from it at least to double that sum. I planned to invest this money to bring me in a small annual income which, together with my copying, would allow me to live without any more writing. I had still two works on the stocks. The first was my *Political Institutions*. I looked into the state of this book, and found that it still required several years' more labour on it. I had not the courage to continue with it, and to postpone my resolution until it was finished. Accordingly I abandoned it, deciding to extract from it whatever could be extracted and then to burn the rest; and pushing eagerly ahead with that task, without any interruption to *Émile*, in less than two years I put the finishing touches to *On Social Contract*.* * *

* * *

* * * I was obliged to wait until the contract for *Émile* was completed; and while I waited I put the finishing touches to *On Social Contract*, which I sent to Rey, fixing the price for the manuscript at a thousand francs, which he gave me.[1] Perhaps I should not pass over one little incident concerning this same manuscript. I handed it, well sealed, to Duvoisin, a Vaudois minister and chaplain at the Dutch Residence, who came to see me sometimes and undertook to send it to Rey, with whom he was in touch. The manuscript was written in a very fine hand, and was so small that it fitted easily into his pocket. However, as he passed the excise barrier [just outside Paris, where taxes were collected], it fell into the hands of the clerks, who opened it, examined it, and returned it to him immediately on his claiming it in the name of the ambassador. This gave him the opportunity of reading it himself, which, as he naively informed me, he did, and at the same time praised the work most highly. Not a word of criticism or censure did he utter, though he was no doubt reserving for himself the part of Christian avenger for the moment when the work appeared. He resealed the manuscript, and sent it to Rey. * * *

9. *Ibid.*, p. 478.　　　　　1. *Ibid.*, p. 517.

[In 1762, the controversy over *On Social Contract* and, more especially, *Émile*, brings the French to the point of prosecuting him, and he tries to decide how to react to the warrant for his arrest.]

*   *   *

Conscious that I had secret and powerful enemies in the Kingdom, I considered that despite my love for France, if I wished to live at peace I must depart.[2] My first impulse was to retire to Geneva, but an instant's reflection was enough to dissuade me from doing anything so stupid. I knew that the French ministry had even more power in Geneva than in Paris, and would no more leave me in peace in one place than the other if they had decided to persecute me. I knew that my *Discourse on Inequality* had excited a hatred for me on the Council, the more dangerous because no one dared to express it. Lastly I knew that when *The New Héloïse* appeared they had hurriedly banned it at the request of Doctor Tronchin. But seeing that nobody was following their example, even in Paris, they became ashamed of their foolishness and withdrew their prohibition. I had no doubt that they would find the present opportunity more favourable, and do their best to profit by it. Notwithstanding outward appearance, I knew that in every Genevese heart there lurked a secret jealousy, only waiting for the chance to be assuaged. Nevertheless patriotism called me back to my own country, and if I had been able to convince myself that I could live there in peace I should not have hesitated. But neither honour nor reason allowed me to seek refuge there as a fugitive; and I decided to retire to a nearby place and wait in Switzerland until I saw what course they would take about me in Geneva. It will soon be seen that I was not left in doubt for long.

Mme de Boufflers strongly disapproved of this decision, and made fresh endeavours to persuade me to go to England. I remained unshaken. I have never liked England or the English; and all Mme de Boufflers' eloquence, far from overcoming my repugnance, served for some reason to increase it. * * *

[The controversy which erupted in Switzerland and the territories of Berne where Rousseau had taken refuge after the condemnation of *Émile* prompt the Bernese authorities to force him to leave. Rousseau left intending to go to Berlin, but was persuaded instead to go to England.]

*   *   *

At last, having with difficulty procured a carriage, I left that murderous land on the following morning, before the arrival of the deputation with which they intended to honour me, and even before I could see Thérèse, to whom I had sent a message when I expected to stay in Bienne, to join me there.[3] I had barely time to countermand this by a short note, informing her of my new disaster. It will be seen in the third part of my *Confessions*, if ever I have strength to write it, how though I thought I

2. *Ibid.*, pp. 536–37.   3. *Ibid.*, p. 605.

was setting out for Berlin I was in fact leaving for England, and how the two ladies [Mme de Boufflers and Mme de Verdelin] who were trying to control me, after having driven me by weight of intrigue from Switzerland, where I was not sufficiently in their power, finally managed to deliver me over to their friend [David Hume]. * * *

Reactions to Rousseau

Collected in this section are writings by Rousseau's contemporaries and successors which offer varied perspectives on his life and work. These readings also shed light on Rousseau the person and expose the framework within which debate on Rousseau's politics was originally set.

FRANÇOIS MARIE AROUET DE VOLTAIRE

1694–1778

Voltaire was a prolific, witty, and stylish writer best known for the short novel *Candide* (1759). The early correspondence between Rousseau and Voltaire dating from around 1745 is full of mutual admiration. In the end, however, their friendship could not withstand their intellectual differences, Rousseau's feelings of persecution, and friends who constantly helped poison the minds of the two men against each other. After their bitter quarrel over the significance of the earthquake in Lisbon in 1755, their estrangement deepened. Once Voltaire became convinced that Rousseau had betrayed the cause of the *philosophes*, he began to write against Rousseau and his works, and his assessments were sometimes brutally critical.

The famous letter satirizing the *Discourses*, which is quoted below, reveals Voltaire's dissatisfaction with Rousseau's condemnation of civilization. Still, it is less rancorous than later letters would be. Much of this letter is actually devoted to the ways in which original thinkers have always been persecuted.

* * *

To Jean-Jacques Rousseau. Les Délices, near Geneva. August 30,
1755.

I have received your new book against the human race.[1] I thank you for it. You will please mankind to whom you tell a few homely truths but you will not correct it. You depict with very true colors the horrors of human society which out of ignorance and weakness sets its hopes on so many comforts. Never has so much wit been used in an attempt to make us like animals.

1. François Marie Arouet de Voltaire, *The Selected Letters of Voltaire*, trans. and ed. Richard A. Brooks (New York: New York Univ. Press, 1973), pp. 179–81.

The desire to walk on all fours seizes one when one reads your work. However, as I lost that habit more than sixty years ago, I unfortunately sense the impossibility of going back to it, and I abandon that natural gait to those who are worthier of it than you and I. Nor can I embark on a search for the savages of Canada, first because the maladies to which I have been condemned make me require a European doctor; secondly, because warfare has reached that country and the example of our nations has made the savages almost as wicked as we. I confine myself to being a peaceful savage in the solitude I have chosen near your homeland where you ought to be.

I agree with you that literature and the sciences have sometimes caused great harm.

The enemies of Tasso made his life a series of misfortunes; those of Galileo made him suffer in prisons at the age of seventy for recognizing the earth's motion and even more shameful was their compelling him to issue a retraction.

As soon as your friends began the *Encyclopedic Dictionary*, those who dared compete with them called them deists, atheists, and even Jansenists. If I ventured to include myself among those whose works have only been rewarded with persecution, I would show you a bunch of wretches eager to bring about my ruin from the day I first presented the tragedy of *Oedipus*; a library of ridiculous slander printed against me; a former Jesuit priest whom I had saved from capital punishment repaying me with slanderous satires for the service I had rendered him; a man even guiltier having my work on the *Age of Louis XIV* printed with notes in which the most shameless of deceptions are spouted in the crassest ignorance; another man selling a book dealer a so-called universal history under my name, and the book dealer greedy and stupid enough to print this shapeless tissue of blunders, false dates, facts, and mangled names; and finally, men cowardly and wicked enough to attribute that rhapsody to me. I would show you society infected by this new breed of men unknown to all of antiquity who, incapable of embracing an honest profession either as lackeys or as laborers but unfortunately able to read and write, become brokers of literature, steal manuscripts, and disfigure and sell them. I could complain that a jest written over thirty years ago on the same subject which Chapelain was silly enough to treat seriously, is now being circulated because of the faithlessness and infamous avarice of those wretches who have disfigured it with as much stupidity as malice and who, after thirty years, are selling that work (which is certainly no longer my own and has become theirs) everywhere; I would add lastly that they have dared rummage through the most respectable archives and steal a part of the memoirs I had deposited when I was historiographer of France and that they sold the product of my work to a Paris book dealer. I would depict to you ingratitude, deception, and pillage pursuing me to the foot of the Alps and even to the edges of my grave.

But also admit that these thorns attached to literature and to one's good name are but flowers compared to the other ills which have always flooded the earth. Admit that neither Cicero, Lucretius, Virgil, nor Horace were responsible for the banishment of Marius, of Scylla, of that libertine Anthony, of that imbecile Lepidus, of that uncourageous tyrant Octavius Cepias who has been nicknamed, in so cowardly a fashion, Augustus.

Admit that the bantering of Marot did not bring about St. Bartholomew's Day and that the tragedy of the *Cid* did not cause the wars of the Fronde. Great crimes have only been committed by celebrated ignoramuses. What makes and will always make of this world a valley of tears is the insatiable and indomitable pride of men, starting with Thamas Couli Can[2] who could not read and write up to the customs official capable of only making calculations. Literature nourishes the soul, rectifies it, consoles it, and it is even responsible for your glory as you write in opposition to it. You are like Achilles who flew into a passion against glory and like Father Malebranche whose brilliant imagination wrote against imagination.

M. Chapius informs me that your health is quite poor. You ought to come and restore it in the native air, enjoy freedom, drink with me the milk of our cows, and graze on our grass. I am, very philosophically and with the most affectionate esteem, your very humble and very obedient servant.

Voltaire

[In the following letter, Voltaire praises De Montenoy's play *Les Philosophes (The Philosophers)*, in which the actor Preville amused the Parisian theatre audience by coming on stage on all fours to satirize the person and philosophy of Rousseau.]

*   *   *

To Charles Palissot de Montenoy. Les Délices. June 4, 1760.

I thank you for your letter and your work.[3] Please get ready for a long reply; old men like to babble a little.

I will begin by telling you that I consider your play well written. I even imagine that the philosopher Crispin walking on all fours must have created considerable merriment, and I believe that my friend Jean-Jacques will be the first to laugh. This is gay, not at all malicious, and besides since the citizen of Geneva is guilty of treason against the theatre, it is quite natural for the theatre to give him his just desserts. * * *

2. Nadir Shah (1668–1747) was Shah of Persia   3. *Op. cit.*, p. 211.
1736–47.

[The conflict between Voltaire and Rousseau escalates.]

To Jean Le Rond D'Alembert. June 17, 1762.[4]

Excessive pride and envy have destroyed Jean-Jacques, my illustrious philosopher. That monster dares speak of education! A man who refused to raise any of his sons and put them all in foundling homes! He abandoned his children and the tramp with whom he made them. He has only failed to write against his tramp as he has written against his friends. I will pity him if they hang him, but out of pure humanity, for personally I only consider him like Diogenes's dog or rather like a dog descended from a bastard of that dog. I do not know whether he is abhorred in Paris as he is by all the upright people of Geneva. You may be sure that whoever abandons the *philosophes* will come to an unhappy end. * * *

[Voltaire attacks Rousseau's ideas on equality and government.]

To Louis-François-Armand du Plessis, Duc de Richelieu. Geneva. June 22, 1762.[5]

Sire,

* * * I assure you that although I am in the native city of Jean-Jacques Rousseau, I find that you are so right and I do not share his opinion at all. Only he is mad enough to say that all men are equal and that a state can survive without a hierarchy. He has carried the madness of his paradoxes so far as to say that if a prince were to find the hangman's daughter honest and pretty, he ought to marry her and his marriage ought to be universally approved.

I flatter myself that you make a distinction between Parisian men of letters and this madhouse philosopher. But you know that there is a bit of jealousy in literature as in the other estates. * * *

[In a letter written to Philippe-Antoine de Claris on December 26, 1776, even a rumor of Rousseau's death does not soften Voltaire's attitude. Rousseau actually died in Paris on July 3, 1778, a few weeks after Voltaire's death.]

* * * Jean-Jacques really did the right thing by dying.[6] People claim it is not true that a dog killed him; he recovered from the wounds that his friend the dog had inflicted on him, but it is said that on December 12 he took it into his head to do some climbing in Paris with an old Genevese named Romilly. He ate like a devil and, getting indigestion, he died like a dog. A philosopher is a trifling thing. * * *

---

4. *Ibid.*, pp. 230–31. A mathematician and philosopher, D'Alembert (1717?–1783) along with Diderot (1713–84), was co-editor of the *Encyclopedia*, the principle vehicle of the Enlightenment attack on traditional concepts of religion and philosophy in support of the rationalist approach to the world and human problems.

5. *Ibid.*, p. 231.

6. *Ibid.*, p. 308.

DAVID HUME

1711–1776

A Scottish philosopher of broad scope, most influential for his *Treatise of Human Nature* (1739–40), Hume describes his dispute with Rousseau as "the most critical Affair which, during the Course of my whole Life, I have been engaged in." When Rousseau had found himself under the threat of arrest, Hume offered him refuge. Early letters reveal Hume's genuine concern for the French thinker's welfare and his understanding of Rousseau's personality. The relationship between the two slowly became embittered, however, because Rousseau imagined that he was the victim of a conspiracy in which Hume was the principal villain. Hume was finally provoked into reacting angrily against Rousseau's accusations.

In a letter written from Paris on December 28, 1765, to Rev. Hugh Blair, Hume announces that Rousseau has agreed to come to London. Blair (1718–1800) was a popular preacher, lecturer, and literary critic of the day.

* * *

I must, however, be in London very soon, in order to give an Account of my Commission; to thank the King for his Goodness to me, and to settle the celebrated Rousseau, who has rejected Invitations from half of the Kings and Princes of Europe, in order to put himself under my Protection.[1] He has been at Paris about twelve days; and lives in an Apartment prepard for him by the Prince of Conti, which he says gives him Uneasyness by reason of its Magnificence. As he was outlawd by the Parliament, it behov'd him to have the King's Pass-port, which was at first offerd him under a feignd Name, but his Friends refusd it, because they knew, that he woud not submit even to that Falshood. You have heard that he was banishd from Neuf-chatel by Preachers, who excited the Mob to stone him. He told me, that a Trap was laid for him with as much Art as ever was employ'd against a Fox or a Poll cat. * * * He also told me, that last Spring, when he went about the Mountains, amusing himself with Botany, he came to a Village at some Distance from his own: A Woman met him; who, surpriz'd at his Armenian Dress (for he wears and is resolvd to wear that Habit during life) ask'd him what he was and what was his Name. On hearing it, she exclaimd; Are you that impious Rascal, Rousseau: Had I known it, I shoud have waited for you at the End of the Wood with a Pistol in order to blow out your Brains. He added, that all the Women in Switzerland were in the same Dispositions; because the Preachers had told them, that he had wrote Books to prove that Women had no Souls. * * *

On leaving Neuf-chatel, he took Shelter in a little Island, about half a League in Circumference, in the midst of a Lake near Berne. There livd in it only one German Peasant with his Wife and Sister: The Coun-

1. J. Y. T. Greig, *The Letters of David Hume*, (Oxford: Clarendon Press, 1932), I, pp. 527–30.

cil of Berne, frightend for his Neighbourhood, on account of his democratical, more than his religious Principles, orderd him immediatly to withdraw from their State. * * *

It is impossible to express or imagine the Enthusiasm of this Nation in his favour. As I am suppos'd to have him in my Custody, all the World, especially the great Ladies teaze me to be introduc'd to him: I have had Rouleaus thrust into my hand with earnest Applications, that I woud prevail on him to accept of them. I am perswaded, that were I to open here a Subscription with his Consent, I shoud receive 50,000 Pounds in a fortnight. * * * People may talk of antient Greece as they please; but no Nation was ever so fond of Genius as this; and no Person ever so much engag'd their Attention as Rousseau. Voltaire and every body else, are quite eclipsd by him. I am sensible, that my Connexions with him, add to my Importance at present. Even his Maid, La Vasseur, who is very homely and very awkward, is more talkd of than the Princess of Monaco or the Countess of Egmont, on account of her Fidelity and Attachment towards him. His very Dog, who is no better than a Coly, has a Name and Reputation in the World.

As to my Intercourse with him, I find him mild, and gentle, and modest, and good humoured; and he has more the Behaviour of a Man of the World, than any of the Learned here, except M. de Buffon who in his Figure and Air and Deportment, answers your Idea of a Marechal of France, rather than that of a Philosopher. M. Rousseau is of a small Stature, and wou'd rather be ugly, had he not the finest Physiognomy in the World, I mean, the most expressive Countenance. His Modesty seems not to be good Manners; but Ignorance of his own Excellence: As he writes, and speaks, and acts, from the Impulse of Genius, more than from the Use of his ordinary Faculties, it is very likely that he forgets its Force, whenever it is laid asleep. I am well assurd, that at times he believes he has Inspirations from an immediate Communication with the Divinity. He falls sometimes into Ecstacies, which retain him in the same Posture for Hours together. Does not this Example solve the Difficulty of Socrates's Genius, and of his Ecstacies? I think Rousseau in many things very much resembles Socrates. The Philosopher of Geneva seems only to have more Genius than he of Athens, who never wrote any thing, and less Sociableness and Temper.

*　　*　　*

[Hume wrote to John Home of Hinewells on March 22, 1766, giving some of his firsthand insights into Rousseau's personality.]

*　　*　　*

Rousseau left me four days ago. He goes to live in a House of Mr Davenport, a worthy Gentleman of 5 or 6000 pounds a year, who gives him one of his houses in Derbyshire, in which he himself seldom lives, and takes 30 pounds a Year of board for him and his Gouvernante.[2]

2. *Ibid.*, II. 26–7.

Surely Rousseau is one of the most singular of all human Beings, and one of the most unhappy. His extreme Sensibility of Temper is his Torment; as he is much more susceptible of Pain than Pleasure. His Aversion to Society is not Affectation as is commonly believd: When in it, he is commonly very amiable, but often very unhappy. And tho' he be also unhappy in Solitude, he prefers that Species of suffering to the other. He is surely a very fine Genius: And of all the Writers that are or ever were in Europe, he is the man who has acquird the most enthusiastic and most passionate Admirers. I have seen many extraordinary Scenes of this Nature. He sat for his Picture at my Desire. * * *

[Another letter to Blair, dated March 25, 1766, gives some additional insights into Rousseau's personality and the ambiguous English attitudes towards his works.]

* * * I think [The New Héloïse] his Master-piece; tho' he himself told me, that he valu'd most his Contrat sociale; which is as preposterous a Judgement as that of Milton, who preferd the Paradise regaind to all his other Performances.[3] * * *

I now understand perfectly his Aversion to company, which appears so surprizing in a Man well qualify'd for the Entertainment of Company, and which the greatest Part of the World takes for Affectation. He has frequent and long Fits of the Spleen, from the State of his Mind or Body, call it which you please, and from his extreme Sensibility of Temper. During that Disposition, Company is a Torment to him. When his Spirits and Health & good Humour return, his Fancy affords him so much & such agreeable Occupation that to call him off from it gives him Uneasyness; and even the writing of Books, he tells me, as it limits and restrains his Fancy to one Subject, is not an agreeable Entertainment. He never will write any more; and never shou'd have wrote at all, coud he have slept a nights. But he lies awake commonly, and to keep himself from tiring he usually compos'd something which he wrote down when he arose. He assures me, that he composes very slowly and with great Labour and Difficulty.

He is naturally very modest, and even ignorant of his own Superiority: His Fire, which frequently rises in Conversation, is gentle and temperate; he is never, in the least, arrogant & domineering, and is indeed one of the best bred Men I ever knew. * * *

*   *   *

[Rousseau suspected Hume of joining Voltaire and others in trying to dishonor him. His main accusation against Hume seems to be that his Scottish host tried to make him comfortable and obtain a pension for him. By the time Hume writes this letter to Richard Davenport on July 8, 1766, he has become quite angry and hurt over Rousseau's odd behavior and ingratitude.]

3. Ibid., pp. 28–31.

Dear Sir

I am favour'd with yours of the 6th Instant; but not a Word from Rousseau, nor indeed do I expect to hear from him.[4] I see, that this whole Affair is a Complication of Wickedness and Madness; and you may believe, I repent heartily, that I ever had any Connexions with so pernicious and dangerous a Man. He has evidently been all along courting, from Ostentation, an Opportunity of refusing a Pension from the King, and at the same time, of picking a Quarrel with me, in order to cancel at once all his past Obligations to me. The worst is, that I am detain'd in Town by this foolish Affair, to which there is no Prospect of an Issue. For as it is utterly impossible for him, even by the utmost License of Lying, in which he seems very little scrupulous, to give the smallest and most distant Reason for his Quarrel, I presume he will never write me at all. Cou'd I therefore encroach so far on your Goodness as to desire you, if you think proper, to suggest to him, that I am impatient to have an Answer. I also repeat my Request to have, if possible, Copies of all my Letters to him since he left London. I cannot sufficiently express my Satisfaction in your Conduct, and my Vexation at the Uneasiness this Affair must have given you.

[This excerpt is from another letter to Richard Davenport, dated July 15, 1766.]

Dear Sir

I receiv'd to day a Letter from Rousseau, which is as long as wou'd make a two Shillings Pamphlet; and I fancy he intends to publish it.[5] It is a perfect Frenzy. He says, that M. d'Alembert, Horace Walpole and I had entered into a Conspiracy to ruin him, and have ruined him. He says, that his first suspicions arose in France, while we lay in two beds in the same room of an Inn. There I talked in my Sleep, and betrayed my bad Intentions against him. * * * I am really sorry for him; so that, tho' I intended to be very severe on him in my Answer, I have been very sparing; as you may see. I wou'd not, however, have you imagine that he has such an extreme Sensibility as he pretends. He wrote to General Conway, that he was oppress'd with such a grievous Calamity as deprivd him of the Use of his Senses and Understanding: This was about the time of your first Arrival at Wootton; when you wrote me, that he was perfectly gay, good-humourd and sociable: So that these Complaints of his Misery and Sufferings are a mere Artifice. I find in many other Respects that he lies like the Devil: You cannot imagine what a false and malicious Account he has the Assurance to give me of the Transaction between him and me the last Evening he was in Town, which I related to you. I am afraid indeed you have a very bad Pennyworth of him; but if I may venture to give my Advice, it is, that you wou'd continue the charitable Work you have begun, till he be shut up altogether in Bedlam, or till

4. Raymond Klibansky and Ernest C. Mossner, *New Letters of David Hume* (Oxford: The Claren- don Press, 1954), pp. 134–35.
5. *Ibid.*, pp. 142–43.

he quarrel with you and run away from you. If he show any Disposition to write me a penitential Letter, you may encourage it; not that I think it of any Consequence to me, but because it will ease his Mind and set him at rest.* * *

JAMES BOSWELL (1740–1795) AND SAMUEL JOHNSON (1709–1784)

James Boswell was a Scot, who, like many of his contemporaries, developed the habit of keeping a journal early in life. He became acquainted with Dr. Samuel Johnson during one of his sojourns in London, and their friendship became one of the most important events in his otherwise rather unhappy life. His *Life of Samuel Johnson* (1791) grew out of his journals and is considered the greatest of English biographies. It is composed year by year in "Scenes" which narrate events, describe Johnson's works, cite letters (primarily by Johnson), and depict various encounters and conversations. As a whole, the biography emphasizes Johnson's role as moralist, arbiter of taste, and professional author.

Samuel Johnson, the great English literary critic, is also known for his essays, *The Rambler*, A *Dictionary of the English Language*, and *Lives of the Poets*. He is recognized as the last spokesman for classical values in eighteenth-century England. Far from sympathetic to the newest literary trends of his day, Johnson particularly disliked the cult of primitivism that was becoming fashionable. He pronounced Rousseau's defense of primitive life a ridiculous search for novelty and the unique or particular, which could not withstand the test of experience.

In the first passage from Boswell's *Life*, Johnson reacts to Rousseau's complaints in the *Discourse on Inequality* about the inequities of social life. This conversation took place on the evening of July 20, 1763, when Boswell had invited his uncle, Dr. Boswell, Johnson, and a Mr. Dempster to dine with him.

* * *

Rousseau's treatise on the inequality of mankind was at this time a fashionable topic.[1] It gave rise to an observation by Mr. Dempster, that the advantages of fortune and rank were nothing to a wise man, who ought to value only merit. JOHNSON. "If a man were a savage, living in the woods by himself, this might be true; but in civilised society we all depend upon each other, and our happiness is very much owing to the good opinion of mankind. Now, Sir, in civilised society, external advantages make us more respected. A man with a good coat upon his back meets with a better reception than he who has a bad one. Sir, you may analyse this, and say, What is there in it? But that will avail you nothing, for it is a part of a general system. Pound St. Paul's church into

1. James Boswell, *The Life of Samuel Johnson LLD*, (London: John Murray, 1831), II. 224–28.

atoms, and consider any single atom; it is, to be sure, good for nothing: but, put all these atoms together, and you have St. Paul's church. So it is with human felicity, which is made up of many ingredients, each of which may be shown to be very insignificant. In civilised society, personal merit will not serve you so much as money will. Sir, you may make the experiment. Go into the street, and give one man a lecture on morality, and another a shilling, and see which will respect you most. If you wish only to support nature, Sir, William Petty fixes your allowance at three pounds a year; but as times are much altered, let us call it six pounds. This sum will fill your belly, shelter you from the weather, and even get you a strong lasting coat, supposing it to be made of good bull's hide. Now, Sir, all beyond this is artificial, and is desired in order to obtain a greater degree of respect from our fellow creatures. And, Sir, if six hundred pounds a year procure a man more consequence, and, of course, more happiness, than six pounds a year, the same proportion will hold as to six thousand, and so on, as far as opulence can be carried. Perhaps he who has a large fortune may not be so happy as he who has a small one; but that must proceed from other causes than from his having the large fortune: for, *coeteris paribus*, he who is rich, jn civilized society, must be happier than he who is poor; as riches, if properly used, (and it is a man's own fault if they are not,) must be productive of the highest advantages. Money, to be sure, of itself is of no use; for its only use is to part with it. Rousseau, and all those who deal in paradoxes, are led away by a childish desire of novelty. When I was a boy, I used always to choose the wrong side of a debate, because most ingenious things, that is to say, most new things, could be said upon it. Sir, there is nothing for which you may not muster up more plausible arguments, than those which are urged against wealth and other external advantages. Why, now, there is stealing; why should it be thought a crime? When we consider by what unjust methods property has been often acquired, and that what was unjustly got it must be unjust to keep, where is the harm in one man's taking the property of another from him? Besides, Sir, when we consider the bad use that many people make of their property, and how much better use the thief may make of it, it may be defended as a very allowable practice. Yet, Sir, the experience of mankind has discovered stealing to be so very bad a thing, that they make no scruple to hang a man for it. When I was running about this town a very poor fellow, I was a greater arguer for the advantages of poverty; but I was, at the same time, very sorry to be poor. Sir, all the arguments which are brought to represent poverty as no evil, shew it to be evidently a great evil. You never find people labouring to convince you that you may live very happily upon a plentiful fortune. So you hear people talking how miserable a king must be; and yet they all wish to be in his place.

* * *

Mr. Dempster having endeavoured to maintain that intrinsic merit *ought* to make the only distinction amongst mankind. JOHNSON. "Why,

Sir, mankind have found that this cannot be. How shall we determine the proportion of intrinsic merit? Were that to be the only distinction amongst mankind, we should soon quarrel about the degrees of it. Were all distinctions abolished, the strongest would not long acquiesce, but would endeavour to obtain a superiority by their bodily strength. But, Sir, as subordination is very necessary for society, and contentions for superiority very dangerous, mankind, that is to say, all civilized nations, have settled it upon a plain invariable principle. A man is born to hereditary rank; or his being appointed to certain offices gives him a certain rank. Subordination tends greatly to human happiness. Were we all upon an equality, we should have no other enjoyment than mere animal pleasure."

I said, I consider distinction of rank to be of so much importance in civilized society, that if I were asked on the same day to dine with the first Duke in England, and with the first man in Britain for genius, I should hesitate which to prefer. JOHNSON. "To be sure, Sir, if you were to dine only once, and it were never to be known where you dined, you would choose rather to dine with the first man for genius; but to gain most respect, you should dine with the first duke in England. For nine people in ten that you meet with, would have a higher opinion of you for having dined with a duke; and the great genius himself would receive you better, because you had been with the great duke."

He took care to guard himself against any possible suspicion that his settled principles of reverence for rank, and respect for wealth, were at all owing to mean or interested motives; for he asserted his own independence as a literary man. * * *

*   *   *

[Boswell introduced his friend Rev. Temple to Dr. Johnson when they met at the Mitre on Saturday, February 15, 1766. Boswell mentions the visit he paid to Rousseau on the continent in 1763–64. Johnson and Boswell provide differing perspectives on the French writer, whose views on religion had, by this time, been officially condemned in Paris and Geneva, causing him to seek the refuge in England offered by David Hume.]

*   *   *

Our next meeting at the Mitre was on Saturday the 15th of February, when I presented to him my old and most intimate friend, the Rev. Mr. Temple, then of Cambridge.[2] I having mentioned that I had passed some time with Rousseau in his wild retreat, and having quoted some remark made by Mr. Wilkes, with whom I had spend many pleasant hours in Italy, Johnson said, sarcastically, "It seems, Sir, you have kept very good company abroad, —Rousseau and Wilkes!" Thinking it enough to defend one at a time, I said nothing as to my gay friend, but answered with a smile, "My dear Sir, you don't call Rousseau bad company. Do you really think *him* a bad man?" JOHNSON. "Sir, if you are talking

2. *Ibid.*, pp. 314–15.

jestingly of this, I don't talk with you. If you mean to be serious, I think him one of the worst of men; a rascal, who ought to be hunted out of society, as he has been. Three or four nations have expelled him: and it is a shame that he is protected in this country." BOSWELL. "I don't deny, Sir, but that his novel *[Émile]* may, perhaps do harm; but I cannot think his intention was bad." JOHNSON. "Sir, that will not do. We cannot prove any man's intention to be bad. You may shoot a man through his head, and say you intended to miss him; but the judge will order you to be hanged. An alleged want of intention, when evil is committed, will not be allowed in a court of justice. Rousseau, Sir, is a very bad man. I would sooner sign a sentence for his transportation, than that of any felon who has gone from the Old Bailey these many years. Yes, I should like to have him work in the plantations." BOSWELL. "Sir, do you think him as bad a man as Voltaire? JOHNSON. "Why, sir, it is difficult to settle the proportion of iniquity between them."

This violence seemed very strange to me, who had read many of Rousseau's animated writings with great pleasure, and even edification; had been much pleased with his society, and was just come from the continent, where he was very generally admired. Nor can I yet allow that he deserves the very severe censure which Johnson pronounced upon him. His absurd preference of savage to civilised life, and other singularities, are proofs rather of a defect in his understanding, than of any depravity in his heart. * * *

* * *

[While dining together on Saturday, September 30, 1769, Boswell and Johnson discuss the quality of savage life as depicted in the *Discourse on Inequality*, and Johnson declares that Rousseau was simply trying to shock his audience, all the while knowing that he was talking nonsense.]

* * *

On the 30th of September we dined together at the Mitre.[3] I attempted to argue for the superior happiness of the savage life, upon the usual fanciful topics. JOHNSON. "Sir, there can be nothing more false. The savages have no bodily advantages beyond those of civilised men. They have not better health; and as to care or mental uneasiness, they are not above it, but below it, like bears. No Sir; you are not to talk such paradox; let me have no more on't. It cannot entertain, far less can it instruct. Lord Monboddo, one of your Scotch judges, talked a great deal of such nonsense. I suffered *him*; but I will not suffer *you*. BOSWELL. "But, Sir, does not Rousseau talk such nonsense?" JOHNSON. "True, Sir; but Rousseau *knows* he is talking nonsense, and laughs at the world for staring at him." BOSWELL. "How so, Sir?" JOHNSON. "Why, Sir, a man who talks nonsense so well, must know that he is talking nonsense. But I am *afraid* (chuckling and laughing), Monboddo does *not* know that he is talking nonsense." BOSWELL. "Is it wrong then, Sir, to affect

3. *Ibid.*, III. 73–74.

singularity, in order to make people stare?" JOHNSON. "Yes, if you do it by propagating error: and, indeed, it is wrong in any way. There is in human nature a general inclination to make people stare; and every wise man has himself to cure of it, and does cure himself. * * *

GIACOMO CASANOVA

1725–1798

Despite his involvement in political and amorous scandals, Casanova's wit and charm gained him access to many of Europe's most famous and powerful men and women. He dabbled in poetry and drama, but his greatest work is his autobiography *Mémoires (History of My Life)*, notable for its easy hedonism, creation of a living myth, and overall depiction of eighteenth-century society. Upon its publication in 1821, the book became an international bestseller. In the passage below, Casanova describes a meeting with Rousseau in the summer of 1759 and recounts a story that illustrates Rousseau's sometimes peculiar behavior.

*   *   *

About this time Madame d'Urfé took a fancy to make the acquaintance of J. J. Rousseau; we went to Montmorency to visit him, taking some music, which he copied wonderfully well.[1] People paid him twice as much as they would have paid another copyist, but he guaranteed that there would be no errors. It was the way he made his living.

We found a man who reasoned well, whose manner was simple and modest, but who was entirely undistinguished either in his person or his wit. We did not find what is called a pleasant man. We thought him rather impolite, and it took no more for Madame d'Urfé to set him down as vulgar. We saw a woman of whom we had already heard. She scarcely looked at us. We went back to Paris laughing at the philosopher's eccentricity. But here is a faithful account of a visit paid him by the Prince of Conti, father of the Prince who was then known as the Count of La Marche.

The charming Prince goes to Montmorency by himself, on purpose to spend a pleasant day talking with the philosopher, who was already famous. He finds him in the park, he accosts him and says he has come to dine and spend the day with him in unconstrained conversation.

"Your Highness will eat poor fare; I will go and order another place set."

He goes, he comes back, and after spending two or three hours walking with the Prince he conducts him to the room in which they are to dine. The Prince, seeing three places laid:

1. Giacomo Casanova, *History of My Life*, trans. Willard R. Trask (New York: Harcourt, Brace & World, Inc., 1968), V. 223–24.

"Who," he said, "is the third person with whom you want me to dine? I thought we should dine alone together?"

"The third person, Monseigneur, is another myself. It is a being who is neither my wife nor my mistress nor my servant nor my mother nor my daughter; and she is all those."

"I believe it, my dear friend; but since I came here only to dine with you, I will leave you to dine with all those other selves. Good-by."

Such are the absurdities of philosophers when, trying to be remarkable, they only succeed in being eccentric. The woman was Mademoiselle Levasseur, whom he had honored with his name, except for one letter of it, under the mask of an anagram. * * *

ADAM SMITH

1723–1790

Smith, the first systematic defender of a free market economy in the *Wealth of Nations* (1776), was also a legendary absent-minded professor of moral philosophy at the University of Glasgow in Scotland. In the following letter to the editor of the *Edinburgh Review*, published in 1756, Smith praises Rousseau's *Discourse on Inequality*, by comparing it favorably to Bernard de Mandeville's *Fable of the Bees*.

* * *

The original and inventive genius of the English has not only discovered itself in natural philosophy, but in morals, metaphysics, and part of the abstract sciences.[1] Whatever attempts have been made in modern times towards improvement in this contentious and unprosperous philosophy, beyond what the ancients have left us, have been made in England. The Meditations of Des Cartes excepted, I know nothing in French that aims at being original upon these subjects. * * * This branch of English philosophy, which seems now to be intirely neglected by the English themselves, has of late been transported into France. I observe some traces of it, not only in the Encyclopedia, but in the Theory of agreeable sentiments by Mr. De Pouilly, a work that is in many respects original; and above all, in the late Discourse upon the origin and foundation of the inequality amongst mankind by Mr. Rousseau of Geneva.

Whoever reads this last work with attention, will observe, that the second volume of the Fable of the Bees[2] has given occasion to the system of Mr. Rousseau, in whom however the principles of the English author are softened, improved, and embellished, and stript of all that tendency to corruption and licentiousness which has disgraced them in

---

1. Adam Smith, *Essays on Philosophical Subjects*, eds. W. P. D. Wightman and J. C. Bryce (Oxford: The Clarendon Press, 1980), pp. 249–51.

2. Bernard de Mandeville (1670–1733) was an Anglo-Dutch philosopher whose *Fable of the Bees, or Private Vices Public Benefits* first appeared in London in 1723. Rousseau cites Mandeville's work in the *Discourse on Inequality*. See pp. 28–29.

their original author. Dr. Mandeville represents the primitive state of mankind as the most wretched and miserable that can be imagined: Mr. Rousseau, on the contrary, paints it as the happiest and most suitable to his nature. Both of them however suppose, that there is in man no powerful instinct which necessarily determines him to seek society for its own sake; but according to the one, the misery of his original state compelled him to have recourse to this otherwise disagreeable remedy; according to the other, some unfortunate accidents having given birth to the unnatural passions of ambition and the vain desire of superiority, to which he had before been a stranger, produced the same fatal effect. Both of them suppose the same slow progress and gradual development of all the talents, habits, and arts which fit men to live together in society, and they both describe this progress pretty much in the same manner. According to both, those laws of justice, which maintain the present inequality amongst mankind, were originally the inventions of the cunning and the powerful, in order to maintain or to acquire an unnatural and unjust superiority over the rest of their fellow-creatures. Mr. Rousseau however criticises upon Dr. Mandeville: he observes, that *pity*, the only amiable principle which the English author allows to be natural to man, is capable of producing all those virtues, whose reality Dr. Mandeville denies. Mr. Rousseau at the same time seems to think, that this principle is in itself no virtue, but that it is possessed by savages and by the most profligate of the vulgar, in a greater degree of perfection than by those of the most polished and cultivated manners; in which he perfectly agrees with the English author.

The life of a savage, when we take a distant view of it, seems to be a life either of profound indolence, or of great and astonishing adventures; and both these qualities serve to render the description of it agreeable to the imagination. The passion of all young people for pastoral poetry, which describes the amusements of the indolent life of a shepherd; and for books of chivalry and romance, which describe the most dangerous and extravagant adventures, is the effect of this natural taste for these two seemingly inconsistent objects. In the descriptions of the manners of savages, we expect to meet with both these: and no author ever proposed to treat of this subject who did not excite the public curiosity. Mr. Rousseau, intending to paint the savage life as the happiest of any, presents only the indolent side of it to view, which he exhibits indeed with the most beautiful and agreeable colours, in a style, which, tho' laboured and studiously elegant, is every where sufficiently nervous, and sometimes even sublime and pathetic. It is by the help of this style, together with a little philosophical chemistry, that the principles and ideas of the profligate Mandeville seem in him to have all the purity and sublimity of the morals of Plato, and to be only the true spirit of a republican carried a little too far. * * *

THOMAS PAINE

1737–1809

Paine is renowned for his spirited vindications of the American and French Revolutions in such controversial works as *The Rights of Man* (1791–92), which caused its author to be charged with sedition by the English government. In the following he enlists Rousseau in the ranks of writers who paved the way for the revolutionary awakening of France.

* * *

The despotism of Louis XIV, united with the gaiety of his court, and the gaudy ostentation of his character, had so humbled, and at the same time so fascinated the mind of France, that the people appear to have lost all sense of their own dignity, in contemplating that of their Grand Monarch: and the whole reign of Louis XV, remarkable only for weakness and effeminacy, made no other alteration than that of spreading a sort of lethargy over the nation, from which it showed no disposition to rise.[1]

The only signs which appeared of the spirit of liberty during those periods, are to be found in the writings of the French philosophers. Montesquieu, President of the Parliament of Bordeaux, went as far as a writer under a despotic government could well proceed: and being obliged to divide himself between principle and prudence, his mind often appears under a veil, and we ought to give him credit for more than he has expressed.

Voltaire, who was both the flatterer and satirist of despotism, took another line. His forte lay in exposing and ridiculing the superstitions which priestcraft, united with statecraft, had interwoven with governments.

It was not from the purity of his principles, or his love of mankind (for satire and philanthropy are not naturally concordant), but from his strong capacity of seeing folly in its true shape, and his irresistible propensity to expose it, that he made those attacks. They were however as formidable as if the motives had been virtuous; and he merits the thanks rather than the esteem of mankind.

On the contrary, we find in the writings of Rousseau and the Abbé Raynal, a loveliness of sentiment in favor of liberty, that excites respect, and elevates the human faculties; but having raised his animation, they do not direct its operations, but leave the mind in love with an object, without describing the means of possessing it.

* * *

But all those writings and many others had their weight; and by the different manner in which they treated the subject of government—

1. Thomas Paine, *The Rights of Man* in *The Complete Writings of Thomas Paine*, ed. Philip S. Foner (New York: The Citadel Press, 1945), I. 298–99.

Montesquieu by his judgment and knowledge of laws, Voltaire by his wit, Rousseau and Raynal by their animation, and Quesnay and Turgot by their moral maxims and systems of economy, readers of every class met with something to their taste, and a spirit of political inquiry began to diffuse itself through the nation at the time the dispute between England and the then colonies of America broke out. * * *

IMMANUEL KANT

1724–1804

Immanuel Kant, a German professor of philosophy, was the first to criticize systematically the Enlightenment's unbounded faith in reason. His *Critique of Pure Reason* (1781) explores the workings of speculative thought in order to identify its scope and limits. Kant then turned to ethics and drew out the implications for human conduct of his analysis of reason. Rousseau's imaginative portrayal of man's hidden nature inspired Kant by directing his attention to the realm of inner experience. In Book I, chapter 8 of *On Social Contract* Rousseau had made liberty depend on self-legislation. Kant extended Rousseau's idea by making morality depend on obedience to universally applicable self-imposed rules.

The following excerpts are occasional remarks about Rousseau's influence which Kant inserted into the manuscript of *Observations on the Feeling of the Beautiful and the Sublime* (1764).

* * * Rousseau proceeds synthetically, and begins with the natural man; I proceed analytically, and begin with the moral man.[1] However the heart of man may be constituted, our only question here is, whether the state of nature or of the civilized world develops more real sins and more facility to sin. The moral evil can be so muffled that only lack of greater purity, but never a positive vice, exhibits itself in actions (he is not necessarily vicious who is not holy); on the other hand, positive vice can be so developed as to become abhorrent. The simple man has little temptation to become vicious; it is luxury alone which is very attractive, and when the taste for luxury is already very great, the respect for moral sensibility and for the understanding cannot restrain one.

*   *   *

I am an investigator by inclination. I feel a great thirst for knowledge and an impatient eagerness to advance, also satisfaction at each progressive step. There was a time when I thought that all this could constitute

1. All these observations are from Immanuel Kant, *Fragmente aus dem Nachlässe*, in vol. VIII of *Immanuel Kant's Sämmtliche Werke*, ed. G. Hartenstein (Leipzig: Leopold Voss, 1868), pp. 618, 624, 630. The translation of the first two excerpts is taken from Edward Franklin Buchner, *The Edu-cational Theory of Immanuel Kant* (1904; rpt. New York: AMS Press, 1971), pp. 230–31, 236; the other two are translated in Ernst Cassirer, *Kant's Life and Thought*, trans. James Haden (New Haven: Yale Univ. Press, 1981), pp. 88–89.

the honor of humanity, and I despised the mob, which knows nothing about it. Rousseau set me straight. This dazzling excellence vanishes; I learn to honor men, and would consider myself much less useful than common laborers if I did not believe that this consideration could give all the others a value, to establish the rights of humanity.

* * *

I must read Rousseau until the beauty of expression no longer moves me, and then I can look at him rationally.

* * *

The first impression which the reader who is not merely reading idly and passing time gets from the writings of J. J. Rousseau is that he is in the presence of an uncommonly acute mind, a noble sweep of genius, and a soul filled with a degree of feeling so high as to have been possessed all together by no other author, of whatever age or nationality. The succeeding impression is astonishment at the peculiar and nonsensical notions, so opposed to what is generally current, so that it readily occurs to one that the author, by his extraordinary talents and the sorcery of his eloquence, wanted to display himself as an eccentric fellow, who surpasses all his intellectual competitors through bewitching and startling novelty.

* * *

Newton first saw order and lawfulness going hand in hand with great simplicity, where prior to him disorder and its troublesome partner, multiplicity, were encountered, and ever since the comets run in geometrical paths.

Rousseau first discovered amid the manifold human forms the deeply hidden nature of man, and the secret law by which Providence is justified through his observations.

JOSEPH DE MAISTRE

1753–1821

Born in Savoy, de Maistre became a leading French spokesman for the ultra-Catholic counterrevolution. During the Revolution he emigrated, ultimately to Russia, where he remained until 1817 to write the many works, such as *The Saint Petersburg Dialogues*, which were acclaimed by a Europe disillusioned with revolution. De Maistre was a true reactionary who wanted to return to a feudal past. He abhorred the Revolution and the ideas of those, such as his arch-villain Rousseau, who he thought had caused it. In his works he condemns these ideas forcefully as contrary to human nature, social order, and divine command.

The following excerpts come from his *Study on Sovereignty* (c. 1796) and

The Pope (1819). Here de Maistre disputes Rousseau's philosophical analysis of the nature of man in the *Discourse* and the origin of the social order in *On Social Contract*. He also attacks Rousseau for certain inconsistencies in his ideas of the lawgiver and his attitude toward democracy.

* * *

Rousseau and all the thinkers of his stamp imagine or try to imagine a people *in the state of nature* (this is their expression), deliberating formally on the advantages and disadvantages of the social state and finally deciding to pass from one to the other.[1] But there is not a grain of common sense in this idea. What were these men like before the *national convention* in which they finally decided to find themselves a sovereign? Apparently they lived without laws and government; but for how long?

It is a basic mistake to represent the social state as an optional state based on human consent, on deliberation and on an original contract, something which is an impossibility. To talk of a state of *nature* in opposition to the social state is to talk nonsense voluntarily. The word *nature* is one of those general terms which, like all abstract terms, are open to abuse. In its most extensive sense, this word really signifies only the totality of all the laws, power, and springs of action that *make up* the world, and the *particular* nature of such and such a being is the totality of all the qualities which make it what it is and without which it would be some other thing and could no longer fulfill the intentions of its creator. Thus the combination of all the parts which make up a machine intended to tell the time forms the *nature* or the essence of a *watch*; and the *nature* or essence of the *balance wheel* is to have such and such a form, dimensions, and position, otherwise it would no longer be a balance wheel and could not fulfill its functions. The *nature* of a viper is to crawl, to have a scaly skin, hollow and movable fangs which exude poisonous venom; and the *nature* of man is to be a cognitive, religious, and sociable animal. All experience teaches us this; and, to my knowledge, nothing has contradicted this experience. If someone wants to prove that the nature of the viper is to have wings and a sweet voice, and that of a beaver is to live alone at the top of the highest mountains, it is up to him to prove it. In the meantime, we will believe that what is must be and has always been.

"The social order," says Rousseau, "is a sacred right which is the basis of all others. Yet this right does not come from *nature*: it is therefore founded on convention."[2]

What is *nature*? What is a *right*? And how is an *order* a *right*? But let us leave these difficulties: such questions are endless with a man who misuses every term and defines none. One has the right at least to ask him to prove the big assertion that *the social order does not come from nature.* "I must," he says himself, "establish what I have just advanced."

1. Joseph de Maistre, *The Works of Joseph de Maistre*, trans. and ed. Jack Lively (New York: Macmillan, 1965), pp. 96–97, 101–102, 125, 143–44.

2. *On Social Contract*, Book I, chapter 1.

This is indeed what should be done, but the way in which he goes about it is truly curious. He spends three chapters in proving that the social order does not derive from family society or from force or from slavery (chapters 2, 3, 4) and concludes (chapter 5) *that we must always go back to a first convention.* This method of proof is very useful: it lacked only the majestic formula of the geometers, *"which was to be proved."*

It is also curious that Rousseau has not even tried to prove the one thing that it was necessary to prove; for if the social order derives from nature, there is no social compact.

"Before examining," he says, "the act by which a people chooses a king, it would be as well to examine the act by which a people is a people: for this act, being necessarily previous to the other, is the true foundation of society" (chapter 5). This same Rousseau says elsewhere, "It is the inveterate habit of philosophers to deny what is and to explain what is not."[3] Let us on our side add that it is the inveterate habit of Rousseau to mock the philosopher without suspecting that he also was a *philosopher* in all the force he gave to the word; so, for example, the *Social Contract* denies from beginning to end the nature of man, which *is*, in order to explain the social compact, which *does not exist.*

*   *   *

Rousseau wrote a chapter on *the legislator* in which all the ideas are confused in an intolerable way. In the first place, this word *legislator* can have two different meanings: usage allows us to apply it to the extraordinary men who promulgate constitutional laws, and also to the less remarkable men who pass civil laws. It seems that Rousseau understood the word in the first sense, since he talks of the man "who dares to undertake to institute a people and who constitutes the Republic." But soon after he says that *"the legislator is in all respects an extraordinary man* IN THE STATE." Then there already is a state; the people is then constituted; it is thus no longer a question of *instituting* a people but, more or less, of reforming it. * * *

Rousseau confuses all these ideas, and states in general that the legislator is neither an official nor a sovereign. "His task," he says, "is a superior function that has nothing in common with human rule."[4] If Rousseau means that a private individual can be consulted by a sovereign and can propose good laws which might be accepted, this is one of those truths so trivial and sterile that it is useless to bother with them. If he intends to hold that a sovereign cannot make civil laws, * * * this is a discovery of which he has all the honor, no one ever having suspected it. If he means to prove that a sovereign cannot be a legislator in the strongest sense of the term, and give truly constituent laws to a people, by creating or perfecting their constitutional system, I appeal to the whole history of the world.

*   *   *

3. *The New Héloïse*, part 4.   4. *On Social Contract*, Book II, chapter 7.

* * * Who has ever said worse of democracy than Rousseau, for he declares point-blank that it is made only for a society of Gods.[5] It remains to be seen how a government which is made only for *gods* can yet be proposed to *men* as the only legitimate government, for if this is not the meaning of the social contract, the social contract has no meaning.

But this is not all: "How many things," he says, "difficult to bring together are required by this government. First, a very small state, in which the people can easily assemble, and where each citizen can easily know all the others; second, great simplicity of manners to prevent a multiplicity of problems and difficult discussions; then a high degree of equality in rank and fortune without which equality in rights and authority would not last for long; finally, little or no luxury."

At this point, I shall consider only the first of these conditions. If democracy is suitable only for very small states, how can this form of government be put forward as the only legitimate form of government and as, so to speak, a *formula* capable of resolving all political problems?

* * *

Rousseau is exquisite when he starts his *Social Contract* with the resounding maxim *Man was born free, and everywhere he is in chains*.

What does he mean? Apparently he does not intend to speak of the fact, since in this very phrase he affirms that EVERYWHERE *man is in chains*. Then it is a question of *right*, but this is what is necessary to prove *in opposition to the fact*.

The foolish assertion *Man was born free* is the opposite of the truth. Until the establishment of Christianity, and even until this religion had sufficiently penetrated men's hearts, slavery was everywhere and always considered as a necessary part of the government and the political system of nations, in republics as in monarchies, without it occurring to any philosopher to condemn it or to any legislator to abolish it by a constitutional or other law.

JOHN ADAMS

1735–1826

John Adams had the misfortune to serve as President between the terms of Washington and Jefferson, and to preside over the demise of the Federalist party. His unfortunate reputation as a public figure has overshadowed his renown as a political thinker. Adams was widely read, a prolific writer, and an acute analyst of political events.

Adams's views of society and government were based upon the assumption that man is by nature a social creature who is subject to his passions. To Adams, equality held for the rights and duties incumbent upon mankind,

5. *Ibid.*, Book III, chapter 4.

but not for the distinctions of rank and property. He argued that only mixed
government could insure social stability because its design reflects the natural order of society and the nature of man. Hence, Adams disparaged Rousseau's views about man's natural goodness, the evils of property, and the
general will. In a letter to Thomas Jefferson, written on July 13, 1813, Adams
expresses his impatience with the notion that all men are naturally equal.

* * * Inequalities of mind and body are so established by God Almighty
in his constitution of human nature, that no art or policy can ever plane
them down to a level.[1] I have never read reasoning more absurd, sophistry more gross, in proof of the Athanasian creed, or transubstantiation,
than the subtle labors of Helvetius and Rousseau to demonstrate the
natural equality of mankind. *Jus cuique*, the golden rule, do as you
would be done by, is all the equality than can be supported or defended
by reason or common sense. * * *

[The following excerpt comes from another letter written to Jefferson on July
16, 1814, in which Adams discusses religious and political fanaticism before
turning to Plato and Rousseau and their views on property.]

*   *   *

I am very glad you have seriously read Plato; and still more rejoiced
to find that your reflections upon him so perfectly harmonize with mine.[2]
Some thirty years ago I took upon me the severe task of going through
all his works. With the help of two Latin translations, and one English
and one French translation, and comparing some of the most remarkable passages with the Greek, I labored through the tedious toil. My
disappointment was very great, my astonishment was greater, and my
disgust shocking. Two things only did I learn from him. 1. That Franklin's ideas of exempting husbandmen, and mariners, etc., from the
depredations of war, was borrowed from him. 2. That sneezing is a cure
for the hickups. Accordingly, I have cured myself, and all my friends,
of that provoking disorder, for thirty years, with a pinch of snuff.

Some parts of some of his dialogues are entertaining like the writings
of Rousseau, but his Laws and his Republic, from which I expected
most, disappointed me most.

I could scarcely exclude the suspicion that he intended the latter as a
bitter satire upon all republican government, as Xenophon undoubtedly
designed, by his essay on democracy, to ridicule that species of republic.
In a letter to the learned and ingenious Mr. Taylor, of Hazlewood, I
suggested to him the project of writing a novel, in which the hero should
be sent upon his travels through Plato's republic, and all his adventures,
with his observations on the principles and opinions, the arts and sciences, the manners, customs, and habits of the citizens, should be
recorded. Nothing can be conceived more destructive of human happi-

1. Charles Francis Adams, ed., *The Works of John
Adams, Second President of the United States*
(Boston: Little, Brown and Co., 1856) vol. 10, p.
53.

2. Albert Ellery Bergh, ed., *The Writings of Thomas
Jefferson* (Washington, D.C.: The Thomas Jefferson Memorial Association, 1907), vol. 13, pp. 156–
59.

ness; more infallibly contrived to transform men and women into brutes, Yahoos, or demons, than a community of wives and property. Yet in what are the writings of Rousseau and Helvetius, wiser that those of Plato? The man who first fenced a tobacco yard, and said this is mine, ought instantly to have been put to death, says Rousseau. The man who first pronounced the barbarous word *Dieu*, ought to have been immediately destroyed, says Diderot. In short, philosophers, ancient and modern, appear to me as mad as Hindoos, Mahometans, and Christians. No doubt they would all think me mad, and, for anything I know, this globe may be the Bedlam, *Le Bicatre* of the universe. After all, as long as property exists, it will accumulate in individuals and families. As long as marriage exists, knowledge, property, and influence will accumulate in families. Your and our equal partition of intestate estates, instead of preventing, will, in time, augment the evil, if it is one.

* * *

Nothing seizes the attention of the staring animal so surely as paradox, riddle, mystery, invention, discovery, wonder, temerity. Plato and his disciples, from the fourth-century Christians to Rousseau and Tom Paine, have been fully sensible of this weakness in mankind, and have too successfully grounded upon it their pretensions to fame. * * *

BENJAMIN CONSTANT

1767–1830

A French Swiss, like his fellow countryman Rousseau, Constant made his literary and political career in France. As a liberal member of the Chamber of Deputies during the Restoration, he spurned the theory of divine right as well as that of unlimited popular sovereignty. His *Spirit of Conquest* (1814) examines the new kind of despotism developed by Napoleon which claimed to rest on popular sovereignty. In his *Principles of Politics* (1815), excerpted here, Constant traces this theory of popular sovereignty to Rousseau's *On Social Contract*. Although Constant found Rousseau's defense of rights and liberty laudable, he held that Rousseau's concept of liberty was that of the ancients and could not be adapted to the modern world. He argues here that Rousseau's theories of liberty and popular sovereignty lead only to despotism.

* * *

Certainly, in a society where the people's sovereignty is accepted as a basic principle, no man and no class may subject the others to his or their particular will; but it is not true that society as a whole possesses over its members an unlimited sovereignty.[1]

The generality of citizens constitutes the sovereign in the sense that

1. Benjamin Constant, *The Principles of Politics*, trans. John Plamenatz in *Readings from Liberal* Writers (London: George Allen and Unwin Ltd., 1965), pp. 199–200.

no individual, no fraction, no partial association can assume the sovereignty unless it has been delegated to him or them. But it does not follow that the citizens generally, or those in whom they have vested the sovereignty, may dispose absolutely of the lives of individuals. On the contrary, there is a part of life which necessarily remains personal and independent, which of right is beyond the competence of society. Sovereignty can be only limited and relative. At the point where personal independence and life begin, the jurisdiction of the sovereign ceases. If society goes beyond this point, it is as guilty as the despot whose only title is the sword of the destroyer; society cannot pass beyond the sphere of its competence without usurpation, nor the majority without factiousness. The assent of the majority is not always enough to make its acts legitimate: there are some which nothing can justify. When authority commits such actions, it matters little from what source the authority is alleged to come, or whether it belongs to an individual or a nation; even when it is exercised by the whole nation, except for the citizen oppressed, it is not the more legitimate for that.

Rousseau failed to recognize this truth, and his error has made of his *Social Contract*, so often invoked in favor of liberty, the most terrible support of all kinds of despotism. He defines the contract made by society with its members as the complete and unreserved alienation of each individual with all his rights to the community. To reassure us about the consequences of so absolute a surrender of all aspects of our life to an abstract being, he tells us that the sovereign, that is to say the social body, cannot injure either its members in general or any one of them in particular: that, since each gives himself entire, the condition is the same for all, and none has an interest in making it burdensome to others; that each in giving himself to all gives himself to nobody, that each acquires over all his associates the rights which he grants to them, and gains the equivalent of all that he loses together with greater power to preserve what he has. But he forgets that all these preservative attributes which he confers on the abstract being he calls the sovereign derive from its including within it all individuals without exception. But, as soon as the sovereign has to make use of the power belonging to it—that is to say, as soon as authority has to be organized for practical purposes—the sovereign, since it cannot itself exercise this authority, must delegate it; and all these attributes disappear. Since the action taken in the name of all is willy nilly done by one person or by a few, it is not true that in giving oneself to all one gives oneself to no one; on the contrary one gives oneself to those who act in the name of all. Whence it follows that, in giving oneself entire, one does not enter a condition which is equal for all, because there are some who alone benefit from the sacrifice of the others. It is not true that no one has an interest in making the condition a burden to others, since there are associates to whom the condition does not apply. It is not true that all the associates acquire over others the rights which they grant to them over themselves; they do not all gain the equivalent of what they lose, and what results from their sacrifice is, or may be, the establishment of a power which takes from them what they have.

Rousseau himself took fright at these consequences. Appalled by the immensity of the social power he had created, he did not know in what hands to place that monstrous power, and could find as a safeguard against the danger inseparable from sovereignty thus conceived only an expedient which made its exercise impossible. He declared that sovereignty could not be alienated or delegated or represented; which amounted to saying that it could not be exercised. This was to annihilate the principle he had just proclaimed.

* * *

Where sovereignty is unlimited, there is no way of protecting the individual against the government. It is in vain that you claim to subject governments to the general will. It is they who give utterance to that will, and all precautions become illusory.

The people, says Rousseau, are sovereign in one respect, and subjects in another; but in practice these two respects merge into one another. Authority can easily oppress the people taken as subjects in order to compel them in their sovereign capacity to express a will prescribed to them by authority.

No political organization can remove this danger. It is in vain that you separate the powers: if the sum total of power is unlimited, the separate powers have only to make an alliance, and there is despotism without a remedy. What matters is not that our rights should be inviolable by one power without the approval of another, but that the violation be forbidden to all the powers. * * *

PIERRE-JOSEPH PROUDHON

1809–1865

Pierre-Joseph Proudhon was a French writer and political activist who elaborated the theory of anarchism. During the Revolution of 1848 he sought to apply that theory from his post as a representative to the Constituent Assembly, as the editor of a widely read newspaper, and by establishing a "People's Bank" which was to provide free credit.

He wrote the *General Idea of the Revolution*, the source of these excerpts, from the prison to which he had been sentenced for sedition. In this work he goes beyond the vigorous denunciation of opponents such as Rousseau to describe succinctly how an anarchist society could be organized. Such a society would be governed by contract instead of laws and divided into decentralized communes and industrial associations, through which the working class would wield its share of power.

* * * Is it necessary now to say that, out of the multitude of relations which the social pact is called upon to define and regulate, Rousseau saw only the political relations; that is to say, he suppressed the fundamental points of the contract and dwelt only upon those that are secondary?[1] Is it necessary to say that Rousseau understood and respected not one of these essential, indispensable conditions,—the absolute liberty of the party, his personal, direct part, his signature given with full understanding, and the share of liberty and prosperity which he should experience?

For him, the social contract is neither an act of reciprocity, nor an act of association. Rousseau takes care not to enter into such considerations. It is an act of appointment of arbiters, chosen by the citizens, without any preliminary agreement, for all cases of contest, quarrel, fraud, or violence, which can happen in the relations which they may subsequently form among themselves, the said arbiters being clothed with sufficient force to put their decisions into execution, and to collect their salaries.

Of a real, true contract, on whatsoever subject, there is no vestige in Rousseau's book. To give an exact idea of his theory, I cannot do better than compare it with a commercial agreement, in which the names of the parties, the nature and value of the goods, products and services involved, the conditions of quality, delivery, price, reimbursement, everything in fact which constitutes the material of contracts, is omitted, and nothing is mentioned but penalties and jurisdictions.

Indeed, Citizen of Geneva, you talk well. But before holding forth about the sovereign and the prince, about the policeman and the judge, tell me first what is my share of the bargain? What? You expect me to sign an agreement in virtue of which I may be prosecuted for a thousand transgressions, by municipal, rural, river, and forest police, handed over to tribunals, judged, condemned for damage, cheating, swindling, theft, bankruptcy, robbery, disobedience to the laws of the State, offence to public morals, vagabondage—and in this agreement I find not a word of either my rights or my obligations, I find only penalties!

But every penalty no doubt presupposes a duty, and every duty corresponds to a right. Where then in your agreement are my rights and my duties? What have I promised to my fellow citizens? What have they promised to me? Show it to me, for without that, your penalties are but excesses of power, your law-controlled State a flagrant usurpation, your police, your judgment, and your executions so many abuses. You who have so well denied property, who have impeached so eloquently the inequality of conditions among men, what dignity, what heritage, have you for me in your republic, that you should claim the right to judge me, to imprison me, to take my life and honor? Perfidious declaimer, have you inveighed so loudly against exploiters and tyrants, only to deliver me to them without defence?

*   *   *

1. Pierre-Joseph Proudhon, *General Idea of the Revolution in the Nineteenth Century*, trans. John   Beverley Robinson (London: Freedom Press, 1923), pp. 115–119, 121.

Rousseau is so far from desiring that any mention should be made in the social contract of the principles and laws which rule the fortunes of nations and of individuals, that, in his demagogue's programme, as well as in his Treatise on Education, he starts with the false, thievish, murderous supposition that only the individual is good, that society depraves him, that man therefore should refrain as much as possible from all relations with his fellows; and that all we have to do in this world below, while remaining in complete isolation, is to form among ourselves a mutual insurance society, for the protection of our persons and property; that all the rest, that is to say, economic matters, really the only matters of importance, should be left to the chance of birth or speculation, and submitted, in case of litigation, to the arbitration of elected officers, who should determine according to rules laid down by themselves, or by the light of natural equity. In a word, the social contract, according to Rousseau, is nothing but the offensive and defensive alliance of those who possess, against those who do not possess; and the only part played by the citizen is to pay the police, for which he is assessed in proportion to his fortune, and the risk to which he is exposed from general pauperism.

It is this contract of hatred, this monument of incurable misanthropy, this coalition of the barons of property, commerce, and industry against the disinherited lower class, this oath of social war indeed, which Rousseau calls *Social Contract*, with a presumption which I should call that of a scoundrel, if I believed in the genius of the man. * * *

* * *

After having laid down as a principle that the people are the only sovereign, that they can be represented only by themselves, that the law should be the expression of the will of all, and other magnificent commonplaces, after the way of demagogues Rousseau quietly abandons and discards this principle. In the first place, he substitutes the will of the majority for the general, collective, indivisible will; then, under pretext that it is not possible for a whole nation to be occupied from morning till night with public affairs, he gets back, by the way of elections, to the nomination of representatives or proxies, who shall do the lawmaking in the name of the people, and whose decrees shall have the force of laws. Instead of a direct, personal transaction where his interests are involved, the citizen has nothing left but the power of choosing his rulers by a plurality vote. That done, Rousseau rests easy. Tyranny, claiming divine right, had become odious; he reorganizes it and makes it respectable, by making it proceed from the people, so he says. * * * Moreover there is not a word about labor, nor property, nor the industrial forces; all of which it is the very object of a Social Contract to organize. Rousseau does not know what economics means. His programme speaks of political rights only; it does not mention economic rights.

* * *

Let me say, in conclusion, that, to the shame of the eighteenth century and of our own, the *Social Contract* of Rousseau, a masterpiece of oratorical jugglery, has been admired, praised to the skies, regarded as the record of public liberties; that Constituents, Girondins, Jacobins, Cordeliers, have all taken it for an oracle; that it served for the text of the Constitution of '93, which was declared absurd by its own authors; and that it is still by this book that the most zealous reformers of political and social science are inspired. The corpse of the author, which the people will drag to Montfaucon, on the day when they shall have learned the meaning of these words: Liberty, Justice, Morality, Reason, lies glorious and venerated in the catacombs of the Pantheon, where never one will enter of these honest laborers who nourish with their blood their poor families; while the profound geniuses set up for their adoration send, in lubricious frenzy, their bastards to the almshouse. * * *

LEO TOLSTOY

1828–1910

Tolstoy, the famous Russian novelist, idolized Rousseau, especially for his views on the state of nature expressed in the *Discourse on Inequality*. In 1905 Tolstoy was one of the first people asked to join the new *Société Jean-Jacques Rousseau*, and his response was one of four letters published in the first volume of its *Annales*.

Yasnaia Poliana, Toula, 7/20 March 1905

Sir,

It is with the greatest pleasure that I enroll myself as a member of your Society.[1]

I send you my best wishes for the success of your work.

Rousseau has been my master since the age of fifteen.

Rousseau and the Gospel have been the two great positive influences on my life.

Rousseau never grows old. Recently, I happened to reread some of his works, and I felt the same sentiment of spiritual elevation and admiration that I felt when I read him in my early youth.

I thank you, Sir, for the honor you do me by enrolling me as a member of your Society, and I send you my very best regards.

Leo Tolstoy.

COMMENTARIES

The commentaries that follow have been chosen to help readers reach their own conclusions about some of the more vexing issues raised by Rousseau. Three types of commentary are provided: interpretations of Rousseau's political intentions, analyses of his attitude toward equality, and discussions of how his principles might be applied in the present day.

The first two essays, by Jean Starobinski and Ralph A. Leigh, identify Rousseau's political intentions by setting the selections chosen for this edition into a larger frame. Starobinski considers the full range of Rousseau's political writings, from the early *Discourse on the Arts and Sciences* to *Considerations on the Government of Poland*, which Rousseau wrote late in life. Leigh's focus is *On Social Contract*, and he examines and refutes its best entrenched opponents, from Benjamin Constant to Jacob Talmon. These essays both portray Rousseau as at heart a democrat.

The essays by Robert Nisbet, Judith N. Shklar, and Robert Paul Wolff, also proceed from a view of Rousseau as a kind of democrat. However, through analysis of his attitude toward equality, and of the structure and value of the democratic institutions he sought, they each reach different conclusions. For Nisbet, Rousseau is a subversive leveller who puts radical democracy in the service of an unqualified egalitarianism which corrodes the social fabric by dissolving its organic fiber. Shklar sees Rousseau as backing a limited democracy, confined by the idea that equality must protect the disadvantaged and secure unity and peace. For Wolff, Rousseau's democracy, while impeccably egalitarian and participatory, is morally unacceptable, because it coerces minorities through majority rule. These three essays raise the main points of the controversy over the democratic elements in Rousseau's thought.

All of the commentators mentioned so far share the view that Rousseau is concerned more with establishing political principles than with working out their applications. The final two essays in this collection, by Simone Weil and Benjamin R. Barber, re-examine twentieth-century political life in light of Rousseau's principles. Weil identifies political parties in 1930s France as organizations which must be abolished and replaced in part by affinity groups if a Rousseauist democracy is to succeed. Barber, considering conditions in the present-day United States, points not to parties but to representation as the chief obstacle to the public-spirited citizenship on which Rousseauist democracy depends. Barber goes even further than Weil in suggesting controversial replacements for the institutions he deems undemocratic. Both authors, by arguing for reform in Rousseau's name, spur us to clarify the implications of his principles and soberly estimate their value.

JEAN STAROBINSKI

Winner of the 1984 Balzan Prize, Jean Starobinski is a professor of French literature at the University of Geneva. His *Jean-Jacques Rousseau: la transparence et l'obstacle* (1972) and his *Montaigne in Motion* (1982) are complementary works which focus on how Rousseau and Montaigne analyze the problem of false appearances. Starobinski is also well known for his interdisciplinary approach to the Enlightenment in *1789: The Emblems of Reason* (1973). The essay which follows gives an excellent overall view of Rousseau's political writings and was originally published in Samuel Baud-Bovey, ed., *Jean-Jacques Rousseau* (Neuchâtel: Editions de la Baconnière, 1962), pp. 86–99. It is translated by Julia Conaway Bondanella. Footnotes are by the editors.

The Political Thought of Jean-Jacques Rousseau

* * *

In Rousseau's political thought, we can distinguish four elements or, if one prefers, four distinct moments which I shall endeavor to analyze. First, a critique of contemporary society, expressed to some degree everywhere but particularly in the first *Discourse*, *The New Héloïse*, and *Emile*.[1] Secondly, a philosophy of history, which will be found in the *Discourse on Inequality*. Thirdly, a definition of the fundamental principles of a social organism: this is *On Social Contract*. And finally, an attempt to apply these principles in certain concrete conditions: in Corsica and Poland.[2]

Let us start at the beginning, which is revolt and the critique of society. Everything, in effect, begins with the experience of social outrage and revolutionary protest. The *Discourse on the Sciences and the Arts* denounces an unhappy condition and an imposture. Men seem to live in concord and harmony; in reality, they give themselves over to cunning war, they dream only of doing evil, and, under the mask of civility, each conscience pursues the death of the other (as Hegel will declare later). Primitive peoples, the unpolished citizens of Sparta or of early Rome, knew another existence. They lived in a union of the heart, in perfect transparency; they offered themselves to the examination of their gods just as they offered themselves to their fellow citizens. Their happiness consisted in living in such a manner that nothing ever prevented full communication between consciences. No shadow, no lie was ever

---

1. The *Discourse on the Sciences and the Arts* (1750) is a treatise written in response to a contest sponsored by the Academy of Dijon for essays on the effects of the progress of civilization upon morals; with Rousseau's entry, which won the prize, its author became famous. *Julie, or the New Héloïse* (1760) is a sentimental epistolary novel describing the love affair between a man of low birth and a woman of station, her subsequent marriage to a man of her own class, and the pathos which followed this marriage. *Émile* (1762), a treatise on education, was condemned by both the Parlement of Paris and the Council of Geneva, and as a result of this latter attack, Rousseau renounced his Genevan citizenship.

2. *Constitutional Project for Corsica* (1762) and *Considerations on the Government of Poland* (1772).

interposed. For us, alas, everything has changed; we live in servitude and defiance. Everything opposes us, down to the interests which seem to join us together. From whence does this evil emanate? It is inseparable from luxury, and luxury goes along with the unbridled progress of the sciences and the arts. Certainly, Rousseau makes clear, the sciences and the arts are not harmful in themselves; it is necessary to reserve them for a few great minds who will understand all the danger that exists in passing from pure knowledge to its application. And since everything seems to declare that corruption is irrevocable, it would do us little good to banish the sciences and the arts. A degenerate humanity cannot return to virtue; we cannot go backwards, we can only attempt to slow down an evolution which tends toward the worst. From this first *Discourse*, Rousseau formulates the grand outlines of what will be called his historical pessimism. The interest of this *Discourse*, if not its originality, lies in the close rapport he establishes between the moral aspect and the economic aspect of human relations. Social disparity (the inequality of wealth) and psychological separation (the rupture between consciences) go together. The man who can no longer exist without a superfluity of possessions is the slave of opinion. He needs to shine before others, to impose himself upon them by his rank or by his ostentation. From that moment on, essence and appearance become more and more separated, there is no more true friendship, no more good faith, no more piety. This laceration does not exist only between civilized man and his neighbor, it also exists in the interior of each conscience: we are alienated, we are separated from our truth, we are separated from ourselves, we have lost our unity. It is a quest for unity that the entire corpus of Rousseau's works presents to us.

In a reader of 1750, the first *Discourse* must have touched a sensitive point and reawakened a good deal of bad conscience. How can one otherwise explain the clamorous reception this little bit of generous and somewhat confused eloquence received, nourished throughout with reminiscences of Seneca and Plutarch? Rousseau revealed and defined a general malaise; the number and obstinacy of his opponents furnishes us with supplementary proof. The *Discourse* held out a mirror in which the public of 1750 recognized itself, for better or for worse.

I thus arrive at Rousseau's philosophy of history. Let us allow Rousseau to explain to us in his own words how, after the critique of society, he then came to formulate a general interpretation of history. I borrow these lines from the *Letter to Monseigneur de Beaumont:*[3] "As soon as I was in a condition to observe men, I watched them act and listened to them speak; then, observing that their actions did not resemble their words, I searched for the reason for this dissimilarity, and I discovered that since essence and appearance were, for them, two conditions as different as acting and speaking, this second difference was the cause of the other and had itself a cause which remained for me to seek. I found

3. A polemical tract he composed in 1762 in response to attacks upon his *Émile*.

it in our social order which, in every detail contrary to nature which destroys nothing, constantly tyrannizes it and constantly causes it to reclaim its rights. I followed this contradiction to its conclusion, and I saw that this alone explained all the vices of men and all the evils of society. From this I conclude that it was not necessary to suppose man to be evil by his nature, since one can mark the origin and the progress of his wickedness." This is certainly the intention of the *Discourse on the Origin and the Foundations of Inequality Among Men*: this great text, the one which has been the least well understood, is presented as an "historical study of morals." This time, Rousseau is going to describe the genesis of the corruption from which our society suffers; he is going to trace its "genealogy." In order to do so, it is necessary to return to the primitive condition of man. But a prejudicial question poses itself: this primitive condition, this state of nature—did it ever really exist? Perhaps not; perhaps man has always lived in society; perhaps man has always changed himself. Let us, nevertheless, formulate the hypothesis of a "state of nature." This is a necessary hypothesis. Why? Because it is necessary to have at hand what philosophers call a regulative concept in order to judge our present condition and, in general, in order to compare the different forms of social life. If history and culture have transformed us, we can only appraise the amplitude of this transformation by defining, first of all, what man was (or could have been) before all the changes were brought to bear upon his constitution. It is necessary to presuppose, as the linguists say, a *zero degree* condition in order to appreciate the departures from the norm. How, then, to formulate this definition of natural man? It is necessary, by hypothesis, to subtract everything which has been acquired, all the additions, to deduct all the artificial acquisitions which constitute civilized existence. Once this operation has been completed (by an effort of philosophical imagination), we shall have at our disposal a fixed reference point, a term of comparison. From that moment on, each civilization, each stage of human culture could be evaluated according to its degree of relative departure from the primitive state. Civilization is a variable point of departure in relationship to a fixed point—an original point—which is real or supposed. Everything which differs from the ideal definition of natural man thus appears to us as an effect of the free activity of man; everything which is not included in the definition of his nature will be a human enterprise, a result of human effort, an "artifice." Man has transformed himself, he is no longer the man of nature, he has become "the man of man." It is necessary to recognize him, in order for us to grieve over this and to make the best of a bad situation.

Completely primitive man, as Rousseau describes him, is a happy man. His fate, in many respects, is preferable to that of civilized man. He knows no sickness, he does not fear death, he does not feel the torments of jealousy * * * In reading the seductive imaginary descriptions that Rousseau provides for this infancy of the world, one might imagine that Rousseau decided, and invited us to decide, in favor of the condition of the savage. Nothing of the sort. All one can affirm at most is that he feels a profound nostalgia for this existence. But the primitive condition, as Rousseau knows, has been lost—irrevocably lost. It is not, therefore, a question of seeing in it a norm, that is to say, a value which it would be necessary to attempt to realize or to rediscover once again. One cannot go back: Rousseau declares this in many places in his works. The return to nature which has often been believed to be discovered in Rousseau, is to be found nowhere in his works, unless we wish to say simply that he prefers the country to the great city. When Rousseau describes, in the *Discourse on Inequality*, the solitude of the savage, he in no way presents it as the life modern man ought to lead. It is simply that he would have preferred not to have ever left that state: but the fall has taken place, and one can say that the loss of his original quietude is an accident which is the equivalent, equally far back in time, to the loss of Paradise.

Let us imagine creatures still close to their animal nature. Perhaps— as a note in the *Discourse* explains—the orang-outang is even a specimen conserved from this original state. These naked men do not live in society. They are scattered about; each man lives for himself in the immense expanse of the great primitive forest in which nature is generous. There is no toil, no necessary work, between the natural needs of man and what nature offers him; the equilibrium is perfect. Of course, this man already differs from the animals in a particular way: his liberty. Natural law, which speaks directly to his conscience, enjoins him to preserve himself and to have pity for the suffering of his fellow creature. Here is all of natural morality. For the rest, the savage has no memory, no foresight, he lives in the present moment, he possesses no language, he neither reflects nor reasons, he couples fortuitously, without the union of male and female transforming itself into a durable marriage (Voltaire was quite scandalized by this). In one sense, this condition is miserable, but in another sense, Rousseau describes it as a paradisiacal plenitude and presence. A presence immediate to itself, the immediate presence of nature to man, without obstacles, without intermediaries imposed. It is also necessary to add another thing: the man of nature does not consciously do evil. Rousseau tells us that this man is naturally good. But more than goodness, we can observe in him a total ignorance of good and evil. It is the innocence of pre-moral life, guided by the instinctive movement of piety and sympathy.

But the equilibrium has been broken, and this has not taken place as a result of the fault of man. A day arrived when humanity in expansion was forced to confront, to the extreme south, less favorable climates. Here is the rather strange hypothesis that Rousseau formulates. On that day, the good-will and spontaneous gifts of nature ceased. Rigorous winters and scorching summers menaced human existence. Everything occurred as if man had been *weaned* by nature. Man was challenged, and it was necessary that he do something if he wished to survive. It was necessary for him to surmount obstacles which were now mounted against him. He now must put the resources of his *perfectibility* to work. He must now invent techniques and set himself to work. This obliges him to reason. He learns to compare objects; he will learn how to construct tools. But if he compares objects, he also compares himself to his fellow creatures. It is thus that self-love is born, and with self-love, an infinity of vices. Nothing in all this is natural. These are acts of human liberty, an art provoked by an encounter with an obstacle. This man becomes this creature who changes his nature and transforms the milieu surrounding him, and who, in changing his nature transforms himself. It was first of all a question of life or death; it was necessary to overcome hostile circumstances. But the movement has begun and will no longer cease. Man has learned to desire beyond his primitive needs. And through the excess of his desire, he will reach the material power and the moral impoverishment which are today his lot.

It would be difficult overly to praise the depth and originality which Rousseau exhibits in the description of the different stages through which humanity travels from its hypothetical origins up to our state of society. Rousseau here shows himself to be the true inventor of the sociological interpretation of history. He also bears witness here to a very acute sense of the relations uniting different orders of facts which were not usually juxtaposed or compared. Economic facts, moral facts, psychological facts, all of this is unfolded within a unique development. It is there that he creates what one would rightly name a "dialectic conception of history."

Let us analyze the consequences of this remarkable theory. Having placed the definition of man in nature at the lowest level, Rousseau will attribute to the "man of man," to the artificial and indefinitely perfectible man, all that which is not included in the state of nature. The work of man, reflection; human institutions, family, and patriarchal life; human inventions, property and, above all else, society and civil order. To say that man is not a being who is *naturally sociable*, as Rousseau does, is not to say that man should not live in society, it is to say quite simply that Rousseau does not derive the rules of social life from any transcendental authority, from any preexisting *natural law*: these rules emanate only from his free will, and it is necessary to realize that therein lies his work, for better or for worse.

In the actual history of humanity, things have changed for the worse. Man would have been better off to have remained in the "state of early society." Rousseau thus designates the patriarchal communities, living on hunting, fishing, and gathering, ignoring the division and the specialization of labor. That was "the true youth of the world," the healthiest state for man. That was the condition in which the navigators and the explorers discovered the American tribes; it was also (we should add) the state that historians of antiquity designate by the name of "Neolithic." But a "fatal chance occurrence" overtook this age. Humanity did not stabilize its evolution at this stage; men discovered metals and applied them to the cultivation of the earth; the division of labor was imposed, and this had as its result the division of conditions and consciences. Landed property was instituted and soon covered the earth; from then on there were rich and poor, masters and slaves; some wished to raise protests, and these degenerated into bloody wars. Notice that up to this point in the history of humanity, we have not yet entered into what Rousseau calls civil society, but we have already long ago left the first state of nature. There is a long interval between this first state of nature and the foundation of civil society: Rousseau calls it several times "a second state of nature." To mitigate this disorder and to safeguard his possessions, the rich man has imagined a sort of associational contract or a contract of subjection, thanks to which the forces of society would be placed at the service of order and security, but for the exclusive benefit of the rich. This mystifying contract, far from abolishing the law of the strongest, has only bestowed upon them the sanction of the law; it has aggravated inequality in making it legal. And here we are finally, such as we are, victims of opinion, subjugated to unjust masters, divided in the profoundest part of ourselves. The *Discourse on Inequality* ends on a cry of revolt: "it is manifestly contrary to the law of nature, however it is defined, for a child to command an old man, for a fool to lead a wise man, and for a handful of men to abound in superfluities while the starving multitude lacks the bare necessities."

Is this evil without remedy? To know that man is naturally good is a paltry consolation if history denatures us and renders us irrevocably bad. For small republics, for Geneva in particular, there is perhaps a means of obtaining a reprieve in this evolution. As for the great monarchies where power has become despotic, they head toward their downfall. Under the absolute will of a tyrannical master, men "become equals once again because they are nothing." And "everything here is reduced to the law of the strongest alone, and, consequently, to a new state of nature which differs from the one with which we began, in the sense that the former was the pure state of nature and this last is the fruit of excessive corruption." Without a miraculous renovation—Rousseau never excludes this miracle—everything ends in bloodshed, everything tends toward catastrophe. Such is, for Rousseau, the *goal of history*, very different from that which modern philosophers propose to us. It is evident that he is very far from believing, as so many of his contemporaries did, in automatic progress: let us be glad that he delivered us from this belief. But it would be false to imagine that he believes in an automatic decline: man is free, and the use of this liberty is dangerous. Man alone decides: * * * Perhaps with a supplementary effort of artifice and culture, one might be able to reeducate man in order to reconcile him to the primitive exigencies of his nature which he has forgotten, now hidden, but which have never completely disappeared. Rousseau will exploit this grand idea of a reconciliation with nature through the perfection of culture in *Emile*; it will animate the political theory of Kant who, according to Eric Weil, will carry Rousseau's ideas farther than Rousseau. There is, therefore, a possible remedy, but through what means can it be found?

Through politics itself? Would this be only a dreamed-of compensation, in the manner of the *intimate society* whose image appeared in *The New Héloïse?* Does not Jean-Jacques end by preferring to manifest his refusal in the solitary reverie, in the knowledge which is both painful and delicious of his own justification, of his perfect personal authenticity, maintained and affirmed in the midst of a world given over to evil?

Will *On Social Contract* point toward an urgent path to follow? No. It is not offered as a program of action. It is presented to us as a declaration of principles whose conditions of application are not connected to the concrete situation of France or of other European countries. Rousseau legislates in the abstract. He proposes no remedy for a corrupted society. He simply states the great civic virtues in the absence of which, for his part, there will only exist revolt, refusal, and nonacceptance. To the concrete world, he opposes a political ideal in the name of which he judges and condemns the world. At the same time, he proposes this ideal as a universal model, as a norm. In *On Social Contract*, there is an implicit negative aspect: "I reject everything which is not included in this ideal city." On the other hand, this ideal city is not an unrealizable utopia; it is a timeless possibility. Here is what the city in which Jean-Jacques would be proud to be a citizen should be. Here is the work par excellence that men worthy of this name ought to realize. As long as it has not been realized, Rousseau can only be in opposition.

The main idea of *On Social Contract*, the one which we are all living with today, is that there is no legitimate community unless it is founded upon *law*. This seems very simple. Let us cite here a commentator who is well known, Eric Weil: "The society of of men is a society of law: Rousseau's discovery is contained in this single proposition. Certainly the school of natural law had proclaimed it: man possesses certain rights which cannot be lost, rights which he could not renounce even if he wished to do so. But for Rousseau, it is not a matter of these rights alone. Man in the state of nature has no rights because he is alone. . . . Law is born with society, and society, in Rousseau's eyes, cannot form itself without forming itself into a state . . . it is a question of reasonable liberty, of reason in action, and this law is its own foundation. It exists only in a community and on the condition that the community itself be a community of law."

But let us listen to Rousseau, let us allow him to speak. "I assume men to have reached the point at which the obstacles to their preservation in the state of nature have a resistance greater than the forces each individual can use to maintain himself in that state. At this point, that primitive state could no longer subsist, and the human species would perish if it did not change its way of living. Now, since men cannot engender new forces but merely unite and direct the existing ones, they have no other means of preserving themselves than to form by aggregation a sum of forces that can overcome this resistance, bring them into play by means of a single motive power, and make them act in concert. This sum of forces can arise only from the cooperation of several men, but since each man's strength and liberty are the primary instruments of self-preservation, how will he commit them without harming himself and without neglecting the care he owes himself? This difficulty, in relation to my subject, can be set forth in these terms: " 'To find a form of association that defends and protects the person and property of each associate with all the common strength, and by means of which each person, joining forces with all, nevertheless obeys only himself and remains as free as before' " (*On Social Contract*, I. 6). Such is the fundamental problem to which *On Social Contract* gives the solution.

"If, then, we eliminate whatever is not essential to the social pact, we shall find that it can be reduced to the following terms: *Each of us puts his person and all his power in common under the supreme control of the general will, and, as a body, we receive each member as an indivisible part of the whole*" (*On Social Contract*, I. 6). We have passed from the individual ("each of us") to the collectivity which declares: we. We have passed from the *series* to the *group* (Sartre). An organic operation, a metamorphosis wherein a body constitutes itself by the unanimous enthusiasm of its members.

Let us first of all remark that this is solely a question of a contract by association, and that this contract, in Rousseau's eyes, is fundamental. Earlier theoreticians frequently imagine a double contract: they envision a contract by association which constitutes a nation, after which this nation establishes a new contract with one of its members, who thus receives the title of king. Sovereignty thus is found to be divided between the people and the prince. Other philosophers, such as Hobbes, had imagined a contract giving all sovereignty to a master charged with maintaining order in the nation. This, Rousseau rejects. In constituting the nation, the collective body, the common "I," the contract imagined by Rousseau also defines the only legitimate source of law, the only sovereign: the people and the general will. At the moment in which the State is constituted, this will results from a unanimous agreement of all its citizens. Later Rousseau will arrive at the idea that the "general will" may not coincide with what Rousseau calls the "will of all"; perhaps even—and the instance becomes embarrassing—the interest of the State will be defended by an enlightened minority, and it will be this minority which will express what Rousseau calls the "general will." But let us not enter into these difficult questions: they are considerable, and commentators have labored over them for a long time. Let us simply remark that at the beginning, there is a spontaneous, unanimous adhesion in the founding act of the nation. In this act, each of us participates equally in the declaration of the general will, and by this participation in sovereignty, each of us is a *citizen*. The laws which concern the collectivity will be decreed by the general will, and insofar as we are collectively the objects of the law, we shall then be *subjects*. We are therefore sovereign and subject at the same time. The people are at the same time sovereign when they declare the law and subject when they obey it. This subjection implies no restriction upon liberty whatsoever. Men entered freely into the constitutive contract; the general will is the expression of their reasonable liberty (reasonable: that is to say, anxious to express the universal). Note this well: what each of us bestows upon the collectivity at the moment of the contract consists of his person and his possessions; he does not sacrifice at any moment his reason. And this is what prevents us from making Rousseau the ancestor of nationalism.

Let us allow Rousseau to speak once again. "What man loses by the social contract is his natural liberty and an unlimited right to everything that tempts him and to everything he can take; what he gains is civil liberty and the ownership of everything he possesses. In order to avoid being mistaken about these compensations, we must carefully distinguish between natural liberty, which is limited only by the strength of the individual, and civil liberty, which is limited by the general will; and between possession, which is only the result of force or the right of the first occupant, and ownership, which can be based only on a real title. Besides the preceding, another benefit which can be counted among the attainments of the civil state is moral liberty, which alone makes man truly his own master, for impulsion by appetite alone is slavery, and obedience to the law that one has prescribed for oneself is liberty" (*On Social Contract*, I. 8).

Sovereignty is *inalienable*; the people cannot at any moment strip themselves or let themselves be stripped of this fundamental right to declare the law. If necessary, the people can abolish earlier edicts. They are not tied down by past agreements. The general will is "always in the right"; it cannot err, but it can recover its consciousness. A second point, equally important: sovereignty cannot be delegated; it belongs to the people as a body and to them alone. The government, which Rousseau sometimes calls "the magistrate," is only an agent of the sovereign. It possesses only a simple executive power; its acts will be constantly controlled by the legislative power. The sovereign can depose the government when this seems suitable. In the almost narcissistic relationship between the collectivity of the citizens as sovereign and the collectivity of subjects (who are the same men), the government is an obtrusive intermediary. Rousseau always detested intermediaries, but here the intermediary is unfortunately indispensable. In his thought, the government will be under the domination of the sovereign, and it will display a singular weakness. "What, then, is government? An intermediary body established between the subjects and the sovereign for their mutual dealings, charged with the execution of the laws and with the maintenance of liberty, both civic and political" (*On Social Contract* III. 1). The ideal would be a *direct* exercise of sovereignty by the people.

I should like to underline yet a last point: the government is not alone in depending upon the general will; all of the life of the city and religion itself should be controlled by the general will or at least subordinate to it. *On Social Contract* concludes with a chapter on "civil religion," which caused a scandal in Geneva in 1762. It was this text which justified the condemnation of the book. Why? Because the chapter on civil religion subjugates religion to the superior interests of the city. While he set aside private opinions, "which the sovereign does not need to know," Rousseau declares the principles of a "completely civil profession of faith, the articles of which are for the sovereign to determine, not precisely as religious dogmas, but as sentiments of sociability, without which it is impossible to be a good citizen or a faithful subject" (*On Social Contract* IV. 8). This idea worried Christians and irritated atheists.

Here one can perceive an aspect of *On Social Contract* which was to exercise a enormous attraction upon the men of the French Revolution. Rousseau transposes into political life, at the level of civic spirit and patriotism, the fervent emotions which belonged to the proper domain of religion. In Rousseau, the need for unity is such that he cannot separate the political order from the spiritual order; he melts them together in order to make of them a single and burning necessity.

But what will result from this doctrine? What will this thought produce in history? Nationalism? That has been affirmed. Totalitarianism? People have pretended as much. Democracy? That appears to be truer. Let us be careful of conjecture. Rousseau formulated his principles, but he did not draw out of them the concrete consequences. He did not wish to do so. He cared very little for realizations of his doctrine. He allowed others to be inspired by him and to interpret him in different ways. As for Rousseau, it was sufficient for him to have given an ideal pretext to his sense of revolt which he had lacked until that moment. However, when the Corsican Buttafoco, in 1764, asked him to prepare a draft constitution, and when in 1771, Count Weilhorski came to beg him to outline a program of political reforms for Poland, Rousseau accepted. He was no doubt flattered to play the role of lawgiver, of the providential and divine man called to install (to "institute") or to reform a nation. And he did not work in the abstract in this instance. He collects documents; he surrounds himself with maps, history books, he asks for time to reflect, he wishes to know the climate, the resources, the industries of the country, he even dreams of a trip. Read the *Considerations on the Government of Poland* and you will see there a Rousseau attentive not to proceed in a too rapid or brutal manner, careful not to overturn traditional institutions. He will suppress serfdom only in a slow and progressive fashion, regardless of how hostile he may be to all forms of servitude. While waiting to constitute a federated republic, he will not act against the prerogatives of the nobility or of the king, which he will touch only with extreme prudence. Thus, his *Considerations* have been utilized in the interests of a conservative or reactionary politics. All the reforms he suggests, however, constitute a very obvious application of the principles of *On Social Contract*. There is a difference of style and not of spirit between the dry declarations of *On Social Contract* and the subtle procedures counseled to the Poles. But what an attentive reading of this text can especially show us is the persistent presence of the grand themes which dominated the entire life and imagination of Jean-

Jacques. He needs unity, as we have observed; he needs plenitude, immediacy, transparency. That is what counts above all else. It matters very little if this need expresses itself in a solitary existence, in the intimate society of Clarens, or on the scale of an entire nation. He wishes for Poland to bestow upon herself a national and "exclusive" spirit, which manifested itself primarily by the conservation of a national costume. And how will he revive this spirit? By festivals, by great popular reunions where the nation will bestow upon itself the spectacle of its joy. (Recall the crucial role of the festival in *The New Héloïse* and in the *Letter to d'Alembert*).[4] The civic happiness of which Rousseau dreams is nothing other than the amplified image of the intimate happiness of his childhood: to see and to be seen in absolute trust and openness. Rousseau's taste for small republics prefers that each individual live there virtuously *under the gaze of all*. We read in *The Considerations on the Government of Poland*: "Almost all small States, republics or monarchies, prosper for the sole reason that they are small, that all their citizens know each other and observe one another." Thus, the young Polish nobles should get used to growing up and even to playing "*under the eyes* of their fellow citizens." The administration should act "*under the eyes* of the legislator"; the representatives to the Diet must see themselves in advance "*under the eyes* of their constituents," etc. When Rousseau sets out the principles of the economic system he recommends for the Poles, he will do so in order to celebrate, one more time, autarchy, self-sufficiency, and absolute independence. Rousseau never wished to depend upon anyone, and Poland must restrain as much as possible its commerce with foreign nations. Money itself should be as rare as possible in the nation: Rousseau—as we know—dreaded being subject to cash, not to say anything of capital. He imagined, at Clarens, an autarchic economy wherein loans were made only in kind. Poland, as he hoped, will live under the same virtuous and frugal regime. The State will solemnly recompense good citizens, not with money but with honorific tokens in base metal. And rather than retract anything from the purity of his principles, Rousseau is prepared to sacrifice the independence of the country for which he has made himself the lawgiver. If its neighbors invade and occupy the country, what does it matter? That is preferable to possessing a strong army which runs the risk of turning against the authorities. The homeland will continue to live in the hearts of the oppressed citizens. By a strange coincidence, the Poland of 1772, for which Rousseau is proposing laws, is a rather faithful image of Jean-Jacques himself, encircled, surrounded, beseiged by his persecutors, and by his enemies—real or imagined. And the refuge within the inviolable interior conviction which he recommends to the Poles is the consolation which he sought and discovered by himself.

There exists in more than one circumstance, therefore, a very clear

4. In this work (1758), Rousseau attempted to demonstrate that the establishment of a theater in Geneva would necessarily corrupt civic morality.

convergence between the political ideas of Rousseau and the most unusual tendencies of his personality. It is always necessary to avoid pretending to explain the philosophical originality of Jean-Jacques by the singular aspects of his personality, by his preferences and his intimate desires. To do so would be to refuse to take seriously his political thought as such; this would reduce it to nothing but the imagination of a particular kind. An unjust judgment. Even if he can be reproached for not having confronted the essential problem which is that of the conditions for the realization of his ideas, even if the political theory of Rousseau suffers from an incompleteness which weakens it in a regrettable manner, his remains the merit of having opened the era of modern reflection upon the nation and the function of the state. His remains the merit of having been the first to pose, with all the clarity one might desire, problems of anthropology and historical sociology. Can we ask the same man to be simultaneously the one who invents and the one who brings to fruition?

R. A. LEIGH

Appointed to a personal Chair at the University of Cambridge in 1973, Ralph A. Leigh, now retired, is the respected editor of Rousseau's complete correspondence, a work of multidisciplinary scope, which includes not only letters from and to Rousseau but a variety of other relevant documents. As a student during the prewar years in Paris of the noted experts on the Enlightenment, Paul Hazard and J.-M. Carré, Leigh very early in his career focused upon Rousseau. The article included here is a cogent argument against the notion that *On Social Contract* advances the cause of totalitarianism. It was first published as "Liberté et autorité dans le *Contrat social*" in *Jean-Jacques Rousseau et son oeuvre* (Paris: Klinckseik, 1964). The present English translation was done by Alan Ritter.

Liberty and Authority in *On Social Contract*

*   *   *

In any political theory the problem of liberty and authority is so crucial that the solution offered can serve as a touchstone or a dividing line. Obedience and freedom seem to be mutually exclusive. Reconciling them is like squaring a circle. What exactly is Rousseau's view on this question? Here we face a strange enigma. From Benjamin Constant to Jules Lemaître, with St. Marc Girardin, Lamartine, Taine, Faguet, and Brunetière between them, the same bell tolls: Rousseau's *On Social Contract* is a blueprint for insupportable tyranny.[1] But though these critics are unanimous in denouncing the vicious character of *On Social Contract*, they are far from agreement when it comes to diagnosis.

1. Except for Constant and Lamartine they were all literary critics. Benjamin Constant (1767–1830), author of the novel *Adolph*, was the intellectual spokesman for the cautious French liberalism of the early nineteenth century. The poet Alphonse de Lamartine (1790–1869) was a political activist, especially during the 1848 revolution, when he was a leader of the democratic cause [Editor].

Sometimes we are told that *On Social Contract* justifies the annihilation of the individual for the sake of an all powerful, omnicompetent state; sometimes the claim is that Rousseau extolls a direct, popular government, entirely subversive of order and authority. . . . Recent history and current political events have won renewed support for a variant of these claims. Not long ago, in a book which attracted a great deal of attention on our side of the English Channel, Rousseau's *On Social Contract* was named responsible, in large measure, for what the author of the book, Jacob Talmon, called "totalitarian democracy." "Totalitarian democracy," according to Talmon's definition, "imposes on the individual an exclusively social mode of existence. . . . It is a dictatorship resting on popular enthusiasm. . . . Rousseau's conception of the general will becomes the motive force of totalitarian democracy."[2] Without going as far as Talmon, some have recently thought they could discuss Rousseau's vision of "man as entirely politicized," or of "man as entirely socialized."

We think all of this involves a misunderstanding. That, at the level of history, *On Social Contract* had a certain influence upon authoritarian and even totalitarian theories of the state is possible, and, certainly, this is an important and interesting question. But it is not the one that we propose to consider today. Our question is entirely different. Setting aside its historical repercussions, is or is not the doctrine in *On Social Contract* inherently totalitarian? In answering this question we will give the advantage to those who champion "tyrannical" interpretations of the book. That is, we will renounce all the advantages that can be drawn from Rousseau's other writings. It would be too easy to rely on Rousseau's own comments on his work; it would be too easy to point out that he was correcting the proofs of *On Social Contract* almost at the same time as those of *Emile* and that, if the doctrine in *On Social Contract* had to be classed as totalitarian, this would be the strangest case of philosophical schizophrenia in the annals of Western civilization. All of this, one could object, is irrelevant to the question. Since *On Social Contract* can be read by itself, without knowledge of any other works by Rousseau—the proof is that this is exactly what some of his interpreters have done—this work must be examined as if it were an independent, entirely autonomous text. It will only be permissible to talk of Rousseau's intentions to the extent that these intentions can be found in the work itself. Let us submit to these rules and see where we can go.

Now, even if we accept this seemingly impossible challenge, it is clear that so far as it concerns Rousseau's intentions there is not much need to argue. "I wish to discover," he says, "if, in the civil order, there can be any legitimate and fixed rule of administration, taking men as they are and laws as they can be." This "citizen of a free state" will, he tells us, "in this inquiry, always strive to reconcile what right permits with what interest prescribes, so that justice and utility may not be divided"

2. J. L. Talmon, *The Origins of Totalitarian Democracy* (London, 1952).

(Book I, Introduction). But justice and utility are not everything: there is also liberty. Introduced in the status of free citizen which Rousseau assigns to himself in his Foreword, the word *liberty* makes its entrance onto the stage as early as the first chapter of the first book of the work, but it is closely followed by the word *order*. If liberty is the greatest good, order is defined as "a sacred right which serves as the basis of all the others" (Book I, chapter 1). Here, then, the drama's two protagonists are placed face to face, ready to begin a dialogue. For the moment liberty has the floor: "To renounce one's liberty is to renounce one's humanity, the rights of humanity and even its duties. . . . to strip [a man] of all freedom of will is to strip his actions of all morality" (Book I, chapter 4). How, then, reconcile liberty, without which one is not human, with order, without which society cannot subsist? In a celebrated formula Rousseau delights in pressing the difficulty to its limit: "To find a form of association . . . by means of which each person, joining forces with all, nevertheless obeys only himself *and remains as free as before*" (Book I, chapter 6, Leigh's italics). Let us for the moment consider here just the last part of this sentence, since it is Rousseau's intentions that interest us. Now, disregard the equally celebrated formula in which he gives the solution to the problem and watch him contemplate, not without a certain satisfaction, the consequences which flow from this formula: "What man loses by the social contract is his natural liberty and an unlimited right to everything that tempts him and to everything he can take; what he gains is *civil liberty* and the ownership of everything he possesses. . . . another benefit which can be counted among the attainments of the civil state is *moral liberty* which alone makes man truly his own master, for impulsion by appetite alone is slavery and obedience to the law that one has prescribed for oneself is liberty" (Book I, chapter 8, Leigh's italics).

There is no room for argument. Hence, even Rousseau's most intractable enemies are seldom bold enough to claim that this man, who constantly has liberty on his lips, has tyranny in his heart. And certainly, when one reads sentences in *On Social Contract* like "Vile slaves smile with a mocking air at the word liberty" (Book III, chapter 12), one may, if one likes, shrug at such candor or grandiloquence, but one cannot impugn Rousseau's good faith. Those who see in *On Social Contract* a vindication of despotism, whether collective, personal, or administrative, are therefore forced to evade the difficulty in one way or another. One can say, for example, that this thinker was an imbecile or even a madman, who did not know what he was saying, that this master of language expressed himself so badly that ambiguity and contradiction had to result from the terms he used. One can claim that, despite his good intentions, Rousseau miscalculated the means needed to achieve them. One can insinuate—and a half century of vulgarized psychiatry has prepared us, if not predisposed us, for this solution—that Rousseau's mind harbored dark forces which seized his pen without him knowing it and made him unwillingly say the opposite of what he thought he wanted to say. But before we try to explain a phenomenon so strange as a work by an apostle of liberty which culminates in a vindication of tyranny, let us make sure this phenomenon exists. What, then, is it about Rousseau's city that is found to be so despotic, so tyrannical? Where is the crack through which drains liberty, that most precious essence, which Rousseau boasts of having so well preserved?

Obviously, there is first of all that notorious "total alienation" prescribed in the contractual formula itself: "the total alienation of each associate with all his rights to the whole community" (Book I, chapter 6). Let us frankly admit that at first glance there is something appalling here. But this may not be the first time that Rousseau "started with a novelty and ended with a commonplace." In fact, this total alienation of our property and our rights makes no real change in our immediate social situation; the change is merely titular—a change of name which morally consecrates a matter of fact. As Rousseau himself explains, "Instead of alienating anything, [men] have only made an advantageous exchange" (Book II, chapter 4). From our privileged, twentieth-century perspective, we could even say that there is no point to this maneuver except in the context of social contract theory, which uses the natural-social distinction. Both before and after the social contract, we have rights and property, but after the contract the community rather than nature secures them. We should add that in Rousseau's theory this alienation which he calls "total" certainly does not give the community unlimited power over its members. To be sure, the sovereign power must in principle be absolute in all of the spheres where it is legitimately exercised, because, if there were a group or individual in the state which could resist the sovereign power in those spheres, not only would that power not be sovereign, but it would soon collapse into anarchy.[3] But, first of all, the sovereign power is not competent to act in all spheres of human life, and, secondly, it has natural limits, Rousseau assures us, which arise from the very nature of the contract. This is what he explains in the chapter justly entitled "On the *Limits* of Sovereign Power" (Book II, chapter 4, Leigh's italics).

But before studying the scope and value of these limits, we should recall what Rousseau means by "sovereign state." He does not mean a group of individuals which imposes its will on the people. Nor does he mean a government of any particular form. A sovereign state is simply all the members of a community. If I may make use for my own purpose of a phrase perhaps wrongly attributed to Louis XIV, the state is us. But, someone will say, in trying to avoid the tyranny of government, Rousseau ran afoul of the opposite danger—tyranny of the mob. No, because the sovereignty of the people can only be exercised legitimately through acts called laws, law being the expression of the general will. Hence

3. "For if rights were left to private individuals and there were no common superior who could decide between them and the public, each person, being in some respects his own judge, would soon claim to be so in every instance; the state of nature would subsist, and the association would necessarily become tyrannical or ineffectual" (Book I, chapter 6).

popular sovereignty is not exercised arbitrarily, haphazardly, irrelevantly, at the whim of feverish assemblies or tumultuous crowds. It is exercised with respect to proposed laws, which are submitted to the people in assemblies duly convoked at times or under conditions prescribed by the constitution.[4] The converse of this proposition is just as important as the proposition itself. The sovereignty of the people cannot be exercised except by voting on laws or by consenting to them, always in accordance with constitutional provisions.[5] Thus, there are checks and balances between the government and the people, between authority and liberty. The people do not govern and the government is not sovereign.

What, then, should be thought of those of Rousseau's interpreters who make him the official theorist of government by an unleashed mob? Listen for a minute to Mr. Talmon:

> [According to Rousseau] a fixed, rigid and universal pattern of feeling was to be imposed in order to create man of one piece, without contradictions, without centrifugal and anti-social urges. The task was to create citizens who would will only what the general will does, and thus be free, instead of every man being an entity in himself, torn by egoistic tensions and thus enslaved.

Talmon is obviously thinking here of the Nazis' infamous *Gleichshaltung* and of the political doctrines of the so-called peoples' democracies.[6] And a little later he adds:

> There is nothing that Rousseau insists on more than the active and ceaseless participation of the people and of every citizen in the affairs of the State. The State is near ruin, says Rousseau, when the citizen is too indifferent to attend a public meeting. Saturated with antiquity, Rousseau intuitively experiences the thrill of the people assembled to legislate and shape the common weal. . . . He was unaware that total and highly emotional absorption in the collective political endeavor is calculated to kill all privacy, that the excitement of the assembled crowd may exercise a most tryannical pressure, and that the extension of the scope of politics to all spheres of human interest and endeavor . . . was the shortest way to totalitarianism. Liberty is safer in countries where politics are not considered all-important and where there are numerous levels of non-political private and collective activity, although not so much direct popular democracy, than in countries where pol-

---

4. ". . . it is impossible, in such cases, to be too careful about observing all the formalities required to distinguish a regular and legitimate act from a seditious uproar, and the will of an entire people from the clamor of a faction" (Book III, chapter 18).

5. "But aside from these assemblies, which are made legal by their date alone, any assembly of the people that has not been convoked by the magistrates appointed for that purpose and in accordance with the prescribed procedures must be held to be illegitimate" (Book III, chapter 13).

6. *Gleichshaltung* was the Nazis' term for their political surveillance and control of all activities including those normally considered private [Editor].

itics take everything in their stride, and the people sit in permanent assembly.[7]

One thinks one is dreaming when one reads such interpretations of *On Social Contract*. Not only is Talmon wrong about the meaning of the terms used by Rousseau and about some crucial points in his theory, he also makes him say the exact opposite of what he really says.

It is clear that Rousseau explicitly rejects direct popular government, which, using his vocabulary, he calls "democracy." It is not only the illegitimate form of this government which he condemns under the name ochlocracy, but also the legitimate form. Well before reaching this conclusion he had advanced this maxim: "To be legitimate, the government must not be confused with the sovereign, but must be its minister" (Book II, chapter 6, note 4). Further on the condemnation becomes explicit: "It is not good for the one who makes the laws to execute them, or for the body of the people to divert its attention from general objectives and turn it to particular ones. . . . Taking the term in the strict sense, true democracy has never existed. . . . It is impossible to imagine that the people would remain constantly assembled to attend to public affairs" (Book III, chapter 4). Finally, there is the well-known aphorism with which he concludes: "If there were a people of gods, it would govern itself democratically. So perfect a government is not suited to men" (Book III, chapter 4).

"It is impossible to imagine that the people would constantly remain assembled to attend to public affairs." But it is precisely this that Rousseau envisaged and sought, according to Talmon. One feels quite helpless when confronted with an interpretation of a theory which claims that its author defends a thesis which, on the contrary, he plainly rejects as absurd.

Furthermore, Rousseau never said that the state is lost as soon as the citizen becomes too apathetic to attend "a public meeting." That would have been incredibly silly. What he says is altogether different: "In a well-run republic, everyone rushes to the assemblies; under a bad government, no one likes to take a single step to get there, because no one takes any interest in what is done in them" (Book III, chapter 15). The word Rousseau uses here is the word "assembly." It refers not to public meetings in general, but to assemblies authorized by the constitution, where the citizen is called on to vote on proposed laws submitted to him. At bottom, the idea Rousseau is expressing here is the irreproachably banal one repeated in a hundred different ways by newspapers and party leaders in our modern democracies each time citizens are called to the polls.

But Talmon's most serious error is to think that *On Social Contract* prescribes or leads to the *Gleichschaltung* of the individual, the death of all personal life, the absorption of all realms of human activity by politics and the imposition on everyone of "a fixed, rigid and universal pattern

7. Talmon, pp. 39, 47.

of feeling." Quite the contrary, in his chapter "On the Limits of Sovereign Power," Rousseau explicitly states: "But beyond the public person, we have to consider the private persons who compose it, whose life and liberty are naturally independent of it. It is a question, then, of clearly distinguishing the respective rights of the citizen and the sovereign, and the duties the former have to fulfill as subjects from the natural rights they should enjoy as men" (Book II, chapter 4).

Let me comment briefly on this text without regard to Talmon's errors. In opposition to certain interpreters of his thought, Rousseau here states very precisely that in contractual society natural law remains in force. The general will itself is therefore unable to make acts legitimate which are contrary to natural law. This is how Rousseau escapes the reproach directed against him on this point by Benjamin Constant, in a pamphlet which appeared in 1815 and which has had considerable influence.[8] One can certainly regret that Rousseau did not elaborate his point. It is nonetheless one of those theoretical axioms which he did little more than formulate and which he did not emphasize, but which anyone trying to understand him must not overlook.

Whatever the precise role assigned to natural law in Rousseau's state, it is obvious from the text we have just cited that in the lives and personalities of members of a community Rousseau allows for the existence of a private sector over which the general will has no hold. Rousseau's man is not only a citizen, he is also an individual. This dualism is fundamental to *On Social Contract*, according to the second of the axioms I have just mentioned. Rousseau refers to it more often than to the first axiom. He tells us, for example, that "each individual can, as a man, have a particular will contrary to or different from the general will he has as a citizen. His private interest may speak to him quite differently than the common interest." The same passage speaks of "his absolute and naturally independent existence" (Book I, chapter 7). Recall in this connection that for Rousseau the particular will and the particular interest of the members of a community are not in themselves at all vile or suspect. They are natural facts, the sources of political problems, consequences of that human nature with which the philosopher and the lawgiver must learn to come to terms. Without the interplay of particular interests and the common interest, says Rousseau, there would be no political problem, "politics would cease to be an art" (Book II, chapter 3, note 1). Society itself is based on nothing but its members' interests. Rousseau does not condemn particular interests except when they usurp the place of the general interest, when particular wills replace the general will. To overlook the private sector of the personalities of the members

8. "There is part of life which necessarily remains personal and independent, which is of right beyond the competence of society. . . . The assent of the Majority is not always enough to make its acts legitimate: there are some which nothing can justify. . . . Rousseau failed to recognize this truth." Benjamin Constant, *Collection complète des ouvrages publiés sur le Gouvernement representatif et la Constitution actuelle de la France* (Paris, 1818), I. 178. But Rousseau did not "misunderstand this truth." On the contrary, he would have agreed completely with Constant's theses on this point.

of the community makes everything Rousseau writes about the general will and the will of all unintelligible—what I am saying is that it makes the whole book unintelligible. Rousseau, "in taking men as they are," never envisaged a state of affairs where politics embraces everything, confiscates private life for the state's profit and drowns the minds of individuals in the whirlpool or the grave of a collective mind. The objections which Talmon makes against him on this score are completely unjustified. Unjustified—although here as elsewhere one can understand how these mistakes arose.[9] Rousseau unquestionably prefers societies undivided by fundamental conflicts, strongly united societies where the word *community* keeps all its meaning. Certainly, this uprooted man understood the full value of rootedness, the full psychological value for an individual of feeling himself a member of a distinctive community, of belonging to it at the same time that it belongs to him, of feeling himself to be a member of a society where, without becoming lost or dissolving into it, he has his role to play and his own place. Should we be angry with Rousseau for understanding this? Should we criticize him? Would it not be more appropriate to praise him here as elsewhere for being both a prophet and a critic of modern times, the forerunner of our sociologists and psychiatrists? Did he not here put his finger on the cause of one of the twentieth century's deepest sources of discontent—the displacement of communities by anonymous, amorphous formations, which evoke nothing but complaints and demands, and to which we can no longer feel bound.

Persistence of natural law even in a city founded on contract, inviolability of the citizen's private life: here are guarantees that deserve consideration. But there are others which flow from the nature of the contract itself. First, there is the doubly general character of law: "it must emanate from all to be applied to all," thus securing a political equality which must, among other things, keep any individual from being singled out for harmful treatment. Next, there is the fact that laws can only apply to matters which bear on the common interest. The scope of absolute sovereignty is thus further limited—to an indeterminate degree, to be sure, but still it is limited. This is a third axiom of Rousseau's thought, but in this case, uncustomarily, he gives it many formulations. "The right which the social pact gives the sovereign over the subjects does not go beyond . . . the limits of public utility" (Book IV, chapter 8).

"In the republic, says the Marquis d'Argenson, each man is perfectly free with regard to that which does not harm others. This is the invari-

---

9. Talmon seems to rely on the following text: "The better constituted the state, the more public concerns prevail over private ones in the minds of the citizens. There are even many fewer private concerns, because the sum of common happiness furnishes a more considerable portion of each individual's happiness, and there remains less for the individual to seek through his own private efforts" (Book III, chapter 15). (Next comes the text we have already cited, "In a well-run republic everyone rushes to the assemblies. . . .") Nevertheless, as the structure of this passage shows ("the better . . . the more"), what is being described here is a theoretical sequence. This is, in fact, one of the few passages in *On Social Contract* that can be called utopian. But clearly, since even here Rousseau does not contemplate suppressing the individual's private life, there is even less reason to think he contemplates doing so "taking men as they are."

able limit; it cannot be set any more exactly" (Book IV, chapter 8, note 6). "The sovereign . . . cannot impose on the subjects any restraints that are useless to the community." "It is agreed that each person alienates through the social pact only that part of his power, possessions, and liberty that will be important to the community" (Book II, chapter 4). All this seems very well put. Unfortunately, Rousseau appears at first sight to cancel the effects of these restrictions by adding: "the sovereign alone is judge of what is important." But he salvages his position right away by recalling and elaborating a gloss essential to the contract itself: "Since the condition is equal for all, no one has an interest in making it burdensome for the others."

"No one has an interest in making it burdensome for the others." Here, in the final analysis, is what protects us from disagreeable surprises in Rousseau's city. And this reminds us of something that is not always well understood. In his *On Social Contract* Rousseau does not describe a particular legitimate society. What he tries to do is not to design machinery, but to evoke a spirit and establish criteria. *On Social Contract* does not provide a blueprint which is supposed to enable us to manufacture just, free societies, if by that is meant complete societies, each identical to the others, emerging from the sociological production line like mass-produced cars. On the contrary, there can be an infinite number of societies, quite different from each other, but all legitimate according to the criteria of *On Social Contract*. Let there be no mistake: it is not about forms and institutions that I wish to speak; it is well known that for Rousseau as for Montesquieu these depend on each society's particular circumstances—historical, geographic, economic, etc. I am talking about what is revelant to my subject: the *weight* of the social authority that the individual must bear. Now, who cannot see that this weight depends solely on the general will of the particular community being considered? Thus, one society might ban the theater or games (as Geneva did in the eighteenth century), another, in our own times, might well ban smoking in public places, if the general will so decided. (Such a ban is being considered in our country today). It is not impossible to conceive, as a limiting case, of a society of sadomasochists who would delight in loading themselves with crushing burdens, or of a community at the other end of the political spectrum so lacking in foresight as to chose to do without useful and even necessary services, rather than consenting to the taxes needed to pay for them. In both cases one can speak of oppression. But is Rousseau to blame? He did a very good job, it seems to me, of laying out the rules of the game. It is up to us to play. It is not always possible to save peoples, any more than individuals, from the consequences of their own folly.

These reflections lead me to the civil religion, which has always constituted the most scandalous part of *On Social Contract*. It is a curious thing that what has caused offense has changed over the two centuries that have passed since the book was published. What mainly offended Jean-Jacques' contemporaries was his criticism of Christianity. Pure

evangelical Christianity, according to Rousseau, was, if not the antisocial religion par excellence, at any rate a religion which failed to strengthen
the "social bond" and which in certain cases could even threaten state
security. In our times a different passage from the chapter constitutes the
main stumbling block, even for readers favorably disposed toward Rousseau. This passage seems to have gone almost unnoticed 200 years ago.
Let us reread it, in order to identify the cause of offense:

> There is, therefore, a purely civil profession of faith, the arti-
> cles of which are for the sovereign to determine, not precisely
> as religious dogmas, but as sentiments of sociability, without
> which it is impossible to be a good citizen or a faithful subject.
> Without being able to obligate anyone to believe them, the
> sovereign can banish from the state anyone who does not believe
> them; it can banish him not for being impious but for being
> unsociable, for being incapable of sincerely loving the laws
> and justice, and of sacrificing his life, if need be, for his duty.
> If after having publicly acknowledged these same dogmas,
> someone behaves as though he does not believe them, let his
> punishment be death; he has committed the greatest of crimes;
> he has lied before the laws (Book IV, chapter 8).

I confess that I find this text a bit alarming, but less so than certain
others have. I note, for example, that the civil religion is not a religion
but a "purely *civil profession* of faith." I also note that, according to
Rousseau, one can and should tolerate "all those [religions] which tolerate others, insofar as their dogmas are in no way contrary to the duties
of a citizen." I note further that liberty of conscience is respected, to a
very great extent: "Considered in relation to society, which is either general or particular, religion can also be divided into two kinds, namely,
the religion of man and the religion of the citizen." And I also note that
when society is satisfied by the profession of civil faith, "each may have,
in addition, such opinions as he pleases, without it being the sovereign's
business to know them." Liberty of conscience, I have said, is respected
to a very great extent, and I well understand the misgivings which such
a formulation can arouse. But can liberty of conscience ever be complete? No more, it seems, than can civil liberty. What, for example,
should be done about the Doukhobors? Is not the solution that has been
proposed as a last resort—mass emigration—a Rousseauist one? [1] Returning
to the chapter on civil religion, I note in conclusion that the sentence
which in our day is criticized most severely does not speak of condemn-
ing a person to death for not *believing* the profession of civil faith after
having duly subscribed to it. A person is only to be punished with death
if he *acts* as if he does not believe in the profession. The offense is best
described not as a lack of faith, but as a failure to keep faith. The crux

1. The Doukhobors, a pacifist and mystical sect
of Russian Christians, were severely persecuted
under the Tsars. After a successful petition campaign led by Leo Tolstoy, they were allowed to
emigrate. By 1899 a settlement of 12,000 had been
established in Canada [Editor].

of the matter, though, is to identify the type of conduct which infallibly shows that a person does not believe in the profession of faith. This, I think, can only be determined by referring to a state's criminal code and, in the context of the problem we are studying, to the fifth chapter of the second book of *On Social Contract*, where we read, "Only a person who cannot be preserved without danger can rightfully be put to death, even as an example." In other words, I do not think that the chapter on civil religion established new offenses. What it does (though it is hard to tell, since Rousseau did not clarify his ideas on this point) is to mention criminal and even political acts which are incompatible with membership in a community and which would, in any event, call for the death penalty. Is the chapter on civil religion then simply tautological? Not exactly. The problem, Rousseau tells us, is to make the citizen love his duties. The profession of civil faith thus rests at bottom on an idea that was quite banal and quite common in the eighteenth century: religion in the service of society. It is a kind of coinsurance.

Now, having studied the terms of this disconcerting declaration, and having shown how it does not entail all of the sinister consequences that are sometimes ascribed to it, is it not appropriate to go further? If we look a bit closer, do we not see that those celebrated articles of the profession of civil faith—the existence of God, the afterlife, with its rewards and punishments, the sacredness of the contract, etc.—cannot possibly be deduced from the contract? They are gratuitous, added on, even, in a sense, at odds with Rousseau's political theory. In fact, Rousseau has here stepped out of his role as a political philosopher and encroached on the legislator's. For, as he himself admits, it is the sovereign's job to establish the provisions concerning social sentiments that it considers necessary. Here we encounter again the principle of diversity that we described earlier. The profession of civil faith may very well be different in different communities. One community, being pious or even puritanical, could require a maximum number of provisions; another could dispense with them altogether; and a third could be satisfied with the one negative dogma specified by Rousseau, the one which forbids intolerance. Would the societies which resulted from this be any the less legitimate according to *On Social Contract*'s own criteria? Of course not. The only objection Rousseau could make against a society which rejected all of these dogmas is that it would jeopardize its viability. But that would be his own personal opinion, which anyone could freely reject.

Let me conclude with a brief summary. * * * The only thing I have tried to do here is to bring together a number of texts which it seems to me do not square with the thesis that I consider unacceptable (and for many other reasons beside this one). Far from handing over the contractual state's citizens bound and gagged to any sort of tyranny, Rousseau carefully considered the problem of social freedom and its relations with authority. His ideal was a state in which "the people are free without being masters, and the magistrate commands without tyrannizing."[2] Could it not in fact be said, on the basis of rereading certain passages from *On Social Contract*, that Rousseau's thought, so far as it concerns liberty and authority, is not totally unanalgous to the thought of certain theologians who have no difficulty reconciling divine grace with man's free will? In a sense, for Rousseau, liberty *is* authority ("the essence of the body politic lies in the reconciliation of obedience and liberty" Book III, chapter 13), just as, for some theologians, free will is nothing other than grace itself, acting through us.

At any rate, our analysis has had the aim of showing that there is material in *On Social Contract* to give pause to those of Rousseau's interpreters who complain of oppression. The doubly general character of law, its supremacy and its inviolability, political and civil equality, the distinction between the government which is not sovereign and the sovereign people which does not govern, recognition of the double nature of social man, who is both an individual and a citizen, the persistence of natural law in the contractual state, the limits of sovereign power—there really must be blindness or bad faith involved in discussing the theory of *On Social Contract* without mentioning these numerous guarantees of civil liberty. To conclude that they are insufficient is conceivable, but at least these guarantees must be evaluated and weighed.

As for what remains of that notorious "total alienation," once it has been mitigated by all these corrections and restrictions, I have only this to say. Do not the democratic states of Western Europe all follow this doctrine? Do they not all act as if, in case of need, they may demand that we sacrifice our time, our property, our liberty, and even our lives? Are we not all, in democratic regimes, "forced by the whole body" to obey the laws, which is to say, in Rousseau's language, "forced to be free"? And are these regimes any more totalitarian or despotic for all that? Let us congratulate Rousseau for having here once again been a prophet of the modern age, for having leaped beyond classical nineteenth-century liberalism, for having glimpsed that a society where the state seldom or never intervenes can be just as oppressive or unjust as a society where the state intervenes constantly and everywhere.

The truth is that when the arguments of critics hostile to *On Social Contract* are closely examined, a rather significant point becomes clear. Almost all of these critics, having summarized Rousseau's principles in their own way, quickly slide into a much more thorough analysis of the pernicious consequences caused by abusive applications of these principles. But to enter the realm of abuses is to leave the realm of *On Social Contract*, which is the realm of right. It is too easy to refute an author by showing that distortions of his ideas have been, or can be, catastrophic. . . . The state is us: the law is our own will (Book II, chapter 6). Any social system that does not give these principles flesh and bones

2. Letter to Coindet, February 9, 1768.

is unfaithful to the spirit of *On Social Contract* by Jean-Jacques Rousseau.

ROBERT NISBET

Robert Nisbet taught sociology for many years at the University of California, Riverside. In 1974, he was named Albert Schweitzer Professor of Humanities at Columbia University. His many books, all focusing on Western social and intellectual history, include *The Quest for Community* (1953), *Tradition and Revolt* (1968), and *The Social Philosophers* (1973), in which Rousseau is portrayed as much more of a totalitarian than in the essay presented here. Now retired from teaching, Nisbet, in recent years, has become an academic luminary of the neoconservatives. *Prejudices: A Philosophical Dictionary* is his most recent book. "Rousseau & Equality" is a selection from *Encounter* (February 1974).

Rousseau & Equality

*   *   *

Rousseau shrinks from nothing in his passion to found a social order on the rock of equality. Only in a few religious figures in history do we find a like combination of zeal, relentless purpose, and willingness to take whatever steps are necessary to ensure salvation for mankind. After Rousseau, equality would be the Procrustean bed on which conceptions of freedom, justice, rights, and compassion would be placed by an unending and constantly increasing line of intellectuals in, first the West, then most other parts of the world.

Before commencing the analysis of Rousseau's writings that I shall follow in this essay—one based on the chronological sequence of his most important political writings—it is useful, I think, to mention quickly three basic, constitutive, and overriding themes in his social and political philosophy. In one degree or other, all three are to be found in the *Discourses* and the *Social Contract*, which are the works I shall limit myself to for the most part here.

First, the hatred of what can best be called intermediate society. That is, the ascending hierarchy of institutions, from family through parish, guild, and profession all the way to social class, the fabric of traditional elements of the social bond, such as friendship, mutual aid, and other kinds of elemental interdependence, and, most of all, the network of traditional authorities, which can be seen as lying intermediate to man and the political state.

Second, a love sometimes reaching adoration of the individual, conceived as liberated from the historically-developed constraints and coercions of traditional society, and placed in a new, nurturing context of association so tightly woven that man's re-endowed, true self will never again be subjected to the corruptions, torments, and conflicts which Rousseau had found to be the very stuff of ordinary society.

Third, an almost mystic dedication to omnipotence—whether in the person of legislator, tutor, or *eminence grise or in the form of the General Will, rooted in a reconstituted and hence incorruptible populus*—so broad and so penetrating, so omniscient, as to be able not only to emancipate the individual from the fetters of traditional society but to become the indispensable basis of a new political community where men can, in Rousseau's words, "be forced to be free" and also equal in their rights, duties, possessions, and membership.

These are the fundamental themes of Rousseau's political and social thought. In one degree or shape they can be found in the line of writings that stretches from the first Discourse through the *Social Contract* and also in such works as *Emile*; the romance, *Héloïse*; and, far from least, the *Confessions.* The flexibility, the versatility, of the themes taken together is obvious. As I tried to point out some three decades ago, they provide Rousseau's linkage with "totalitarianism." But their utility is greater and deeper than that. They can be seen in non-totalitarian manifestations of the political community, in expressions of the ideology of permanent revolution that have been, ever since the French Revolution, a fixed undercurrent of Western society, in writings as recent as those of the New Left, and, depending upon time, circumstance, and place, in incontestably liberal and democratic movements. The combination of social nihilism, absolute individualism, and adoration of legitimate, unlimited power is a formidable one. It is precisely this combination that offers undergirding for Rousseau's equalitarianism and endows him with such consummate relevance, such contemporaneity, at the present time.

Knowing how to read Rousseau is, as I discovered long ago, vital. Too often readers go directly to the *Social Contract.* This is a mistake, for it is bound to remain a collection of epigrammatic, often digressive, and frequently opaque utterances unless one reaches the book by pretty much the same route that Rousseau took over a twelve-year period in order, eventually, to write it. This is a route that includes the *Discourses* above all else, and it is these, together with the *Social Contract,* that will occupy us for the most part in this essay. Any other references will be brief and for purposes of added emphasis only; one can learn just about all there is to be learned about Rousseau the philosopher of equality from these texts.

The first of the *Discourses* was published in 1750, and it yielded Rousseau a prize from the Academy of Dijon, which had set the question: *"Has the Restoration of the Arts and Sciences had a Purifying Effect upon Morals?"* Rousseau's answer, as is well known, was in the negative. But the real significance of this short piece has little to do with the question as stated by the Academy, and it is failure to recognise this point that has often led to neglect or merely superficial understanding of the first *Discourse.* What we have in fact, fully and often brilliantly stated, is a countercultural position that would not require many textual changes for it to have immediacy in our own time. The first *Discourse* is, as I say, only passingly and tepidly interested in the arts and sciences as such and their negative role in human happiness. It is, most deeply and pervasively, an attack upon the values, institutions, and intimate social relationships of the society Rousseau had, as a young man, entered in France and about which he had such agonising conflicts of regard. In this *Discourse* we are given a picture of French society—with full implications reaching all civilised society—that is skilfully textured, with the full range of tones and accents reaching from egoistic corruption to inauthenticity. That last is not Rousseau's word; but it will serve as a reasonably exact synonym of a word that very definitely is Rousseau's: *hypocrisy*. The society around him, Rousseau tells us, is riven with "jealousy, suspicion, fear, coldness, reserve, hate, and fraud." But surmounting even these is "hypocrisy."

Now, what is the cause of this hypocritical or inauthentic society? In a word "inequality." It is in this *Discourse*—though I do not say in this work alone—that the *leit-motiv* is introduced. Listen to Rousseau on the source of the corruption that for him spreads through all society:

> whence arise all those abuses, unless it be from that fatal inequality introduced among men by the difference of talents and the cheapening of virtue. This is the most evident effect of all our studies, and the most dangerous of all their consequences.

Dangerous indeed, for whatever else the *ancien régime* was, it was hierarchical: in social structure, in religion, and also, it might be noted, in the intellectual-*philosophe* community, one that as Rousseau learned to his occasional humiliation tended to regard equality as a virtue only insofar as it did not affect their own status in the salons of Paris. Inequality, then, for Rousseau in 1750—as for Christopher Jencks or John Rawls in the America of two centuries later—is the cause of the conflict, hypocrisy, the corruption (the inauthenticity, in a word) he had in his own personal life come to hate and to feel humiliated by.[1]

Let us pass now to the second *Discourse*, this one published in 1755, also in response to a topic presented by the Academy at Dijon: "*What is the Origin of Inequality Among Men, and Is it Authorised by Natural Law?*"

Any reader today of Professors Rawls and Jencks is bound to feel at home with such a question. He is bound to feel even more at home with Rousseau's extended answer. I happen to regard this, the second *Discourse*, as the single most brilliant piece of sociological writing in the

1. When this article appeared, Jencks, a sociologist, and Rawls, a philosopher, had just published influential books alarming to Nisbet, who feared they would promote the radical egalitarianism that he traces in his article to Rousseau. See Christopher Jencks, *Inequality* (New York: Basic Books, 1972) and John Rawls, *A Theory of Justice* (Cambridge, Mass.: Harvard Univ. Press, 1971) [Editor].

18th century; never mind what we may feel its long-run consequences to have been on Western social structure and culture. Here Rousseau uses with extraordinary advantage a methodological device known in the 18th century as "conjectural" or "natural" or "speculative" history, or what Rousseau himself calls "hypothetical" history. In its way it is the precursor of the 19th century's cherished social evolutionary or developmental works. In its way it is also the precursor of what Professor Rawls makes fundamental in his A *Theory of Justice*, that is, the hypothetical "original position" from which he deduces so many monumental, or at least statuesque, propositions regarding the good and the desirable for 20th-century society in the West.

> Let us begin, therefore, by setting all the facts aside, for they have no bearing on the question.[2]

This sentence, at the very beginning of the second *Discourse*, has been so many times derided. And yet, given the then regnant methodology of science so far as the study of man was involved, it is perfectly intelligible and justifiable. All Rousseau implied by the statement, as his succeeding words make quite evident, was the irrelevance and immateriality of ordinary historical data, given the issue that for him—as for Professor Rawls—was vital. What is the nature of man? What would man have become? What would society today be if there had not taken place some "fatal accident" that diverted man's history from equality and goodness to the corrupt, tyrannous, and hypocritical—above all, inequalitarian—society whose poisoned fruits we are obliged to live on today?

It is not true (as Arthur O. Lovejoy pointed out in detail many years ago) that for Rousseau the primal state of nature was mankind's happiest stage of existence—it was a later one, after language, morality, and the elemental arts had come into being, that Rousseau thought probably the happiest for man. But it is true that this primal state, as best it could be reconstructed through a speculative, rationalist psychology and ethnology, was the one which Rousseau used as his "laboratory" in which to examine the true nature of man.

There are many things to be found in second *Discourse*, including a distinct pre-Marxian recognition of the curse placed upon mankind by the rise of private property and condemnation of man thereby to an alienated existence. The speculations on the origin and development of language, of morality, the arts, and the earliest forms of social structure are, without exception, ingenious and reflect a degree of learning Rousseau is not always credited with. Necessarily, I must concentrate here on what is essential in that *Discourse* so far as my subject is concerned. That is the rise of social inequality, yes, but also the immediately precipitating *conditions* of inequality. And these are what Rousseau called "combinations," that is, social interdependences which involved authority, hierarchy, and other elements of the social bond that for Rousseau

---

2. *Discourse on Inequality*, p. 9. [The editors have added references to the texts in this volume.]

were chains upon man's true nature, despoilers of the freedom he had known earlier in his evolution.

> As long as men . . . applied themselves only to tasks that a single man could accomplish and only to arts that did not need the cooperation of several hands, they lived free, healthy, good, and happy lives. . . . But from the moment any one man needed help from another, and as soon as they perceived that it was useful for one man to have provisions for two, equality disappeared, property was introduced, work became necessary, and vast forests were changed into pleasant fields, which had to be watered with human sweat and in which slavery and misery were soon seen to spring up and grow with the crops.[3]

Observe in that passage the emphasis upon, not property or work as such, but upon social interdependences, upon aspects of the social bond rising from work or mutual need, which, in words he uses just before the quoted passage, refers to "combinations fatal to innocence and happiness." True, by Rousseau's own declaration, it was the discovery of agriculture and the metallurgical arts, and with these the rise of private property, which provided background—necessary background. Nevertheless, it is Rousseau the sociologist rather than Rousseau the economist who is foremost here. It is the Rousseau who had very early come to despise and fear the ordinary ties of civil society, with all their tiny but potent webs of authority and hierarchy, their traps of inequality, who is offering us analysis that had begun in the first *Discourse*.

Once the "combinations fatal to innocence and happiness" began to proliferate in early society—began to take from man his true nature and replace it with something alien to his being—then

> it was necessarily to one's advantage to seem to be other than what one was in fact. To be and to appear became two completely different things, and from this distinction sprang imposing ostentation, deceptive cunning, and all the vices which follow in their train.[4]

In that statement, obviously, we are brought back to the theme of the first *Discourse*, the point of departure of the second. In the first we were told that the hypocrisy, uncertainty, and corruption of the social order around him sprang from inequality. In the second *Discourse* we have what is by the standards of the time a superlative essay in anthropology and social psychology that seeks to demonstrate how deep the roots of inequality are in the human condition and, therefore, how radical must be the remedy. That remedy is provided us in the third *Discourse*, to which I shall come in a moment. There is, however, an anticipatory statement in the *Discourse on Inequality* in which, noting the defects of all early efforts at the reform of the political state that had been brought

3. *Ibid.*, pp. 39–40.   4. *Ibid.*, p. 42.

eventually into existence by social inequality, strife, and conflict, he writes prophetically:

> It [the state] was continually patched up, whereas it would have been necessary to begin by clearing the area and discarding all the old materials, just as Lycurgus had done in Sparta, in order afterwards to raise a solid edifice. [5]

It has been so often said of Rousseau that his desire was to return men to the state of nature that one almost despairs of setting the matter straight. Never anywhere to my knowledge did Rousseau so much as hint at any desirability of mankind's abandoning of civil society and, in effect, returning to forests and fields of the primordial condition. The "state of nature" for Rousseau was never anything more than, first, a term for the primal condition that has never ceased to fascinate philosophers and social scientists: and, second, a touchstone of moral excellence that could be applied to existing societies.

What Rousseau sought, with powerful effect, was no retreat from civilisation but, rather, *a form of government* that would, at one and the same time, liberate man from social inequalities and their tyrannies of spirit and, equally important, establish a form of association from which all such inequalities and tyrannies would be forever banned. And, as men have on so many occasions in Western history (our own day included), Rousseau turned to politics as the redemptive means.

More accurately I should say that Rousseau availed himself of the theme of political redemption that had been in his mind from his youth. In the *Confessions* he tells us that in 1743, while an aide in the French embassy at Venice, well before he commenced any of his important social and political writings, the thought came to him one day

> that everything was radically connected with politics, and that however one proceeded, no people would be other than the nature of its government made it.

Not by an iota did Rousseau ever deviate from that conviction. In the first *Discourse* there is adulation expressed for ancient Sparta, its people freed of the corrupting influences of the kind of society and culture Athens knew, and in another connection unmistakable admiration for "military virtues." In the second *Discourse*, having made clear, in words which Marx and Engels must surely have studied with care a century later, that the political state came into being as the means of seeking to contain, to moderate the conflicts in society generated by social inequality, Rousseau emphasises the destructive effects of the political state upon men's liberty.

> All ran headlong into their chains, hoping to ensure their liberty, for, along with enough reason to be conscious of the

5. *Ibid.*, p. 46.

advantages of political institutions, they did not have enough
experience to foresee their dangers.[6]

It is, however, in the third *Discourse*, "On Political Economy", published shortly afterwards, that the inspiration of 1743 becomes fully
articulated.

Rarely if ever in history, at least since Plato, has the idea of the total
political community been advanced so compellingly, has the theme of
redemptive political power reaching the very roots of human personality
been presented so temptingly, or the notion of a total human virtue
fashioned by political psychology been set before readers so enchant-
ingly. I know of no work unless it be Plato's *Republic* that so consecrates
man to the redeemer-state. It is not possible here to deal adequately with
the rich insights into the relation between power and personality that
Rousseau furnishes us, between politics and morality, and the many
other elements of this work which have worked their way tellingly into
modernity, especially into the whole radical thrust of the modern intellectual's mind. I must stay, all too briefly, with the elements which are
most apposite to the problem of inequality in society.

If the third *Discourse* is best thought of as an 18th-century "Theory of
Justice", its regard equal between liberty and equality which for Rousseau (as for Professor Rawls) are the two constitutive principles of legitimate society, it has to be said that Rousseau's grasp of the political
implications of equalitarian justice is far more sophisticated, or at least
a great deal more open and candid than anything that can be found in
Rawls' work. Rousseau was under no illusions that an equalitarian society could come into existence merely through men's contemplation of
abstractly stated principles of justice, or even through systematic education in any ordinary sense of that word. What was required, as Rousseau
sees shrewdly and states brilliantly, was a totally new conception of power,
one that instead of being remote superstructure would penetrate the most
intimate recesses of the social order, indeed of the human mind.

> If it is good to know how to make use of men as they are, it is
> better still to make them into what one needs them to be; the
> most absolute authority is that which penetrates a man's inner
> being and is exerted no less on his will than on his actions.[7]

For at least fifteen years (beginning, as I have noted, when Rousseau
was an aide in Venice) that theme had been virtually inseparable from
Rousseau's passion for equality and his hatred of all the inequalities which
are the very stuff of civil society. Precisely as the religious millennialist
knows how indispensable is God the absolute sovereign—omnipotent,
omniscient, omnipresent—to the salvation of man, so does Rousseau
know how vital is the absolute sovereign in political terms. Without it,
as he recognised almost mystically and eschatologically, all talk of jus-

6. *Ibid.*, p. 44.   7. *Discourse on Political Economy*, p. 66.

tice, liberty, virtue, and equality is but idle rhetoric. I dare say Rousseau would regard most of what is today being written in dedication to equality (including, I fear, Professor Rawls' *A Theory of Justice*) as lacking in essential substance, as being emasculated by refusal to deal candidly with the problems of political power and of political psychology necessarily involved in any forthright proposal for building the social order on the rock of equality. Very well indeed did Rousseau know how deeply rooted in man's character is the impulse to *inequality* and how diversely manifest in the entire social fabric is this impulse. As only a supreme power can save man from original sin in the religious realm, only an equal power can save man from society's inherent and pervasive inequality.

What is this power? The General Will, a power not the less absolute, total, and penetrating for its declared roots in the people—that is, the people first purified, cleansed of the false wills and desires and attitudes which history has implanted in their minds and personalities, and, as it were, psychologically reconstituted. By definition the General Will, in contrast to the Will of All, is the will that emerges when the members of the political community are able to give their allegiances and their thoughts completely to the community, when they have become liberated from the false consciousness that directs them to think and act as individuals or as representatives of partial interests in the social order. The General Will has nothing to do with a majority as such, least of all with the mere counting of votes.

"The first and most important maxim of legitimate or popular government", Rousseau tells us in the third *Discourse*,

> in other words, of a government whose aim is the good of the people, is therefore, as I have said, to follow the general will in all things. . . . How, someone will ask me, can the general will be known in cases in which it has not expressed itself? Must the whole nation be assembled at every unforeseen event? It will be all the less necessary to do so, because it is by no means certain that its decision would be the expression of the general will, because this means is impracticable for a large people, and because it is rarely necessary when the government is well intentioned, for the leaders know very well that the general will is always on the side most favorable to the public interest, that is to say, the most equitable, so that it is necessary merely to be just to be assured of following the general will.[8]

Rousseau would adapt that somewhat in later writings, including the *Social Contract*, seeking a means whereby voting might reveal the General Will, even suggesting that the majority must be followed. But from beginning to end in Rousseau there is the clear distinction between the

8. *Ibid.*, pp. 63, 66.

General Will, alone sovereign, incorruptible, and the guardian of public interest, discernible by its common interest rather than by number of heads, and what is revealed by voting and by representation. For representation Rousseau had only contempt. Correctly, he saw representative institutions as the yield of that feudalism he and other *philosophes* hated in all respects. It is impossible to read Rousseau—and this holds in such works as *Emile* and *La nouvelle Héloïse*, in his drafts of constitutions for Corsica and for Poland, in the famous diatribe against D'Alembert, as well as in the third *Discourse* and the *Social Contract*—without becoming aware of his obsession with the kind of power Tocqueville was to describe, in a classic passage, as "absolute, minute, regular, provident, and mild." Whether it is Rousseau in his role of tutor to Emile or of Legislator in the chapter of that title in the *Social Contract*, or any of the other roles he assumed from time to time, power—cast in therapeutic terms, power as redeemer, purifier, guardian as well as sovereign in the ordinary sense, power above all as the community in which reconstituted human beings would have equal rights—is the indispensable element, the *vis generatrix* and the *vis conservatrix*, of a just social order.

But what separates Rousseau's envisagement of political power from that of anyone else (with the possible exception of Plato, whom Rousseau adored) is the linking of power with morality, with liberty, and, of course, with equality. Rousseau is never less than the political psychologist in his treatment of power in relation to human beings.

> Do you want the general will to be carried out? Make certain that all particular wills are in accord with it, and, since virtue is only this conformity of the particular will with the general, to say the same thing in a word, make virtue reign.[9]

> Now, training citizens is not just a day's work, and turning them into men requires that they be educated as children. Suppose someone tells me that anyone who has men to govern should not seek outside their nature a perfection of which they are incapable; that he should not wish to destroy the passions within them; and that the execution of such a plan would not be any more desirable than it is possible. I will agree all the more with this, because a man without passions would certainly be a very bad citizen, but it must also be agreed that even if men cannot be taught to love nothing, it is possible to teach them to love one object rather than another, and what is truly beautiful rather than what is deformed. If, for example, they are trained early enough never to consider their own persons except in terms of their relations with the body of the state, and not to perceive of their own existence, so to speak, except as a part of that of the state, they may finally succeed in identifying themselves in some way with this greater whole;

9. *Ibid.*, p. 67.

in feeling themselves members of the homeland; in loving it with that exquisite sentiment which every isolated man feels only for himself; in perpetually lifting up their souls toward this great objective, and thus in transforming into a sublime virtue that dangerous disposition from which all our vices arise.[1]

How profoundly the uses of power recommend themselves to Rousseau in his character of political psychologist can be seen in a passage of the third *Discourse* where he treats of the relation of public power to the family. The context is the system of education which for Rousseau is total, beginning in infancy, not terminating until death. The government, he writes, should not abandon

the education of children . . . to the knowledge and prejudices of their fathers, because it is a matter of greater importance to the state than to their fathers . . . the state remains, and the family dies out."[2]

If the public authority, by taking the place of fathers and assuming this important function, acquires their rights by fulfilling their duties, the fathers have all the less reason to complain about it, because, in this regard, they are doing absolutely nothing but changing a name, and because they will hold in common, as citizens, the same authority over their children as they exercised separately as *fathers*, and will be obeyed no less well while speaking in the name of the law than they were while speaking in the name of nature.[3]

Rarely in the history of power has the social molecule been so completely broken as in that passage on the family. It is important, though, to keep in mind that what actuates Rousseau is not power for its own sake, not power as sole possible refuge from a Hobbesian state of nature, but power as the necessary instrument by which to liberate man from inequality and its myriad corruptions and conflicts and also to create for man an equalitarian community. Above anyone else in the history of political thought Rousseau gave to the word *citizen* a majesty previously reserved for such words as Father, Brother, Priest, King, and Lord. And, for Rousseau, the central essence of citizenship is equal participation in power—the power that, as we have seen, suffuses the community, reaching every corner and crevice.

Necessarily, attention must be given to matters of property and possession in the political community. This we find in the final section of the third *Discourse*.

It is not enough to have citizens and to protect them; it is also necessary to consider their subsistence.[4]

1. *Ibid.*, pp. 72–73.   3. *Ibid.*, p. 73.
2. *Ibid.*, p. 73.   4. *Ibid.*, p. 75.

Rousseau does not ban property from personal possession; at least not the residual property, the necessary possessions, all men must have in their individual names.

> Certainly, the right of property is the most sacred of all the citizens' rights and more important in certain respects than liberty itself.[5]

There is no reason to believe that Rousseau was other than sincere in that statement. But neither is there any reason to believe that by "private property" he had much else in mind than what he further on calls "the common necessaries of life." Socialism would be too strong a word for the kind of public weal Rousseau describes in this section of the third *Discourse*, but by the time one has finished reading Rousseau's artful prescriptions for taxation, based as they are on his hatred of all luxuries—within which he places the arts—and his passionate exclamations on behalf of the common man, one is obliged to come up with a conception not very far off from socialism; one that is in almost equal measure puritan and communal.

Equalitarianism is the warp, of course, on which his proposed system of taxation is woven. Space prevents any detailed account here of this proposed system; I shall content myself with two or three of Rousseau's recommendations, all of which should please our contemporary equalitarians. First, those who "possess only the common necessaries of life should pay nothing at all." But taxation should be extended to everything, to all the "superfluities" an individual might have over and above the common necessaries. Those who object on the ground that rank is not thereby taken into account (and that what may seem "superfluous" to the common man is not by any means superfluous to another) receive short shrift from Rousseau. The "grandee has two legs just like a cowherd and, like him again, but one belly."

It is easy enough to withhold sympathy, of course, for what Rousseau calls a "grandee." Our sympathy might be stretched, though, when a little later in the discussion we find Rousseau treating just as sternly what he calls "the useless professions." Here he makes plain that among these are artists and others involved in any way in "public entertainments" ("dancers, singers, players" not excluded). Rousseau's hatred of the public arts was almost total, as his notable *Letter to D'Alembert* (1758) suggests in detail and as his recommendations to the citizens of Corsica suggest in even more austere fashion. And we cannot forget Rousseau's jibes and jeers at the scholars of his day, those whom he contemptuously refers to in the first *Discourse* as comprising "herds of textbook writers," "mountebanks exhibiting themselves in public," and mere hawkers of wares. There is no reason to believe that Rousseau would regard the arts and sciences as other than baneful manifestations of social inequality.

*   *   *

5. *Ibid.*, p. 75.

At no point did Rousseau ever imagine (as have so many of our liberals and progressives during the present century) that the good society can be had for the asking, had for simple legislation and appeal to popular reason. There is a passage in the *Social Contract* that I shall come to in a moment, one in the chapter on The Legislator, that gives awful emphasis to what Rousseau knew to be required in the way of psychological surgery and transplant. Here it will suffice to cite a few more words on the subject of the General Will in the third *Discourse*. To follow the General Will

> it is necessary to know it, and, above all, to distinguish it clearly
> from the particular will, starting with oneself. This distinction
> is always extremely difficult to make, and only the most sub-
> lime virtue is capable of shedding sufficient light on it.[6]

Many today might wonder from how many ill-fated, even tragic and destructive political designs we might have been saved during the past two centuries if their architects had but paused to look for even a part of the "sublime virtue" in human consciousness that Rousseau had wisely made a condition of the good society, and for the achievement of which he was willing to declare what was in effect permanent revolution.

The *Social Contract* was, we are told, treated with a good deal of indifference by the reading public when it appeared in 1762. One can easily see why. Too many of its electric and quite essential passages are separated by meandering streams of exposition and often pedantic digression. The reason lies, no doubt, in the fact that the book was a kind of compromise between Rousseau's desire to publish a truly systematic work of great length on "political institutions" and his unconquerable passion to instruct the public without let. Despite its classic status, its demonstrable influence upon the political mind in not merely the West but quite literally the entire world, the book is unsatisfactory in many ways and cannot compare in strictly philosophical terms with Hobbes' *Leviathan*, say, or Montesquieu's *Spirit of the Laws*, books which Rousseau admired almost as much as he did Plato's *Republic*.

Nevertheless, the *Social Contract* achieved, after Rousseau's death, a unique popularity by virtue of the magnetic appeal it exerted upon minds like Robespierre and Saint-Just. Apparently it even had substantial following among the rank-and-file of the Revolution. A contemporary tells us that hardly a paragraph in the book failed to be quoted at one time or other in the newspapers, and that excited groups of citizens could be seen reading and discussing the book on the streets of Paris. No matter what one may think of the work taken as a whole or set against the grand project Rousseau had wished to complete, it has some of the most brilliant passages and torch-like phrases to be found anywhere in the history of thought. What follows here is not intended to be another assessment of the book, even in briefest terms. All I want to do is show the relation-

6. *Ibid.*, p. 63

ship of the book to those ideas and themes we have thus far been concerned with here, those pertaining to equality and its vital contexts.

As in his earlier writings, the two themes of liberty and equality are dominating. And also as in these earlier writings, the referent of each theme is the individual in his relation to traditional society and all its hierarchies and networks of authority. *"Man is born free; and everywhere he is in chains."* Those are the thrilling words with which the first chapter begins. The chains are, of course, the interdependence founded on place, kinship, class, religion, work, and composed of the tiny but puissant links of friendship, mutual aid, social exchange, conformity, and other aspects of the social bond which Rousseau had come to detest for their generation of inequality, corruption, and conflict and their debasement of the individual.

The problem, we are told, is

> To find a form of association that defends and protects the person and possessions of each associate with all the common strength, and by means of which each person, joining forces with all, nevertheless obeys only himself and remains as free as before.[7]

The problem might seem insuperable by the criteria of all ordinary conceptions of liberty, but it is within easy reach of the Rousseauian vision of the *populus* and the individual, each refashioned by the permanent revolution of the General Will. Rousseau, it must be admitted, is fully aware of the requirements—somewhat more so than the equalitarian *philosophes* of our own day who tend to shrink, it sometimes seems, from the political-psychological implications of their chosen premises and moral objectives. What is demanded, Rousseau says calmly, is

> the total alienation of each associate with all his rights to the whole community, for, in the first place, since each person gives himself entirely, the condition is equal for all, and since the condition is equal for all, no one has an interest in making it burdensome for the others.[8]

That is the social contract—conceived in and dedicated to the absolute equality that Rousseau cherished in the deepest parts of his mind, capable of being fulfilled, as Rousseau well knew, only through the instrument of a profounder, more penetrating, more absolute power than any ever before known in human society but a power, by its very nature, that could liberate man completely from all the tyrannous inequalities which he regarded as inseparable from traditional society. Rousseau is perfectly aware of what he is doing in the name of equality and liberty. The social compact reduces itself, he goes on, to this:

7. *On Social Contract*, Book I, chapter 6.   8. *Ibid.*

Each of us puts his person and all his power in common under the supreme control of the general will, and, as a body, we receive each member as an indivisible part of the whole.[9]

Then comes, in full effect and brilliant clarity, the passage that lets us know precisely what the costs of equality must be:

In order, therefore, that the social pact may not be an empty formula, it tacitly includes the commitment, which alone can give force to the others, that anyone who refuses to obey the general will shall be compelled to do so by the entire body; this means nothing else than that *he will be forced to be free,* for such is the condition which, by giving each citizen to the homeland, *protects him against all personal dependence,* a condition which determines the workings of the political machine, and which alone renders legitimate civil commitments, which would otherwise be absurd, tyrannical, and subject to the most enormous abuses. [Italics added][1]

Observe in the passage the recurrence of the theme we have seen to lie in the three *Discourses* (and which lies in other works as well, including *Émile* and *La nouvelle Héloïse,* along with his letters and the two draft constitutions): the intolerability of personal dependence, that is, normal social interdependence with its incessant threat to equality, and the recurrence of the theme that had come to him in almost blinding revelation while a young man in Venice: the necessity of absolute political power as the means of creating justice and virtue in human affairs. How well Rousseau had learned his sociology from experience! For nothing is more certain than inequality once anything resembling free association, spontaneous social ties, and historically developed institutions come into being on their own.

And how perceptive—and correct!—Rousseau is in his recognition that for the equalitarian social order to come into being, and, above all, to remain in being, relationships among individuals must be as few and tenuous as possible, with, however, each individual's relation to the corporate body, to the state, as close as possible. Once the social compact, resting on the absolute General Will, is established, "each citizen would then be perfectly independent of all the rest, and at the same time very dependent on the [state]."

Like the equalitarian *philosophes* writing today, Rousseau prizes an equality that will exist irrespective of unequal faculties, motivations, and aspirations in life, based as these so often are on natural differences among individuals. The fundamental social compact does not, Rousseau writes, destroy natural inequality. It instead "substitutes a moral and legitimate equality for whatever physical equality nature had been able to impose among men, and, although they may be unequal in strength or in genius,

9. *Ibid.*   1. *Ibid.*, Book I, chapter 7.

they all become equal through agreements and law" (I.9). One need only glance at Professor Rawls' proposals in his A *Theory of Justice* along this very line to see quickly how powerful the Rousseauian constraint remains upon minds intoxicated by moral redemption of man.

Rousseau's continuing superiority lies, though, in his passion for honesty and clarity. At no point does he imply that the social contract, the adoption by man of life consecrated to equality, can be effected through other than means of the most revolutionary character. About the nearest any of our current *philosophes* have come to this realisation is Christopher Jencks' brief and somewhat abstracted conclusion, in the very final pages of his *Inequality*, that the principal obstacle to equality in America today is the refusal of most people even to consider inequality a problem, from which Professor Jencks reaches the further conclusion that if we want to achieve equality, or as he calls it more delicately here, "redistribution",

> we will not only have to politicize the question of income inequality but alter people's basic assumptions about the extent to which they are responsible for their neighbors and their neighbors for them.

Well, Rousseau knew that at the very outset of his labours, and the whole revolutionary strategy of the General Will was designed precisely to "alter people's basic assumptions" in this respect.

Unlike (again) our contemporary *philosophes* he knew this intent to "alter" had immense long-run consequences—the total politicisation of life through the General Will, the abolition of all forms of association, including religion, which might militate against the dogmas of the social compact, the exclusion of the arts and sciences above the most primitive level, the willingness of man to surrender himself and all his rights to the total community, finding "liberty" in equality of participation in the General Will, and, above all else, the continuing refashioning of man's mind and character. In the chapter on "The Legislator"—who is for the work of politics what the tutor is for the work of individual development in *Émile*, what the chilling figure of Wolmar is for the work of human relationships in *La nouvelle Héloïse*—we have Rousseau's superbly candid statement of what must be done. And what a welcome relief it is from the somewhat evasive language we tend to get in our own time on this vital matter!

> Anyone who dares to undertake the founding of a people should feel himself capable of changing human nature, so to speak, of transforming each individual, who by himself is a perfect and solitary whole, into part of a greater whole from which this individual receives, in a way, his life and his being; of altering the human constitution in order to strengthen it; and of substituting a partial and artificial existence for the physical and independent existence we have all received from nature.

He must, in a word, take away man's own forces in order to give him new ones which are alien to him.[2]

Precisely. So declared Robespierre and Saint-Just. So spoke Dostoevsky's Grand Inquisitor. And so have dreamed almost all millennialist revolutionaries since the French Revolution, from Gracchus Babeuf down to Frantz Fanon.

Finally, it must be said for Rousseau—and here too there is valuable instruction for those in our day who would disdain to hypothesise religion in their quest for equality—that he knew full well the necessity of giving equality, and with it the General Will and all the laws flowing from this will, the ineradicable cast of the sacred. Hence the brilliant penultimate chapter on the civil religion. Men must have a religion, Rousseau there tells us, for otherwise the political tie will not remain firm and close. None of the extant, traditional religions will do, however, for their attention is always on the supernatural. Christianity is particularly objectionable, for it lacks the martial virtues which must always be resplendent in the good society. Imagine, Rousseau tells us, "your Christian republic face to face with Sparta or Rome: the pious Christians will be beaten, crushed, and destroyed, before they know where they are, or will owe their safety only to the contempt their enemy will conceive for them. . . ." And in any event Christianity has the fatal political ethic of desiring a large measure of autonomy from the state, a condition clearly intolerable under the General Will.

There must, therefore, be instituted a civil religion, "a purely civil profession of faith." In no way, Rousseau tells us—and here is one place at least where he is being unwontedly dishonest or disingenuous—will this civil religion interfere with men's freedom of conscience in reference to their religious beliefs, Christian or other, "for, as the Sovereign has no authority in the other world, whatever the lot of its subjects may be in the life to come, that is not its business, provided they are good citizens in this life." Subjects owe the Sovereign "an account of their opinions only to such an extent as they matter to the community."

But, as Rousseau must surely have recognised, all struggles between the religious (especially the Christian) and the political in history have concerned precisely religious opinions "as they matter to the community." Not the most despotic of Roman emperors cared a fig for Christian beliefs about the next world. It was this world that mattered, and it was this world that primitive Christianity could only too often seem to be revolutionising. Thus the basic dishonesty, or, certainly, naivety, in the light of the proffered freedom of conscience of the following passage, deadly in its implications to all social and cultural freedom but vitally necessary to any society dedicated to equality and founded upon the General Will:

There is, therefore, a purely civil profession of faith, the articles of which are for the sovereign to determine, not precisely

2. *Ibid.*, Book II, chapter 7.

as religious dogmas, but as sentiments of sociability, without which it is impossible to be a good citizen or a faithful subject. Without being able to obligate anyone to believe them, the sovereign can banish from the state anyone who does not believe them; it can banish him not for being impious but for being unsociable, for being incapable of sincerely loving the laws and justice, and of sacrificing his life, if need be, for his duty. If, after having publicly acknowledged these same dogmas, someone behaves as though he does not believe them, let his punishment be death; he has committed the greatest of crimes; he has lied before the law.[3]

It comes almost as a shock, after that passage and its clearly forestated premises of the Sovereign's responsibility for opinions as "they matter to the community" and, not to be forgotten, of the infallibility and incorruptibility of the General Will, to be told in the next paragraph that among the dogmas of the civil religion is one forbidding intolerance. *Credo quia absurdum* is, obviously, as applicable to the civil as to any other form of religion.

But such naivety or blinding excess of political zeal should not cause us to lose sight of the overall shrewdness and brilliance of Rousseau's chapter on religion.

He understood, as few if any equality-intoxicated *philosophes* of our day seem to understand, that if the dogma of equality is to be instituted and made to survive it must be buttressed by a form of power that draws as much from religious as political substance.

Men will die for a dogma, a great Christian theologian once wrote, who will not even stir for a conclusion.

JUDITH N. SHKLAR

Judith Shklar, professor of government at Harvard University, has written extensively on the history of modern political thought, starting in 1957 with *After Utopia*, which examines recent political theory and its decline. In 1969 she published a study of Rousseau, *Men and Citizens*, which serves as the background for the essay reprinted here. She has also written books on legal theory and on Hegel. *Ordinary Vices* is her most recent book. In 1984 she was named a MacArthur Prize fellow. "Jean-Jacques Rousseau and Equality" appeared in *Daedalus* (Summer 1978).

Jean-Jacques Rousseau and Equality

"Je conçois un nouveau genre de service à rendre aux hommes: c'est de leur offrir l'image fidelle de l'un d'entre eux afin qu'ils apprennent à

---

3. *Ibid.*, Book IV, chapter 8.

se connoitre."[1] Rousseau's mirror was meant to reflect both our private and public faces, and without disguise. What were we to see? The image of man as a self-made victim. Rousseau was preeminently the philosopher of human misery. His entire design was to show how mankind had built a social prison for itself. In the course of this enterprise Rousseau produced a veritable encyclopedia of egalitarian ideas, unique both in its scope and in the personal passion that informs it. For Rousseau chose to write from the vantage point of the wretched. He was not, however, blind to the intellectual difficulties of the very idea of equality, and it is the blending of emotion and intelligence that gives his pages their unique quality. He did not invent the secular idea of equality, but he was its most complete and eloquent defender.

Rousseau chose to speak for and as one of the poor, but he did not share the limitations of their condition. He knew the privileged well and could address them with extraordinarily, perhaps surprisingly, great effect. Certainly he still moves that public. One of the more notable aspects of contemporary egalitarianism is that it is usually promoted by the competent and relatively rich for the sake of the feeble and poor. To say that it is merely the ideological vehicle for the politically ambitious does not suffice to explain the prevalence, especially among the young, of the conviction that inequality must go. The style of argument may be dry and pedestrian often, but the real inspiration is not revealed by words alone. It is compassion, pity, guilt, and shame or an aesthetic disgust at the very thought of so much man-made misery that forces men and women to abandon class, caste, and self-interest "to cast in [their] lot with the victims," in William Morris' words.[2] Wave upon wave of social outrage has swept over successive generations of Anglo-Americans moved by evangelical protestantism, utilitarian benevolence, and simply an immense pity.[3] Pity itself is old as mankind, but as a political force it is new. Rousseau did not invent it, perhaps, but he was the first to explain, to diagnose, and finally to judge it. That is because he made no attempt to disguise the personal and emotional aspects of his whole argument. Equality was not a quasilegal fiction for him, and inequality not something that others suffered. When he announced to his shocked readers that all our vices had their origin in inequality, he meant to take a wholly new view of the moral world: the way it looks from the very bottom of society.[4]

The enduring source of Rousseau's insight into the condition of inequality was personal experience. His fateful decision to make his pri-

---

1. Professor Shklar's footnotes, which refer to the standard French texts of Rousseau's works, have been edited to make them accessible to the readers of this volume. This quotation comes from a brief work by Rousseau entitled *My Portrait* and reads: "I conceive of rendering a new kind of service to men: that is, to offer them the faithful image of one among them so that they will learn how to know themselves" [Editor].

2. William Morris, *Art and Socialism*, *Works XXIII*

(New York: Russell and Russell, 1966), p. 213.

3. E.g., Stanley H. Elkins, *Slavery* (New York: Grosset and Dunlap, 1963), p. 173, and George M. Frederickson, *The Inner Civil War* (New York: Harper and Row, 1965), pp. 15, 81, 86 for what *Uncle Tom's Cabin* achieved before the Civil War.

4. Jean-Jacques Rousseau, "Discourse on the Sciences and Arts" in *The First and Second Discourses*, trans. Roger D. and Judith R. Masters (New York: St. Martin's Press, 1964), p. 58.

vate life into a public document was grounded in the belief that his existence was politically significant. He alone had lived in every class of society without belonging to a single one of them. He had dined with princes and supped with peasants on the same day. Although born a citizen of a republic, he was ending his days as a refugee. * * * He was "the watchmaker's son" against whom all the states of Europe had formed a league. It was therefore he alone who could and did speak of equality as only a universal victim could. * * *

Masters and valets were the two poles of Rousseau's society. He had been a footman in several households, and he could speak of this peculiarly degrading situation as an insider. It was here that he learned to hate violently the ruling classes whose cruelty, pettiness, prejudices, and vices revolted him to the end of his days. It was here also, more significantly, that he acquired his numerous vices. All valets are rogues and cheats. It is inherent in their position, and Rousseau was no exception. Envy, lying, dissimulation, dishonesty, and disloyalty to one's fellow servants are normal for valets. That is the wage for being dependent on others. The master is, in turn, corrupted by power. He becomes cruel and brutal. As a general rule, for there are always a few exceptions, valets are the lowest form of humanity—except for their masters. There was little difference between domestic service and slavery for Rousseau. The two were separated only by the extent of personal dependence. That was the real evil, and it was morally devastating. No bonds of duty or of mutual obligation can be formed where one is completely helpless, the other omnipotent to all intents and purposes.[5]

Rousseau was far more radical than *Figaro*. Beaumarchais' hero has long been recognized as a revolutionary figure. The servant who is smarter than his master had always been a stock figure of the comic stage, but *Figaro* was the first to resent it. That a gifted, competent, and honest man should serve a decadent nobleman was, suddenly, an outrage. That the likeable countess should have a maid, however, was not at all objectionable. For it was not the very existence of domestic service that was wrong. *Figaro* was rebelling against a system that subordinated useful talent to mere birth. He personified a circulation of élites. Rousseau clearly implied more, but he also had had a *Figaro*-like experience. Once, while serving at table he was able to demonstrate to an assembled aristocratic family that he was far better educated than the son of the house. He never forgot the sweet delight of that moment when things were for once "put in their natural order."[6] The unnatural order was, however, what prevailed, and Rousseau's response to it went beyond *Figaro*'s. It reached that revolutionary point that Tocqueville located halfway between an aristocratic and a democratic régime.[7] In the ancien régime the world

5. Rousseau discusses masters and valets in his "Letter to Christophe de Beaumont" and the "Letters to Malherbes" as well as in *The Confessions*, trans. J. M. Cohen (Baltimore: Penguin, 1954), pp. 39–41, 84–89, 476–78, and *Emile or On Education*, trans. Allan Bloom (New York: Basic

Books, Inc., 1979), p. 95 [Editor].
6. *The Confessions*, pp. 96–97.
7. Alexis de Tocqueville, *Democracy in America*, trans. George Lawrence (New York: Doubleday, 1969), pp. 572–80.

"downstairs" mirrors that of "upstairs," and the servant identifies himself with the master so completely that he may well lose any sense of self-hood. Such was the faithful domestic retainer. In a democracy the servant is an employee who receives wages for services in an impersonal quid pro quo exchange in which the opinion of mutual equality prevails. In the period of transition, however, the master is "malevolent and soft," while the servant is "malevolent and intractable." Tocqueville had his reservations about the arrangement that created trusted retainers, and he knew that the democratic equality between servants and masters was only a sort of "fancied" opinion, not an actuality. He thought, as did Rousseau, that contracting for services was an improvement over a wholly servile state. The ex-slave in the North was very much like the base laquays, at the bottom of the old domestic order. They were "obstinate and cringing." The intermediary condition of revolution he deemed the worst. It had been Rousseau's own state, and he did not deny that it had brought him to the lowest moral point, as well as to a state of intolerable resentment.

The slave is only one degree below the valet. In slave households neither master nor slave belongs to a family, but only to a class.[8] The demoralization is the same for all domestic servants, but slavery is, in addition, totally unjust, or to be exact—antijust. It is a situation which cannot be mitigated, because the master cannot be a master without a slave, while the slave has no self at all.[9] The two are locked into a situation of total mutual dependence. That is why slavery is a paradigm for all the lesser states of personal dependence: it reveals so starkly what is wrong with all of them. The social contract is the only cure for them, because it alone depersonalizes, and so moralizes obedience. The necessity for such a step becomes clear when one considers slavery. To begin with, it is wrong, because no man can have the right to sell his life. Only property can be bought, and property is a social creation, while one's life is a gift of nature. As suicide is wrong, so is selling oneself, since in both cases one is trading away something that is not wholly one's own. Certainly the life of children cannot be alienated by their parents. The Aristotelian argument that some people are naturally born slaves mistook the effect for the cause. It is enslavement that makes imbeciles, not the other way around. The most important reason we cannot sell ourselves is, however, moral. No one may simply give up his moral responsibilities, but the slave does just that. Without the power to make choices, he loses his moral personality.[1] His existence is antijust, an offense against the moral order. For enslavement is an assertion of pure force, which can give rise to no ties of duty or obligation, and the slave may rebel, if he can, in a simple act of counterassertion. Slavery is that ultimate point of personal dependence where right and wrong cease to apply.

8. *Emile*, p. 406.
9. *Discourse on Inequality*, p. 42; *On Social Contract*, Book I, chapter 1.

1. *On Social Contract*, Book I, chapters 2–4; *Discourse on Inequality*, pp. 48–50.

Unjust, false, and degrading as slavery is, Rousseau did not forget that the finest of the classical republics depended on slave labor so that its citizens might have the leisure for self-government. That did not prove that slavery could be right, but merely that all civil institutions are subject to imperfections.[2] For slavery, like all the lesser kinds of social dependence, is systematic, not incidental. All the various degrees of inequality create the given social pattern to which individuals adapt. People had sympathized with Rousseau when he was sacked, but it was part of his position to be subject to that injustice, and so no one did anything. The poor are sacrificed to the rich by the maxims of all actual societies and by all legal systems, since these exist to stabilize inequalities of wealth.[3] For in the end, all inequalities can be reduced to rich and poor.[4] Even slavery is possible only because of that difference. That is why there is only one way to root out slavery: no one may be so rich as to buy another and no one so poor as to be tempted to sell himself. That is the basic minimum of equality required for personal freedom.[5] It is not enough to achieve justice. For that, another kind of equality is needed. "Moral and lawful equality" must replace the inequalities, both physical and intellectual, "that nature may have imposed upon mankind."[6]

What did Rousseau mean by natural inequality and "moral and legal equality?" Obviously he did not believe that men were "created equal" or alike. Human beings differ from one another at birth and throughout life.[7] However, in their natural presocial condition, when they are isolated and perfectly free, men's talents do not manifest themselves, nor do they matter. Only when men congregate and their intelligence develops do differences in natural endowment become significant. Then competition replaces egoism, and newly acquired skills and needs bring on the division of labor, mutual dependence, and accumulation of possessions. Inequality now is an established given among associated men, and the institutions of property, law, and government follow.[8] The cement that holds all this together is not egoism, which is a perfectly healthy instinct, but vanity, the desire to shine in the eyes of others and to climb up the social ladder. Otherwise those who benefit least from this system would not accept it so readily.[9] Men are not just oppressed but also deluded. They are, moreover, deeply divided within and among themselves, because the impulses of nature survive in the social state.[1] The exercise of power is an assertion of natural inequality, but might cannot make right. Physical prowess cannot make obligation, only submission. As soon as the oppressed can fight back, they will do so. Conquest, like slavery, is a harsh fact of life, and so is rebellion.[2] To become socialized

2. *On Social Contract*, Book III, chapter 15.
3. *The Confessions*, pp. 304–306.
4. *On Social Contract*, Book I, chapter 9; *Discourse on Inequality*, pp. 44–45, 53–54.
5. *On Social Contract*, Book II, chapter 11.
6. *Ibid.*, Book I, chapter 9.
7. *Emile*, pp. 94–95.

8. *Discourse on Inequality*, pp. 32–34, 38–42.
9. *Ibid.*, pp. 52–53 et passim; *On Social Contract*, Book I, Chapter 2; *Emile*, pp. 212–13.
1. *Emile*, p. 41.
2. *On Social Contract*, Book I, chapters 1–3, Book III, Chapter 10; *Discourse on Inequality*, pp. 44–46.

we need to do more than just cease to be "stupid and limited animals"—we need a moral life.[3]

Even the worst societies have some standards of right and wrong, which create some notion of duty. The trouble is that the rules have no other purpose than to freeze people into positions of such inequality that only bonds of fear, not obligation, can develop. How can one have social rules that really serve the interests of all men? How can men be made to obey without anyone commanding, given "men as they are"?[4] If everyone openly agrees to a single set of rules to be equally and impersonally applied to all, then the citizens are all perfectly free, for they obey only themselves. To achieve that impersonality of legal rulership, the "total alienation of each associate of himself and his rights to the community" is the first step.[5] Nature must be really abandoned, so that each one can put himself in an identical relation to the whole. That way no one has an interest in making the rules onerous. Everyone receives the same rights and all oblige themselves to obey and to receive the protection of the laws under the same conditions.[6] It is a wholly artificial equality. The criminal is not the equal of the good citizen, but both are measured by the same yardstick. Just as money is a neutral standard which allows us to compare widely different commodities for purposes of fair exchange, so the law allows us to make fair judgments of civil worth.[7] Absolute equality is unthinkable in any society. All have standards, which some men meet and others do not. The question is how to have just rules of distribution according to which we judge some to be good and others bad.[8] * * * The argument is, however, still offered with considerable flourish by the defenders of inequality. That is because it is incompatible with such rejections of all distributive justice as the communist formula, "from each according to his abilities, to each according to his need." That may, in fact, provide the basis for new kinds of rules, but not, as Marx knew, for "men as they are" here and now.[9] The issue is not really equality here, and Rousseau's point is elementary. Since no society can exist without rules, the great question is which are the least onerous.

How much equality is needed for the rule of law? The people know well enough that equality before the law is in their interest, that when exceptions are made it will not be for the benefit of the many. Nevertheless "the force of things" is always against equality, even though it is so obviously best for most men all of the time. Equality is not self-perpetuating, and the problem is therefore not how much equality, but how to maintain the degree of equality necessary to prevent injustice.[1] The

3. On Social Contract, Book I, Chapter 8.

4. Ibid., Book I, chapter 1, Book II, chapter 6; On Political Economy, pp. 63–64.

5. On Social Contract, Book I, Chapter 6.

6. Ibid., Book I, chapter 7, Book II, chapters 4, 6, Book III, chapter 16.

7. Emile, p. 189.

8. Discourse on Inequality, p. 53; Ralf Dahrendorf, "On the Origin of Social Inequality," in Phi-

losophy, Politics and Society (2nd series), eds. Peter Laslett and W. G. Runciman (Oxford: Basil Blackwell, 1962), pp. 88–109.

9. Lucio Colletti, "Rousseau as Critic of Civil Society," in From Rousseau to Lenin, trans. John Merrington and Judith White (London: New Left Books, 1972), pp. 143–93.

1. On Social Contract, Book II, chapters 1, 11; Discourse on Inequality, pp. 43–47.

point to be avoided is when the rich can bend the law in their own favor. There is no easy way to that end, for although the general will, the will of society considered as a single whole, always tends to equality, each one of us has a particular will which yearns for privilege. This unsocialized self would not in itself be dangerous if it were not organized. The perpetual threat to equality comes from factions, combinations, special associations, all of which become dominating castes.[2] There is a familiar populist sense of conspiracy here, all the more so since Rousseau was personally obsessed by it. Who was to rescue mankind from these multiple threats? The state as a paternal savior was the only possible hope. That introduces a new idea of freedom. Partial associations are bound to create personal dependencies, and these are so much power withdrawn from the "body of state."[3] Freedom is defined, here, as the unimpaired strength of the state, not as personal choice. Dependence on private persons is a loss of freedom now, *because* it diminishes the state, not because it enchains the subordinate. Freedom is in reliance on the state's laws which one has made. For one then is *not* doing anything one does *not* want to do, which is Rousseau's definition of freedom in society. It is exceptionally negative. Obeying one's socialized public ego is *not* being forced by anyone else.[4] To that end equality is absolutely necessary, because one cannot identify with the law fully in its absence.

Equality, however, is not enough to ensure that the force of the state be recognized as a liberation. Heavy doses of civic education and manipulation by a great legislator and by censors are needed to keep the civic self alive. Rousseau's medicine may well have been worse than the disease. It is, however, absurd to overlook the psychological truth to which he points. He and many other people who have no self-confidence experience paternal rule as liberating. Protection is not freedom, but it certainly may feel just like it. Nevertheless, anyone who thinks that pluralism and diversity of views and manners are the very core of freedom will look upon Rousseau's definition of freedom as a simple abuse of the word.[5] The liberty of those who can cope on their own is one that rejoices in conflict and competition. To those who see themselves as unalterably weak and subject to oppression by an endless army of predators, this prospect is a nightmare. Rousseau chose to see society from their perspective, and his view of freedom follows from it.

In fact Rousseau was not oblivious to some of the difficulties that a policy of preventing inequality might create. To suppress potentially dangerous particular associations requires a strong government. That immediately creates a problem, for the government is also a "particular association." It has, like all the others, whether they be military or religious, loyalties and interests that are at odds with those of the general

---

2. *On Social Contract*, Book II, chapter 3, Book IV, chapter 1.
3. *Ibid.*, Book 2, chapter 11; *Constitutional Project for Corsica* in Rousseau, *Political Writings*, trans. Frederick Watkins (Edinburgh: Thomas

Nelson and Sons Ltd., 1953), 288–90, 327–28.
4. *On Social Contract*, Book II, chapters 12–13.
5. E.g., Isaiah Berlin, *Two Concepts of Liberty* (Oxford: Clarendon Press, 1958).

public.[6] The means of domination are always readily at hand. The purposes and the actual tasks of governments are therefore usually incompatible. Governments are necessary to enforce the law, not to make it; that is to be done by the sovereign people.[7] As executive agents, governments should in principle have no arms of their own. However, their work is such as to make them the masters, rather than the servants of the people. They must prevent the rise of wealth and poverty which would quickly make a mockery of the social contract. For once there are rich and poor, every law serves the former. To achieve equality the government must command ample forces, and with that the awful equality of despotism may eventually come.[8]

For all their defects, Rousseau could imagine governments that could successfully impose and maintain equality. The conditions that he set might seem utopian, but in fact they amount to the very opposite: an exact estimate of the full cost of equality. There would be very little division of labor in a subsistence economy with no foreign trade as part of a society that would have no arts or sciences or any civilization to speak of. The price of equality is the elimination, preferably through taxation, of any surplus. Rousseau knew perfectly well that no modern European, certainly not any of his Genevan fellow citizens, was interested enough in equality to accept such harsh terms. Corsica might try to create equality at such a cost, but no one else would. Rousseau was exceptionally honest here. He had no intention of claiming that equality could be had cheaply, or that civilized people could really afford it. If Corsica was to attempt a policy of equality, all opportunities for the accumulation of riches must simply be eliminated. In a permanently underdeveloped, agrarian society, that is readily avoided. Under this "rustic system" each one produces enough for himself and his family and is discouraged by taxation from doing more. Under primitive noncommercial conditions there will be no atrophy of incentives to work, for self-sufficiency requires a lot of hard labor. The state will be rich, the people poor, and there will be a minimum of inequality.[9] Contemporary political theorists who see Rousseau as the prophet of Third World democracy have not taken full account of these views. The hope that Third World countries might retain enough traditional social cohesion to avoid the class divisions of the former colonial powers may, or may not, be reasonable. Since these countries are determined to become developed technological societies, however, they are not taking Rousseau seriously. He at least took it for granted that the equality of rustic systems such as Corsica's could not survive even commerce and money, not to mention industrial economies. Whatever the rhetoric, the élites

6. On Political Economy, pp. 61–63; On Social Contract, Book III, chapter 2.
7. On Political Economy, pp. 60–61; On Social Contract, Book II, chapter 2.
8. On Political Economy, pp. 71–72, 82–83; Cor-

sica, pp. 308–309, 317–18; Discourse on Inequality, pp. 43–47, 55–56.
9. On Political Economy, pp. 74–76, 82–83; Corsica, pp. 297–300, 302–303, 308–10, 317–18.

of these countries and their Western champions owe little to Rousseau's vision of agrarian equality.[1]

Rousseau's preference for the rustic system was inspired not only by his egalitarianism, but also by a deep moral distaste for luxury. To be sure, luxury was, in the first instance, the effect of inequality, but once superfluity existed, it was a powerful stimulus to ever greater inequalities. That was not all. Luxury was directly corrupting. It made men soft and self-indulgent. It destroyed the martial spirit and eroded civic virtue.[2] These views had long been a standard feature of that civic humanism which was central to early modern radicalism.[3] Robespierre was to be both its epitome and nemesis, whereas Rousseau was perhaps its last genuine prophet. If any remnants of this Spartan moralism survive, it is among those who revile the consumer society as demoralized and politically debilitating. Rousseau was, however, far more severe than these contemporary critics. Luxury included the arts and sciences, and not only soporific *Kitsch*. It was high culture that provided the garlands to hide the chains which imprisoned the people. It entertained the ruling classes and gave artists a means to gain public reputations. It kept citizens from their social duties, and ruined their private morals. Art as a spectator sport was isolating and ruptured the ties of social life. Finally it provided audiences with a pseudomorality. After weeping at the spectacle of suffering, they felt that they had actually done good deeds. The best that could be said for the theater was that in a corrupt city, like Paris, it kept the dissolute off the streets, where they would commit crimes. Rousseau thought that art alienates people, because it provides an imaginary world to which one can escape, away from family, work, and social duty. Nothing could be more opposed to this than Marcuse's complaint that the rationalized domestication of art has robbed us of its revolutionary antibourgeois power. For him it is precisely high art that enables one to recognize the shoddiness of all actuality.[4] To Rousseau art looked like a mere escape from actuality, which is our one and only world. But then Rousseau did not look forward to revolution from above. In fact he did not look forward to anything. Change is always a disaster: for societies, because the normal course of history is from bad to worse, for the individual, because social mobility is psychologically destructive.[5]

Science, Rousseau thought less harmful than high art. For most men it is an unsuitable waste of time, but the great scientist is not corrupted as artists and writers are. Scientists are not mere peacocks and flatterers of the great. Moreover, Rousseau could imagine popular art that was not destructive. The Swiss peasant locked in his cabin might sing, fiddle, and do a little science without harm. On the contrary, it kept him and

---

1. E.g., C. B. Macpherson, *Democratic Theory* (Oxford: Clarendon Press, 1973), pp. 157–69, and *The Real World of Democracy* (Oxford: Oxford University Press, 1972), pp. 23–24, 56–67.
2. *Discourse on the Sciences and Arts*, passim.
3. J. G. A. Pocock, *The Machiavellian Moment* (Princeton, N.J.: Princeton University Press, 1975).
4. Herbert Marcuse, *One Dimensional Man* (Boston: Beacon Press, 1964), pp. 56–74.
5. *Corsica*, pp. 309–10; *Emile*, p. 41; *On Political Economy*, pp. 76–77.

his family happy and united.[6] Finally there were the public festivals. The Greek drama was a national spectacle uniting citizens in common remembrance of their past. Modern country fairs again provide a lot of communal pleasure and renew ties of friendship among hard-working people. This is certainly not a full-blown ideology of popular culture, but it is its beginning and it stems from Rousseau's own experience as both a successful artist and a failed citizen.

In the end luxury was part of the system of rich and poor. Intellectual luxury was an excess of self-development, as material luxury was the production of superfluities. Neither would arise if men did not wish to be superior to their fellows. The best answer to it was civic education and sumptuary laws, imposed especially on the well-to-do.[7] That returns us to the difficulty of governmental usurpation. It is an unavoidable evil, but it can be postponed. Both the form of the government and the vigilance of the sovereign people can do much to put off the fate that overcame even the best of republics.[8] The best form of government varies from place to place, in keeping with the considerations that Montesquieu had discussed. In principle, however the most just government is the one that departs least from the general will which seeks equality. That would be direct democracy, but it is possible, if at all, only in a primitive Swiss Canton—not generally. Men fit to govern themselves would need no government at all.[9] The best alternative is an elective aristocracy chosen for brief periods of office by the whole people. In general that would mean that the wealthier members of society will be elected, but from time to time a poor man should be chosen to prove that merit is not ignored.[1] This system is not to be confused with representative government in which deputies make laws, which is a destruction of popular sovereignty, since political justice and freedom depend on popular legislation.[2] Representation may be one way to govern large polities, but these cannot enjoy much freedom. The citizen is an insignificant cipher, and the rigor of the law must be severe to reach a great, dispersed population.[3]

Given the difficulties of democratic government, there is always the potential for tyranny, and only a watchful citizenry can prevent its emergence. This is why active political participation is necessary.[4] The people do not assemble to make new laws. That is to be avoided, as is all change. The popular assemblies exist to preserve the republic, not to alter or adapt its laws.[5] Their chief purpose is to express their confidence in or dissatisfaction with the magistrates and to reconfirm the original laws. Sporadic and limited as these gatherings are, they clearly are designed to protect the interests of the people at large, and everyone is expected

6. *Discourse on the Sciences and Arts*, pp. 62–63.
7. *Corsica*, pp. 323–24; *On Political Economy*, pp. 72–73.
8. *On Social Contract*, Book III, chapters 10, 11, 18.
9. *Ibid.*, Book III, chapters 2, 4, 8, Book IV, chapters 1, 3.

1. *Ibid.*, Book III, chapters 5, 6.
2. *Ibid.*, Book III, chapter 15.
3. *Ibid.*, Book II, chapter 4, Book III, chapter 6.
4. *Ibid.*, Book III, chapters 11–13, Book IV, chapter 5.
5. *Ibid.*, Book III, chapter 3, Book IV, chapter 1.

to attend and to take an active part in the proceedings.[6] They are clearly very democratic, but they do not aim at the sort of politics today called participatory democracy. First of all, Rousseau's assemblies do not govern and do not frame policies; that is left entirely in the hands of the elected magistrates. The function of participation is also different. It does indeed aim at forming a new and better individual citizen, but not by encouraging the "realization of his creative capacities."[7] The citizen is to be relentlessly socialized, to remain patriotic, and to achieve personal and social integration by identifying directly and constantly with the polity. He is to be made and kept a patriot all the time. When the citizens no longer rush to the assembly, all is lost.[8] Civic commitment also expresses itself in unanimity. When there is a small minority vote, it does not matter; a few individuals have erred, and a large majority is likely to be close to the general public will. The real disaster is when a majority has lost its general will. Then the republic is dead, killed by the particular wills to inequality—for men may agree to that also.[9] Mutuality of obligation tends to evaporate, but assemblies can halt that.

Rousseau's democracy was not designed to promote a long conversation in a "public space," bringing compromise, social change, self-fulfillment, and power to one and all. It was far from being eccentric. New England town meetings in the eighteenth century were also meant to achieve consensus. Differences were generally called unhappy, and the primacy of peace rendered discord, argument, and parties unacceptable. The meetings were not presented with a choice of competing interests or opinions. They met to reassert the unity of townsmen. In the absence of coercive authority the town meeting shaped obedience by creating harmony, which was achieved by careful compromises and pressures well before the meeting took place. Neither the defense of private interests nor the projection of personal ideas was welcome.[1] Given the small size and exclusiveness of the towns, these meetings were not, however, extensively "managed." The advocates of participatory democracy today tend to accept far more specialization of functions, and to provide a great deal of direction to those who are to be improved by participating. Its educative ideal is, moreover, highly personalized and dynamic. There is none of that in Rousseau. His civil-soldierly peasants may not be plain New Englanders, but the psychic benefit of participation for them is also social integrity and mutual peace. The elimination of emotional and social conflict is the great objective. Why this requires so much civic heroism is not altogether clear, but at least Rousseau did not expect the poor to become a heroic proletariat. Certainly creativity, individual self-fulfillment, and personal completion were not what he had in mind. In the end the simple domestic contentment of the peasant-citizen was his ultimate test of good government, and he in fact expected men to remain

6. *Ibid.*, Book III, chapter 18, Book IV.
7. Macpherson, *Democratic Theory*, p. 184, is one example among many.
8. *On Social Contract*, Book III, chapter 15.

9. *Ibid.*, Book III, chapters 11–12.
1. Michael Zuckerman, *Peaceable Kingdoms* (New York: Random House, 1970), pp. 65–72, 93–102, 154–56 et passim.

"as they are."[2] That did not mean pluralism or freedom, but censors, tutorial legislators, civic religion, and mutual watchfulness. To Rousseau it seemed a price worth paying for political cohesion and emotional peace.

The emphasis on political unanimity and on common mores and beliefs and on an essentially plebiscitary system, reveals the distance between Rousseau and the New England towns of his time. It is a difference rooted in Rousseau's low opinion of the social capacities and general intelligence of most people. Community is therefore not an independent ideal for him, the end which equality is meant to serve. Indeed if by community we mean not only shared attitudes, but also constant interaction between individuals, Rousseau was against it. The benefits of solitude were, in his eyes, too great for that. One of the advantages of the Swiss mountain cantons was that its people were kept indoors and apart by the weather for almost half the year. To avoid parties or any divisive ongoings each member of the assembly must, before voting, isolate himself to seek only his own opinion.[3] Each citizen is inextricably bound to the state, but each one is alone, a discrete unit in relation to the whole. There are indeed to be plenty of festivities in a good society, but the main purpose of these, beyond fun and games, is to arrange marriages. The community is one that has only private and no public functions. It enhances ties of affection in hours of leisure, but work and politics are individualized; for relations of dependence and exploitation would otherwise arise. There is, moreover, one community in which there is no equality at all—the family. Women are to be inferior to their husbands. Equality is between households, not between spouses.[4] That had something to do with Rousseau's fear that women tended to dominate men. Indeed the primacy of isolation expresses a profound sense of weakness and inadequacy. In solitude one is at last safe from the domination of others. This is not the solitude of Prometheus, but the self-protective flight of the incurably weak who are afraid of being bossed.[5] Mutuality is achieved by avoiding face-to-face relationships, and the impersonality of legal relations becomes a substitute for politics.[6] That may not appeal to those who feel a great deal of confidence in their ability to hold their own in a free political arena, but it may have an obvious advantage for those whose chief hope is to escape subjugation, especially in the form of personal dependence.

Not only are most individuals too weak to protect themselves against the strong among them. They are not even able to see and pursue their own best interest. The general will, the public will of the people does tend to equality, but alas, "the force of things is always against it."[7] That

2. *On Social Contract*, Book III, chapter 9.
3. *Ibid.*, Book II, chapters 3, 12.
4. *On Political Economy*, pp. 59–60.
5. Rousseau, *The Reveries of the Solitary Walker*, trans. Charles E. Butterworth (New York: Harper, 1982), "Fifth Walk," pp. 62–73, "Sixth Walk," p. 83.

6. See John Charvet, *The Social Problem in the Philosophy of Rousseau* (Cambridge, England: The University Press, 1974) for an excellent critique of this aspect of Rousseau's thought.
7. *On Social Contract*, Book II, chapter 11.

is so because "the people are stupid."[8] The people are simply a collection of potential victims. They are nevertheless better, healthier, and more decent than the rich and powerful. They are also all that matters. Let all the kings and philosophers disappear and everything would go on much as usual.[9] These are indeed the perennial attitudes of "populism," and Rousseau was surely its original voice. American agrarian populism shared his truculence, the demand that the simple decencies should receive the respect they deserve, and a certain moralistic distaste for intellectuals. But the hope that, given the opportunity, each man could rise by his own efforts was there also. It was wholly absent in Rousseau and in most European populism.[1] Indeed Rousseau was far better able to accept failure and rejection than his overwhelming success. "Let no one say that my life is of no interest because I am a man of the people," he wrote about his *Confessions*.[2] He knew of course that he had made his life sensationally fascinating, but he preferred to present himself as not only the spokesman, but also as one of the people. He had, after all, begun as "the son of a watchmaker."

The picture of the people as an undifferentiated mass which must be protected against the depredations of financiers and tax-gatherers is certainly inspired by the most intense feelings of class hatred, but it is not the militancy of the Marxian proletariat. Rousseau's people are to look backward from technology and development to a harmony that history has always missed. To be sure Rousseau knew as much about social alienation as the author of *On the Jewish Question*. Marx was, however, right not to acknowledge any affinity for Rousseau, who was ahistorical and only wanted to escape from, not to transform, the new world that was coming into being. Rousseau's egalitarianism did, however, serve that all-purpose antiestablishment fervor which has colored every subsequent ideology and has survived them all. Populism is a sort of trade-unionism of the victimized, a response to the people seen in terms of its sufferings, but there are also far less structured reactions. Pity is likely to be the most immediate feeling, and Rousseau certainly meant to arouse it in his readers.

It has lately been argued that Rousseau invented political pity, and that he supplied Robespierre and Saint-Just with the rhetoric of "compassionate zeal" on behalf of the wretched.[3] That may be something of an exaggeration, but there is no doubt that Rousseau did much to advertise pity as a means of creating bonds of solidarity. He did, however, have much more to say on the subject.[4] Pity is one of man's natural feelings. Natural man identifies immediately with the suffering being, whether it be another man or an animal. He knows intuitively that he

---

8. *Ibid.*, Book II, chapter 6.
9. *Emile*, pp. 225–26.
1. Richard Hofstadter, "North America," and Peter Wiles, "Symptom not a Doctrine," in *Populism*, ed. Ghita Ionescu and Ernest Gellner (London: Weidenfeld and Nicolson, 1969), pp. 1–27, 166–79.
2. Rousseau wrote this in a preliminary version of

The Confessions, but it did not appear in the final version.
3. Hannah Arendt, *On Revolution* (New York: Viking, 1965), pp. 68–76, 83–87.
4. I am much indebted to Clifford L. Orwin's unpublished Harvard Ph.D. dissertation "Humanity and Justice: The Problem of Compassion in the Thought of Rousseau" (1976).

too is a potential sufferer, and he feels briefly the pain he sees. That is to be expected, because suffering is the universal experience. To be human is to suffer. In simple people, whose passions are not overwhelming, and whose intelligence is limited, this capacity for compassion survives in society. Among the rich and clever it atrophies. When there is a street fight the market women will separate the brawlers; the scholar just shuts the noise out. Nevertheless, pity remains a sweet emotion in society; but it is not quite the same sentiment that it was in nature. Now that we compare ourselves to each other all the time, there is always an element of self-satisfaction in pity; we are glad that it is not we who are suffering when we pity another person. That does not render pity socially worthless. On the contrary, even though it be flawed, it is still the only feeling likely to bind us to one another. It serves among the people to bring them together, and it would render the wealthy less odious if they would not bear the sufferings of others quite so patiently. It is, in fact, common among the rich to claim that the poor are too stupid to suffer, and so to absolve themselves from the pangs of pity. That is the mature, adult response. In our society adolescence is the only age when pity is felt intensely; later, callousness is rationalized. Education might attenuate that, but in the long run there must be less inequality, so that only the people remain, if pity is to accomplish its binding task.[5]

The place of pity in society is socially ambiguous. It is a tie between the dissociated, but it is no substitute for duty. Without duty there can be no polity, but there would be no impulse to treat people fairly without mutual identification, which requires compassion. Indeed, Rousseau's own enduring hatred for injustice had its germ in a compassionate encounter with a hospitable peasant who lived in fear of tax agents.[6] It is, however, very dangerous to let pity degenerate into weakness. Compassion must be generalized and depersonalized until it is transformed into justice. Pity cures us of hatred, cruelty, and envy, but it is no replacement for justice, which depends not on feeling, but on an unremitting adherence to rules. Moreover, the kindness that pity expresses creates ties of dependence. The feeble cling to their benefactors without gaining strength, while the latter soon feel intolerably burdened by the objects of their generosity. Rousseau for once spoke as a patron and admitted that he had been too weak and too inconstant to endure the obligations that he had incurred by his casual acts of benevolence. He simply ran away from his charges.[7] Pity is too uncertain and fluctuating to guide us in society. We need duty and justice that depend on law, not sentiment, which reduces the weak to suffering clients. In nature we do not need attitudes that support enduring relationships. Pity is fleeting there also, lasting only as long as the sight of suffering is present. Then it goes away. It creates no bonds and can be evoked as readily by an animal in pain as by another human being. It is no more enduring

5. *Discourse on Inequality*, pp. 27–29, 38–39, 43–44; *Emile*, pp. 221–253.
6. *The Confessions*, pp. 158–60.

7. *The Reveries of the Solitary Walker*, "Sixth Walk," pp. 75–80.

among socialized men. Rousseau had been patronized often enough to know the difference between friendship and justice among equals and the benevolence that the strong may lavish occasionally on those whom they wish to help.

Justice, unlike pity, makes the weak independent. By belonging to a polity, they gain the strength of citizens, which protects them against the strong in body and mind. Compassion binds the weak together, as vanity tears them apart, but these ties of natural emotion are quite inadequate in society. They cannot protect legitimate interests, nor sustain the public good. Without pity we would not be joined, but once we have come together, only justice can make society tolerable. That is why the poor must be protected even against pity, lest they fall prey to the vices of helplessness. Beggars are the support of tyranny. If the poor, who are never disguised, are far from amiable, the rich, when they are seen as they really are, are horrible. Rousseau had little use for the consumers of pity, but he hated far more those who refused to respond to suffering. Without equality there could be no healthy compassion, just as without pity there could be no justice.

Political pity has been with us for more than two hundred years, fired by religious revivals, sentimental literature, guilt, and much more. That it is no substitute for justice will come as no surprise to those who know the history of America's exslaves. Rousseau is not to blame for the inadequacy of pity, which he both stimulated and dissected. On the contrary, by identifying with the dispossessed, he could shudder at the harshness of the rich and yet know perfectly well that this was not the great question of politics. The real issues clustered around the historically inevitable experience of inequality. What makes his account of the majestic progress of inequality and oppression so complete and compelling is his refusal to abandon the source of his energy, his unquenchable sense of personal injury. He was with matchless success able to reveal the experiences of the endemically unsuccessful. Other philosophers write about those less fortunate than themselves in measured sentences, and they often do persuade us of their case. But they do not shake us, as Rousseau does, with his epic prose. He alone is the Homer of the losers.

ROBERT PAUL WOLFF

Robert Paul Wolff, professor of philosophy at the University of Massachusetts at Amherst, besides publishing influential interpretations of Kant's epistemology and ethics, has also written on topics in contemporary political philosophy such as the theory of justice of John Rawls. Most recently he has published *Understanding Marx, A Reconstruction and Critique of "Capital."* In the following selection from *In Defense of Anarchism* (New York: Harper and Row, 1971), Wolff approaches Rousseau from the usefully unconventional perspective of an anarchist by asking whether even Rousseau's democracy is a legitimate state.

Rousseau's Majoritarian Democracy

*   *   *

The most ambitious defense of majoritarianism in the literature of democratic theory is that offered by Jean-Jacques Rousseau in Book IV of *On Social Contract*. The fundamental problem of political philosophy, according to Rousseau, is to discover whether there is "a form of association that defends and protects the person and possessions of each associate with all the common strength, and by means of which each person, joining forces with all, nevertheless obeys only himself and remains as free as before."[1] The solution to this problem is the social contract by which men first constitute themselves a polity. By means of the contract, the many particular and divisive wills of the prepolitical community are transformed into the general will of the collective body. Each contracting party pledges himself to place "his person and all his power in common under the supreme control of the general will and as a body we receive each member as an indivisible part of the whole."

A will is distinguished by Rousseau as general by virtue both of its form and its content, or aim. Formally, a will is general insofar as it issues in commands having the form of general law rather than particular edict. Thus, Rousseau considers only the laws of the society to be products of the general will; applications of the laws to particular cases are made by the government, which operates under a mandate from the collective will of the people. Materially, a will is general insofar as it aims at the general good rather than at the particular goods of separate individuals. An individual can be said to have a general will, or to strive for a general will, if he aims at the general good rather than his own good, and if he issues commands having the form of law. Similarly, the group as a whole has a general will when it issues laws which aim at the general good. In this way, Rousseau distinguishes a true political community from an association of self-interested individuals who strike bargains among their competing interests, but nowhere strive for the good of the whole. (The same distinction is said to be embodied in the division of function between the Congress, which represents sectional and class interests, and the president, who is supposed to be guided by the national interest.)

It is Rousseau's claim that when a political community deliberates together on the general good and embodies its deliberations in general laws, it thereby acquires legitimate authority over all the members of the deliberating body, or parliament. Thenceforward, each member of the society has a moral obligation to obey the laws which have been willed by the collectivity. That obligation can be suspended only when the general will is destroyed, which is to say only if the parliament of all the

---

1. This is essentially the problem which I have called the deduction of the possibility of political philosophy. Rousseau appears to be the first political philosopher to recognize explicitly the conflict between the demands of moral autonomy and legitimate authority. My treatment of the problem owes a great deal to the *Social Contract*, Book I, chapter 6.

people ceases to aim at the general good or to issue laws.

Rousseau, in keeping with the tradition of democratic theory, introduces the device of majority rule into the founding contract. But he recognizes that the legitimacy of laws enacted by a majority of the parliament cannot be traced merely to the binding force of a promise. In Book IV of *On Social Contract*, therefore, he returns to the problem:

> Apart from this original contract, the vote of the majority is always binding on all the others; this is a consequence of the contract itself. But it may be asked how a man can be free while he is forced to conform to wills which are not his own. How are the opponents free while they are bound by laws to which they have not consented? (Book IV.2)

Rousseau continues:

> I reply that the question is not properly put. The citizen consents to all the laws, even to those that pass against his will, and even to those which punish him when he dares violate any of them. The unchanging will of all the members of the state is the general will; through it they are citizens and free. When a law is proposed in the assembly of the people, what they are being asked is not precisely whether they approve or reject the proposal, but whether or not it is consistent with the general will that is their own; each expresses his opinion on this point by casting his vote, and the declaration of the general will is derived from the counting of the votes. When, therefore, the opinion contrary to my own prevails, this merely proves that I was mistaken, and that what I considered to be the general will was not so. If my private opinion had prevailed, I would have done something other than what I had willed; it is then that I would not have been free.

The air of paradox which surrounds this passage has enticed or repelled students of Rousseau ever since *On Social Contract* appeared. The notion of man being "forced to be free," which was employed by later idealist political philosophers to justify the state's repression of the individual "in the interest of his own true self," can be traced to this argument. Actually, as I shall try to show, there are no sinister implications to Rousseau's argument, although it is not valid.

The foundation of the argument is a distinction, whose lineage runs at least to Plato, between doing what one wills and doing what one wants. An individual may be said to do what he wills so long as he manages to perform the action which he sets out to perform; but he may thereby fail to do what he wants, if the outcome of the action is other than he anticipated. For example, suppose that I arrive at a train station just as my train is scheduled to leave. Not knowing which track I am to leave from, I rush up to a conductor and shout, "Which track for Boston?" He points at track 6, but I misunderstand him and dash off for track 5, where a train for Philadelphia is also on the point of leaving. The conductor, seeing my mistake, has only two choices: he can allow me to board the wrong train, thereby permitting me to do what I will, or bodily hustle me onto the right train, thereby forcing me to do what I want. Rousseau's description seems perfectly apposite. If the conductor makes no move to stop me, I will fail to do what I want to do, and in that sense not be free.

Consider another case, that of an intern who is on duty in the emergency ward of a hospital. A case comes in which he misdiagnoses as poisoning. He orders a stomach pump, which is about to be applied when the resident in charge happens by, recognizes the case as actually one of appendicitis, for which the stomach pump would be fatal, and countermands the intern's order to the nurse. Here, the intern's aim is of course to cure the patient, and he is assisted in achieving it by the resident's counterorder, which (in a manner of speaking) forces him to treat the patient correctly. Had he been permitted to follow his own diagnosis, he would have accomplished precisely the end which he most wished to avoid.

Plato, it will be recalled, uses this same argument in the *Gorgias* and *Republic* in order to demonstrate that the tyrant is not truly powerful. The tyrant, like all men, wants what is good for him. Power, then, is the ability to get what is good for oneself. But the tyrant, through a defect of true moral knowledge, mistakenly thinks that it is good for him to indulge his appetites, deal unjustly with his fellow men, and subordinate his rational faculties to his unchecked desire and will. As a result, he becomes what we would today call a neurotic individual; he compulsively pursues fantasy-goals whose achievement gives him no real happiness, and he thereby shows himself to be truly powerless to get what he wants.

The three cases of the man catching a train, the intern diagnosing a patient, and the tyrant have three common characteristics on which are founded the distinction between getting what one wills and getting what one wants. First, it is supposedly quite easy to distinguish between the goal of the individual's action and the means which he adopts to achieve it. (This is, of course, debatable in the case of the tyrant; it would hardly be denied in the other cases.) Hence, we can speak meaningfully of the agent's willing the means and wanting the end, and therefore of his doing what he wills but failing to get what he wants. Second, the goal in each case is some state of affairs whose existence is objectively ascertainable, and about which one can have knowledge. (Again, Plato's example is open to dispute; this is precisely the point in the development of his ethical theory at which he makes use of the doctrine that there is such a thing as moral knowledge.) It follows that a man may sometimes know less well what he really wants (i.e., what will really accomplish his own goals) than some independent observer. Finally, in all three cases we are to assume that the individual places a purely instrumental value on the means which he adopts, and would be willing to give them up if he believed that they were ill suited to his ends.

Life is full of significant situations in which we strive to achieve some objective state of affairs, and in which we would therefore be sorry if our mistaken views about the means to those ends were to be adopted. For example, if a member of Congress genuinely wishes to reduce unemployment, and if his traditionalistic convictions about the virtues of a balanced budget are overriden by a liberal majority which seeks to spend the nation into prosperity, *and if unemployment is thereupon reduced*, then (personal pride to one side) we may expect him to be glad that his views were in the minority, for he can now see that "If my private opinion had prevailed, I would have done something other than I had willed; it is then that I would not have been free."

And we can now see what Rousseau intended in the passage quoted above. He assumes that the assembly of the people is attempting to issue commands which have the form of law and aim at the general good. This is a legitimate assumption for Rousseau to make, since he is only interested in discovering whether a community which *does* aim at the general good thereby confers legitimacy on the laws which it passes. The further question, whether one can often find an assembly which holds to the ideal of the general good instead of pursuing diverse particular interests, concerns the application of Rousseau's theory. Democratic theorists frequently devote great attention to the problem of devising safeguards against the ineradicable partisanship of even the most enlightened men. Although that is indeed a serious matter, their concern tends to mask their unexamined assumption that a majoritarian democracy of thoroughly public-spirited citizens, if it ever could exist, would possess legitimate authority. This is merely one more reflection of the universal conviction that majority rule is self-evidently legitimate. By recognizing the necessity for an independent justification of majority rule, Rousseau plays in political philosophy the role which Hume plays in the theory of knowledge.

Rousseau supposes further that it is an objectively ascertainable fact whether a proposed law has the proper form and aims at the general good. He thinks, finally, that the proper test of these matters is a vote, in which the majority must inevitably be correct. Hence, when a member of the assembly "gives his suffrage," he is not expressing his *preference*, but rather offering his opinion on the character of the proposed law. He may perfectly well prefer a different measure, which serves his interest better, and nevertheless vote for the proposal because he believes it to aim at the general good. Since the majority are always right, a member of the minority will *by that fact* be revealed as supporting inappropriate means to his own end; in short, the minority are like the individual who dashes for the wrong train, or the intern who prescribes the wrong treatment.

The flaw in this argument, of course, is the apparently groundless assumption that the majority are always right in their opinion concerning the general good. (Rousseau's appeal to this assumption is contained in the innocuous-looking words "and the declaration of the general will is derived from the counting of the votes.") What can possibly have led Rousseau to such an implausible conclusion? Experience would seem rather to suggest that truth lies in the minority in most disputes, and certainly that is the case in the early stages of the acceptance of new discoveries. At any rate, if the nature of the general good is a matter of knowledge, then there would appear to be no ground for assuming that the majority opinion on any particular proposal for the general good will inevitably be correct.

I think we can trace Rousseau's error to a pair of complicated confusions. First, Rousseau has not adequately distinguished between an assembly which attempts to aim at the general good, and one which actually succeeds. In a chapter entitled "Whether the General Will Can Err," he writes:

> It follows from what has gone before that the general will is always in the right and always tends toward the public utility, but it does not follow that the decisions of the people are always equally correct. A person always wills his own good, but he does not always see it; the people is never corrupted, but it is often deceived, and it is only then that it appears to will what is bad. Book II. 3.

The confusion lies in failing to distinguish three possible conditions of the assembly. First, the citizenry may vote on the basis of private interest, in which case they are not even attempting to realize the general good. That is what Rousseau calls an "aggregate will." Second, the people may strive to achieve the general good, but choose poor laws because of their ignorance, or simply the unpredictability of important aspects of the problems which they face. Insofar as everyone does his best to realize the general good, the collectivity is a genuine moral and political community. Finally, the assembly of the people may aim at the general good and hit it. They may deliberately choose to enact laws which do in fact offer the best way to achieve the good of the community.

Now, there may be some ground for claiming that an assembly which is in the second condition has legitimate authority over its members; one might argue that it acquires authority by virtue of the universal commitment of its members to the general good. But Rousseau's proof of the legitimacy of the majority will only work if we assume that the assembly is in the third condition—that whenever it is guided by the majority it actually succeeds in moving toward the general good. In that case, it really would be true that a member of the minority could get what he willed (the general good) only by failing to get what he voted for.

The confusion between trying to achieve the general good and succeeding is compounded, I would like to suggest, by a second confusion which leads Rousseau to overlook what would otherwise be a rather obvious error. There are three questions which one might suppose the assembly to be presented with. Rousseau mentions two: Which law do you prefer? and Which law tends to the general good? A third question might also be asked: Which alternative will win? Now the peculiarity of this last question is that the majority opinion *must be correct*. If everyone's vote is a prediction about the outcome, then the members of the minority will hardly desire their choice to prevail, for by so doing they would violate the principle of majority rule to which they are presumably committed. The phrase "general will" is ambiguous in Rousseau's usage, even though he takes great care to define it earlier in his essay. It should mean "will issuing laws which aim at the general good," but it frequently has for him the more ordinary meaning "preponderant opinion" or "consensus of the group." When the assembly is asked "whether (the proposition before them) is conformable or not to the general will," we may view them either as being asked for their opinion of the value of the proposition for the general good, or else as being asked to make a prediction of the outcome of the vote. I suggest that Rousseau himself confused these two senses, and was thereby led into the manifestly false assumption that the majority opinion of the assembly would successfully express what the minority were really striving for, and hence be binding on everyone who voted for or against.

We appear to be left with no plausible reason for believing that a direct democracy governed by majority rule preserves the moral autonomy of the individual while conferring legitimate authority on the sovereign. The problem remains, that those who submit to laws against which they have voted are no longer autonomous, even though they may have submitted voluntarily. The strongest argument for the moral authority of a majoritarian government is that it is founded upon the unanimous promise of obedience of its subjects. If such a promise may be supposed to exist, then the government does indeed have a moral right to command. But we have discovered no *moral* reason why men should by their promise bring a democratic state into being, and thereby forfeit their autonomy. The implicit claim of all democratic theory, I repeat, is that it offers a solution to the problem of combining moral liberty (autonomy) with political authority. This claim is justified for the special case of unanimous direct democracy. But none of the arguments which we have considered thus far succeed in demonstrating that this claim is also valid for majoritarian democracy.

This is not to deny that there are many reasons for favoring democracy of one sort or another under the conditions which prevail today in advanced industrial societies. For example, one might reply impatiently to all the foregoing argumentation that majority rule seems to work well enough, and that minorities do not show signs of feeling trampled upon, for all that they may be frustrated or disappointed. To which one need only reply that the psychology of politics is not at issue here. Men's feelings of loss of autonomy, like their feelings of loyalty, are determined by such factors as the relative degree of satisfaction and frustration of deeply held desires which they experience. Modern interest-group democracy is, under some circumstances, an effective means of reducing frustrations, or at least of reducing the connection between frustration and political disaffection. But many other forms of political organization might accomplish this result, such as benevolent autocracy or charismatic dictatorship. If democracy is to make good its title as the only morally legitimate form of politics, then it must solve the problem of the heteronomous minority.

SIMONE WEIL

Simone Weil (1909–1943) was a French teacher and writer whose commitment to socialism and the labor movement led her to work for a year on a factory assembly line. Her reflections on this experience are available in English in a collection of her writings, *Oppression and Liberty*. Toward the end of the 1930s she was drawn to a very personal kind of Christian mysticism. The unfinished essay presented here with a few deletions was written in 1943, during the German occupation of France, when she was working for the French Resistance in London by helping to plan for reorganizing her country after the war. She died the same year, of tuberculosis, made worse by her refusal to eat more than the inadequate ration of food which she believed was being allocated to her compatriots in occupied France. The original article was first published in *La Table Ronde* (February 1950). This translation is by Alan Ritter.

A Note on the Complete Abolition of Political Parties

*   *   *

Our republican ideal is derived entirely from Rousseau's notion of general will. But the meaning of that notion was almost immediately lost, because it is complex and requires close attention.

Aside from a few chapters, not many books are as beautiful, strong, lucid and clear as *On Social Contract*. Few books are said to have had as much influence, but in fact everything has happened and continues to happen as if it had never been read.

Rousseau started from two obvious facts. One is that reason discerns and chooses what is just and what is blamelessly useful and that the motive for every crime is passion. The other is that reason is the same in all men, whereas passions are usually different. It follows that, if each individual, faced with a general problem, reflects all alone and expresses an opinion, and if opinions are thereafter compared, they will probably coincide so far as each is just and reasonable and differ so far as they are unjust and erroneous.

It is only by virtue of this sort of reasoning that universal consensus can be admitted to be a sign of truth.

There is only one truth. There is only one justice. Errors and injustices are indefinitely various. Hence people converge toward what is just and true, whereas lies and crimes cause them to diverge indefinitely. Since union is a material force, one can hope to find in it a resource for making truth and justice materially stronger than crime and error here on earth.

A suitable device for doing this is needed. If democracy is such a device, it is good. Otherwise it is not.

An unjust will common to an entire nation was in no way superior in Rousseau's eyes—and he was right—to the unjust will of a single man.

Rousseau thought only that, most often, a will common to an entire people does in fact conform to justice, because particular passions are mutually neutralized and balanced. That for him was the only reason to prefer the will of a people to a particular will.

It is in just this way that a body of water, though made up of particles which continually move and collide, is perfectly in balance and at rest. It sends back the reflections of objects with irreproachable fidelity. It indicates the horizontal plane perfectly. It reliably measures the density of objects that are dipped in it.

If impassioned individuals, inclined by their passion toward crime and deceit, are similarly combined into a truthful, just people, then it is good that this people be sovereign. A democratic constitution is good if it first establishes this state of equilibrium among the people and only then arranges for the will of the people to be carried out.

The true spirit of 1789 consists not in thinking that something is just because the people want it, but that under certain conditions the will of the people is more likely than any other to conform with justice.

There are several conditions that must be met before the idea of the general will can be applied. Two have a particular claim on our attention.

The first is that when people become aware of willing something and expresses this will, there is no collective passion among them.

It is perfectly obvious that Rousseau's reasoning fails as soon as there is collective passion. Rousseau knew this well. Collective passion is an infinitely more powerful impulse toward crime and deceit than any individual passion. Bad impulses in this case, far from neutralizing each other, grow exponentially. Their pressure is almost irresistible, except perhaps for authentic saints.

A body of water, put in motion by a violent, impetuous current, no longer reflects objects, no longer has a horizontal surface and no longer measures densities. And it matters very little whether it is swept by a single current or by five or six, which collide and make eddies. It is equally disturbed in each case.

If a single collective passion seizes hold of a whole country, the whole country unanimously commits the crime. If two or four or five or ten collective passions divide it, it is split into a number of criminal gangs. The divergent passions are not neutralized as occurs when a powder of individual passions melts down into a solid mass; the number is much too small; the force of each one is much too great for neutralization to occur. The struggle exacerbates them. They collide with a truly infernal din, which makes it impossible to hear even for a second the always almost imperceptible voice of justice and truth.

When there is collective passion in a country, any particular will is probably closer to justice and reason than the general will, or rather, its caricature.

The second condition is that the people must express its will concerning problems of public life and must not be restricted to choosing persons, or, even worse, to choosing irresponsible groups of officials. For the general will is totally unrelated to such a choice.

If, in 1789, the general will was partially expressed, even though a system of representation had been adopted, because no one could conceive of an alternative, the reason is that a great deal was happening besides elections. All that was vital throughout the country—and the country then overflowed with life—sought to express ideas through the agency of the *cahiers de revendications*.[1] The representatives had made themselves known for the most part while this cooperative thinking was going on; they retained its zeal; they sensed how attentive the country was to their words, how anxious to make sure that they accurately expressed its aspirations. For a while—a short while—they were really nothing but organs for expressing public thought.

Such a thing never happened again.

The mere statement of these two conditions shows that we have never known anything that even faintly resembles a democracy. In what we name with this word the people have neither the opportunity nor the means to express an opinion about any problem of public life; and everything that particular interests disregard is left to collective passions, which are systematically and officially encouraged.

The way the words *democracy* and *republic* are used requires us to examine closely these two problems:

How can we give the individuals who make up the French people a recurrent opportunity to express their judgment on the great problems of public life?

How can we keep collective passion from sweeping over the people during the time it is being consulted?

If these two problems are not considered, it is pointless to talk of republican legitimacy.

Solutions are not easy to imagine. But it is obvious, after close examination, that any solution implies to begin with the abolition of political parties.

* * *

In order to evaluate political parties according to the criterion of truth, justice, and the public good, we must begin by identifying their essential characteristics.

Three can be listed:

1. These were grievance lists drawn up by the three orders of clergy, nobles, and commoners during the elections to the Estates General, the body which took the first and decisive steps in the French Revolution [Editor].

A political party is a machine for manufacturing collective passion.

A political party is an organization constructed so as to exercise collective pressure on each of the human beings who are its members.

The primary aim, and, in the last analysis, the only aim of any political party is its own growth, without any limits.

Owing to these three characteristics, any party is totalitarian in origin and aspiration. If it is not actually totalitarian, that is only because those that surround it are no less so than it is.

These three characteristics are facts of experience evident to anyone who has entered at all into the life of parties.

The third is a particular case of a phenomenon that always occurs where a collectivity dominates thinking beings. What is involved is the inversion of the relationship between end and means. Everywhere, without exception, everything that is generally regarded as an end is by nature, by definition, in essence and very obviously, only a means. One can cite as many examples as one likes in every realm: money, power, status, national grandeur, economic production, university degrees and many others.

The good alone is an end. Everything that exists in the world of facts belongs to the class of means. But collective thought is incapable of rising above the world of facts. It is brutish thought, it grasps the notion of goodness just well enough to make the error of regarding one or another means as an absolute good.

This is what happens with parties. A party is in principle an instrument for serving a certain conception of the public good.

This is true even of those which are linked to the interests of a social group, because there is always a certain conception of the public good by virtue of which the public good and these interests will come to coincide. But this conception is extremely vague. This is always true with hardly any difference in degree. The most inconsistent parties and the most strictly organized ones have equally vague doctrines. No one, no matter how profoundly he had studied politics, would be able to give a precise, clear exposition of any party's doctrine, including his own.

* * *

A political party's end is a vague, unreal thing. If it were real, a very great effort would be needed to understand it, because a conception of the public good is not an easy thing to grasp. A party's existence is palpable, obvious and no effort is needed to recognize it. It is therefore inevitable that a party consider itself to be its own end.

From then on there is idolatry, because God alone is legitimately an end in Himself.

The transition is easy. One takes it as axiomatic that the necessary and sufficient condition for a party to effectively serve the conception of the public good for whose sake it exists is that it possesses a great deal of power.

But in fact no finite amount of power can ever be regarded as sufficient, especially once it has been acquired. Owing to a lack of ideas, a party finds itself in a state of constant impotence which it always ascribes to the lack of power at its disposal. Even if it were the absolute master of a country, international necessities would impose strict limits on it.

Thus the essential tendency of parties is totalitarian, not only with regard to nations, but with regard to the whole earth. It is precisely because any party's conception of the public good is a fiction, an empty thing, lacking in reality, that it forces the party to seek total power. Everything real has inherent limits. Things that do not exist at all can never be limited.

That is why there is an affinity, an alliance, between totalitarianism and lying.

No doubt, many people never dream of total power; the thought of it would frighten them. It is dizzying, and a certain nobility is needed to affirm it. Such people, when they take an interest in a party, are satisfied with seeking its growth, though as something that admits of no limit. If there are three more members this year than last, or if appeals for funds have brought in 100 francs more, they are satisfied. But they want this growth to continue indefinitely. Never would they believe that under any circumstances their party could have too many members, too many voters, or too much money.

Revolutionary temperament leads to holistic thinking. Petty bourgeois temperament leads to settling upon an image of slow, continuous, limitless progress. But in both cases a party's continuous growth becomes the sole criterion used in all cases to define good and evil. It is exactly as if the party were a force-fed animal to fatten, and as if the universe had been created in order to force-feed it.

One cannot serve God and Mammon. If one has a criterion of goodness different from goodness, one loses the idea of goodness.

Once a party's growth is established as a criterion of goodness, collective pressure is inevitably exerted on men's thoughts. This pressure is exerted palpably. It is publicly displayed. It is avowed and proclaimed. All this would horrify us if habit had not made us so callous.

Parties are organisms publicly and officially constituted so that they kill the sense of truth and justice in human souls.

Collective pressure is exerted upon the general public through propaganda. The avowed purpose of propaganda is to persuade and not to enlighten. Hitler saw very well that propaganda is always an attempt to enslave minds. All parties make propaganda. One that did not would vanish owing to the fact that the others made it. All avow that they make propaganda. None is bold enough in its lying to affirm that it is trying to educate the public, to form the people's judgment.

True, parties talk about education with respect to those who have come to them, sympathizers, young people, new members. This word is a lie. What it refers to is training to pave the way for the party to strengthen its hold on the minds of its members.

Imagine a member of a party—a representative, a candidate for a post as a representative, or a simple party worker—who publicly makes the following commitment: "Whenever I examine any political or social problem, I promise completely to disregard the fact that I am a member of a certain group and to devote myself solely to discovering the public good and justice."

This declaration would be very badly received. His fellows and even many outsiders would accuse him of treason. The least hostile would say, "Why, then, did you join a party?" thus acknowledging implicitly that in joining a party one gives up searching exclusively for the public good and justice. This man would be expelled from his party, or would at least lose its endorsement; he would certainly not be elected.

But, even more to the point, it does not seem possible that such a statement would be made. In fact, if I am not mistaken, it never has been. If words seemingly similar to these have been spoken, it was only by men seeking to govern with the support of parties other than their own. Such words then bespoke a sort of breach of honor.

On the other hand, one finds it altogether natural, reasonable and honorable for someone to say, "as a conservative," or, "as a Socialist, I think that. . . ."

This, it is true, is not peculiar to parties. One does not blush either to say, "as a Frenchman I think that," or "as a Catholic I think that. . . ."

Some little girls who declared themselves committed to Gaullism as the French equivalent of Hitlerism, added, "Truth is relative, even in geometry." They expressed the central point.

If there is no truth, it is legitimate to think one thing or another by virtue of being one thing or another. If you have black, brown, red, or blond hair, just because you have it, you also express certain ideas. Thought, like hair, is then the product of a physical process.

But if you recognize that there is a truth, it is not permissible to think anything except what is true. You then think something, not because you happen in fact to be French, or Catholic, or a Socialist, but because the irresistible force of the evidence obliges you to think that way and not otherwise.

If clarity is lacking, if there is doubt, it is then obvious that, given the state of the available evidence, the issue is doubtful. If a slight probability favors one side, it is obviously favored by a slight probability, and so on. In every case, insight gives anyone who consults it a clear answer. That the content of the answer has varying degrees of certainty has little importance. It can always be revised; but no correction can be made except by more insight.

If a man who is a member of a party is absolutely determined to be faithful in all of his thinking to insight and to nothing else, he cannot let his party know of this resolve. He is, therefore, in a situation where he must lie to himself.

This is a situation that can only be accepted owing to the necessity of belonging to a party in order to take part effectively in public affairs. But this necessity is then an evil, and it must be stopped by abolishing political parties.

*   *   *

It used to be common to see in advertisements for meetings: Mr. X will present the Communist point of view (on the problem that is the subject of the meeting). Mr. Y will present the Socialist point of view. Mr. Z will present the Radical point of view.

How did these unfortunates manage to understand the point of view they were supposed to present? Who could they consult? What oracle? A group has neither tongue nor pen. Organs for expressing thoughts are all individual. The Socialist collectivity is not to be found in any individual. Neither is the Radical collectivity. The Communist collectivity is found in Stalin, but he is far away; one cannot call him up before talking at a meeting.

No, Messrs. X, Y, and Z consulted themselves. But since they were honest, they first put themselves into a special state of mind, a state similar to that into which they had so often been put by the atmosphere of the Communist, Socialist, or Radical milieu.

If, having put yourself into this state of mind, you let yourself follow your reactions, you naturally produce words that accord with the Communist, Socialist, or Radical "point of view."

Provided, of course, that you sternly forbid yourself from making any attempt to discern truth or justice. If you succeeded in this attempt, you would risk—horror of horrors—expressing a "personal point of view."

*   *   *

But how can one desire truth without knowing anything about it? This is the mystery of mysteries. Words that express a perfection inconceivable to man—God, truth, justice—spoken inwardly with desire and without being joined to any concept, have power to ennoble the soul and flood it with light.

It is by desiring truth blankly and without trying to guess its content in advance that one receives enlightenment. That is all there is to the technique of paying attention.

It is impossible to examine the frightfully complex problems of public life while simultaneously being attentive, both to discerning truth, justice and the public good, and also to retaining the attitude appropriate to a member of some group. Humans are not able to focus attention on both at the same time. In fact, anyone who devotes himself to one gives up the other.

But no suffering awaits him who gives up truth and justice; whereas the party system imposes very painful penalties for recalcitrance, penalties that reach almost everything—career, feelings, friendships, reputation, the external side of honor, sometimes even family life. The Communist party has brought the system to perfection.

Even for someone who does not surrender inwardly, the existence of penalties unavoidably warps discernment. Because, if he wants to resist his party's control, this will to resist is itself a motive foreign to truth and that must be distrusted. But so must this distrust, and so on. A state of true attentiveness is so difficult for man to achieve and is so extraordinary that any disturbance of personal feelings is sufficient to obstruct it. From this arises the pressing obligation to protect one's internal faculty for making judgments as much as one can against tumultuous personal hopes and fears.

If a man makes very complex numerical calculations while knowing that he will be whipped whenever he gets an even number as his result, he is in a very difficult situation. Something in the bodily part of his self will press him to give his calculations a slight shove in order always to get an odd number. In attempting to resist, he will risk getting an even number even where it is incorrect. Caught in this wavering, his attention is no longer intact. If his calculations are complex enough to require his full attention, he will inevitably make many mistakes. It will not help at all if he is very intelligent, very brave, or very concerned with truth.

What should he do? The answer is simple. If he can escape from the people who threaten him with whipping, he should flee. If he could have avoided falling into their hands, he should have avoided it.

It is exactly the same with political parties.

When there are parties in a country, circumstances arise sooner or later under which it is impossible to take part effectively in public affairs without joining a party and playing its game. Anyone who takes an interest in public affairs wants to be effective. Hence those who are disposed to care about the public good either renounce thinking about it and turn to other things or endure the grind of party life. In the latter case no less than in the former, they develop concerns which exclude that for the public good.

Parties are marvelous mechanisms by virtue of which not one mind anywhere in the country gives attention to trying to discern goodness, justice and truth in public affairs.

The upshot is that, except in a few lucky cases the only measures decided upon and carried out are contrary to the public good, to justice and to truth.

If the devil were entrusted with organizing public life, he would not be able to conceive of anything more ingenious.

If reality used to be somewhat less dismal, that was because parties had not yet devoured everything. But was it in fact less dismal? Was it not exactly as dismal as the picture sketched here? Has this not been proved by events?

It must be admitted that the technique used by parties for oppressing mind and spirit was introduced into history by the Catholic Church in its struggle against heresy.

A convert who enters the church—or a believer who deliberates with himself and decides to remain—has glimpsed truth and goodness in its dogma. But in crossing the threshold he professes at the same time not to be struck by the *anathema sit,* that is, to accept as a whole all of the articles of so-called "strict faith." He has not studied these articles. Even a whole life blessed with a high degree of intelligence and education would be too short for such a study, considering that it requires examining the historical circumstances of each condemnation.

How can one accept assertions that one does not understand? It suffices to submit unconditionally to the authority that makes them.

That is why Saint Thomas declines to support his assertions with anything but Church authority to the exclusion of all other arguments. For, he says, nothing more is needed for those who accept it; and no argument will persuade those who reject it.

Thus, clear insight, that discerning faculty granted from above to the human soul as an answer to its desire for truth, is pushed aside, condemned to servile tasks, such as adding numbers, and excluded from any investigation into man's spiritual fate. The motive for thought is no longer an unqualified, undefined desire for truth, but a desire to conform to a teaching established in advance.

That the church founded by Christ has done so much to stifle the spirit of truth * * * is a tragic irony. This has often been noted. But another tragic irony has been less noted: the revolt against the stifling of minds by the Inquisition took a course which led it to continue the work of stifling minds.

The Reformation and Renaissance humanism, both products of this revolt, contributed a great deal, after three centuries of gestation, to arousing the spirit of 1789. The result, after some delay, was our democracy based on the play of parties, each of which is a little secular church, armed with the threat of excommunication. The influence of parties has contaminated all mental life in our time.

A man who joins a party has probably noticed things about the party's activities and propaganda that seem just and good to him. But he has never studied the position of the party on all the problems of public life. When he joins the party, he accepts positions that he knows nothing about. Thus, he submits his thinking to the party's authority. As he gradually becomes acquainted with its positions, he will accept them without examination.

His situation is exactly the same as that of someone who adheres to Catholic orthodoxy as conceived by Saint Thomas.

If a man who asked for a membership card said, "I agree with the party on this and that point; I haven't examined its other positions and I will suspend judgment until I have examined them," he would undoubtedly be asked to come back again later.

But in fact, except in very rare cases, a man who joins a party docilely accepts the attitude that he later expresses in these words, "As a monarchist, or as a Socialist, I think that. . . ." This is very easy, because it amounts to not thinking, and there is nothing so comfortable as not thinking.

As for the third characteristic of parties, namely, that they are machines for manufacturing collective passion, it is so obvious that there is no need to establish it. Collective passion is the only fuel available to parties for external propaganda and for exerting pressure on each member's soul.

Everyone admits that party spirit blinds us, deafens us to justice, and incites even in honorable people the cruelest animosity toward innocents. Everyone admits this, but no one thinks of abolishing the organisms that create such a spirit.

Nevertheless, narcotics are prohibited.

There are still people who are addicted to narcotics, but there would be even more of them if the state organized the sale of opium and cocaine in tobacco shops with posters to encourage consumers.

The conclusion is that the institution of parties seems certainly to be an almost unalloyed evil. They are bad in principle, and their practical effects are bad.

The abolition of parties would be an almost pure good. It is eminently legitimate in principle and does not seem liable in practice to have anything but good effects.

Candidates would say to voters, not, "I have this label," (something that in practice tells the public absolutely nothing about their concrete attitude toward concrete problems), but: "I think this, that or the other thing about this, that or the other great problem."

Those elected would form and disband associations as prompted by the natural and shifting play of affinities. I can very well agree with Mr. A. on the issue of colonization and disagree with him on the issue of small farms; and just the opposite can occur with Mr. B. If we are talking about colonization, before the session I will go chat a bit with Mr. A; if we are talking about small farms, with Mr. B.

The artificial crystallization into parties coincided so little with real affinities that a deputy could disagree with a colleague from his party on all specific issues and agree with a man from another party.

In Germany in 1932, how often were a Communist and a Nazi struck by mental vertigo when, talking in the street, they discovered that they agreed on all the issues!

Outside of Parliament, since there would be journals of opinion, there would quite naturally be circles of sympathizers around them. But these circles would have to be kept in a fluid state. It is fluidity that distinguishes an affinity group from a party and keeps if from having a bad influence. When someone associates in a friendly way with the person who edits a journal and with those who often write for it, or when he writes for it himself, that person knows that he is in contact with that journal's circle. But he does not know whether he himself is part of it; there is no clear distinction between the inside and the outside. Further off are those who read the journal and know one or two of those who write for it. Further off are regular readers who draw on it for inspiration. Still further off are occasional readers. But no one would ever dream of thinking or saying, "As someone who is linked to such and such a journal, I think that. . . ."

When collaborators on a journal run in elections, they should be forbidden from referring to their journal. The journal should be forbidden from endorsing them, or from directly or indirectly supporting their candidacy, or even from mentioning it.

Every group of "friends" of such a journal should be prohibited.

If a journal used the threat of exclusion to keep its collaborators from working for any other publication whatever, it would be suppressed as soon as the fact was proved.

All this implies press regulations that make it impossible for publications to exist on which it is dishonorable to work.

Whenever a circle tried to crystallize by giving a definite character to the status of a member, it would be legally repressed once the fact had been established.

Of course, there would be clandestine parties. But their members would have a guilty conscience. They would no longer be able to testify in public to the servility of their spirits. They could make no propaganda in the party's name. The party would no longer be able to hold them within a network of interests, feelings and obligations that had no exit.

Whenever a law is impartial, fair, and based on a view of the public good that the people can easily grasp, it weakens whatever it forbids. It weakens it owing simply to its existence, apart from the repressive measures which seek to insure its application.

This intrinsic majesty of the law is a factor in public life which has long been overlooked and which must be utilized.

There do not seem to be any drawbacks in the existence of clandestine parties that are not found to a much greater extent in legal parties.

Speaking generally, attentive examination from all points of view seems not to reveal drawbacks of any kind to the abolition of parties.

* * *

Their abolition would have purifying effects on much besides public life. For party spirit had succeeded in contaminating everything.

The institutions that determine how the game of politics is played always influence a country's whole way of thinking, owing to the spell cast by power.

We have reached the point in every sphere of almost never thinking except by taking a position "for" or "against" an opinion. Then we seek arguments, depending on the case, either for or against. This is exactly analogous to joining a party.

Just as, in the realm of political parties, there are democrats who accept several parties, so in the realm of opinions broadminded people see value in opinions with which they say they disagree.

This amounts to having lost all understanding of what is right and what is wrong.

Others, having taken a position in favor of an opinion, refuse to examine anything that weighs against it. This is analogous to totalitarian spirit.

When Einstein came to France, everyone in a more or less intellectual milieu, even including the scientists themselves, divided into two camps, for and against. Every new scientific idea has its partisans and its opponents within scientific circles, all animated to a regrettable extent by party spirit. Moreover, within these circles there are factions and coteries, crystallized to varying degrees.

In art and literature this is even more noticeable. Cubism and surrealism were types of parties. One was a proponent of Gide just as one was a proponent of Maurras.[2] To make a name for oneself it is useful to be surrounded by a band of admirers, animated by party spirit.

Furthermore, there was not much difference between membership in a party and membership in a church or hostility to religion. One was for or against belief in God, for or against Christianity, and so on. The point had been reached, in religious matters, of talking about militants.

Even in schools no one knows any more how to stimulate children to think except by asking them to take a stand for or against. They are presented with a sentence by a great author and are asked: "Do you agree or not? Develop your arguments." During the examination these unfortunates, having to finish their essay in three hours, cannot spend more than five minutes asking themselves whether they agree. And it would be so easy to say to them: "Think about this text and express the thoughts that come to your mind."

Almost everywhere, and often even with regard to purely technical problems, the process of taking a stand, of taking a position for or against, has replaced the process of thinking.

This is a plague, which originated in the political world and has spread across the whole country to almost all realms of thought.

It is doubtful that this plague, which is killing us, can be cured, unless we start by abolishing political parties.

BENJAMIN R. BARBER

Benjamin Barber, who is both a professor of political science at Rutgers University and a practicing playwright, first took up questions of Rousseau's applicability in *The Death of Communal Liberty* (1974), a study of direct democracy in a Swiss mountain village. In *Strong Democracy* (1984) he erects the theoretical underpinnings for the proposals advanced in this excerpt from an essay published in 1978 by The Poynter Center of Indiana University, Bloomington.

Political Participation and the Creation of Res Publica

* * *

Traditional democratic theorists have always been suspicious of representative institutions, thinking them bad compromises at best, and, at

2. André Gide and Charles Maurras were prominent antagonists in the French intellectual life of the decades before World War II. Gide, a renowned novelist, championed the humanist republican left, Maurras, a caustic journalist, the nationalist, antiparliamentary right [Editor].

worst, in Rousseau's vision, destroyers of liberty. "The moment a people allows itself to be represented," he warns in *On Social Contract*, "it is no longer free." Americans have permitted themselves to be everywhere represented, in everything represented, by (almost) anyone represented; as a consequence they have lost the freedom of self-government and must make do with the far more pallid liberty of debating the size, efficacy, equity, and accountability of the institutions with which they have allowed themselves to be replaced.

Although the representative formula in its original founding conception had an activist, participatory overtone, its primary goal was the containment of power. Participation was never a dominant value among constitutional theorists preoccupied with using power without becoming subject to it, and the potentially continental scale of the new republic simply confirmed that prejudice. Representation seemed an ideal device with which to mediate the conflicting demands of effective leadership in a vast republic, and accountability and restraint in a republican democracy.

The compromise was never spectacularly effective even as an instrument of control, but it served both efficiency and accountability reasonably well. If the people could not police themselves, they could and did police the police at the ballot box. If power could not always be controlled at the moment it was exercised or abused, it could be tamed *ex post facto* on election day. As a guarantor of popular sovereignty in some ultimate sense then, representation has worked—at a price.

The price has been self-government and citizenship, and its cost has become increasingly evident as the scale and complexity of American society has demanded ever more participation while permitting ever less. It is true, from the point of view of accountability, the securing of interests, and the limitation of power, there is little that direct political participation can do that representation cannot do better—and much more agilely and efficiently as well. The mandated representative embodies his constituency's interests and guarantees them a voice in the pluralist pressure system. The Burkean representative, heeding the voice of the whole nation as well as of his constituents, removes the burden of public thinking from individuals, allowing them to pursue private interests secure in the notion that the nation's interests are well tended. Both forms of representation, however, while they act as tacit limits on government, remove citizens from the public marketplace and encourage them to regard themselves as private persons with rights rather than responsibilities, and interests rather than obligations. Watchdogs, which is what the subjects of a representative democracy quickly become, are only part-time citizens at best—active on election day, but able to pursue other interests the rest of the year, as long as a single baleful eye is kept fixed on the now alien realm of public affairs. The mournful cry that can now be heard through much of America is the baying of watchdogs, properly agitated by the intrusive irresponsibilities of their representatives, but unable by training or disposition to do anything but wail.

Clearly participation can and must be more than a warning system designed to sound brash alarms when the government becomes a trespasser against the private sector, or a burglar of private property (inequitous taxation) or public funds (vested interest spending), or disappears in the night with the Constitution as a hostage (Watergate). There is an alternative tradition of thinking which has its roots in philosophers of civic virtue like Rousseau and Kant and articulate defenders in social critics like Peter Bachrach and (the late) Arnold Kaufman, a tradition which treats political participation as a vital condition of meaningful citizenship rather than an instrument of limited government. The goal of participation, understood in this fashion, is civic education and the cultivation of a people who are self-governing both as individuals and as citizens. This is an objective which representation, far from serving, can only obstruct. For the perspective of civic education treats the participatory act not as an instrument of securing interests or effecting policy goals or controlling power but as a unique concomitant of citizenship. Specifically, it achieves three things: public thinking; an appreciation of the interdependence of freedom and obligation; and autonomous self-government.

To participate actively in public affairs is first of all to learn how to think and act publicly—an art almost unknown in modern America. Our social scientists tell us there is no such thing as a public interest, and even public officials see their public duties as residues of private failures—they undertake to do what the private sector cannot do, or undo what the private sector has done badly. Certainly, there is no such thing as a public, let alone "public opinion" (which signifies private opinions that have been counted up and classified). Nor, in the absence of a vigorous tradition of continuing political participation, can there be. To participate politically is then to become sensitized to what citizens share in common as Americans or as New Yorkers or as West Siders or as block association members; to find common ground not because you give some to get some or because advantages can be traded off (the private bargaining model), but because there are certain interests held in common that are disclosed only when citizens gather communally (the public deliberation model); to realize there are values in the fraternal camaraderie and the enlivening disputatiousness of public political discussion that have nothing to do with solving problems or developing policies or enacting legislation; to discover that it is possible to belong to a community without surrendering an identity and to share considered ideals without becoming enthralled to ideology; quite simply, to become public persons, citizens—and then learn that citizenship enhances individuality instead of jeopardizing it.

Second, to participate actively in public affairs is to recognize that to speak of freedom without thinking of responsibility is no less absurd in politics than in morals and education. When we choose to permit our responsibilities to be represented, we soon find that our freedom is being represented as well. The government on which we bestow the burden of ruling for us says "yes, we will govern for you . . . and we will be free for you too." With the freedom, comes the responsibility; away with the responsibility goes the freedom. The representative system would like to separate the two—keep liberty while shifting the burden of duty. But a republic is a vessel of all things public *(res publica)*: it exists only because there *is* a public, an active citizenry with public concerns. Any other form of government ceases to be republican. It is in this sense (the critics of democratic distemper cannot seem to grasp) that republican government must necessarily commit itself to civic virtue and vigorous political participation. When a public is no longer to be found, the republic itself is in grave danger of being lost. Participation is then not a luxury but a necessary precondition of republican life: it alone guarantees the survival of political liberty as a function of political responsibility, and of public citizenship as the foundation of republican politics.

Third and last, to participate actively in public affairs is to assure the growth and maintenance of individual autonomy, of (to use an ancient formulation) self-government of the soul as well as of the polis. To be autonomous, both Rousseau and Kant have taught, is to be governed by laws that we choose for ourselves. This means to be self-governing as moral beings we must also be self-governing as political beings—that we must have actively participated in the choice of the principles that govern our lives. There can be no question here of representation: mandating a deputy to choose laws by which I then must live entails a serious attenuation of self-government. For however much generic legitimacy a founding contract in which we do participate may convey to representative parliaments, original consent is not present choice; any more than tacit consent is active assent. This is why Rousseau regarded representation as the death of autonomy, and continuous participation as the precondition of self-government for individuals and communities.

*   *   *

The question then is quite simple: is it possible, within the general framework of the Constitution and in the face of inhospitable conditions, to create an institutional nexus within which participation might be encouraged—without immediately changing deep-seated attitudes of alienation? What kind of institutions, compatible with a representative system that will inevitably dominate state and federal politics, can be devised that will nourish political activism and continuous participation? If none can be found, this analysis issues only in a terminal prognosis: the republic is dead; long live the republic. There are, however, possibilities—some evident in present trends, some suggested by technology and incentive systems, some merely conjectural as institutional experiments. On them hangs the fate of res publica—the long neglected public side of American life.

Participatory Institutions and the Creation of Res Publica

There are three classes of institutions which together would constitute a significant program for the support of political participation—institutions designed for *common deliberation*, for *common legislation*, and for *common work*. These three, cultivated in an environment of supportive zoning regulations, incentives, and technology, would go a long way towards rooting civic education, public thinking, and citizenship in our constitutional traditions. This would not require that representative institutions be eliminated, albeit in many cases, above all at the local level, it would allow them to be superseded. Nor would it depend upon radical attitudinal changes, though it might well help to bring them about. In short, the program seems no less feasible than it is desirable.

Common Deliberation: the value of open hearings, public forums, town meetings, neighborhood gatherings, block parties, and other assemblies that engage the entire citizenry of a delimited community is fairly widely recognized. The mechanisms by which they are structured and conducted do not have to be invented any more than the norms by which they are justified need to be legitimized. What perhaps does require stressing is their intrinsic (as against their instrumental) value. Anyone who has attended a block association meeting, an open community school board meeting, a town assembly, or even a neighborhood political club caucus will recognize how many needs unconnected with the policy objectives of the organization can be met by the fellowship, communication, and sense of commonality that can envelop a spirited gathering. Certain community action groups have sponsored open "town meetings" and "community days" in which women and men have for the first time discovered they are citizens, and citizens that they are neighbors—and then, as citizens and neighbors, gone on to learn how difficult and engaging an art public thinking can be. Political clubs, church groups, farm associations, even barber shops, general stores, and public saloons, as well as other traditional institutional vehicles of American pluralism once served at least some of these purposes, but their religious or political partisanship or their semi-elite structures or their recreational ethos were never very ideal to the purposes of public thinking, and in any case they are moribund today to varying degrees.

Foundation funding, block grants, and other federal and state monies could be put to no better use at this moment than the sponsorship of community-initiated, community-run public meetings. In urban areas, the block association is the obvious starting point, although it needs to move a long way from local self-protection society insularity before it can become a forum for public thinking and an instrument of civic education. In towns and villages, local assemblies convoked at regular intervals—not necessarily with any immediate legislative or policy mission—could provide a local identity which in many rural areas is lacking. Although ultimately such bodies would inevitably and properly become interested in the control of power and resources, initially their objectives would be educative and redemptive: to "save" citizenship as it were, apart from the resolution of crisis issues (which alone seem to prompt public meetings nowadays). At this level they could presumably expect to attract wide non-partisan support.

Common Legislation: the most obvious limitation of common assemblies as tools of citizenship training is that they are oriented to deliberation and public thinking but not to action and public doing. Fellowship and camaraderie *are* ends in themselves but they cannot be cultivated in and for themselves. They emerge rather as by-products of group action— by-products which may, to be sure, appear more valuable than "primary" objectives like effecting policy changes, but which nonetheless ensue only from them. Thus, common deliberation without common legislation and common work will finally be seen as a futile exercise in chumminess that serves neither participation nor politics—and rightly so.

Common legislation suggests legislation that is commonly enacted rather than merely "in the common interest"—as all legislation in a representative democracy can claim to be. Under ideal circumstances, common legislation emerges directly out of common confrontation and common deliberation—as happens in the Swiss *Landesgemeinde* or the New England Town Meeting. Where possible, this model deserves to be employed. Where numbers, geographical diffuseness, and other adversities render it unfeasible, its standard surrogates, the referendum and the initiative, can be used. It is remarkable in an arsenal of institution weapons as varied and experimental as ours how little attention has been paid to these two canons of direct democracy. If the referendum has been used at all, it has been used as one more check on public power—a potential veto with which constituents can remonstrate with mischievous representatives who have overinterpreted their mandate.

Yet the referendum can be a powerful catalyst of democracy, particularly in large-scale societies where direct political participation is problematic; only, however, if it is understood to entail a great deal more than pulling an extra lever on election day. A referendum that does not demand (if not inspire) thoughtful public deliberation becomes the tool of special interests and probably diminishes the quality of political democracy. A device that was once used in parts of Switzerland and might be adapted to American use puts referenda questions to the public in a form that enjoins more knowing and thus participatory responses: in place of the standard yea/nay alternatives that permit the public to confirm or veto but hardly to participate in legislative action, this device offers a more varied and searching set of choices. In an American setting it might look something like this:

A BILL TO PROVIDE FUNDS FROM SALES TAXES FOR ALCOHOLISM TREATMENT CENTERS

1 ( ) YES: I support the bill on principle and believe it is a first priority.

2 ( ) YES: I support the bill, but do not feel strongly; not a first priority.

3 ( ) NO: I disapprove of the bill on principle.

4 ( ) NO: I approve of the bill on principle but do not

believe it is a priority. Deferred action suggested.

5 ( ) NO: I approve of the bill on principle but disapprove of it in this form. Rewriting and resubmission suggested.

Now the yeas and nays would be counted in the aggregate and the bill would thus pass or fail as legislation in the usual way. But the insistence on reasoned responses would achieve two crucial objectives. First, those responsible for the legislation (whether representative assembly or citizen initiated) would receive important information about why their measure won or lost, and could evaluate the likely effects of the win or loss on the political system. A bill defeated primarily by nays in the 5 column would clearly be a candidate for immediate revision and resubmission; a bill passed by a small majority of yeas in the 2 column but opposed by a large minority of nays in the 3 column would suggest what political scientists call asymmetrical intensity—a casual, disinterested majority overruling an intense, impassioned minority, to the peril of democracy's precarious stability—and thus warn the bill's sponsors to proceed most cautiously with implementation; a bill which split the vote between yeas in the 1 column and nays in the 3, whether won or lost, would reveal a danger zone of profound issue dissensus probably not ready for legislative resolution (abortion or busing would probably elicit such a split). Second, and still more importantly, citizens required to do more than veto or confirm would be compelled to think more subtly and carefully about issues; forced to choose alternatives and rank priorities, they would soon be thinking in the public terms legislators know so well: is A *more* important than B? How can we vote to reduce taxes *and* expand hospital programs? Will my weak support for this measure outrage an intensely opposed minority whose will I have no strong reason to frustrate? These questions epitomize public thinking. They will, in being asked, engage the public in forms of public action vital to citizenship. At the same time, they will weaken the role of corporate and other interests who often become involved in referenda under false pretenses and who will perhaps find it more troublesome to their image to have to draw fine distinctions and explain degrees of motivation.

The referendum is only half of surrogate participation: the other half uses the initiative to turn respondents into activists who can lead as well as follow in the enactment of legislation. By setting certain limits appropriate to the level of government and the constitutional pertinence of the proposed bill, the more eccentric and feckless measures can be kept off the public calendar (sponsoring petitions requiring appropriate numbers of signatures). For the rest, the public would be free to petition to put legislation passed by representative bodies to the referendum, to put their own initiatives to the public, and to put by-law and other state and local government constitutional amendments (but probably not federal constitutional amendments) to the test of public judgment.

There are obvious costs of increasing the amount of public participation in legislation, and a price would have to be paid in risking inefficiency, obstructionism, fashion-mongering, interest group intervention, and an overly cautious tendency to veto rather than support innovative legislation. In the 1976 election, referenda to ban handguns (Massachusetts), revive the California Agricultural Relations Board (Initiative 14), impose stricter standards on nuclear reactors and wastes (Washington, Oregon, Ohio, Arizona, and Montana), and permit the union shop (Arkansas) all failed to secure public approval—an experience mirrored by the largely negative and obstructionist use to which the Swiss referendum has been put. But in Michigan and Maine disposable soft-drink containers were banned, in New Jersey casino gambling in Atlantic City was legalized, and in many states bond issues thought to be vulnerable to the public's fiscal conservatism were passed. Whether or not there is some initial price to be paid in progressive legislation, the referendum and initiative seem worth developing as tools of public decision-making. Citizenship that remains an innocuous form of camaraderie will neither educate Americans to the responsibilities of action nor relieve them of their sense of public impotence. As subjects become citizens they may, during the transition, often behave as subjects—at some cost to themselves and perhaps to public justice. But there is little reason to think they will make *more* mistakes than those to whom they too readily surrender their responsibilities, and every reason to think that until they are permitted to make their own mistakes they will be forever cut off from the possibility of self-government. Democracy would be easy if it required only that popular prudence be tolerated: in fact it requires a much greater tolerance for popular folly. The safeguards built into the American system (federalism, separation of powers, judicial review, etc.), none of which should or would be touched by these proposals, give it a natural tolerance for folly—how else would it have survived the people's remarkable menagerie of presidential and congressional representatives over the last two hundred years? Having survived them, it is perfectly capable of surviving the people themselves as they learn the difficult art of self-government.

Common Work: thinking about problems in their public setting and participating in their legislative resolution constitutes a large part of democratic politics. But despite the American tendency to treat them as the whole of what it means to participate politically, they are incomplete. For the most significant and enlivening form of political participation involves citizens in the execution and implementation of policies and decisions they have deliberated and enacted. When men or women must themselves do what as legislators they decide must be done, their legislation is informed by the realities of action—just as their action is spurred by the motivation of deliberation. The separation of powers, like so many American institutions, has done a great deal more to protect us from the abuse of power at the national level than to educate us to its prudent public use at the local level. Citizens permitted at least in their own localities to experience the organically integral character of public speech, public decision, and public action would not only learn something about government but be able to teach their representatives something about *self*-government.

Common work is just that: work done on common project by common labor; work done by as well as for the public. Wherever the strength and integration of a village or a district or a neighborhood permit common legislation, the conditions are present that facilitate common work. In urban neighborhoods the possibilities are endless: transforming abandoned, trash-buried lots into pocket parks; rehabilitating storefronts as community education centers or senior citizen clubs or athletic and social meeting places; developing neighborhood teams skilled in carpentry, masonry, plumbing, and electricity to cooperate with tenants and owners in urban homesteading programs (which have been critically disadvantaged by the costs of professional rehabilitation and the absence of tenant and owner skills). In towns and rural areas, still more ambitious public projects may be feasible—on the model of traditional barn-building and roof-raising events. In 1974 the town of Thebes, Illinois, used a grant from the Department of Agriculture to rebuild an historic old courthouse, using local women and men who were unemployed for all the actual labor. Congressman Paul Simon insisted it was "a lesson for the nation," and so it should have been:

> By taking people off of welfare and unemployment and giving them an opportunity to do something constructive, that community and this nation have preserved an important historical shrine. Men and women who otherwise would have been drawing money from the Federal Government for doing nothing had the opportunity to work. Every one of them can look to that bluff and see that fine old courthouse and take great pride in having been part of the reconstruction.

Simon looks at the nearly 20 billion spent on Federal unemployment compensation per annum, and the 25 billion expended on welfare, and wonders why that is regarded as a more prudent use of funds than underwriting public projects undertaken by those who would otherwise be unemployed. Is there anyone who did not wonder when New York City laid off its school crossing guards for what purposes their children's safety had been jeopardized? Would the city (thus the nation) save more in salaries than it paid out in unemployment and welfare compensation? And what price would be put on the dignity and self-reliance lost in the process of turning contributing job-holders into passive wards of the state?

Indeed, it is in the area of services that labor involving common work is most needed; and it is here that the unemployed, the unskilled, and the retired might most easily be trained to participate—not merely by virtue of holding jobs, but by holding jobs with a significant public utility. A block watcher's association made up of senior citizens occupying street front apartments (who spend most of their time watching anyway!), linked by telephone to a responsible area coordinator familiar with members' idiosyncracies and in touch with the police, could help to revitalize the neighborhood presence that Jane Jacobs has argued is indispensable to neighborhood safety. Child care centers staffed by mothers on a rotating basis would free so-called "welfare mothers" for employment in other neighborhood or district-wide public projects (as well as for jobs in the private sector). Experimental programs in drug-prevention, family assistance, and remedial education have repeatedly demonstrated not only the feasibility of paraprofessional participation by neighborhood residents, but the crucial centrality of such participation to their success.

Patently it will not be possible for participants in such programs to participate in deliberating and enacting the sponsoring legislation—although the Department of Health, Education and Welfare is increasingly sensitive to the need to involve potential "clients" of various programs in their planning and design. But there are many laws already on the books which are enforceable only in a climate of community understanding, consent, and participation. Most cities have ordinances requiring shopowners and building superintendents to keep sidewalk and curb areas in front of their property clean: enforcement of these laws by neighborhood sanitation teams equipped to help cooperative owners and authorized to ticket recalcitrant ones could clean up the streets and leave city-wide sanitation workers free to concentrate on training, coordination, administration, and servicing of entirely public ways. (Much the same argument could be made for transportation and, to a lesser degree, police services; certainly police departments ought to be increasing the number of substations, insisting on local residents (as New York's defunct Lyons Law did) for their patrolmen, and maximizing auxiliary and other citizen-input functions instead of doing the opposite).

Whatever form they take, and whether or not they arise out of common deliberation and common legislation, programs of common work are valuable both to participants and to the communities they serve. They make communities more self-sufficient (and thus self-governing) and ease the burden on central administration; they address residents as citizens rather than clients or wards and encourage them to regard themselves in the same way; they direct attention away from fractious private interests by focusing on common problems capable of common solution; they provide dignifying work for those in the present economy whose age or race or training disenfranchises them—first economically and then, inevitably, politically; they confront every kind of dependency with the discipline of self-help and thus lay the foundation for self-government; they prove citizenship can work if citizens are willing to work and that participation reaps permanent rewards when it is permanently practiced; finally, by completing the cycle of citizenship begun with common deliberation and common legislation, it provides a complete institutional framework for civic action and civic responsibility at the national level—where participation is harder but the stakes much higher. There is a growing resentment at the efforts of government to redistribute income by fiat; those from whom the government takes may not deserve what they have, but neither do those to whom the government gives earn what they get—nor, indeed, are they allowed to earn it. Americans are forced to give and forced to take but they are neither allowed to contribute nor permitted to earn; they are treated as exploiters or exploited, to be scolded or coddled by an avuncular government, but rarely as citizens responsible for their own destinies. They in turn demean their government as a grasping Scrooge or as a foolish spendthrift or as a perpetually soft touch (the idiot aunt who gives too many presents and is contemned by her beneficiaries), quite dissociating themselves from its pathologies—which they prefer not to see, only mirror their own. Common work earns a common share and helps to justify the redistributions by which a society assures that shares will be held in common. It permits giving and legitimates taking: indeed, it shows them to be but the economic reflection of the two sides of citizenship—duties and rights; just as it forces citizens to see their own faces, for better or for worse, in the fragile glass pane of their government.

Supporting Institutions

These are, of course, ideals rather than realities. There is a vast distance between them and the present condition of citizen apathy, frustration, and resentment. Despite the activities of community action groups and the occasional successes of community work projects, large-scale local participation is not going to be self-generating. This means that available supporting institutions will have to be strengthened and directed if programs of political participation are to be realized. Zoning and districting laws, tax and economic incentives, and technology, while presently serving mainly to discourage mutualism and political participation, can be adapted to play more supportive roles.

Traditional federal districting and current metropolitan zoning have been largely superseded by demographic and economic change. Integral economic regions and organic neighborhoods are more often fragmented than integrated by formal governmental boundaries. The great metropolitan area of New York is spread across three states, 16 metropolitan districts, and 880 municipalities that distort the interdependence of the area and make adversaries of communities with common problems and potentially common goals. The prudent speak of "trans-statism," and organizations like the Tri-State Commission and the Port Authority (in New York) try to break down insular thinking and administrative obduracy, but without a more systematic attempt to encourage macro-regional thinking and cooperation at the economic level and micro-regional thinking and cooperation at the political level, such rationality will remain a distant ideal. Cities and townships are for the most part too small to reflect regional economic interdependence (industry, transportation, communications, education, and taxation) but far too large to accommodate neighborhood political activism of the kind on which citizenship depends. Tax districts, education districts, State Assembly and City Council districts, drawn to correspond with the economic needs of regions and the political needs of citizens, would look very different and would provide a vital supporting framework for the growth of political participation.

Economic incentives are familiar devices in the American governmental system. But they rarely appear in support of participation, mutualism, and citizenship. Creative participation in private profit-taking is generously rewarded in the belief that a vigorous economy makes for a vigorous nation. Creative participation in public activities directed at the common weal ought surely to be at least as well compensated. The shop owner who keeps a clean pavement deserves a break on his property tax (the city would more than make it up in savings in its sanitation service); the union willing to help train neighborhood residents in work skills they could not afford to buy from the unions in any case ought to receive transportation vouchers or other public service advantages for its members; the commuter willing to use public transportation ought to be encouraged with special fares, while the car driver ought to be penalized (Berkeley's scheme to levy a daily road-use tax is praiseworthy, as are reduced commuter-pool turnpike tolls, express bus lanes, and so forth). These measures are mostly indirect, however. Political participation can also be directly supported—explicitly subsidized. In a nation that has lost its participatory habits and is rapidly losing its voting habits as well, it may even make sense to *pay* subjects to exercise their citizenship, both at the polls and in community meetings. Payment made in vouchers exchangeable for discounts on publicly oriented activities— night schools, transportation, newspaper and magazine subscriptions, community cultural events, and perhaps food stamps—would endow the compensation system with a double utility: as a reward system, it would generate political activity; as a voucher system it would direct private activity towards publicly significant ends. It might seem odd to have to bribe men and women in private to persuade them to appear in public, to blackmail them into assuming their rights; yet at present it pays to be private in America; we must make it pay to be public in the hope that mature citizens will soon come to understand citizenship is more than its own compensation.

Like Luther's reason, America's technology is a wholesome whore— willing to cater to all tastes and serve all needs. Unfortunately, it has too often been regarded as the exclusive mistress of mass society, immune to the seductive powers of participatory democrats. These romantic Luddite prejudices are entirely misplaced. Political participation depends on effective communications, efficient transportation, accurate information, and careful data management—particularly in large-scale societies where citizens cannot know each other face to face and where neighborhoods and regions cannot be traversed on foot in an hour or even a day (the criteria of traditional democracy). Technology is a potential servant of each of these goals, and the natural adversary of none. At the core of Marshall McLuhan's fashionable banalities about the global village indwelling in the vacuum of a cathode ray tube is a simple truth: as the world grows more populated, more complex, more diversified, and more diffuse, the villain that has made it so—technology—increasingly becomes its own remedy. Like the secret potions sipped by Alice on first dropping down the rabbit hutch into Wonderland, technology first blows the world up into a huge, unmanageable giant, only to shrink it down to manageable pea size again. Television is an obvious political resource of the first magnitude, not to sell candidates to the public but to help the public discover itself; not to pacify weary subjects but to engage active citizens: here the public-access channels are perhaps most promising. The networks have toyed with national viewer polls and citizen response programs, but the potential uses of programming for citizen education, public debate, and even referendum voting (with ballot lever-equipped sets) have not really been explored at all. Television is but a single example: public planning, architecture, demography, information retrieval systems, polling, and urban policy making are all advantaged by technological progress, and in turn advantage participatory democracy. Indeed, without technology, modernity would have long ago condemned democracy to historical oblivion.

The chief drawback from which this program suffers is the parochialism of local political participation. Although it may well be true, as Burke had it, that "to be attached to the subdivision, to love the little platoon we belong to . . . is the first principle (the germ as it were) of public affections," and although local citizenship can be an effective training ground for wider citizenship, it is also true that local affections can breed national antagonisms, that a community neighborhood of insiders creates an alien world of outsiders beyond it. How often have block associations purged their streets of crime by driving muggers down the avenue to less well organized blocks—and felt pride rather than regret about it? Public thinking is relative, reflecting the breadth and scope of the populace embraced in a neighborhood or district or state or nation. If Bostonians learn in their local schools of political participation only to "think Boston," how will democracy in America at large be served?

Public Thinking as National Thinking—A Universal Citizen Corps

These are crucial objections which suggest then that an institutional solution to our crisis that depends entirely on neighborhood thinking—though it may provide useful checks on virulent forms of national citizenship (chauvinism)—will be inadequate. What is required is supplementary institutional support for citizenship at the national level that would utilize rather than compete with neighborhood involvement.

William James sought to invoke the idea of a moral equivalent of war. More pertinent to our concerns would be a moral equivalent of military conscription: a universal citizen corps in which every young American might serve for two years. Women and men would be expected to undergo basic training in physical fitness, general rural and urban survival skills, and communication as preparation for public service in teams deployed throughout America, where possible, cooperating with neighborhood and regional forces. Training might also encompass some specialization (at which point volunteers for military service might be siphoned off), so that project teams would be prepared to undertake a wide variety of services to the public weal. In some cases, this training would initiate career commitments, in others it would remain a tool of public service for a limited period (an interval between studies); but in every case it would permit the young to express their democratic idealism actively, and call on the best traditions of public-spiritedness. American youth has always responded as it was treated: when thought to be callow, privatistic, and self-interested, it was; when treated as altruistic, generous, and idealistic, it behaved that way.

A universal citizen corps would compel the young to expect much of themselves—benefiting both them and the public weal. It could offer many of the undisputed virtues of military service—becoming acquainted with a wide variety of Americans, experiencing fellowship and camaraderie, expressing ideals of duty and service, developing notions of a citizenship wider than the neighborhood, and experiencing the traumas of maturation in a setting of service where introspection is balanced by active living and work. Yet in place of military conscription's corollary emphasis on mutuality for the sake of self-defense, obedience for the sake of survival, hierarchy for the sake of efficiency, and outsider-hostility for the sake of motivation, it could offer a far more generous and democratic creed: fellowship and equality rather than hierarchy, common discovery and cooperation rather than obedience, a rewarding altruism rather than the self-interest of survival; in sum, mutuality for living rather than self-abnegation for death, service in the name of citizenship and self-government rather than blind duty in the name of the abstract nation.

Again, there is a good deal to be said for imitating the Swiss model and reactiviting teams at specified intervals throughout the working life of their members—more for the sake of their civic commitments than for services they might render in the two- or three-week, biennial, or triennial reunions that would be reasonable. Certain precautions against the use of the corps for political purposes might be desirable—the absence of uniforms and insignia, the minimization of substantive political instruction during training, the assignment of teams to cooperative projects with local citizens' groups are examples—and a clear structural design aimed at limiting bureaucratization of the organization would be mandatory. Yet without trying to assess in detail the impact such an innovation would have on the economy, unions, job training, educational institutions, state and local government, party politics, military training, and so forth, it can be regarded as basically feasible: that is to say, within the constitutional framework, both possible and proper. Universal military service has long been regarded as a prerequisite of republican government (Machiavelli or Rousseau or Jefferson can be consulted), and a universal citizen corps could be a remarkably effective surrogate. It could not offer to take America's boys and girls and turn them into men and women, but it might well take men and women and turn them into citizens—participating individuals who believe in political participation because they have come to understand government as an abbreviation for self-government, the state as an extension of their public power, and politics as an expression of their essential commonality.

Conclusion

Our republic, the *res publica*, rests entirely on the capabilities of its public, the vigor and responsibility of its citizenry. Political participation is not a luxury to be dispensed with in troubled times; it is a political necessity without which troubled times can become terminal epochs in the history of democracy. Already in America there are too many signs that apathy has turned into frustration and frustration into backlash. History suggests still more virulent metamorphoses are possible. Passivity today foretells vindictiveness next year. Splenetic anti-governmentalism of a kind not even the presidential candidates could shed last fall is but a revolutionary's stone's throw away from anti-constitutionalism of a kind no American will want to confront next fall.

Political participation is no panacea—for there are no panaceas in a republic. But without it the American *res publica* cannot be created; without it Americans will look more and more to an alien government for totalistic solutions to insoluble problems; without it the habits of citizenship will be wholly lost and the responsibility (and rights) of self-government abjured. Participation will not answer our questions, but it will allow us to raise them once again without fearing for the unity or stability of the nation. Quite simply, it may permit us once again to endure our differences, tolerate our divisions, suffer our compromises, and accept the inevitability of struggle and conflict in a system which cannot afford final solutions—not even to the most pressing of its problems. In learning to live with our problems we can perhaps at least be consoled by the knowledge that final solutions do not in any case exist, except in the monolithic dreams of tyrants or the desperate imaginations of exhausted republicans.

Bibliography

This bibliography consists of a selection of recent works in English on Rousseau's political thought.

Marshall Berman, *The Politics of Authenticity: Radical Individualism and the Emergence of Modern Society* (New York: Atheneum, 1970).

John Charvet, *The Social Problem in the Philosophy of Rousseau* (Cambridge, England: Cambridge University Press, 1974).

Joshua Cohen, "Reflections on Rousseau: Autonomy and Democracy." *Philosophy and Public Affairs*, vol. 15 (Summer, 1986), pp. 275–97.

Maurice Cranston and Richard Peters, eds., *Hobbes and Rousseau: A Collection of Critical Essays* (Garden City: Doubleday, 1972).

Mario Einaudi, *The Early Rousseau* (Ithaca: Cornell University Press, 1967).

Stephen Ellenberg, *Rousseau's Political Philosophy: An Interpretation from Within* (Ithaca: Cornell University Press, 1976).

Richard Fralin, *Rousseau and Representation: A Study of the Development of His Concept of Political Institutions* (New York: Columbia University Press, 1978).

Hilail Gildin, *Rousseau's Social Contract* (Chicago: University of Chicago Press, 1983).

John C. Hall, *Rousseau: An Introduction to his Political Philosophy* (London: Macmillan, 1973).

George Kateb, "The Moral Distinctiveness of Representative Democracy," *Ethics*, vol. 91, (April 1981), pp. 357–74.

Nannerl O. Keohane, *Philosophy and the State in France: The Renaissance to the Enlightenment* (Princeton: Princeton University Press, 1980), chapter 15: "Rousseau: The General Interest in the General Will."

Andrew Levine, *The Politics of Autonomy: A Kantian Reading of Rousseau's Social Contract* (Amherst, Mass.: University of Massachusetts Press, 1976).

Roger Masters, *The Political Philosophy of Rousseau* (Princeton: Princeton University Press, 1968).

James Miller, *Rousseau: Dreamer of Democracy* (New Haven: Yale University Press, 1984).

John B. Noone, Jr., *Rousseau's "Social Contract": A Conceptual Analysis* (Athens, Georgia: University of Georgia Press, 1980).

Susan Moller Okin, *Women in Western Political Thought* (Princeton: Princeton University Press, 1979), Part III, "Rousseau."

Joel Schwartz, *The Sexual Politics of Jean-Jacques Rousseau* (Chicago: University of Chicago Press, 1984).

Judith N. Shklar, *Men and Citizens: A Study of Rousseau's Social Theory* (Cambridge, England: Cambridge University Press, 1969).

Index